THE ENCYCLOPEDIA OF THE
PARANORMAL

AN EXPLORATION OF THE UNEXPLAINED FORCES THAT AFFECT OUR WORLD

RUPERT MATTHEWS, PAUL ROLAND, KAREN FARRINGTON, LUCY DONCASTER AND ANDREW HOLLAND

ARCTURUS

CONTENTS

INTRODUCTION 5

ARCTURUS

This edition published in 2009
by Arcturus Publishing Limited
26/27 Bickels Yard,
151–153 Bermondsey Street,
London SE1 3HA

Copyright © 2009
Arcturus Publishing Limited

ISBN: 978-1-84837-227-6
AD000170EN

Printed in Singapore

INTRODUCTION

Conventional science teaches us that we live in a reassuringly safe and predictable world. The Universe is governed by laws of science that control how objects move, how they interact and the ways in which chemicals combine. It all seems so clear and obvious when explained in the sterile surroundings of a scientific laboratory.

And yet every day out in the real world people are reporting the most bizarre and inexplicable events that seem to break every law of physics. For example, objects are seen to fly through the air without anyone picking them up or throwing them. Researchers blame 'poltergeists', but giving a phenomenon a name does not explain it.

Some humans claim to have quite extraordinary powers. They claim to be able to predict the future, see places hundreds of miles away or even talk to the dead. There is a convincing body of evidence to suggest that a few individuals can perform incredible feats.

Nor is it only in houses that the so-called Goblin Universe can break through into the scientific universe. Out in the remote forests of northwestern North America hundreds of people have reported seeing human-like apes covered in hair and standing eight feet tall. Science would have us believe that it is impossible for any large mammal to survive in North America without everyone knowing about it.

But there are numerous photos and even moving film of this creature that scientists refuse to acknowledge even exists. Let's hope that Bigfoot does not go extinct before scientists have even accepted its existence.

Then there are the visitations to our world that are reported. UFOs are seen all over the globe, some landing and disgorging diminutive humanoids that may be aliens from another world. Ghosts stalk gloomy ancient castles, but also appear in the most modern houses or even by roadsides.

Welcome to the world of the paranormal. Things are not as they appear. Even the most incredible event can be true, and the mundane is never as it seems.

Rupert Matthews, Editor

PARANORMAL HUMANS

Some people seem to have the most amazing powers. They can predict what will happen in the future, talk to the dead or move objects merely with the power of thought. Some of these paranormal humans seek out their powers and use them to their own advantage, but others appear to have their powers thrust upon them and are as bewildered by them as everybody else. But they all have in common the fact that they possess unexplained powers of great force.

MEDIUMS

Humans operate at the lowest frequency of existence on the densest level, the physical plane. Naturally, we tend to believe that what we perceive is real and that anything that we cannot touch, taste, see, smell or hear does not exist. Our world appears solid but, as science has recently discovered, this is an illusion. We cannot see the spaces that exist between matter at the sub-atomic level. Our world is mostly composed of empty space. Although our apparently solid, physical world is an illusion, it is a reality to us while we remain within our physical bodies, but there is another world of finer matter operating at a higher frequency in the spaces in between our own.

However, we all possess an innate sixth sense which is merely an acute sensitivity to the more subtle forces and presences around us and not something abnormal or supernatural. There are some people who are not only aware that they possess this heightened sensitivity but who have developed it to a remarkable degree. We call them psychics and attribute all manner of paranormal powers to them such as precognition (foreseeing future events), psychometry (picking up impressions from personal objects) and remote viewing (projecting consciousness to another location). Those psychics who claim to be able to communicate with the dead are known as mediums and are either regarded as gifted by those who have received comfort and closure from having been given compelling evidence of their loved ones' survival after death, or as charlatans by those who remain sceptical.

> **Mediums are able to facilitate a meeting of minds between this world and the next, until we are willing and able to do this for ourselves**

When the dead try to communicate with us we tend to block them out, either because we fear that acknowledging their presence will disturb our sense of reality or because we need to be grounded in the material world. Many of us have been conditioned to dismiss their influence on our lives as coincidences or as figments of our imagination. However, if we continue to ignore their presence they may intensify their efforts, moving small objects around and contriving to arrange uncanny coincidences. To this end, mediums are able to facilitate a meeting of minds between this world and the next, until we are willing and able to do this for ourselves.

CONVINCING EVIDENCE

Karin Page, founder of the Star of the East spiritual healing centre in Kent, England, had been seeing ghosts since the age of six, but it took a message from the 'other side' to finally convince her.

'One day my elderly mother-in-law promised me that she would come back after her death so that I would have proof of the survival of the soul. I didn't take it seriously at the time, but two months after her passing all the clocks in the house started behaving strangely. They all showed a different time and a travelling alarm clock rolled off the shelf and crashed at my feet just as I was telling my daughter about how oddly they were all behaving. Another day the phone jumped off its holder on the wall and started

So strong is our need to believe that our physical world is the only reality that more significant experiences such as the lucid dream in which we sense ourselves floating or flying are rarely accepted for what they are

swinging from side to side. Then the electric blanket and toaster switched themselves on. Each time I felt a chill in the air. It was Mary trying to tell me that she was with me.

'The final proof came when I went to a spiritualist meeting and was told by a medium, who I'd never met before, that my husband's mother was trying to communicate, that her name was Mary and that she had died of cancer, both of which were true. She just wanted to say thank you for all the time I had looked after her. Then the medium said that Mary sent her love to my husband, my son and his girlfriend and she named them all which left me speechless. The only thing I couldn't understand was when she said, "I'm with Emma now," because I didn't know of an Emma in the family. Mary had never mentioned her. Afterwards I learnt that Emma had been Mary's sister who had died 11 years earlier. Since then I have smelt Mary's talcum powder on many occasions and I know then that she is watching over me.'

POSITIVE BENEFITS

English medium Jill Nash believes that the job of a psychic is to provide evidence of survival on the other side to give comfort to those left behind, not to impress clients with manifestations of ectoplasm and moving objects.

'Initially, I talk to spirits in my mind and ask for their help. I feel their presence and can sense if they are male or female, but I never see them. I'm not communicating with the dead because nobody ever dies. They are the same personalities that they were in life. They are simply discarnate. I ask them to give me names and details that only the client will know which helps the client to relax and open up. Then I close my eyes and visualize drawing that person closer so that I

am absorbed into their aura. When I make the connection I get excited. It's like having a present that you can't wait to open. At that point I usually feel a warmth and I might see a colour or a letter, or a combination of letters. If, for example, I see them surrounded by blue I will know it is a communication issue and I'll ask them if they know of anyone whose name begins with the letter I've seen or a place beginning with that letter that has a significance for them. That's the starting point. It's an entirely intuitive, automatic process. It's like picking at a strand in a ball of wool. It unravels slowly. When the spirit has something to add it impresses itself in my mind. I only receive what the spirit wants me to have at that time. It wouldn't help me or the client to know all the answers. We would stop working things out for ourselves and would only put an effort into something that would guarantee to reward our efforts.

'Unfortunately, I couldn't tell my parents about my psychic experiences when I was young because they were very religious and were frightened of anything which challenged their faith. It made them uncomfortable. I used to sense a presence occasionally and my mother would shut me up by shouting, "I don't want to hear about dead people." But I was never scared because I know nothing really dies. Energy can't die. It can only be transformed.'

'I described the plant and the type of pot it was in and the fact it was underneath the front window of their bungalow'

Jill sees a medium's role as helping the bereaved attain closure by facilitating a reunion with their loved ones.

'On one particularly memorable occasion I opened the door expecting to see a little elderly lady and instead saw her and her late husband. He walked in behind her. She was, of course, unaware that he was with her, but I could see him plain as day, although he was *fainter than a living person, almost transparent and there was nothing to see below the knee. He was tall and slim and when she sat down he stood behind her with a satisfied grin on his face as if he was thinking, "At last, now I can tell her what I have been trying to say to her for months."*

'As soon as we were settled he communicated to me telepathically, mind to

mind, that he wanted me to tell her about a rose. Of course I didn't know what he meant, I hadn't met this lady before. But she did. He had apparently been trying to create a new type of rose by grafting and it hadn't taken while he was alive, but he wanted her to keep the plant alive because he knew it was going to work. I described the plant and the type of pot it was in and the fact that it was underneath the front window of their bungalow. Of course I had never seen their house but I could see it in my mind as he transferred his thoughts to mine.

'He wanted her to know that he was all right and that he was with her if she wanted to say anything or share her feelings. He told me to tell her that he often stood behind her when she sat in her armchair in the evenings and that if she felt something like a cobweb brushing against her cheek or a gentle pat on the head that it was only him reassuring her that he was still around. And as soon as I said that, she admitted that she had felt these things and had wondered if it was him, although she couldn't trust her own feelings or believe that he was really there.'

Jill's experiences have convinced her that the dead remain the same personalities they were on this side of life and recalls an incident with her father's ghost which revealed that he had not lost his mischievous sense of humour when he passed over.

EILEEN GARRETT

The Irish medium Eileen Garrett was one of the most respected mediums of the twentieth century, who possessed remarkable psychic abilities. In one particular séance, she astounded those present – and made headlines around the country – with her uncannily accurate observations. Garrett is also renowned for the assistance she gave to the scientific community in the investigation and explanation of paranormal powers.

Born in 1893 in Beauparc, County Meath, Garrett's early years were troubled, as is often the case among those with psychic abilities. Shortly after she was born both her parents committed suicide, leaving the infant Eileen to be adopted and raised by her aunt and uncle. Her gifts became apparent from a very young age. Not only was she able to see auras of light and energy around living things during her childhood, but she also had a large number of imaginary playmates who took on a very physical appearance to her.

VISIONS OF THE DEAD

It seems that at this time Garrett was also visited by visions of the dead. She later described the first of these occasions, in which she observed one of her aunts, who lived some distance away, walking up the pathway towards her house with a baby in her arms. The aunt told her that she had to go away and that she was taking the infant with her. The following day it was discovered that this aunt had died in childbirth, along with the baby. Such communication with the dead proved to be an increasingly frequent occurrence throughout Garrett's life.

Having contracted tuberculosis as a child, a condition that was to affect her repeatedly for the rest of her days, Garrett moved to the milder climes of England at the age of 15. Before long, she was married to her first husband, Clive, and she bore him four children. Tragically, her three sons all died very young, two of them from meningitis. Her daughter survived, but by this stage the marriage had ended in divorce.

During the First World War Garrett met a young officer through her work at a hospital for wounded soldiers and subsequently remarried. Shortly after he left her to join the fighting at the front, she was visited by a vision of her new husband. Two days later she was informed that he had been killed in action at Ypres.

Amazingly, until this point Garrett had not investigated her remarkable powers to any real extent. However, another period of ill health afforded her the time to consider her unusual abilities and she began to attend séances and table-rapping sessions.

She later recalled that it was at one of these events that she started to feel overwhelmingly drowsy and drifted off into slumber. When she awoke, she discovered that she had actually entered a trance, and that during this state her body had been used by the dead as a means of communicating with living people in the room. Shortly after this she made her first contact with the spirit of Uvali, a 14th century Arab soldier who was to become her primary contact with the spirit world at future séances. Many mediums claim to have a spirit guide of this type, who seems to occupy a role in the spirit world similar to that of the medium in ours.

After a while Eileen's growing reputation as a medium brought her to the attention of a well-known psychic investigator, Harry Price. In October 1930, Price arranged for Garrett to be present at a special séance at the National Laboratory of Psychical Research. It was hoped that she would be able to contact the spirit of the famous writer, Sir Arthur Conan Doyle, who had recently died. In preparation, Price arranged for both his secretary and a journalist, Ian D Coster, to be present to authenticate and document the findings.

It was, therefore, initially disappointing for all concerned when Garrett failed to make contact with Conan Doyle, who had been a spiritualist himself. However, their disappointment soon gave way to astonishment when Garrett proceeded to bring forth the spirit of a man who said that he was Flight Lieutenant H Carmichael Irwin. None of those present had ever heard of Irwin, but it slowly dawned on them that this man had been an officer on the R101, Britain's largest airship, which had crashed in France two days earlier, killing 48 of its 54 passengers.

> When Garrett awoke she discovered she had actually entered a trance, and that her body had been used by the dead as a means of communicating

CONFIDENTIAL INFORMATION

Subsequent news reports of the séance came to the attention of a Mr Charlton, who had been involved in the construction of the airship. Intrigued by what he read, he then asked to see the notes of the séance proceedings. These filled him with amazement, as it transpired that, while in a state of trance, Garrett had produced more than forty specific pieces of highly technical, confidential information. It would have been impossible, Charlton maintained, for Garrett to have had prior knowledge, or understanding, of such matters.

Charlton was so impressed by these discoveries that he alerted his superiors at the Ministry of Civil Aviation, after which it was decided to hold another séance with Garrett. This time, Major Villiers from the Ministry was in attendance while very specific technical questions were put to Garrett to try to gain further information about the air accident. Detailed answers to these questions were relayed through Garrett, who was able to pinpoint the exact cause of the disaster, even naming the very girder that had failed.

The official court of inquiry examined all of the evidence produced by Garrett during the séance and concluded that it seemed to be genuine. Experts declared that it would not have been possible for her to be aware of such precise information about the crash. The only explanation was that she had, indeed, communicated with the spirit world. The whole incident was widely taken as proof that such extraordinary powers do definitely exist. This was seen as a real vindication for the spiritualist community.

Garrett differed from many of her fellow mediums in that there were never any overtly theatrical physical manifestations at her séances. Rather than perform table-rapping or materializations, for example, she merely provided the opportunity to speak with the deceased. It was perhaps this simplicity of her approach that caused so many to support, rather than condemn, her activities, with several scientists risking their reputations to do so.

Following this widespread acceptance of her abilities, in 1932–33 Garrett agreed to participate in extensive psychoanalytical experimentation at the New York Psychiatric Unit and Johns Hopkins University, USA. In so doing, she revealed her open-minded attitude towards the human need to understand and explain the workings of the

paranormal, which she embodied and, indeed, she had a very personal desire to gain a greater understanding of her own abilities. She lectured widely, founded the Parapsychology Foundation in 1951, and contributed her thoughts and findings to several publications, including the *International Journal of Parapsychology*, in 1959.

By the time of her death in 1970, Eileen Garrett was held in high esteem, not just for her skill as a medium, but also for her personal qualities. If she were alive today, she would no doubt continue to be as mystified as the rest of the world as to the precise

French firemen hold up a Royal Air Force flag found in the wreckage of the R101: during foul weather, the airship had gone into a dive near Beauvais and hit the ground at 13mph (19kph)

nature of her psychic powers which, in spite of extensive investigations, remain to this day within the realms of the unexplained.

HELEN DUNCAN

The last woman ever to be charged under the Witchcraft Act in the UK was a medium named Helen Duncan. The crime under this act was not so much witchcraft itself, but having falsely claimed superhuman powers that did not come from God. She was found guilty of this crime and imprisoned, despite having produced startling evidence of her genuine psychic abilities during her career as a

medium. The most convincing example of this occurred during the troubled days of the Second World War.

It is reported that, during one of her séances, Duncan appeared to bring forth the spirit of a sailor who had died while serving in the Royal Navy. The serviceman, who bore the words HMS *Barham* on his hat, told the assembled people that the ship had been sunk while in combat with the enemy several days earlier. At that time, however, it was officially denied that the vessel had been sunk. Only later was the truth admitted, the ship had been sunk exactly as Duncan had revealed. The government had kept the

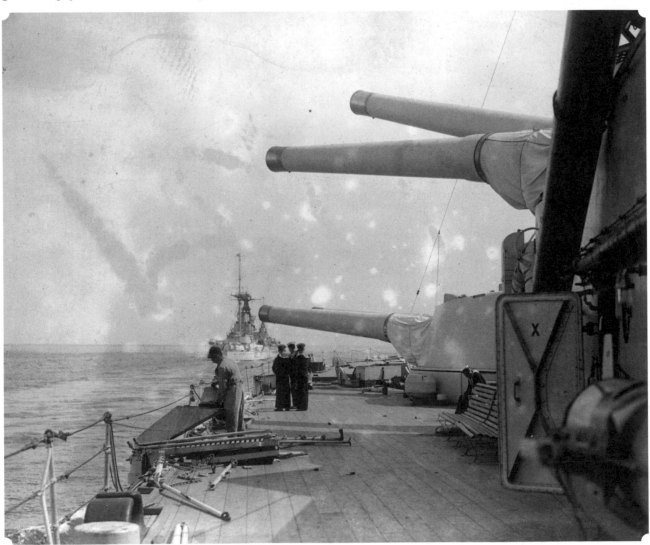

Sailors aboard HMS Barham *before she was sunk in battle: in an attempt to fool the Germans the government at first denied the ship had gone down*

facts secret in an attempt to fool the Germans.

Later that year, Duncan came under the scrutiny of the law. Fellow spiritualists have since alleged that this was due to the authorities' concerns over the possible risk to military security posed by her extraordinary powers. Police arrived at one of her séances, interrupting proceedings and searching the scene. Although they found nothing, she was nevertheless brought to court, where a variety of fraud charges were levelled against her.

In a move that caused some consternation among the public, and outrage among Duncan's community of fellow spiritualists, Duncan was prosecuted under the Witchcraft Act of 1735, and imprisoned. The fact that the authorities were willing to use such an outdated and draconian law suggests a sense of desperation on their part, or at least an ulterior motive. Interestingly, in 1951, the Witchcraft Act was repealed and replaced with the more modern and specific Fraudulent Mediums Act – almost certainly as a direct result of the Duncan prosecution.

Once freed from jail, Duncan immediately began working as a medium once more. Yet her involvement with the police was not over, as in 1956 they again raided her séance in Nottingham while she was in a deep trance. She seemed to react very badly from the shock of being interrupted while in this state, and a doctor had to be called to treat her. Within five weeks of the raid, she was dead.

To this day, there is a campaign to clear the name of Helen Duncan among the spiritualist community, who are enraged by the way she was treated and by the nature of her untimely death.

EUSAPIA PALLADINO

One of the most closely studied of all mediums has been the Italian psychic, Eusapia Palladino. Born in Naples in 1854, Eusapia had a troubled childhood. Her mother died shortly after she was born and, when she was twelve, her father was murdered. It was in the year following this incident that her unusual powers began to manifest themselves. While the young Eusapia was attending her first séance as a visitor, the furniture was said to move towards her

and even levitate, acts that were to set the pattern for what was to follow.

PRODIGIOUS TALENT

The tale of how Palladino rose to psychic prominence is surprisingly convoluted and begins in 1872 in London, long before she had ever set foot there. Here, the English wife of an Italian scientist named Damiani was attending a séance, at which a communication was made with a particular spirit who stated that there was a medium of prodigious talent residing in Naples, and that she was the reincarnation of his daughter. On their return to Italy, the Damianis resolved to seek out this medium. Their enquiries eventually led them to Eusapia Palladino, who was already well known in her community for considerable psychic powers.

In spite of this portentous message, it was still a considerable time before Palladino's talents came to be witnessed by the world at large. Finally, in 1892, word of her unusual abilities reached the famous Italian criminologist Cesare Lombroso, who decided to carry out some investigations into her abilities. After a long series of thorough tests, the initially sceptical Lombroso and his colleagues announced that Palladino was, indeed, a true psychic. This endorsement from one of the foremost Italian scientists of the day caused many people from around the world to travel to Italy to witness her demonstrations for themselves. From this point on, Palladino's fame was assured.

Descriptions of her séances reveal that Palladino was able to perform a remarkable range of psychic activities. Entering a deep trance, she would move furniture around the room, bring forth, out of nowhere, disembodied hands that might touch members of the audience, or convey messages through writing or tapping sounds. Observers noted that the nature of these events seemed to reflect her state of mind at the time, with more violence being demonstrated if she seemed perturbed during the session.

Almost all scientific observations indicated that Palladino was an authentic psychic, so there was naturally a great uproar when she was inspected by the Society for Physical Research in Cambridge, and was declared to be cheating. The scientific community was dismayed, particularly in view of the fact that so many eminent men had given her their backing. However, a subsequent inspection by different experts reached the conclusion that Palladino was genuine after all.

It is to science that sceptics turn in order to expose sham spiritualists and, therefore, the fact that the scientific establishment of the day generally found in Palladino's favour must count strongly towards her credibility. All the evidence points to the fact that Eusapia Palladino was a genuine psychic phenomenon whose mysterious powers are, even today, an endless source of intrigue.

MADAME HELENA PETRONA BLAVATSKY

If any figure in the history of the paranormal was as controversial as she is remarkable that figure must be the woman who called herself Madame Helena Petrona Blavatsky. Her writings, views and predictions arouse heated debate and astonishment even today. To many she is considered a powerful psychic, a cultural messenger and even a prophet. As with all controversial figures in history there are those who attempt to debunk her incredible achievements and abilities, but when faced with the evidence, it is particularly hard not to believe that she was genuinely psychic. During her lifetime a wealth of literature by her and about her was created, and she brought about a revolution in Victorian spiritual thinking that affects us all today.

Madame Blavatsky was born in 1831 to a family of aristocrats in Dnepropetrovsk, Ukraine, although she spent most of the rest of her life travelling. The staff and servants of her family home later recalled how unusual she was as a child and how they credited her with possessing powers spoken of in their ancient rustic superstitions. She was reported to be a strange and troubled child, prone to sleepwalking, fits and headaches, all of which are common symptoms among those who have experienced visions or otherworldly communications.

Helena Petrona Blavatsky

ILLEGITIMATE CHILD

By the age of 18, Blavatsky was married to a man much her senior, but she quickly grew tired of him and embarked on a life of adventure and travel, leaving her family and country behind. There are numerous versions of Blavatsky's life story, especially concerning the less documented part of her early years. In this time she was alleged to have borne an illegitimate child and to have been the mistress of numerous men. However, despite this behaviour, which was utterly scandalous for the era she lived in, Blavatsky still achieved great fame and respect in society. She was undoubtedly afforded this leeway due to her status as a person who was profoundly different.

Blavatsky spent most of her sixty years travelling over huge expanses of the globe, studiously absorbing the culture and spiritual thinking of various different sections of humanity. Among the countries she visited were lands as diverse as Canada, Mexico, the West Indies, the USA, Japan, Egypt, Tibet and India, to name but a few.

Many of the skills she acquired while on this enlightening world tour were to have a bearing on her later life. She worked at one point with a circus and at another as an assistant to a medium who performed séances. However, it was her work alongside Eastern spiritualists that she claimed was the most influential force in her life.

MYSTICAL SECRETS

Blavatsky told of how she spent several years in both Tibet and India, studying as the student of great spiritual masters. She claimed that several 'mahatmas' took her into their trust, and that she became their apprentice. Her unique abilities were recognized by these great mystics and she was granted unprecedented access to ancient mystical secrets reserved only for the initiated. It was from these roots that she explained her extraordinary abilities of prophecy and communication with the spirit world.

These Eastern travels were a crucially important aspect of Madame Blavatsky's life for more reasons than this, however, and have left us a legacy of knowledge even today. She stated that it was here that she acquired the most important knowledge of her life. With this spiritual learning as her base, she introduced the first real taste of the wisdom and understanding of Eastern religions to the Western world, in particular ideas of karma, reincarnation and the hidden higher powers of the mind.

On her eventual return to the West after her spiritual apprenticeship, Blavatsky propounded the idea of reincarnation – a concept that was totally alien to Western Judeo-Christian spiritual thinking. She explained how she believed in the spiritual journey of the soul through many different bodies on the road towards perfection. She did not believe in humans reincarnating as animals, but rather that the human soul slowly evolves, improving itself until it can gain extraordinary superhuman powers.

She maintained that a small number of these highly evolved superhuman beings existed in Tibet and India and that they were guiding the fate of the world. The mythical Tibetan paradise of Shambala is said to be inhabited by these luminous superhuman beings who have attained greatness after many reincarnated lifetimes. Blavatsky stated that they were the sole possessors of the hidden 'ancient wisdom' that originated from highly advanced human civilizations of the past. She insisted that they had been guarding this knowledge and using it to benefit mankind.

The nature of what she described endorses certain aspects of Tibetan and Hindu philosophy. Both Tibetan monks and Indian Yogis attempt to reach a higher state of consciousness through dedicated training and the application of their minds through meditation. Many such monks and Yogis are capable of extraordinary superhuman feats as a result of the mystical power they have cultivated within themselves.

Blavatsky was later to crystallize her view of this Eastern spiritual thinking, and combine it with her own sense of mysticism, into a system called the 'Theosophical Movement', which she founded with a number of her followers in 1875. The teachings of this movement are still adhered to by a number of people around the world today. According to Blavatsky herself:

> 'The chief aim of the ... Theosophical society [was] to reconcile all world religions, sects and nations under a common system of ethics, based on eternal verities.'

Blavatsky's aim was unity. It seems that she was seized with a kind of moral fervour, recognizing the inherent wisdom of this ancient and peaceful school of thinking. She realized that for any change to come about in wider society she must publicize this wisdom as much as possible. There is no doubt that this mission benefited greatly from all the publicity she received from her psychic displays.

In some of her demonstrations she was said to have materialized objects such as a cup and saucer. On other occasions she produced written words that were said to originate from the spirit world. The nature of her displays would vary hugely, demonstrating her array of skills and powers. Blavatsky claimed to be able to communicate with her distant Eastern masters by a kind of spiritual telepathy. At one stage she explained how she had seen visions of a tall Hindu who actually materialized before her in Hyde Park, and then became her personal guru and teacher. Claims of this kind were typical of Blavatsky, who liked to create as much mystery around her person as possible to advance her cause.

Some of this has been dismissed by the sceptical as trickery and stage-play, especially as she may have learnt various 'magic' tricks from the performers she worked with. However there is plenty of other evidence of her abilities that is not quite so easy to dismiss. For instance, her writings contained new explanations of world history that differed massively from the accepted view, and predictions for the future that appear to have the essence of truth within them. Despite seeming outlandish at the time, many of her assertions have been proved true, giving her abilities great credibility.

Blavatsky explained to her Victorian audience that much of the 'ancient wisdom' professed by her Eastern teachers actually originated from the great lost civilizations of the past, such as Atlantis. She first mentioned the lost city of Atlantis in her 1877 book *Isis Unveiled*, which sold out on the day of its publication. In the decade following this, the mystery concerning Atlantis became the talk of the Victorian world, with other authors and thinkers such as Ignatius Donnelly approaching the subject with intense intellectual curiosity. Even today there are scientists and explorers searching for traces of this mysterious lost culture.

THE SECRET DOCTRINE

In 1888 Blavatsky went into even greater detail in her next book *The Secret Doctrine*. In this book she displays a thorough knowledge of the deep-sea floor, describing details which were far beyond the known science of her day. Notably she asserted that the recently discovered Mid-Atlantic ridge continued under Africa and into the Indian Ocean. This has since been proved true, as the ridge is the boundary of a tectonic plate. What makes this so remarkable is that the Victorians had no idea of plate tectonics, and

no means of verifying what she said. Technological advances in more recent times have revealed the extent of Blavatsky's genius.

Although this information may seem unrelated to her other teachings on Theosophy, it is actually tied in completely with her general world view. All that Blavatsky had learned from her masters in India and Tibet was from a store of lost knowledge she referred to as the 'great ancient secrets', which had originated from lost civilizations such as Atlantis or Lemuria, and had been guarded for millennia. Only the initiated were allowed access to this knowledge. Blavatsky claimed that the philosopher Plato himself was an initiate of this secret advanced brethren, which is how he knew about the existence of Atlantis.

WORLD DESTRUCTION

Blavatsky's prophecies of events that will befall our own culture make chilling reading. She predicted that there will be: 'a world destruction as happened to Atlantis 11,000 years ago … instead of Atlantis all of England and parts of [the] NW European coast will sink into the sea, in contrast, the sunken Azores region, the Isle of Posiedonis, will again be raised from the sea.'

Although predictions of doom abound in history, when they come from a character as peculiarly convincing as Madame Blavatsky they cannot be ignored. What is more, scientific revelations and discoveries in the fields of climatology and meteorology have revealed the possibility that she may be right. At present the global climate is warming more rapidly than at any point in history. If this causes the polar ice caps to melt completely it could have catastrophic ramifications for the world. Global sea levels could rise by several metres and low-lying areas of land, such as England or Holland, would be inundated, fulfilling the prophecy.

Blavatsky's predictions for the Azores also have definite potential to be fulfilled. The Azores is a particularly active geological area, with plenty of volcanic and tectonic activity. Although we cannot state unequivocally that Blavatsky is correct – or that land will rise from the ocean – she managed to pick one of the places in the world that this is most likely to happen. It is unlikely that she could have deduced this scientifically at the time, so we must assume that she gained this information from some supernatural origin.

Once again there is a mystery based on the inexplicable possession of advanced knowledge. When civilizations, tribes, or even individuals possess knowledge that is in advance of the science of the day, serious questions are posed about its origins. It becomes even more intriguing if they claim that this knowledge originates from a time before civilization is even believed to have existed. How could this knowledge possibly exist without the prior existence of an advanced civilization such as Atlantis?

There is much about Madame Blavatsky's life and achievements that it seems impossible to answer fully. Yet there is the unmistakable ring of truth in much of what she said. The peaceful pursuit of meditation and spiritual advancement in Tibet still amazes many in the West, just as it did the audiences of Madame Blavatsky in the 1800s. Scientific predictions for the future seem to concur with some of her more doom-laden prophecies, and many of her assertions were proved true after her death, leaving us to wonder how she came to know such details. Lack of a better explanation means we must accept that she possessed these 'ancient secrets', and that she was one of the most amazing and mysterious characters in recent history.

DANIEL DOUGLAS HOME

Considered by many spiritualists to be one of the most gifted mediums of all time, Daniel Douglas Home demonstrated his psychic prowess on countless occasions and is remarkable for the incredible range of his ability.

Whereas most spiritualists tend to specialize in the demonstration of a particular type of paranormal activity, nothing seemed beyond the reach of Home's amazing powers.

Home was born in 1833 in Edinburgh, Scotland and, in common with many spiritually gifted people,

Sir William Crookes, the eminent scientist, who tested Home's powers

his talents first manifested themselves during his childhood. His aunt described how, even as an infant, his cradle could be seen to rock itself, unassisted. As a child, he experienced some significant psychic events, and at one stage is said to have seen a vision of his mother that coincided with her death in another city.

Such remarkable powers could not protect him from illness, however, and he was a very sickly child. At the age of nine, he moved from Scotland to Connecticut, USA, to live with his aunt, and it was here that he was diagnosed with tuberculosis. One of the results of this condition was that Home's childhood was a particularly solitary one, during which time he came to believe that he was surrounded by the spirits of the dead. In fact, he would maintain throughout his life that he was supported by certain spiritual benefactors, and that it was these beings that were responsible for his paranormal displays.

The young Home's fascination with the supernatural and the strange happenings of his early years worried his God-fearing aunt, who believed that he must be possessed by the devil. Sadly, while he was still in his mid-teens, he was cast out of her house, and from this time on was forced to seek his fortune in the only way he knew how – by working as a professional medium. He would often be offered board and lodging by a patron in exchange for the performance of séances and displays, at which he would demonstrate his impressive abilities.

Home's repertoire was huge – apart from communicating with the deceased, he would also conjure up from nowhere whole arrays of spectral lights and music. Another of his skills was his extraordinary ability to shrink himself in size, or elongate his body, a phenomenon that was witnessed, and verified, by several people at once.

REMARKABLE DISPLAYS

It was perhaps his displays of telekinesis, though, that were the most remarkable. At several séances, Home caused tables and chairs to move of their own accord and on one occasion he was able to levitate a table to such a height that he could walk beneath it. He maintained, however, that these demonstrations could not actually be classed as telekinesis, for the actions stemmed not from the power of his own mind, but from the actions of friendly spirits with whom he was able to converse easily.

Home made it publicly known at this time that he believed the vast majority of mediums to be fraudulent, and so he took measures to prove that, unlike them, he was genuine. In contrast to other practitioners of the time, Home would conduct his séances in well-lit rooms, or even out of doors. When he demonstrated his ability to move items of furniture, he would challenge the audience to take hold of his hands and feet to prove that he was not touching anything. Many found his displays utterly convincing, particularly those in which he would

summon up spirit hands that would then either touch members of the séance, or write out personal messages for them.

Despite such public demonstrations of his talents, it was not until 1852 that Home's career, quite literally, took off. In a display that seemed to set him apart from his fellow spiritualists, Home showed how he was able to levitate off the ground for a prolonged period of time. According to the account of a journalist, F L Burr, who witnessed the event, Home levitated no fewer than three times, and on the last attempt actually rose up to touch the ceiling. Home later asserted that the levitation should be attributed to the power of his spirit companions, who had chosen to lift him into the air in this way.

Home's fame spread far and wide, and he set off on a European tour, eventually reaching Russia, where he married. During his travels, he performed séances for some of the leading figures of the day, notably Emperor Napoleon III of France and the Empress Eugenie. Both were amazed by his abilities. At one stage, Home even appeared to make contact with the deceased Napoleon Bonaparte, who signed his name on paper. The Emperor was enormously impressed by this, announcing to all that the handwriting was genuinely that of Bonaparte himself.

Arguably the most famous and impressive of Home's feats was performed in London, at the home of Lord Adare, in 1866. Apparently without warning, Home slipped into a trance and began to levitate. He then proceeded to float out of one of the open windows before drifting back in through another. This demonstration ensured Home's popularity and fame, especially as the assembled audience was possessed of considerable credibility and influence.

What is clear is that Home was a supremely talented individual. Some sceptics have asked, however, whether his skills as a medium were genuine or whether his abilities lay more in the area of deception. It has been suggested that Home may have induced some powerful kind of mass hallucination in his audiences through the power of suggestion.

Home was so confident of his own abilities that he agreed to subject himself to some rigorous investigations. Sir William Crookes, a well-known scientist of the day with a particular interest in spirituality, studied Home's activities over a two-year period. During this time, Home apparently managed to make an accordion play while it was sealed inside a cage which had been specially designed by Crookes to block out the magnetic energies that he believed were the root of Home's power. Finally, Crookes was forced to admit that he could find no scientific explanation for Home's remarkable powers.

BETTY SHINE

At the outbreak of the Second World War Betty Shine was evacuated to the comparative safety of the English countryside with thousands of other children whose parents were desperate to save them from the dangers of the London Blitz. One night a stray bomb landed near the house in which she was staying, blowing in all the windows and sending a large shard of glass into the headboard just an inch above her head. The shock appears to have stimulated her psychic sensitivity because the following night Betty began to see 'misty people' passing through her bedroom door, across the room and through the opposite wall. Even though they seemed oblivious to her she found their presence oddly reassuring and accepted her extraordinary psychic experiences as entirely natural. At the time she thought that everyone shared the same clairvoyant gifts until a friend assured her that seeing dead people was unusual to say the least.

At first Betty was reluctant to pursue her calling as a medium and healer, but by the time she had reached adulthood the build-up of suppressed psychic energy was making her physically ill. When she finally opened up to the power within she was overwhelmed by self-generated phenomena such as moving objects and disturbances which are commonly associated with poltergeist activity. 'I was seeing spirit faces everywhere – on the walls, in the carpet, everywhere and I would hear voices too as if I was suddenly able

Thousands of children were evacuated from London during the Second World War. For Betty Shine, it was to prove a particularly life-changing experience

to hear people talking in the next room, only they weren't in this world but the next.'

On one occasion she sensed a dark entity overshadowing a female patient and heard its voice in her own head saying, 'I will never leave her, she's mine.' As soon as she began praying for protection, Betty saw a bright white light appear around the entity putting it into silhouette. It was a man and as he was pulled away by some unseen force into the light he screamed. At the same moment, the woman instinctively covered her ears, though she later told Betty that she hadn't actually heard anything. After the session the woman told Betty that she had once been married to a possessive, sadistic man who had pursued her for years after she had left him before finally suffering a fatal heart attack on her doorstep. After his death she remarried but still felt his suffocating overbearing presence and had become chronically depressed. A few weeks after the exorcism the woman returned to Betty's healing centre radiant and relieved, finally free of the black cloud she felt had been smothering her for years.

THE PSYCHIC CLERIC

It is believed by some that everyone attends their own funeral in spirit, if only to see who has turned out to say goodbye. It is not uncommon for family members to see the deceased who often appear bemused at what they perceive as the fuss being made over their empty shell. Catholic sacristan Tina Hamilton often senses the presence of discarnate spirits during the funeral services over which she presides at St Thomas Church, Canterbury, England.

'I rarely see them, but I hear them and sense the force of their personality which has survived the death of the physical body. Sometimes I may even feel an arm around my

Who knows what uninvited guests are at the funeral of a loved one?

shoulder. If it is a particularly strong presence they might try to communicate in which case I will hear them as another voice in my head. These are not my own thoughts. The tone of voice is quite distinct from my own. They tell me that they feel more alive than they did in life and will express frustration at not being able to be seen by their friends and family.

'Many express surprise at the number of people who have come to pay their respects, while others seem amused at seeing a relative who didn't like them but who has reluctantly turned up out of a sense of duty.

'Curiously, it's usually their sense of humour that touches me most strongly. I suspect it stems from the relief of having been unburdened of their earthly responsibilities and fears and the sense that they are now free from the constraints of the physical body.

'I have been presiding over funeral services for more than 50 years and can truly say that I have never sensed a spirit that appeared disturbed, although I once conducted the funeral service for a teenage suicide who came through to say how sorry she was for having brought her parents so much pain. She asked me to tell them that it wasn't their fault. She had been suffering from depression and other problems which her family later confirmed to have contributed to her death.'

THE SOUL RESCUER

Exorcisms are rarely performed these days. The most common method of clearing a haunted house of earthbound spirits today is a technique known as 'soul rescuing'.

British psychic Pamela Redwood typifies the new breed of 'sensitives' who can sense spirits – malign

or otherwise – and work quietly to rid homeowners of their uninvited guests, bringing both parties peace of mind. She explains:

'What is sad is when someone cannot return to the light after their death because they are so attached to their life. I have cleared several houses where there have been disturbances or where the owner complains that they cannot live there because a certain room is cold even in the summer. They call me in and the first thing I pick up on is a thickness in the atmosphere as if it is charged with an invisible presence. Sometimes my spirit guides will give me different colours and I will see that soul taken up through the ray of colour by my guides into the light and then the atmosphere will clear as if the room has been aired.

'I used to take the spirit up through my own body as I thought that I had to act as a channel for its return to the light but now the guides do it for me. Which is just as well as it could be very exhausting to be a host to someone else's spirit even for a few minutes. I would feel as if I'd absorbed their essence into my own being, but occasionally if they were reluctant to go I would still have them with me when I went home. My daughter is very psychic and she would see me hobbling down the garden path, bent double like an old hag with a spirit on my shoulder and calmly say to her dad, "Mum's back and she's brought a ghost home."

'You have to treat earthbound spirits as if they were still alive as they are the same personalities that they were in life. I once had to persuade the spirit of a pipe-smoking stubborn old man to pass over by promising him that he would have all the tobacco he could smoke if he went over to the other side!'

JOHN EDWARD

The young American medium John Edward (whose hugely popular TV show *Crossing Over* has been syndicated around the world) is one of a new generation of 'celebrity psychics'. His affability and commonsense approach have dispelled the suffocating gloom of Victorian spiritualism that gave mediumship a bad name with its candlelit séances and obsession with ectoplasm. His extraordinary experiences demonstrate that spirits are not an unsettling paranormal phenomenon but simply discarnate individuals who initiate contact with the living because they wish to assure their grieving loved ones that they are fine and to encourage them to move on with their own lives.

The first hint that John possessed an unusual talent came at an early age when he casually commented on events in his family history. These were events which he shouldn't have known about as they had occurred before he was born, yet he assured his parents that he remembered being there at the time. By the age of five he had informed his teachers that he could see a radiance around them. It was only much later that he learnt that not everyone could see these coloured auras. The first flowering of his psychic gifts began with visions of his maternal grandfather who had died in 1962, seven years before John was born. He saw the old man sitting at the dinner table next to his grandmother who took John's announcement that the old man was present as a comfort, even though she couldn't see her husband herself. John soon graduated to premonitions that relatives would drop by unexpectedly – a talent his mother soon learnt to take seriously and be grateful for.

MYSTERY WOMAN

Then one day, while he was still in his teens, he witnessed his first significant materialization. His aunt Anna had teased him into reading the tarot cards which she regarded as little more than a child's magic trick. But when John looked up from the cards he saw a woman standing behind his aunt. She was a stout lady in her sixties, wearing a black dress and a flower-shaped brooch and she appeared to have only one leg. John's description gave Aunt Anna a start. She immediately identified the mystery woman as her mother-in-law who had lost her leg through diabetes. Aunt Anna had never met her and neither had John because the old lady had died before he was born. But that was only the beginning.

The number of readings John was asked to give put enormous demands on his time, but the most taxing aspect was the sheer intellectual effort he had to make in order to interpret the subtle signs the spirits were showing him. Often they would use obscure references because they couldn't communicate directly, but on one occasion John learnt that there was a danger in trying too hard. During a reading for a recently bereaved lady, her dead husband kept showing John a bell. The reading had been going well up to that point and she had been able to verify everything John had passed on to her.

John Edward in a publicity shot for his TV show

John Edward hosts Crossing Over, *which is very popular with celebrities – for example, Deborah Gibson (right) – and the public alike*

But he was puzzled by the bell. He asked if she or her husband had had any connection with Philadelphia or Ben Franklin. Did they know of anyone called Ben or Franklin? It was only when John said that he kept seeing the image of a bell but couldn't think of another association for that image that the woman understood and became tearful. On the morning of his death her husband had given her a souvenir bell he had picked up on a business trip. 'If you ever need me, ring this and I'll be there,' he had said. Then he kissed his wife goodbye and went to work. He was killed in a car accident later that day. Sometimes a bell just means a bell.

As his fame spread, first by word of mouth and then through his TV show, John found his appointments diary filled to overflowing and the spirits crowding in, jostling for his attention in their eagerness to have their messages passed on to their loved ones. They would pull him to one side of the room and home him in on a particular member of the audience, then tease him with tantalizing clues. The atmosphere was good-natured, although often emotional, as friends and family members recognized a pet name or a half-forgotten incident which the spirit recalled to validate the evidence of their survival. Occasionally, the experience was dramatic. A victim of a car accident came through to give her version of events, offering unknown evidence implicating another driver, whose involvement was subsequently verified by the police.

More often, though, spirits speak of mundane matters which sceptics argue is proof that mediumship is a dangerous delusion. If it was a genuine communication from the afterlife, they argue, then surely the spirit would have something profound to say about life after death. Instead, they usually talk of routine family matters. John Edward contends that such minor personal details are more important for the grieving family as what they really need is proof that they are talking to their loved ones.

OUIJA BOARDS

The Ouija (which is said to take its name from a combination of the French and German words for 'yes') was produced as a parlour game in 1898 at the height of the spiritualism craze by the Fuld brothers of Baltimore.

Invented by Elijah Bond, who was working for the Fulds, this Ouija Board is a trade name for a particular product, the name has come to mean any of several similar devices. Some see these as harmless toys, and the original Ouija Board is the second highest-selling board game with 25 million sold in Europe and the USA to date. Others view them as dangerous ways to meddle in the paranormal and deplore the fact that the Ouija Board continues to be available in toyshops and novelty stores around the world despite its dubious reputation.

MYSTIC SYMBOLS

The Fuld brothers may have been inspired by a similar technique used by the ancient Egyptians to contact their ancestors. The Egyptians used a ring suspended by a thread which they held over a board inscribed with mystic symbols. The inquirer then asked their questions and noted which symbols the ring indicated. Another inspiration may have been the Chinese Fuji, a board marked with Chinese words over which a pointer moved allegedly of its own volition.

The ouija board works in a similar way. A board is

marked with letters of the alphabet, numbers from 0 to 9 and the words 'yes' and 'no' – there are usually a number of mystical symbols of no real meaning that help give it a spooky look. Participants place a finger on a pointer called a planchette which moves on casters or sometimes is felt to give a slight twitch – it is supposedly manipulated by the spirits. The user asks a question, the answer to which is then spelled out by the planchette as it moves around the board.

MESSAGES FROM BEYOND

Those who believe that the ouija is delivering messages from the spirit world suggest that the board somehow enables people who are not psychic enough to be mediums to make contact with the spirits. Whether the pointer is moved directly by the spirits, or by one of the users who is guided by the spirits is irrelevant to this explanation. The ouija has no power in itself, but serves to channel the latent psychic powers of the users.

Detractors argue that the supposed spirit messages originate in the participants' unconscious and that what appears to be a twitching of the planchette is in fact caused by involuntary muscle contractions known as ideomotor actions. Whatever the source, there is no doubt that messages – many of them predicting death – have been recorded using this method.

Among the more famous users of the ouija was Mrs Pearl Curran, who first used a ouija in May 1913. In her first session, Mrs Curran made contact with what appeared to be a spirit able only to spell out the words 'pat c' repeatedly. This spirit, if that is what it was, soon learned how to use a ouija more effectively and revealed that its name was Patience Worth. This spirit rarely revealed much about herself, preferring to dictate poetry. From the little that could be gleaned, it seemed that Patience Worth had had a fairly miserable time on Earth. She had been born in Dorset around 1640 or so, but at an early age had moved with her family to live in one of the English colonies in North America. Soon after arriving she had been killed by a raiding party of local Native

Americans. No wonder she preferred to write. A typical example of her poetry in these early sessions was 'Lavender and Lace':

A purple sky; twilight
Silver fringed of tremorous stars;
cloud rifts, tattered as old lace
And a shuttling moon – wan-faced seeking.

Twilight and garden shadows;
The liquid note of some late songster;
And the scent of lavender and rue
Like memory of the day aclinging.

TALKING TO SPIRITS

Worth later dictated over 1.6 million words through Mrs Curran. Most of the work was published under the name of Patience Worth, at first with no indication that the author was apparently dead at the time she did the writing.

The novels received some critical acclaim and sold well, but sales rocketed once Mrs Curran confessed that the books had been dictated to her through a ouija board. Several of the books were historical novels containing obscure, but true information that Worth claimed to have gained from talking to spirits who had lived at the time. There seemed no way that Mrs Curran – who had not enjoyed much formal education herself – could have known this information.

Whatever the origins of Worth's work, it was only one example of apparent literary work from beyond the grave. In 1917 Emily G. Hutchings was using a ouija when she seemed to make contact with the recently deceased American writer Mark Twain. The Twain spirit dictated to her a novel, which Hutchings sought to publish under the name of Mark Twain. Unsurprisingly, Twain's family went to court to halt publication of the book in his name, arguing that it was a fraud. Most critics agreed that it was so bad that it could not have been written by Twain dead or alive.

Some researchers fear that malevolent entities will use a ouija as a way of making contact with a human.

Talking to the world beyond: the use of a ouija board appears to open up the possibility of communication with disembodied spirits

The entity would pretend to be a harmless or friendly departed human spirit in order to beguile the user into continuing contact. Slowly, however, the entity will twist the messages given so as to inveigle the hapless human into demonic activity and evil acts. Certainly some users can become compulsive in their need to use the ouija, disrupting their family and work lives as the ouija becomes an addiction. Whether this is the fault of a demon or of the user's own psychological problems is a moot point.

DEMONIC FORCES

There have been an alarming number of violent attacks and teenage suicides involving unstable and impressionable individuals who claim to have been acting on the instructions of demonic forces contacted through a ouija board. It is marketed as a 'fun' game in which the 'players' consult the 'Mystifying Oracle', but the evidence suggests that in the wrong hands it can become dangerously addictive and can be profoundly disturbing to those who are psychologically unsound.

It has been compared to punching in a random phone number and hoping to connect with a family member, old friend or guru. Your call is far more likely to be picked up by a stranger who may find the temptation to tease or torment too good to resist. Even if the discarnate spirits who are attracted by this activity are not malevolent or intent on mischief, they may nevertheless influence how the players interpret their messages simply by the fact that they are earthbound and therefore must themselves be distressed or addictive personalities. This would account for the predominance of negative messages. Benign spirits are presumably beyond the influence of the board, enjoying their eternal rest.

The board itself may not be intrinsically bad, but it attracts the irresponsible and the immature who are not able to handle what they receive. If you have natural mediumistic ability, you won't need the board or any other focus object to induce the light trance state which will make you receptive to spirit communication.

In 1917 Emily G. Hutchings tried to publish a novel allegedly from the pen of Mark Twain (above) – he died in 1910. See page 27

Horror film fans will recall that it is through the use of the ouija board that the little girl in *The Exorcist* becomes possessed. This movie is not alone in using a ouija for dramatic effect. In the movie *What Lies Beneath*, Michelle Pfeiffer and her friend try to contact the ghost in her house with a ouija, while the character Monica in the TV show *Friends* is shown using one on occasion. More recently the movie *Ouija*, released in 2007, uses events surrounding a ouija as the main plot device with supernatural and horrific consequences. However you view it, the ouija board spells danger.

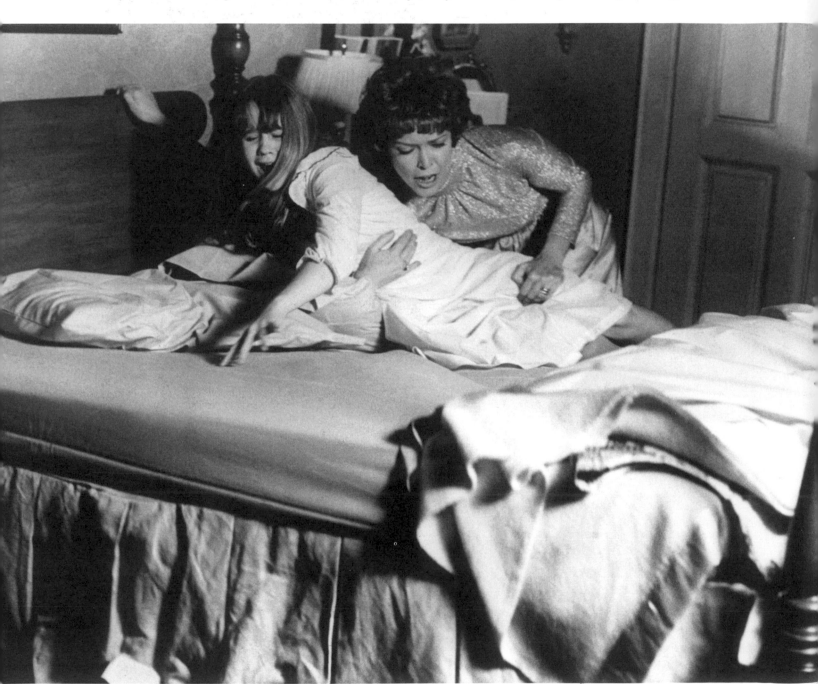

Ellen Burstyn and Linda Blair (left) in a scene from the 1973 movie The Exorcist: *it was through the use of a ouija board that the main character became possessed*

PREDICTIONS AND SEERS

The desire to predict the future is deeply rooted in human nature. People have always been fascinated by the art of prophecy and throughout the ages have attempted to discern what the future might hold for them. Sometimes they try to achieve this by consulting an individual who possesses the unique ability to see into the future – a seer or an oracle.

There are many different methods of divination, which are practised by societies all over the world. Belief in the power of the prophet is strong, as case after case demonstrates that there is some truth behind this mysterious phenomenon.

NOSTRADAMUS

Of all those who have claimed to be able to predict the future, none has gained greater fame than the 16th century Frenchman known today as Nostradamus. But even he could not foresee that his words would have such a long-lasting effect, remaining pivotal in the beliefs of many people up to five centuries after his death.

The words penned by Nostradamus during his many years as a seer have been translated, pored over and debated. Still, no one is sure how much weight to lend them. While some of his predictions appear wildly speculative and have not yet come to pass, others seem to have neatly summed up events with spine-chilling clarity.

Nostradamus was born Michel de Nostradame in St Rémy de Provence on 14 December 1503. He was from a prosperous middle-class family and his father is generally described either as a lawyer or grain merchant – he may have been both. Young Michel

Nostradamus (1503–1566) couched his prophecies in a mysterious combination of French, Latin, Greek and Italian in order to avoid condemnation by the Catholic Inquisition

proved to be a brilliant young scholar, showing particular skill in languages and the sciences. He also read voraciously. The family had recently converted from Judaism to the more prevalent Roman Catholic faith, so Michel grew up with a thorough knowledge of both belief systems.

However, Nostradamus' first passion was medicine, and at the age of 18 he entered the University of Montpelier to train as a physician. He became a successful doctor, married and fathered two children, but his medical skills were not sufficient to save his young family from the clutches of the dreaded plague. After the death of his wife and children, the bereft Nostradamus became a wandering scholar, travelling throughout southern France and Italy.

It was while he was in Italy that the first sign of his future career became apparent. He came across a group of Franciscan monks herding cattle and for some reason thought that one of them was the pope. He knelt down to address one of the monks as 'your holiness'. The men, however, were only monks and soon put Nostradamus correct. Years later the monk singled out by Nostradamus, Felice Peretti, became Pope Sextus V.

When Nostradamus reached the age of 44, he ended his itinerant lifestyle and settled in the Provencal town of Salon. He married a wealthy widow and began his career in prophecy in earnest. His aim was nothing less than to prophesy the future of mankind, and eight years later he produced the first of more than a dozen books of predictions. The books are called *Centuries* because each is made up of a hundred verses, or quatrains.

Nostradamus saw no conflict between his religion and his prophecies. However, he knew that others would not share this open-minded attitude. So he set about disguising his predictions by couching them in a mysterious combination of French, Latin, Greek and Italian. Furthermore, he used metaphors and anagrams to produce baffling and impenetrable riddles.

Despite the mysterious nature of the predictions, Nostradamus' *Centuries* became popular reading material, particularly among the nobility and royalty, and his reputation grew ever greater. During his lifetime, he came to prominence for one prediction in particular, which gained him both friends and enemies.

> *The Young Lion will overcome the older*
> *one on the field of combat in a single battle,*

> *Inside a cage of gold his eyes will*
> *be put out,*
> *Two wounds made one,*
> *He dies a cruel death.*
> *(Century 1, Quatrain 35)*

Just four years after this prophecy was written, King Henry II of France died during a joust when a lance pierced his gilded visor and caused two mortal injuries. Many believed that Nostradamus had caused the death of the King, and demanded that the prophet be tried for heresy. Fortunately for Nostradamus, the king's widow, Catherine de Medici, did not share their view. She was so impressed by his powers that she hired him as physician to her son and heir.

But Nostradamus was not only adept at predicting events during his own lifetime. Several of his verses seem to have predicted events that took place long after his death in 1566. Take this one:

> *The blood of the just will be demanded*
> *of London,*
> *Burnt by the fire in the year 66,*
> *The ancient Lady will fall from her*
> *high place,*
> *And many of the same sect will be killed.*
> *(Century 2, Quatrain 51)*

In 1666, the great fire of London destroyed much of the city, including St Paul's cathedral which contained a famous statue of St Mary the Virgin. After the fire some Protestant Londoners blamed Catholic agents of the Pope and demanded that they be executed for arson. This prediction is particularly striking, but many of the others do seem to jigsaw with history. For instance:

> *That which neither weapon nor flame could*
> *accomplish will be achieved,*
> *By a sweet-speaking tongue in a council,*
> *Sleeping, in a dream, the king will see the*
> *enemy not in war,*
> *Or of military blood.*
> *(Century I, Quatrain 97)*

Nostradamus alarms Catherine de Medici, Henri II's queen, with his predictions, as portrayed in an early twentieth-century magazine at a time when spiritualism and the occult were particularly popular

This prediction seems to have a particular resonance with the fate of King Henri III of France. The king, who was on the throne during Nostradamus' lifetime, survived wars and jousts, but in the end he was murdered just after a council meeting by a monk.

Another Nostradamus prediction runs:

The rejected one shall at last reach the throne,
Her enemies found to have been traitors,
More than ever shall her period be triumphant,
At seventy she shall go assuredly to death, in the third year of the century.
(Century VI, Quatrain 74)

Surely this refers to Queen Elizabeth I of England, who at the age of three was declared to be illegitimate by her father, Henry VIII. But when she finally ascended the throne in 1558, in the face of Catholic opposition, her reign was indisputably glorious. She did indeed die aged 70, and the year was 1603.

Although many of Nostradamus' predictions tally with historical events to a startling degree, sceptics have drawn attention to the prophet's ambiguous language, and the fact that he is thought to have copied other prophecies current in his era. The critics claim that, if the cryptic messages of Nostradamus can be applied to real events, then it is nothing more than coincidence. Take, for example, the quatrain thought by many to refer to the coming of Hitler:

Beasts wild with hunger will cross the rivers,
The greater part of the battlefield will be against Hister,
He will drag the leader in a cage of iron,
When the child of Germany observes no law.
(Century II, Quatrain 24)

This quatrain does at first seem to sum up the events of the Second World War during Hitler's dictatorship and to allude to the savage Nazi troops swamping Europe and humiliating conquered leaders. However, Hister is also the exact name of an area close to the Danube. So the prediction can be read with two meanings, although with historical hindsight, it makes better sense when Hister is read as Hitler.

Some of Nostradamus' prophecies have been wrong, most spectacularly the one that implied a catastrophic war would break out in July 1999. Yet despite the ambiguity that surrounds his predictions, thousands of people give due respect to Nostradamus, believing his case has been proven at least in part. And since his predictions continue until 3797, he still has plenty of time to be proved right.

One premonition that he got exactly right was his own death. 'You will not see me alive at sunrise,' he told his assistant on the evening of 1 July 1566. True to his word, by the following morning he was dead.

SHAMBALA

The hidden kingdom of Shambala is described in ancient Tibetan religious texts as a mystical place. Although in geographical terms it is supposed to be located somewhere between the mountains of Tibet and the vast Gobi desert, it is allegedly separated from the world by a spiritual boundary, meaning that only those who are meant to find it will ever reach it. The kingdom has been sought by Tibetan lamas (religious men) for centuries, many putting aside years of their lives in dedicated spiritual preparation.

The Tibetan manuscripts contain detailed descriptions of the secluded land. Maps liken its shape to that of an eight-petalled lotus, with the palace of Kalapa situated in the centre and illustrations reveal that the inhabitants of Shambala are blessed with advanced means of transport such as aircraft and shuttle systems. They also possess sophisticated scientific instruments with which to study the stars.

A Tibetan lama in traditional costume: many lamas put aside years of their lives in dedicated spiritual preparation for a journey to the hidden kingdom of Shambala

Contained in the texts are prophecies relating to the rulers and people of this mysterious kingdom. Precise information is given about the reigns of the 32 kings of Shambala, the dates of the various successions being listed in detail. It is also predicted that, over time, the inhabitants will grow in power and enlightenment, gradually acquiring skills such as the art of telepathy and the ability to travel vast distances at great speed. As they develop, the outside world will correspondingly degenerate, becoming warlike and power-hungry, eschewing the spiritual life for material wealth.

Finally a day of reckoning will come about. At this point, the world will have deteriorated to such a point that it will be dominated by a vicious king who, believing that he is omnipotent, will discover Shambala and attack it. In this battle, the 32nd king of the hidden kingdom, Rudra Cakrin, will lead a vast army of the pure and enlightened to victory, heralding an age of perfection.

Those who believe in the existence of Shambala view factors such as the global spread of materialism and the troubled history of the last hundred years or so as evidence of the accuracy of the predictions contained in the ancient texts. However, as the predicted doomsday year is not until 2425, there is a long time to go until we can know for certain whether the prophets have correctly predicted the future.

I-CHING

The *I-Ching* or *Book of Changes* remains as important today as it was when it first appeared between five and eight thousand years ago. Containing the founding principles of Chinese philosophy, this book, together with the Bible and the Koran, is one of the most studied works in the world and is revered for the great insights held within its pages.

The *I-Ching*, which represents a guide to divination and moral counsel, is central to Chinese and other Asian cultures. The study of this book and the basic Taoist principles that underpin its philosophy also form a major part of the study of

Careful manipulation of the straws produces a meaningful pattern

feng shui, Chinese medicine and most martial arts. By interpreting the *I-Ching*, key decisions about war, love, business and many other personal and political issues can be made.

Early divination in China involved throwing a tortoise shell on to a fire and analyzing the cracks that formed. These cracks were interpreted by comparing them to eight trigrams that are representative of the eight primal forces of the universe. Some believe that the first person to understand this system was Fu Hsi, the legendary first emperor of China. This system then went on to be modified by another mythical emperor, Yu, after seeing a similar pattern on the shell of a tortoise in the Lo River. This Lo Shu map was then interpreted according to a later asymmetrical system that incorporated the four seasons and five elements, and refers to the order of change in the manifest world.

BUCKING THE SYSTEM

The next modification of the system occurred in the Shang dynasty, between 1766–1121BC. Wen Wang, usually referred to as King Wen, was a powerful feudal lord who was imprisoned and sentenced to death by the Shang Emperor, Chou Hsin. While languishing in prison, he is said to have studied the trigrams and combined them to form hexagrams. He then named and organized the sixty-four hexagrams into their present arrangement, as well as providing much of the accompanying explanatory text.

The final modification and resulting present-day name occurred during the 5th century BC. Kung Fu-Tze, better known in the West as Confucius, studied the system and added further philosophical commentary, so overlaying the Taoist principles with Confucian ideas.

There are two principal methods of reading the *I-Ching*, both of which have their basis in the random generation of binary choices. The traditional method is a complex process involving the manipulation of fifty dried yarrow straws, whereby the resultant patterns denote a certain sequence of hexagrams.

The simple, more commonly used method involves the casting of coins. The side which is uppermost when the coin has fallen relates to the drawing of a line, which in turn constitutes the sequence of hexagrams.

The *I-Ching* was first introduced to the West in 1882, when James Legge provided the first English translation. Legge, however, did not approve of the oracular function of the book and it failed to arouse any significant interest until the philosopher Carl Jung brought his attention to bear on it.

Jung discovered that consultations with the oracle on a wide range of topics resulted in consistently meaningful and startlingly accurate insights. He subsequently recorded these findings in an introduction to a German translation of the book in 1929. When Jung's contribution was finally translated into English in 1949, it was received with great enthusiasm and is still widely used and studied.

Today, the *I-Ching* continues to be held in high esteem all over the world largely as a result of its remarkable powers of prophecy and guidance. Although debate surrounds some of its early history, this has not affected its popularity, and it seems likely that this ancient Eastern oracle will continue to be consulted for the mystical wisdom it contains, for many years to come, by seekers after the truth.

> Jung discovered that consultations with the oracle on a wide range of topics resulted in consistently meaningful and accurate insights

Chinese divination bones from the Shang dynasty: the cracks in what were usually ox shoulder-blade bones were interpreted to provide a yes/no or good/bad alternative

BIBLICAL PROPHETS

The Bible contains several main prophetic books, and within each of these is a series of 'Oracles against Foreign Nations'. These highly stylized and poetic sections contain God's predictions about the fate of those nations who commit crimes against humanity and who sin against God. One of the most famous of these can be found in the book of Ezekiel, concerning the fate of the mighty city of Tyre.

Ezekiel continues to prophesy after his deportation by the Babylonians

The prediction was written in 586BC. At that time, Babylon, under the awesome auspices of Nebuchadnezzar, was in the process of consolidating and expanding its empire in the Eastern Mediterranean, and was aiming to gain control of Egypt. Israel was the stepping-stone between Babylon in the east and Egypt in the west, and in 606BC Israel became a vassal state of Babylon. Discontent and nationalism brewed as a result and eventually surfaced as a rebellion against the Babylonian forces.

This was quickly quashed, however, and many of the Israeli ringleaders, including Ezekiel, were deported in 598BC. It was there that Ezekiel made his now-famous prediction.

The city of Tyre was a significant Phoenician seaport, which linked shipping routes from all over the Mediterranean with land caravans from Arabia, Babylon, Persia and India. Ezekiel predicted that, despite its strong defensive position, Tyre and its land-based 'daughter' villages would be totally destroyed. He prophesied: 'For thus says the Lord GOD: Behold, I will bring upon Tyre from the north Nebuchadnezzar king of Babylon, king of kings, with horses and chariots, and with horsemen and a host of soldiers … He will slay with the sword your daughters on the mainland.'

Nebuchadnezzar did attack Tyre, demolishing the mainland parts of the city and laying siege to the island for 13 years. Although the city was not captured, Tyre did agree to become a vassal of Babylon.

THE PAGAN PROPHET

One of the most controversial seers of the Old Testament is Balaam, the pagan prophet whose name means 'devourer of people'. The prophet is often depicted as being blind in one eye and lame in one foot, with his followers distinguished only by merit of possessing the three morally corrupt qualities of an evil eye, haughtiness and greed.

Balaam started his career as an interpreter of dreams, before becoming a magician and finally a prophet. This gift of prophecy enabled him to predict

An illustration of a prophet from the period during which Balaam made his predictions

the exact moment at which God's wrath would occur, and thus his powers could be extremely valuable to the world at large. So great was his reputation as a reliable oracle, that people far and wide asserted: 'he whom thou blessest is blessed, and he whom thou cursest is cursed.'

Anxious to secure Balaam's services, King Balak of Moab – at that time fighting a war against the Israelites – sent messengers to summon the infamous soothsayer. Balaam set off, but the ass on which he rode suddenly stopped when it – but not Balaam – saw an angel of God barring the way. When Balaam whipped the ass, the angel gave it the power of speech so that it could alert the prophet to the presence of the angel. Balaam bowed down before the divine messenger, confessed his sins and offered to return to his homeland. The angel responded by saying that he could continue his journey, but only if he refused to help Balak.

Balaam agreed and continued on his journey to Moab. Here, in response to God's instructions, he ordered Balak to offer sacrifices of seven oxen and seven rams on seven altars positioned on high ground overlooking the land of Israel. Balak did so and was both astonished and furious when Balaam declared blessings on the Israelites and predicted success for them. Balak ceased his aggression against the Israelites. This did not save the city for it was later conquered by King David of Israel.

THE DELPHIC ORACLE

The oracle at Delphi was at the shrine of Apollo, the Greek god of fine arts and the sun. Set high on the hillside of Mount Parnassus, it occupied a prominent position, reflecting the esteem in which it was held in Greek culture.

According to legend, Apollo took control of Parnassus when he was a child, by killing Python, a huge snake, in the battle between the gods of the sky and the earth. Apollo then assumed the form of a dolphin (delphis in Greek, from which the shrine derived its name) and journeyed out into the ocean to capture some sailors who were appointed his first high priests.

Apollo spoke to humans at Delphi through the sybil, or chief priestess. The sybil, who was always a mature woman who had lived a pure life, would take on the name Pythia upon being appointed, after the python slain by the young Apollo. When she sought to speak with Apollo, Pythia would enter a trance before delivering the god's answers. These were sometimes clear messages, but at other times were filled with allusions, allegories and riddles. These were then analyzed and interpreted by the high priests before being relayed to the waiting supplicants.

Some answers given by the Delphic Oracle have become famous. In 480BC, for instance, Athens faced an invasion by a Persian force. The Athenians asked the Delphic Oracle for advice and were told, 'Put trust in the wooden walls of Athens.' The reply did not seem to make sense as Athens was surrounded by stone walls. Then it was realized that the Oracle meant the wooden walls of the Athenian warfleet.

The fleet was sent out and managed to destroy the Persian supply fleet, forcing the main Persian army to retreat.

CONSULTING THE ORACLE

Upon arriving at Delphi, these supplicants would have registered and paid a fee to make an appointment. They would then have been required to purify themselves in the Castalian spring, where a bathing trough still exists, and walk up the Sacred Way to the shrine. A sacrificial offering in the form of a sheep or goat would have been made and the entrails examined for omens by priests. When the pilgrims finally reached the sybil, they were allowed in, one at a time, to ask for her answers to their question.

The Delphic oracle was visited over a period of almost 2,000 years, during which time countless prophecies were delivered on subjects ranging from wars and matters of state to personal affairs, births and deaths. The supplicants came from almost every level of society, a factor that demonstrates the regard in which prophecy was held in the everyday life of those times.

THE SANGOMAS

Deep in the heart of Southern Africa there lives a tradition of healing and divination that is integral to African culture, and is as respected today as it was thousands of years ago. The extraordinary powers of Sangomas, or diviner priests, produce predictions remarkable in their accuracy. It is estimated that around 200,000 such diviners are practising today, helping more than 84 per cent of the Southern African population.

The role of the Sangoma varies and can be divided into two primary categories, although these are by no means rigidly defined. The principal kind of Sangoma is the ancestrally designated diviner who communes with the ancestors, usually by entering a trance, to predict the future. The second type of Sangoma is the herbalist or doctor, who uses traditional methods to cure the sick and has not been called by the ancestors. However, these boundaries are often blurred, as one person may fill both roles.

Novices (*thwasas*) begin their training by enduring and surviving an illness called *ukuthwasa*. This signals that the ancestors, or deceased spirits, have called them to their vocation. The relationship between the novice and the ancestors is forged during the recovery from the illness, and the person assumes a new identity and role in life.

The ancestral link is crucial to the cures and readings that will be made by the Sangoma, as it is believed that the ancestors are the messengers acting as a link between deity and man. The Sangoma, in turn, provides a mouthpiece for the ancestors, and carries out their instructions.

The deliverance of these messages fulfils a major social and political function, as the prophecies provide an acceptable arena for debate about issues that may otherwise be taboo or politically dangerous. Predictions are made on subjects ranging from the

The healing powers of the ancients: a potential customer squats down to examine the wares of a Sangoma, or southern African shaman, which include bones and herbs

state of the crops and the weather to personal problems and health issues. Sangomas maintain that illness can be attributed to one of three main causes – the ancestors, witchcraft and 'pollution' (for example, menstruation or miscarriage). Once the root of the problem has been established, the process of healing can begin.

THE TRANCE STATE

The trance state entered by the diviner is usually central to the process of delivering the oracle. This condition is achieved through a wide variety of ritualistic methods, including rhythmic drumming, clapping and dancing, the inhalation of herbal medicines (*muti*) such as snuff, and the burning of incense (*indumba*). The attire of the Sangoma is also very important, and he will often wear elaborate ostrich feather head-dresses, and tie rattles and beads to his body.

Upon entering the trance, the Sangoma often starts to shake, and his breathing becomes more erratic as the ancestors enter his body. The men then use 'bones' (shells, coins, dice and twigs) as part of the divination ritual, which are thrown on to an impala skin. The position and alignment of the scattered objects are then interpreted, providing the Sangoma with the information required to deliver the oracle or to cure the patient.

THE BRAHAN SEER

Deep in the mists of the folklore of the Scottish Highlands lies the character of the Brahan Seer. This enigmatic figure's uncannily accurate powers of prophecy and his eventual trial for witchcraft made him renowned across the land and continue to amaze people to this day.

With little in the way of written evidence about the seer, his actual identity is unclear. Indeed, many of the tales about him have been preserved through oral tradition alone. Local legend identifies the seer as Kenneth Mackenzie, a labourer born in Baile-na-Gille on the Isle of Lewis around 1650.

It is said that he used to live at Loch Ussie in Ross-shire, where he worked on the Brahan estate,

the seat of the Seaforth chieftains, from about 1675.

Many of the prophecies made by this figure related to the geographical region in which he lived, where the fulfilment of his predictions can be seen to this day. About 150 years prior to the construction of the Caledonian Canal, the Brahan Seer announced: 'Strange as it may seem to you this day, the time will come, and it is not far off, when full-rigged ships will be seen sailing eastward and westward by the back of Tomnahurich, near Inverness.' As, at the time of the premonition, the area in question consisted of rolling hills, the idea was deemed preposterous.

HIGH AND DRY

Another visible example of the seer's prophecies lies in the parish of Petty, where a huge stone once marked the boundary between the estates of Culloden and Moray. In 1799 this colossally heavy stone inexplicably moved into the sea. How or why this occurred remains a mystery, but whatever the cause, the event was specifically foretold by the seer, who predicted: 'The day will come when the stone of Petty, large though it is, and high and dry upon the land as it appears to people this day, will be suddenly found as far advanced into the sea as it now lies away from it inland, and no-one will see it removed or be able to account for its sudden and marvellous transportation.'

The seer seems also to have been adept at predicting numerous important events in the history of Scotland, such as his premonitions of the carnage wreaked at the famous battle of Culloden. While walking in the vicinity, he is said to have stated, 'This bleak moor shall, ere many generations have passed away, be stained with the best blood of the Highlands.'

He also accurately foresaw the demise of the powerful clan Mackenzie of Fairburn and its stronghold, the Fairburn Tower. The seer made the now-famous claim: 'The day will come when the Mackenzies of Fairburn shall lose their entire possessions; their castle will become uninhabited and a cow shall give birth in the uppermost chamber.'

A few generations after the prediction was made,

the family lost its power and wealth, and the tower was taken over by a farmer, who used the upper floor for storing hay. One day, according to numerous eyewitness reports from 1851, a pregnant cow followed a trail of dropped hay up the precarious staircase to the upper level. Having become stuck, the cow gave birth to her calf right there on the top floor, just as the seer had predicted.

This was not the only fall from greatness accurately predicted by Coinneach Odhar (his Gaelic name), since he foretold the end of the male line of the Seaforth clan as a result of the premature deaths of all four sons. He also stated that all of the last lord's possessions would be 'inherited by a white-coiffed lassie from the east and she is to kill her sister'.

And so it happened that, upon the death of the last Lord Seaforth, the estate was passed to the eldest remaining daughter, Mary, who was married to Admiral Hood and lived in India for many years. Upon the admiral's death, Lady Hood returned to her family home wearing a white coif, a traditional Indian mourning garment. Some years later, she lost control of the pony carriage in which she and her sister were travelling, and her sister died.

The Brahan Seer did not live to see the fulfilment of this prediction, however. His fate was sealed when he told Countess Isabella Seaforth, wife of the third Earl of Seaforth, that her husband was having an affair with a Frenchwoman.

This news so enraged Isabella that she ordered that he be tried for witchcraft. Upon hearing the sentence of death passed on him, the Brahan Seer responded with one final prediction. He declared that upon his death, a dove and a raven would meet in the air above his ashes and would instantly alight on them. If, he said, the raven alighted first, then his soul would go to hell. However, if the dove should alight first, then his soul would go to heaven, while that of the Countess would go to hell.

He was executed by being pitched into a barrel of burning tar. According to legend, the spectators were astonished when the two birds did appear above his ashes, and awestruck when the dove alighted first.

A sailing vessel in the Caledonian Canal, which was completed in 1887, 150 years after the Seer's prediction of 'full-rigged ships sailing eastward and westward' in the area

EDGAR CAYCE

Edgar Cayce is one of the most famous seers of recent times. During the course of his remarkable life, he gave in excess of 14,000 readings on topics, ranging from personal health and emotional issues to the lives of ancient civilizations and natural disasters. Born in 1877 in rural Hopkinsville, USA, Cayce became a photographer, but tragedy was to strike him at the age of 21 when he was informed that he was suffering from a rare condition that would cause the gradual paralysis of his throat, and subsequent loss of speech.

MIRACLE RECOVERY

His miraculous recovery from this devastating illness was to be the first of Cayce's incredible cures. Having entered a form of hypnotic sleep, Cayce was able to divine the cure to his illness. To the astonishment and bafflement of his doctors, his suggestions for treatments were totally successful and he made a full recovery.

Having discovered this amazing gift, Cayce quickly realized that he could use it to help others, and he soon became famous throughout the USA as a great healer. Cayce then began to explore other areas of his hypnotically induced powers. In 1923, Cayce met a printer, Arthur Lammers, who was deeply interested in the subject of metaphysical philosophy. Lammers was keen to see what answers Cayce might give to fundamental metaphysical questions.

Cayce agreed to go ahead with this experiment. The 'Life' readings that followed related to information about a person's past life, and were distinct from his 'Physical' readings, which pertained to medical diagnoses and cures. Cayce subsequently declared that the basis for all the great religions was surprisingly similar, as all the people of the world were united by a collective unconscious. Cayce maintained that it was by tapping into this unconscious, or 'universal memory of nature', that he was able to make such a large number of predictions and readings. However, he was sceptical over suggestions that he was able to gain access to an infinite source of collective wisdom, known as the 'Akashic record'. This was, and still is, a contentious idea, and there was no scientific method by which it could be proved, other than by the fulfilment of his prophecies.

Cayce declared that the Sphinx had been built in 10,500BC and that a library concealed beneath would be discovered in the late 1990s. Although no such library has been found, many of his other insights are proving to be more accurate. Cayce's prediction of the destruction and submergence of certain parts of the USA is proving a very real concern among both meteorologists and scientists. Recent information has revealed that one flank of the Cumbre Vieja volcano on the island of La Palma, in the Canaries, is unstable and could plunge into the ocean during the next eruption of the volcano. The effect of this would be the creation of a tsunami which may have the capacity to devastate the east coast of the United States, the Caribbean and Brazil.

An illustration from around 1606, showing a map of the island of Atlantis: Cayce had a remarkable level of insight into past civilizations such as those of ancient Egypt and Atlantis

TITANIC PROPHECIES

The sinking of the liner *Titanic* is a well-known and dramatic story with the freak iceberg and the shortage of lifeboats – but very few realize that, a mere 14 years prior to the accident, a book was published that set out almost the exact details of the entire incident.

The Wreck of the Titan, or *Futility*, was a novel written by a little known author, Morgan Robertson, in 1898. Though barely noticed at the time, the book tells the story of a 70,000-tonne ocean liner named the SS *Titan*, which hits an iceberg on its fourth voyage across the Atlantic. The ship, bearing a number of wealthy and powerful dignitaries, was equipped with fewer than half the necessary lifeboats, and consequently more than two-thirds of the 2,500 passengers on board perished in icy waters when the liner sank.

The parallels with the true story of the *Titanic* are immediately apparent. Moreover, there are further, uncanny, similarities between the fictitious and real vessels, in details such as the weight of the ship, the nationality of the principal shareholders involved, the time of the impact and the number of lifeboats on board.

Incredibly, this was not the only time that a prediction was made about the fate of the *Titanic*. A few years prior to the publication of *The Wreck of the Titan*, a similar story had appeared in a newspaper article. A prophetic note by the editor at the end of the piece warned that 'this is exactly what might take place, and what will take place, if liners are sent to sea short of boats'. In a chilling irony, the man who wrote those words died in the wreck of the *Titanic*.

Could this really be merely a cruel twist of fate, or was some higher power at work?

An article from 1912, depicting lifeboats being lowered after SS Titanic struck an iceberg and passengers were consigned to the icy wastes of the north Atlantic

THE UNKNOWN PROPHET

In 1914, two German soldiers captured a lone Frenchman in the Alsace region of France. They imprisoned and questioned him, and it was during this interrogation that the man made some extraordinary claims about the future. One of the Germans, Andreas Rill, was so amazed by what he had heard that he wrote detailed accounts of the incident in letters to his family.

BIRTH OF THE ANTICHRIST

The unknown prophet predicted not only that the war was going to last for five years, but also that Germany would lose. There would then be a revolution, followed by a period of great prosperity in which, amazingly, money would be flung out of windows to lie untouched on the ground.

Adolf Hitler's rise to power began in the 1920s, but his prediction of a thousand-year Reich fell well short when it ended in 1945

He said that, during this period, an antichrist would be born, who would begin a nine-year reign of tyranny in 1932, passing new legislation and secretly impoverishing the people of Germany. Preparations for a second war, that would last three years, would commence in 1939, and this time Italy would be allied to Germany, rather than fighting against it as it had in the current conflict. Despite this, however, Germany would again lose. The German people would then rise up against the tyrant and his followers, and the man and his sign would disappear. In a year containing the numerals 4 and 5, Germany would be surrounded by its enemies and destroyed.

History proved the amazing veracity of these predictions. The First World War, in which Italy fought against Germany, did last five years, and Germany did lose. This was followed by inflation in which the German currency became so devalued as to be worthless.

TURBULENT YEARS

Adolf Hitler's rise to power began during the 1920s, and in 1933 the National Socialist German Workers' (Nazi) Party commenced its oppressive rule. Preparations for the start of what was to be the Second World War began, as predicted, in 1939 when Germany invaded Poland. This conflict lasted until 1945, when the Germans were surrounded and forced to surrender. Hitler committed suicide and the arrival of the Allies resulted in the end of the reign of the Nazi party.

Rill was amazed to watch history unfold in line with the prophet's statements and, as time went by, the letters to his family became famous for their contents. Indeed, at one point they almost resulted in Rill's internment in a concentration camp. The letters then lay dormant during the turbulent years of the Second World War, before passing to the Freiburg Institute for Border Areas of Psychology and Mental Hygiene. Here, the accuracy of their contents provoked such suspicion that forgery was suspected and, accordingly, the documents were subjected to extensive testing and scrutiny by a team of expert criminologists. Following these investigations, it was

declared that the letters were the genuine documents that Rill had sent home to his family back in 1914.

It was then decided to try to locate the mysterious seer. Professors Hans Bender and Elber Gruber traced Rill's movements in an effort to establish the locality in which the man had been arrested and conducted interviews with Rill's family. Rill's son remembered that his father had himself attempted to locate the nameless prophet, tracing him to a monastery in Sogolsheim, where he was reportedly told that the man had died. The two professors established that the man may have been Frater Laicus Tertiarius, who had died in Sogolsheim Monastery and fitted the facts known of the mysterious prophet.

HITLER'S PROPHET

Countless history books have recorded, analyzed and discussed the events that occurred before, during and after the Second World War, but, of these, few mention the significant part that astrology and prophecy played in determining the course of history.

Prior to the outbreak of war, a prophet and astrologer, Karl Ernest Krafft, was gaining great respect in Germany among his contemporaries. Born in Basel in 1900, Krafft was highly numerate, especially in the field of statistics, and was also passionate about astrology. However, it was the publication of his book, *Traits of Astro-Biology*, that was to raise him to such an extent in the estimation of fellow prophets and occultists. In this work, Krafft expounded his theory on predicting the future, which he termed 'typoscomy'. Essentially, this maintained that a person's destiny could be predicted on the basis of his or her personality.

When the war commenced, Krafft's privileged position was placed in peril. However, his life changed dramatically when a remarkably accurate prediction about Hitler brought him face to face with leading members of the Führer's command. Krafft foresaw that Hitler's life would be in peril at some point between 7 and 10 November 1939. In fact, he was so sure of this that on 2 November of that year he wrote to Dr Heinrich Fesel, a close acquaintance of Himmler, warning him of Hitler's impending fate.

Fesel, not wanting to be associated with the prophet, filed the letter away without mentioning it to Himmler.

BOMB PLOT

On 8 November a bomb exploded in the Munich beer hall just 27 minutes after Hitler had left the building. When the story became known, Fesel immediately supposed that Krafft must have been involved in the plot to kill the Führer, and so gave the letter to Hitler's right-hand man, Rudolf Hess.

decipher Nostradamus' complex quatrains and extract any references which could be inferred as good omens for the Third Reich and which could be used for propaganda purposes.

Then, in 1940, Krafft was called to give a horoscope reading for Hitler. In this, he advised that a planned attack on the USSR be postponed until a later date. In spite of the fact that he had not actually met Krafft personally, Hitler waited until the following June before launching Operation Barbarossa. The success of the attack on the USSR in

Krafft was immediately arrested by the Gestapo, but they found him innocent of conspiring to kill Hitler. At this point, word of Krafft's remarkable powers reached the ears of Josef Goebbels, head of the Ministry for Propaganda, who had recently become fascinated with the works of Nostradamus. Goebbels ordered that Krafft be employed to

The wreckage of the Munich beer hall following the explosion on 8 November 1939, just 27 minutes after Hitler had left the building

the early days of the offensive seemed to prove Krafft's prediction to be correct.

Krafft then insisted that it was imperative that Germany secured victory by 1943 at the latest, or else the war would be lost. Hitler was enraged by his prediction, and cited it as the reason for the sudden defection of Hess in 1941. Krafft was arrested and all occultists and astrologers were rounded up and put in prison.

Upon his release in 1942, Krafft was ordered to study the horoscopes of Allied leaders in order to provide his leaders with vital information about the enemy. Among his many readings was his divination that Montgomery would prove to be stronger than Rommel, an insight which proved to be correct. His final premonition – that a bomb would destroy the propaganda ministry in Berlin – resulted in Krafft being tried for treason. After languishing in prison for many months he contracted typhus and died.

GORDON SCALLION

Another modern seer to achieve popularity is Gordon Scallion. Because of his gifts he has become the author of numerous books, as well as a teacher of consciousness studies, and he has found special fame over the years through his many television appearances.

In common with many prophets, he is said to have obtained his special talents while being struck down by illness. In 1979, having been rendered temporarily dumb following a period of sickness, Scallion is said to have witnessed the unfolding of future events on a type of inner television screen. At this time a mysterious 'shining lady' had apparently appeared before him, informing him of his impending gift.

Having recovered from his illness and regained the power of speech, the visions and predictions continued. After some years spent working as a healer, Scallion noticed that his talent seemed to be shifting, and he found himself able to predict the changing state of the earth.

Of all his numerous predictions, however, perhaps none was more impressive than his foreseeing of Hurricane Andrew in August 1992. The details of his prophecy were remarkably accurate, especially over matters such as the range of dates on which the hurricane might strike, the wind velocity, the path of the storm and the extent of the damage caused.

Blown away: a survivor of Hurricane Andrew surveys the ruins of her former home

In his newsletter, he also accurately predicted the 1984 Mexico City earthquake, the 1988 election of President Bush, the 1987 stock market crash and a series of major earthquakes and volcanic disturbances both in California and Japan.

Further endorsement of his accuracy seems to have been given more recently by the scientific press, which has revealed its concerns about the possibility of impending polar shift and the potential occurrence of a mega tsunami.

On 26 December 2004 the world witnessed the powerfully destructive forces that Scallion predicted. This event, combined with the increasing occurrence of violent weather and devastating earthquakes, would seem to be undeniable proof that Scallion's predictions are coming true.

JEAN DIXON

During the course of her life, Jean Dixon made a large number of predictions, with varying degrees of accuracy. One prophecy about which she was

Jean Dixon in Miami, 1976

entirely correct, however, was her foretelling in 1956 of the assassination of President Kennedy, several years before it actually happened.

It was only after this event that the world really started to pay attention to her remarkable psychic abilities.

ASSASSINATION

Dixon's prediction of the Kennedy assassination was initially vague, but in subsequent predictions, she added more details. She foretold that a Democrat (which Kennedy was) would win the 1960 Presidential election, and that he would then either be assassinated or would die in office. Moreover, she backed up these predictions with a timescale that proved to be correct.

Although Dixon is best known for her pronouncement on the Kennedy assassination, this was not the only event that she accurately foresaw. She also predicted the Soviet Sputnik launch in 1957 and the Apollo rocket disaster that killed several American astronauts in 1967.

In addition, she foretold that in the spring of 1989 the world would witness a terrible shipping accident – and the *Exxon Valdez* oil disaster did indeed occur at this time.

Some of Dixon's other prophecies were not quite so accurate, however. She wrongly predicted an apocalyptic 1980s, in which a devastating meteor strike would hit the earth. Occasionally, Dixon made a prediction that – although incorrect – came very close to being reality.

One such was her prophecy that a plague looked likely to descend on the USA during the late 1970s. Some have suggested that she may have been catching a future glimpse of the arrival of AIDS in the Western world and its devastating effects on public health.

FLEXIBLE REALITIES

Many have wondered whether it is possible to credit Jean Dixon with psychic abilities when the verity of her predictions has varied so much over time.

Her advocates would argue that the future does not

actually run along a set course, but is flexible, and that there are numerous possible realities. Dixon, they maintain, simply presents us with one of these potential scenarios.

If this really is the case as seems plausible, then it would certainly go some way towards explaining how she was so very nearly correct in her predictions of a third world war.

President John F Kennedy and his wife Jackie in the motorcade minutes before his assassination

PSYCHOKINESIS

The power to move things by the power of thought alone – psychokinesis or PK – has long been an ability claimed by various people. In earlier generations the ability was frequently seen in religious or supernatural terms with people who were able to perform telekinetics seen as being favoured by the gods or plagued by fairies. What is today termed poltergeist activity is thought by some to be an unconscious form of PK. The word telekinesis is often used to mean

When things go flying for no reason, poltergeists are often blamed but it could be an unconscious form of psychokinesis

psychokinesis, but strictly speaking telekinesis means the moving of objects by an invisible force such as a ghost, demon or other unseen entity.

More recently attempts have been made to study PK on a more scientific basis. The American laboratory technician Felicia Parise came forward in the early 1970s with claims that objects sometimes moved without her touching them, though she claimed to be unable to control the phenomenon. Early tests seemed to indicate that small objects did move untouched in her vicinity. Parise was encouraged to engage in intense bouts of concentration on individual objects. She reportedly caused a plastic pill container, compass needle and pieces of aluminum foil to move without touching them. However, she found the sessions to be a massive mental and physical effort and soon retired from the tests.

PSYCHIC ABILITIES

About the same time the Indian holy man Swami Rama, a yogi skilled in controlling his heart functions, was studied at the Menninger Foundation when it was reported that he could produce PK events. Swami Rama was equipped with a facemask and gown to rule out the suggestion that he used his breath or body movements. He then successfully moved a knitting needle a distance of several inches. Unfortunately PK was not the subject of the tests that Rama was undergoing and the subject was not pursued.

With the advent of the Cold War it gradually emerged that the Soviets were taking many forms of paranormal abilities seriously, and that included psychokinetics. Anyone demonstrating special psychic abilities was seized upon and exploited in the quest for victory. Ninel Kulagina, was one such character. She was a housewife from St Petersburg who was studied by the Soviets for more than ten years because of her paranormal abilities. During this time she revealed her amazing powers of telekinesis. The fact that Kulagina was investigated for such a long period of time seems to indicate that she was nothing other than entirely genuine.

Film footage still exists of Kulagina causing a compass needle to move by focusing energy through her fingertips. Another of her displays of telekinetic ability was to move matches across a table, or to cause a pile of them to collapse purely by the power of a concentrated stare. But it is the later displays of her remarkable talent that reveal why the authorities

were so interested in her powers. In one experiment, an egg was cracked into a saline solution, and she proceeded to separate the yolk from the white by her powers of telekinesis.

During one of Kulagina's most famous feats, an egg was cracked into a saline solution and she separated the yolk from the white by telekinetic energy

STOPPING THE HEART OF A FROG

In another demonstration which was particularly sinister, Kulagina is said to have stopped the heart of a frog from beating, purely by the power of her mind. To the Cold War scientists, this must have been an incredibly exciting breakthrough in human mental ability and this aptitude would have presented all sorts of horrific possibilities to men who were determined to emerge victorious from this most sinister of global conflicts.

Performing these incredible feats took a serious physical toll on Kulagina, and it is this that apparently persuaded the Soviet doctors of the authenticity of her feats. After she had demonstrated her telekinetic prowess, she reported having experienced a sense of hot energy running up and down her spine and emanating from her hands. During this time, her pulse would apparently race to over 200 beats per minute – the equivalent of doing strenuous exercise, and she is even reputed to have lost weight through such a display. The activities would also affect her blood pressure and she spoke of feeling dizzy and exhausted for several days afterwards, experiencing headaches and blurred vision. Eventually, she was forced to end her involvement with the research after suffering a heart attack, no doubt brought on by her exertions.

Rather more long term were the tests carried out by the Society for Research into Rapport and Telekinesis (SORRAT), a body founded by John Neihardt, an American professor of English with an interest in the paranormal. SORRAT consisted of 20 people who met weekly at Neihardt's home to investigate various aspects of the paranormal. Over a period of months, attempts at PK resulted in the group being able to move a metal tray and a doll so that they hovered in mid-air. Other small objects could be moved about on a table top.

Concerned that outsiders would think trickery was involved, the group recruited a stage magician named William Cox. His task was to devise tests and controls that would exclude the possibility of stage trickery being involved. Cox developed a securely fastened, glass-topped box in which objects could be placed – it was dubbed the PK Minilab.

If the objects could be moved without the box being opened or touched, it was thought, PK must be the only agency in action.

PK activity seemed to focus on Sorrat member Dr J Richards, so Cox concentrated his tests on Richards. Soon the PK minilab was showing that Richards was able to move objects such as a pen, pipecleaners, string and small toys. Cox even managed to take movie footage of the PK in action.

When the PK Minilab was left unattended one day a pen moved from the tabletop to inside the PK Minilab, although it was locked at the time.

The PK Minilab concept was then taken up by British researcher Julian Isaacs, who began work in 1980. Isaac's PK Minilab was more complex than the American version.

It too produced events for which the only explanation seems to be that some form of PK was taking place as objects were moved about inside the glass-fronted box.

IGNORING THE EVIDENCE

Despite such impressive evidence, the scientific establishment refuses to accept that PK is a real phenomenon. More to the point, they refuse to fund investigations on a scale that could prove that objects can be moved by mindpower alone. The field is left to lone researchers who lack adequate funds and whose work is often then criticized for not being carried out with sophisticated and expensive equipment.

> Over a period of months the group were able to move a metal tray and a doll by psychokinesis so that they hovered in mid-air

ESP

Extra Sensory Perception, or ESP, is usually taken to mean the ability to perceive something without using any of the usually accepted senses: touch, hearing, sight, smell or taste. Some researchers prefer to break ESP down into a number of categories, such as clairvoyance (seeing objects that are out of sight), clairaudience (hearing things that are out of earshot). Others see these as being merely different aspects of the same phenomenon and believe that all forms of ESP have a common origin and explanation.

However a researcher chooses to categorize ESP, there is the inevitable problem that the phenomenon defies efforts to define or explain it. For experimenters there is the additional problem that even those most adept at ESP report that it is an ability that is very difficult to control, still less produce to order. Long hours in the laboratory may pass without any ESP event taking place, only for one to occur as soon as the scientific equipment is switched off.

SERIES OF TESTS

Despite this fact many efforts have been made to investigate ESP and those who claim to be able to use it. In 1927 J B Rhine of Duke University conducted a series of tests using Zener Cards. These cards, designed by Karl Zener, carried one of five distinctive designs: a star, a circle, a square, a plus sign or wavy parallel lines.

Rhine's test involved one person drawing a Zener card at random from a shuffled pack and then trying to telepathically send the design to a second person. Chance would dictate that a correct guess was achieved 20 per cent of the time. Most of the time, Rhine's tests did show results at around 20 per cent, but in some instances much higher scores were recorded. Others followed Rhine's lead and produced similarly mixed results. They noticed that the more successful individuals would appear to lose their

Previous page: in 1951 twins Terry and Sherry Young were tested on their ability to 'convey thoughts' through ESP. Terry is attempting to communicate the contents of the card she is holding

powers after three or more rounds of tests. This was put down to increasing boredom with the monotonous task of guessing designs on cards.

New experiments were designed that used what were termed free-response formats, where the target was not limited to a small number of set designs but could be more wideranging. For instance, physicists Russel Targ and Harold Puthoff of Calfornia's Stanford Research Institute decided to investigate clairvoyance, or remote-viewing as they preferred to call it, in the 1970s. They persuaded two well-known psychics, Pat Price and Ingo Swann, to subject themselves to tests.

NAME THAT PLACE

The most detailed test involved Price sitting in a room with Targ while Puthoff drove off in his car. At a prearranged time, Puthoff would stop his car to concentrate on the view. At the same time, Targ would ask the psychic to describe the place where Puthoff was. In seven out of nine instances, Price produced a description that an independent judge was able to use to identify the place visited by Puthoff. In one case, Price actually named the precise location correctly: the Hoover Tower.

Some researchers will put their ESP percipients into what is known as a Ganzfeld state. This involves the person lying down on a comfortable mattress while being blindfolded and wearing earphones that play gentle white noise.

Dr Carl Sergeant of Cambridge University favoured the Ganzfeld technique when attempting to send images of randomly chosen paintings to his students. A student would be put into a Ganzfeld state while Sergeant studied a painting with great concentration. Sergeant ran hundreds of tests with a number of students. Some scored pretty much as chance would predict, but three students consistently did much better than chance would suggest was likely. Those students were then subjected to further tests, achieving results that could be expected to occur by chance with a rate of only 1 in 16,000 times.

Despite these impressive results, and some others,

the majority of tests designed to detect ESP fail to produce meaningful data. Some researchers have noted that the very act of trying to produce ESP will mean that it does not take place. Far more success seems to be achieved when the percipient is relaxed and in familiar surroundings free from stress. Being wired up to test equipment in a laboratory hardly meets these criteria. It is for this reason that many of those most adept at ESP prefer to work alone and at home.

JACK THE RIPPER

While the horrific murders of Jack the Ripper were bloodying the neighbourhood of Whitechapel, Victorian London was paralyzed with fear. The police force was under intense pressure to arrest the perpetrator and bring him to justice, but they had few clues to go on. One man believed he held the key to the gruesome outrages. The age of the psychic sleuth had dawned.

Robert James Lees was born in 1849 in Leicestershire, England. He was a discreet and devout man, not at all the type to seek the limelight or newspaper headlines. In many ways he was the last person to seek the kind of controversy that is attached to serial killers. Yet his conviction about the existence of a powerful spiritual world never wavered, and was closely linked to his intense religious beliefs.

Robert James Lees was a studious and devout character, not at all the type to seek the limelight by claiming to identify Jack the Ripper

KILLER STALKS THE BACKSTREETS

Debate about the Ripper killings still rages today – not least as the murderer was never identified. What is known for sure is that a killer stalked the deprived backstreets of east London, accosting prostitutes and then butchering them. His crimes were typified by his cut-throat methods and the horrific practice of disembowelling his victims, often decorating the vicinity with inner organs. Five deaths were put down to the Ripper, although there may have been more.

The Ripper's confirmed victims were Mary Ann Nichols, Annie Chapman, Elizabeth Stride (right), Catherine Eddowes and Mary Jane Kelly, who were all killed between 31 August and 9 November 1888. Stride and Eddowes were killed on the same night, an occasion that became known as the double event.

The police were baffled by the murders. Lacking the scientific know-how that we use today in criminal investigations, they were nevertheless subject to fierce scrutiny by the press, and under real pressure to solve the case. A sense of melodrama surrounded the manhunt, as the perpetrator stole away from the scenes of carnage like a phantom. Later, he apparently went so far as to send taunting letters and body parts to the police.

The facts surrounding Lees' involvement in the Ripper case are by no means certain. It seems that one day, soon after the double event, Lees had a sudden vision while travelling with his wife on a London bus. He became sure that one of the other passengers was the Ripper himself. Despite his wife's strenuous objections, Lees followed the man and made a note of his home address.

When he took his information to the police, Lees was greeted with derision. In October 1888 he wrote the following in his diary: 'offered services to police to follow up East End murders, called a fool and a lunatic.' The police refused to listen to him until he apparently quoted the contents of one of the letters sent in the name of the Ripper. There was, of course, no way that he could have known what was in the communication, and the police began to take note. They already knew that the address pinpointed by Lees, 74 Brook Street, belonged to an eminent

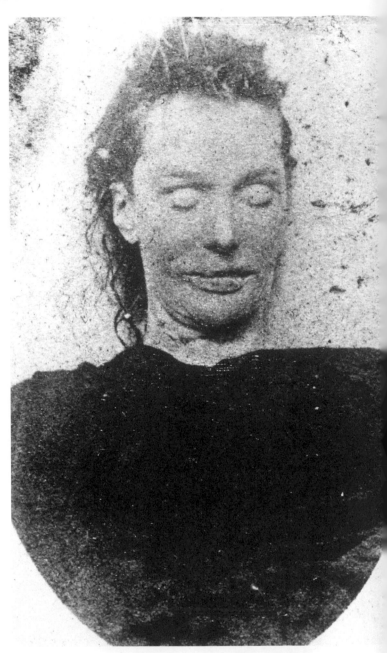

doctor, Sir William Withey Gull. The respected professional seemed at first to be beyond suspicion. Yet Dr Gull's wife told the police that recently he had been subject to violent rages and had even disappeared at the time when the notorious murders were taking place.

It emerged that the doctor was already ill, and he progressed to an asylum where he later died. Following his incarceration the murders halted.

It is this explanation that has earned Lees the

reputation of being the man who identified the Ripper. But although the killer clearly had some anatomical interest or knowledge that might link him to the medical profession, there is actually scant evidence to endorse the tale. Lees barely spoke about the incident. Nor did he include details of the experience in his copious diaries, although it was highly sensitive information and he may have omitted it as a matter of discretion. Much later Lees' daughter revealed that her father had known something of the Ripper case, but she would say no more than that. Observers have both verified and denounced the story of the psychic vision on the bus, and ultimately the police refused to give him official credit for solving the case.

ROYAL KILLER?

So why was there so much doubt about the outcome of the case? In the year preceding the murders, Dr Gull had suffered a stroke. Although it left him in a weakened physical state, one supposition is that the stroke might have altered the balance of his mind, perhaps rendering him capable of heinous acts. However, there is another, even more sensational theory. Gull was a loyal royal physician and there has been considerable speculation that the killer was a member of the royal family, specifically Prince Albert Victor, Duke of Clarence. He was son of the Prince of Wales, grandson to Queen Victoria. Clarence was a self-indulgent, wayward young man. Could it be that the prince himself was the real Ripper, and Gull's obvious anxiety was caused by the duty of protection he felt towards him?

Of course, Dr Gull and the Duke of Clarence were not the only two suspects in the case. Barrister Montague John Druitt was in the frame, especially since he committed suicide shortly after the final Ripper murder. However, there was nothing to suggest that he had the medical know-how to carve up the corpses in the careful manner which the Ripper used.

Aaron Kosminski, a Polish Jew who lived in Whitechapel, was also of interest to the police. They noted that the killings stopped when he was committed to an asylum, where he died in 1919.

Being poor and Jewish, Kosminski would also have been a convenient scapegoat.

The case against two other doctors has been examined. Dr Francis Tumblety, who collected women's uteruses in jars, fled to America where he was popularly believed to be the Ripper. He died of old age in 1923. Dr Thomas Neil Cream was later convicted of two other killings, and implicated himself as he stood on the gallows with the noose around his neck. As the trap doors opened he cried: 'I am Jack the...!' However, he failed to finish the sentence and is widely believed to have been playing for time. Crime writer Patricia Cornwell believes that the artist Walter Sickert was the Ripper, not least for his offensively detailed pictures of mutilated prostitutes. Yet others theorize about a Masonic link.

So what became of Robert Lees? Quite apart from the furore surrounding the Ripper case, he was a well-respected spiritualist in an age when mediums were often exposed as fraudulent. He is even believed to have held séances with Queen Victoria so that she could contact her late and beloved husband Prince Albert. There are claims that he helped police identify the Fenians, an Irish patriotic group who were plotting to blow up the Houses of Parliament.

Perhaps Lees' most remarkable psychic feat was a trilogy of books revealing the secrets of life after death. Bizarrely, Lees claimed no literary credit for these books, which he said were dictated to him over years by a spirit named Fred. When he died in 1931, Lees was a psychic of great reputation, but he left behind many secrets and remains a fascinating enigma to this day.

THE FLASHBACK PSYCHIC

Clutching a single shoe to her breast, Noreen Renier summons up a picture of the appalling tragedy that befell its owner. She spills details of the disturbing scenes that fill her head into a nearby tape recorder, hoping that her words will bring about a breakthrough in a deadlocked investigation.

Noreen is a psychic sleuth, one of very few psychics who are recognized by some members of the police force as an asset in a tricky inquiry. The technique she uses is called psychometry, which

Mayhem ensued during an assassination attempt against Ronald Reagan in 1981. Could events like this have been predicted?

allows her to sense the radio waves emanating from an object after it has been put aside by its owner. As she puts it: 'We all possess unseen energy fields. When we touch an object, we leave behind an invisible fingerprint.' And, according to Noreen, psychometry is something we would all be capable of doing, if only we used the whole and not just part of our brains.

Noreen speaks as a former sceptic. She was so convinced that paranormal claims were fake that she wanted to ban a psychic convention from the Hyatt Hotel in Orlando where she was public relations director. However, her view changed when she met a psychic called Ann Gehman who was able to describe her daughters, her hidden surgical scar and the new chair in her office. This was compelling

evidence that the supernatural world really existed. 'Slowly, this psychic stuff began to take root in my life,' Renier writes in her book, *A Mind for Murder*. 'I didn't understand it, but I couldn't deny it, either. I was completely captivated by the amazing new world that had opened in my mind. I started neglecting my job. All I wanted to do was practise what other people claimed they could do in the books I was reading.'

Eventually she lost her job, admitting with good humour that this was something she didn't predict. She began a fortune-telling business in hotel foyers, clad in gypsy garb. Corny though this sounds, it gave her ample opportunity to hone her talents. As she grew in confidence, she put herself forward for scientific tests to measure her psychic skills. In 1980 she began helping the police with their investigations, either at their request, or of the families involved.

REMOTE VIEWING

In addition to psychometry, Noreen uses remote viewing. That means that she is able to see, hear and feel the world through the senses of another. She can place herself as an eyewitness at the scene of a murder or amid the panic of a fugitive. In investigations, it is vital to take down all the details whilst she attempts to describe the events she is experiencing. Ideally, a forensic artist is standing by as she talks to sketch the face of the killer or rapist – and a tape recorder is running to capture her psychic advice. Afterwards, the memories of her flashbacks are erased from her mind and she returns to normality, sometimes for weeks at a time.

Noreen continues: 'It would be too much to be psychic all the time. So I've found a wrecked plane a thousand miles away, but sometimes I can't find my car keys.' She finds the experience very draining and limits herself to two cases a week. By and large, her work is carried out in the comfort of her own home. Relaxation is key to her success.

The first case that Noreen was involved in occurred when a small town was being terrorized by a rapist, and the local women asked for help. After visiting the homes of two victims, Noreen saw a man in a green uniform with a scar on his knee who drove a vehicle that she could not identify but which, for some reason, turned around constantly. Although her intervention did not directly secure an arrest, her information was proven correct when the culprit was finally caught some months later. He did work in uniform, he was scarred and he drove a cement lorry, all of which Noreen had described.

One of her most impressive and high-profile predictions was that of an assassination attempt on US President Ronald Reagan. Speaking in January 1981 at the FBI academy, she said that in spring the President would suffer piercing chest pains. It was not a heart attack, she was sure, but a gunshot wound from which he would recover. Amazingly, on 30 March that year John Hinkley attacked Reagan, who did make a good recovery. Sceptics point out that much of the information revealed by psychics is vague, so that it can be applied to a host of outcomes. Futhermore, they claim that the practice of psychometry can seriously damage vital evidence. Although the police accept more psychic advice now than ever before, they are generally sceptical of information provided by psychics. Their reluctance is understandable, especially since in the wake of any high-profile homicide, they are deluged with calls from people claiming to be psychic.

Noreen is well used to a measure of scepticism, especially since she herself used to be a sceptic. Even now, she maintains that her skills are not foolproof and admits she thinks that psychic detectives should only be used as a last resort. Her aim is for a success rate of about 80 per cent. Often she does not know herself if the information she gives the police will be of immediate interest to an inquiry or whether it might help solve a crime at some point in the future. Psychic detection is an elusive skill, but sometimes an invaluable one.

IN A TRANCE

A blood-curdling scream splits the night. A weapon falls to the ground and a killer goes on the run. When psychic detective Annette Martin slips into a trance she is able to experience a re-run of these terrible events in minute detail. Hopefully, her second sight will provide police with fresh clues.

Martin was just a child growing up in San Francisco when her psychic skills first became evident. She relates the turning point with trepidation even now. 'I was seven years old, I was playing with my friends, when all of a sudden I looked up to the sky and I saw this huge picture. In it was myself and my friends and they were rushing towards me with rocks and sticks, intent on killing me.' Moments later, her neighbourhood playmates did indeed attack her. She rushed home screaming and crying, forgetting that her parents were out.

'I ran up the steps to my home. I turned around and faced my tormentors when I heard this male voice saying, "Pick up that stick." I thought it was my father but when I turned towards the door there was no one there. The voice spoke to me again, saying, "Pick up the stick and throw it."' Annette did as the voice told her and threw the stick, breaking the nose of the gang leader.

Happily for all involved, the fracas was forgotten within days. However, for Annette it was just the beginning, and was followed by another strange occurrence. 'I was out shopping with my mother when I saw inside this woman's stomach. I saw all these bugs running around and I told my mother that woman should see a doctor. I came into the world being a very dramatic person so my mother thought I was dramatizing.'

It was only when the young Annette accurately predicted the medical condition of a family friend that her parents began to take her claims seriously. Although still a child, Annette had to learn to turn her special powers on and off like a light switch. It is this ability to stop her second sight at will that has allowed Annette to enjoy a normal existence, despite her astonishing career.

The voice she had heard that day on the steps of her house belonged to Cama, a spirit guide who has remained with her ever since. 'I started seeing him when I was aged ten or eleven. He was once a yogi. He is tall and very well built. If I'm doing something and he wants to talk he hollers to me in a very loud voice in his distinctive Middle Eastern tones.' Cama has helped her develop her psychic awareness. 'In the beginning I was just too emotional. My guide Cama kept telling me that when I really learned to control my emotions the information would come through much clearer and easier.'

To enter a trance or altered state Annette simply takes three deep breaths, inhaling through the nose and exhaling through the mouth. When she does police work the trance is deeper and she is in it for longer, sometimes several hours. She works in partnership with Richard Keaton, a private investigator and former police detective.

They met after Annette experienced an extremely frightening vision of a murder and rushed into a sheriff's office to share the information. Keaton, the officer in charge, was initially very sceptical, but he soon put aside his doubts as Annette quoted unpublished details of the case, inside knowledge known only to police officers.

Working together, they combine his aptitude for

Psychic detection is a world away from the life Annette thought she'd lead. Perhaps her musical abilities are linked to her psychic gifts

criminal investigation with her psychic insight. While Annette is in a trance, Keaton questions her closely about details that might seem inconsequential to the onlooker, but which are crucial to those with a detective's mindset. In a trance state, she can revisit the scene of a crime, visualize the victim and even describe an attacker. Together they can discover minute details from the crime scenes she visits in her trance.

As Annette describes it, 'I see scars, moles, diseases that they have, medication that they are taking, which has been extremely helpful because then the police have much more to go on ... I also get conversations. I pick up conversations between the victim and assailant.'

She is able to assume three personalities while she is in a trance: that of the victim, the perpetrator and an observer. Keaton identifies these switches in character as her voice, face and body movements change. When the trance is at an end, Keaton has pages of notes to study.

Of course, the word of a psychic counts for nothing in court. Police may use the detail and information offered by a psychic to capture assailants, but they still have to provide hard evidence to make a case against them. 'I don't believe psychic detectives solve the case. We give the police the pieces of a puzzle. We are just a tool for them,' says Annette.

When 71-year-old Dennis Prado went missing, Pacifica detectives drew a blank, despite an exhaustive investigation lasting two months. His family asked that Annette should be brought in on the case and, although the investigating sergeant was doubtful, the police had nothing to lose. Using a photo and map of Mr Prado's apartment complex, Annette 'saw' that Mr Prado had hiked into the County Park for a stroll and veered off the main path towards a small hill, perhaps to rest and look at the scenery. Along the way he suffered a stroke and dropped dead. Annette marked the location of the body on the map. The County Park covers an area of 8,000km², but Annette's pointer was precise. Using a dog, two rescue volunteers headed for the fateful spot and found Mr Prado's body, as she had predicted they would.

Following one murder in Marin County, California, Annette used her skills to divine the exact spot where the victim had been killed. She sat meditating on the ground for two hours, describing the grisly event and giving police a full description of the assailant. Afterwards, they knew how he had left the crime scene and where he was. They even had a full description of his house.

DOWSING

One activity that is often classed as a form of ESP, though this remains controversial, is dowsing. This is a technique that has been used to find water or minerals underground for thousands of years. Dowsers believe that anyone can acquire this ability – once as natural as sight, but long forgotten by a technology-obsessed society.

Contemporary texts and drawings show that the Ancient Egyptians, Babylonians, Greeks, Romans and Jews all used simple dowsing tools such as split water reeds. The Old Testament tells how Moses and Aaron used a rod to bring forth water from a rock, while among China's royal dynasties the Emperor Kwang Sung of the late third millennium BC was an enthusiastic dowser. Many believe the oriental art of feng shui, which governs building design and layout, emerged from a combination of dowsing and so-called sacred geometry.

THE DEVIL HIMSELF

However by the Middle Ages, and particularly in continental Europe, dowsers were keeping a low profile. The practice was also known as water-witching and anything which smacked of witchcraft tended to attract worrying levels of interest from the Inquisition. As late as 1853, the Roman Catholic Church was warning that 'it was the devil his very self that pulled and twisted the dowsing rod to give the accurate results'.

Despite this claim (or perhaps because of it) Anglican Britain became something of a dowsing centre of excellence, producing some charismatic characters in the process.

A Bristol stonemason, W S Lawrence, earned a useful second income during the 19th century by using a hazel twig to find water and horseshoe-shaped wire to find mineral deposits. By all accounts he was very successful, and enthralled clients would watch him gripped by impressive muscular spasms as he closed in on his target.

Another celebrated exponent was John Mullins of Wiltshire, who turned professional in 1882 with a confident no-find-no-fee promise to clients. His task would be to pinpoint reliable sources of underground water which were crucial to remote farmsteads and houses. Judging by the way his business expanded, he must have convinced many a hard-headed farmer of his abilities.

By the last century, the technique of dowsing was being applied to a range of new challenges. A French Catholic priest, Abbé Mermet, reasoned that if you could find water underground, then that same skill could perhaps be used to diagnose illnesses linked to the human bloodstream. His 'radiesthesia' pendulum technique achieved some recognition among physicians, and later evolved into a discipline known as 'radionics', in which a dowser attempts to tap into the energy field of a patient.

Sceptics were quick to poke fun at all this, and yet dowsing has never been the preserve of New Age eccentrics. During the Second World War, the British Army's Royal Electrical and Mechanical Engineers regiment – the Sappers – trained soldiers to use rods to find water. They reasoned that it did not matter how dowsing worked as long as it did work. The US Army took a similarly pragmatic view and, during the Vietnam war, front-line troops were taught to dowse their way through minefields where no conventional detector was available.

Common dowsing tools today include a hand-held Y-shaped hazel twig (which dips or rises when the user walks across an underground source), L-shaped metal rods (which cross or separate) and a pendulum. Water and mineral deposits are by no means the only targets. Dowsers also specialize in soil testing, locating archeological remains and tracking down lost possessions.

Exactly how and why the technique works is unknown, but according to the International Society of Dowsing Research, one popular theory is that a psychic or telepathic link synchronizes a dowser to the living field which emanates from all people, animals and things. A dowser is said to tune into this energy network by focusing on a clear mental image of what he or she seeks. Subtle or unconscious responses in the nervous system then cause the dowsing tool to move.

Some investigators have cited so-called E-Rays (from the German word *Erdestrahlen* or earth-rays) as a possible explanation. The idea is that these E-Rays originate deep beneath the earth's crust, rising to form an invisible pattern at the surface. Where the pattern is distorted (by, for instance, an underground stream) the dowser makes a subliminal nervous response which is visually amplified by the chosen tool of his trade. Over the years researchers have given E-Rays various names – electromagnetism, biogravitation, electro-kinetic currents, infra-red light sources, neutron radiation, microwaves,

ionizing fields – but the jury is still out on whether these perceived forces can be explained by the current laws of physics.

THE EARTH'S ENERGY FIELD

Similarly, enthusiasts of Curry and Hartmann lines (named after the physicians Manfred Curry, of Switzerland, and Ernst Hartmann, of Germany) are convinced that an energy latticework embraces the entire planet. The precise width between the lines is said to vary according to the position of the sun and moon but is of the order of 20–40cm (8–15.5in).

Academics such as Nils-Axel Morner, head of Paleogeophysics and Geodynamics at Stockholm University, claim they can actually measure E-ray frequencies. Morner uses something called a 'common electrical tone generator' which effectively establishes a line between the source of an E-ray and the generator speaker in his lab. He calculates that Curry lines are at a frequency of 202Hz, Hartmann lines at 142Hz and underground streams at 440Hz.

Morner may be dismissed by many as a maverick, but it is much harder for mainstream science to swat away the beliefs of their most eminent theoreticians, such as Albert Einstein himself. On 4 February 1946, a man called Herman E Peisach of South Norwalk, Connecticut, wrote to Einstein seeking an opinion on whether dowsing was a genuine phenomenon. Mr Peisach's father, a German doctor, had apparently tried it as a diagnostic aid, and believed there was a link between human health and radiation links from water and mineral sources.

Eleven days later, Einstein replied. 'I know very well,' he wrote, 'that many scientists consider dowsing as they do astrology, as a type of ancient superstition. According to my conviction this is, however, unjustified. The dowsing rod is a simple instrument which shows the reaction of the human nervous system to certain factors which are unknown to us at this time.'

With typical humility, Einstein was stating the painfully obvious. The laws of physics, as any student of quantum theory knows, are incomplete. Dowsing may yet come in from the cold.

Dowsers usually hold a Y-shaped hazel twig, which dips or rises when he or she crosses an underground source of water or a mineral deposit

PSYCHIC HEALING

One of the most potentially useful aspects of claimed psychic powers comes from those who claim to be able to cure their fellow human beings using psychic or paranormal means. There have, for centuries, been people who have claimed to be able to effect cures through witchcraft, shamanistic powers or the intervention of various gods, but the rise of practitioners claiming to use psychic powers per se is a largely 20th century phenomenon.

The claims tend to come from parts of the world where conventional medicine is either hard to come by or is out of the financial reach of many poorer citizens. It is seen to fill a gap in the provision of medical care that falls between simple rest and recuperation and conventional medical care.

Some claims of success made by psychic healers are hugely impressive and are backed up by witness statements and satisfied patients enjoying a renewed burst of good health. There can be no doubt that some psychic healers have track records of success and are quite genuine when they make their claims. Nor is there much doubt that some other individuals are trading on the gullibility and desperation of sick people unable to afford conventional drugs. As with so many aspects of the paranormal there is both honesty and fraud to be encountered.

Some efforts have been made by conventional science to explain the results of psychic healing in conventional terms. Leaving aside those claimed psychic practitioners who seem to be outright frauds, there are a number of possibilities to explain what appears to be going on. The first, and most simple, is that the 'psychic' healer is in fact doing little more than applying common sense to a person who may, due to the stresses of sickness and ill health, be incapable of acting responsibly on their own.

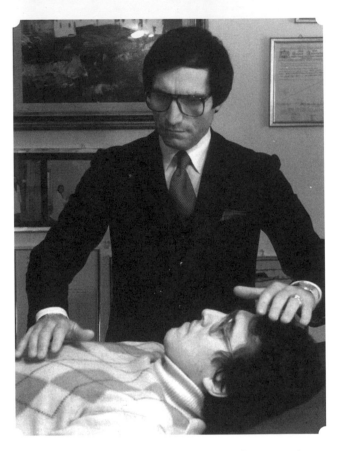

Nicola Cutolo with a patient in 1984: Cutolo is chairman and founder of the Association of Parapsychic Research in Italy. He has achieved outstanding results with many of his patients

Certainly many psychic healers insist that their patients take to their beds for a day or two after a psychic treatment, refrain from any heavy physical labour and generally take things easy. Instructions to eat healthy foods or to drink more water are also often given to patients by the psychic healer. Such instructions coming from a person of some authority can do a great deal of good. A busy farmer's wife with several young children would undoubtedly benefit from rest no matter what her illness. A strict injunction from a psychic healer will often encourage neighbours and relatives to help out and so allow the patient to achieve the rest that has so far eluded them.

Another recognized benefit may be obtained from what is termed the placebo effect. This undoubted advantage is poorly understood, although it is well attested to and recognized by conventional medicine. The effect was first noticed in the 20th century during trials of new drugs. These trials often involved dividing test patients into two groups. One group was given the test drug, the others were given identical-looking pills or injections that contained no drugs at all. These fake pills were known as placebos. The idea was that the group given the placebo would act as a test group against which the success, or otherwise, of the group taking the real drug could be compared.

MIND OVER MATTER

It came as something of a surprise for the early researchers to find that the group taking the placebo also showed clear signs of improvement – even though they were taking no drugs at all. What appeared to be happening was that the mere fact of a person believing that they were receiving effective treatment made them respond as if they were. In short their mind was improving their bodies without the intervention of drugs. How this is achieved is unclear, but the placebo effect is now fully accepted and taken into account during drug trials.

It is certain that some of the successes achieved by psychic healers are due to a similar effect. Because their patients genuinely believe that they are receiving an effective treatment, they respond as if they have. Some psychic healers appear to be better at inducing a placebo effect in their patients – most notably those who genuinely believe that they have psychic healing powers, even if they are at a loss to explain them.

Such rationalizing of psychic healing can account for some instances of cures and improvements, but they cannot explain away the more dramatic instances of psychic healing that have been claimed by some practitioners.

THE GIRL WITH X-RAY EYES

'New Light Sees Through Flesh to Bones' was the headline in one newspaper when, in 1896, Wilhelm Conrad Roentgen (1845–1923) unveiled his new X-

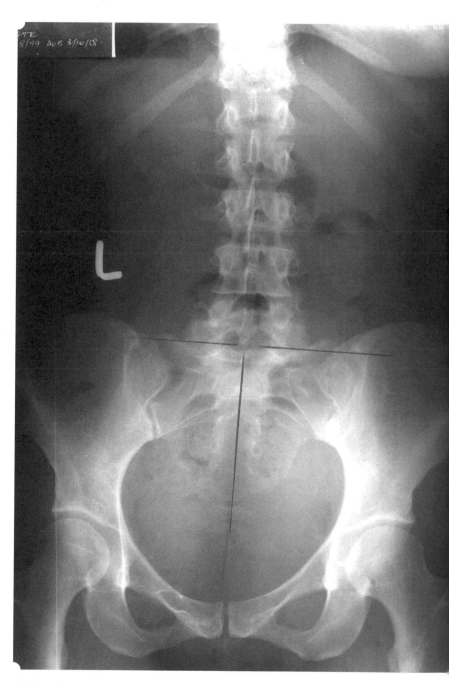

An X-ray showing the lower spine and pelvis of a female patient: could the young Russian girl Natasha Demkina really see into people as clearly as this?

No ordinary eyes: after undergoing international scrutiny of her abilities, Natasha is now concentrating on her medical studies at the university in Moscow

ray machine. His discovery was to change the course of modern medicine. But in 1997, some 100 years later, a young Russian girl claimed to see inside human bodies without the benefit of technology, using her eyes alone.

As a young girl growing up in Saransk, the chief city of Mordovia some 480km (298 miles) east of Moscow, there was little to mark Natasha Demkina out from her playmates. But all that changed when, aged ten, she confessed to her mother that she could 'see' beneath her skin, inside her body. Under Natasha's penetrating gaze, her mum's bones, sinews

and blood-pumping veins were all startlingly apparent.

'At first I was disgusted,' Natasha later admitted. 'Then I became used to it. It seems normal now and, if I don't see anyone for a while, I miss the experience.'

Natasha began to use her unexpected talents to diagnose ailments among friends and family. Her startling success rate soon led people to call her 'the girl with X-ray eyes'. As her reputation spread, Natasha was confronted with more patients than ever. She returned from school each day to discover a line of people outside her house, hoping that she would identify health problems undetected by doctors. She began to charge people a small fee as Natasha dreamed of going to medical school, which would cost more money than the family possessed. Some Natasha enthusiasts claimed she had offered her diagnostic opinion to 10,000 people.

Her bizarre visual surgery finally attracted the interest of an international television company, who asked her to appear on air and expose her skills to camera scrutiny. Ringing in the ears of the television producer were the words of her proud mother Tatyana, 'She has never been wrong in six years.'

In May 2004, the show arranged for Natasha to be put to the test. Unfortunately for Natasha, the notoriously sceptical Committee for the Scientific Investigation of Claims of the Paranormal was involved in drawing up the conditions of the test.

Seven people were selected as subjects for the experiment. Six had different but specific medical issues that would show up on an X-ray – for example, one had an artificial hip while another had internal metal staples. The seventh was, medically speaking, intact. Natasha was given cards with illustrations of the conditions she was expected to identify. Descriptions of them were written in both Russian and English. All seven were expected to remain seated during the test, although Natasha generally saw patients while they were on their feet.

The authors of the test decided Natasha would be deemed successful if she got five out of seven diagnoses correct. The result of the test would not provide definitive evidence that Natasha possessed supernatural powers, the authors decided, but would only determine whether her gift warranted further study.

The experiment was to take place in New York, a long way from home for 17-year-old Natasha. The test was expected to be over in just over an hour, but in the event it lasted four hours. This was unusual, since up until then Natasha had completed most consultations within 10 minutes. Furthermore, she

Aged ten, Natasha confessed to her mother that she could 'see' beneath her skin, inside her body. Her bones, sinews and veins were all apparent

was thought to have chatted to friends and family on her mobile phone, when the rules stated she was to talk to no one.

At the end of the test Natasha was found to have made four correct diagnoses rather than the necessary five. It proved, said Andrew Skolnick, one of the authors of the test, that her gift as a medical intuitive should be called into question. Natasha had contravened the rules of the test, he said, and taken hours to produce a result that simply was not very impressive. Among the medical conditions she had missed was a man with a metal plate in his skull that was reportedly visible to the naked eye. Assertions that she could make cellular diagnoses were disputed by those who organized the test, who said a drawing she submitted of a particular rogue cell was in fact nothing like the real thing.

'COLD READINGS'

The test organizers suspected that during her consultations at home in Russia Natasha made 'cold readings', a technique honed by fortune-tellers of old. It entails the psychic or healer bombarding their subject with questions and alighting on minute clues to draw sweeping conclusions about the state of their health. In the face of such questioning, subjects tend to focus on the correct statements while disregarding the flurry of false information offered beforehand, especially if they are eager to believe. Furthermore, they said she was operating from a position of strength, since it was almost impossible to prove her wrong. In many instances it would take an autopsy to determine whether her medical diagnoses were correct or not.

As far as the test organizers were concerned, all these factors meant that Natasha was no longer of interest. But Natasha's supporters took issue with the results of the test. Her figures, although not up to the required standards of the panel, were nevertheless statistically significant. There was only a one in fifty chance of achieving such a result, which surely put it beyond mere chance. 'Why is it that if I get five out of seven I pass, but if I get four I'm a total failure?' asked a dejected Natasha.

Furthermore, Natasha was operating under stressful, unsupportive conditions when all psychics work better in a relaxed atmosphere. Her sympathizers felt that she had been ambushed by sophisticated sceptics with a vested interest in branding her claims false. Their reputations were, at the end of the day, rooted in disproving paranormal events rather than endorsing them. This was the same crowd who had decided Uri Geller, a famous spoon-bending psychic with armies of devotees, did not have sufficient skill to warrant further investigation either.

In the meantime, Natasha's talents had come under scrutiny elsewhere. She was judged to be entirely convincing by a variety of different audiences, not least the *Sun* newspaper in Britain. Nor is she the only person in the world today to apparently possess X-ray vision. There are a number of psychic healers who make similar claims and offer a list of success stories to back their case.

Afterwards Natasha sank from the limelight, concentrating on her conventional studies at medical school. She was following the ambition she had as a child, to become a doctor, before she attracted so much international notoriety. As she put it, 'The dream is, if I preserve my gift, to use it but on the basis of proper medical knowledge.' With medical training behind her, Natasha may yet return to confound her critics.

ONE FOOT IN THE STARS

Matthew Manning's life story might resemble a strange combination of Harry Potter and *The X Files,* but there is nothing fictional about the scientific data on his extraordinary powers. For almost three decades, this remarkable British healer and psychic has worked with some of the world's leading academics as they try to explain the inexplicable.

Manning first came to public prominence in 1974, following his appearance on a BBC prime-time show *The Frost Interview*. He caused a national sensation with a display of automatic writing – apparently transcribing messages from the dead – which accurately diagnosed health problems suffered by members of the audience. However, for his family, friends and former schoolmates, this feat was unsurprising compared to some of the extraordinary displays of Manning's past.

POLTERGEIST ACTIVITY

In his autobiography, *One Foot in the Stars*, Manning tells how his family first experienced poltergeist activity in February 1967, at their 1950s-style home in Shelford, near Cambridge. Events began unremarkably when a silver tankard threw itself off a wooden shelf overnight, and progressed to the daily movement of everything from ashtrays to armchairs. Eventually, Manning's father contacted George Owen, Professor of Genetics at Trinity College, Cambridge, and a leading authority on poltergeist activity.

Professor Owen assured the family that they were experiencing a natural, though unexplained, phenomenon that would eventually pass, and for a time it seemed he was right. But in the autumn of 1968, when 12-year-old Manning and his family moved to Queens House, an 18th-century home in nearby Linton, the poltergeist returned with a vengeance. In one incident, which Manning describes as 'worthy of a horror film', he watched a bedroom wardrobe inching towards him – then he felt the bed itself vibrate, hover about 15cm (6in) above the ground and then reposition itself.

The following morning, the family went downstairs to find that the kitchen, sitting room and lounge had all been completely ransacked. Over the next few months, dozens of similarly bizarre events occurred, which included random scrawling on walls inside the house and water appearing out of nowhere. At one point, Manning's mother suggested they leave a paper and pen in a locked, empty room

Matthew Manning is a renowned healer and has treated tens of thousands of patients for everything from toothache to migraine and secondary cancer

variety of styles. Among them were pictures supposedly originating from dead masters such as Paul Klee, Thomas Rowlandson and W Keble Martin. Later, Manning produced work resembling that of Picasso, Goya, Beardsley and Dürer, and sometimes his feats were witnessed by teachers from beginning to end. His housemaster Roger Blackmore later told how he had watched Manning at work and questioned him. 'He could answer quite happily,' recalled Mr Blackmore, 'He would talk about the period in which the drawing was based. He didn't appear to be in a trance. He was working as a normal artist of considerable talent.'

Throughout this period, Manning was also producing messages from apparently dead people in widely differing handwriting styles. During the summer holidays of 1971, one of his most regular otherworldly correspondents was a certain Robert Webbe, who seemed to be a previous owner of Queens House (and spoke as though he still was). The following year Manning, concerned about his sick grandmother, established a dialogue with a physician called Thomas Penn, whom he found could be summoned at will. It was Penn whose diagnoses later captivated David Frost's audience in 1974.

Manning tried to satisfy the curiosity of mainstream science, by submitting to a seemingly endless series of tests under laboratory conditions. From late 1976, he toured university campuses in the United States, starting at the University of California and the Washington Research Institute in San Francisco.

to see what happened. A few minutes later they returned to find the words 'Matthew Beware' alongside a Leo zodiac sign.

At first Manning's father, a level-headed architect, tried to find rational explanations for what was going on. But after witnessing so many paranormal events, he grudgingly accepted them as fact.

Despite general agreement among teaching staff that Manning was hopeless at art, he began producing outstanding 'automatic drawings' in a

BEYOND THE REALMS OF CHANCE

His experimental successes were many and varied. They included the ability to influence an electrical impulse on the skin of a frog, sedating or rousing a subject sitting in a separate room, influencing a coin to land heads or tails, and predicting which of ten canisters held water or ball bearings. In this last ESP (extra-sensory perception) test, Manning was correct eight times out of ten in each of three separate runs – far beyond the realms of chance. One experiment in

Manning has cooperated with scientists to see how his powers work

California even showed that he could improve the yield of commercial grass seeds by holding a vial-full in his hand and concentrating.

Perhaps Manning's most astounding result came the following year at the Mind Science Foundation in San Antonio, Texas. Here, a team led by psychologist William Braud sought to establish whether psychokinesis (using psychic power to make things move) could influence human biological systems. His experiments with Manning on slowing the abnormal degeneration of red blood cells suggested that it could.

Braud later observed Manning attempting to destroy cancer cells. Manning operated under strict laboratory conditions and a control subject mimicked his every move. The control failed to have an impact on any of the cells. Manning succeeded in twenty-seven out of thirty attempts, increasing the number of

dead cancer cells by anything between 200 and 1,200 per cent. This was a ground-breaking result. Braud concluded: 'What Matthew has demonstrated is that he can influence cancer cells. There may be parapsychological factors involved that could be used to heal oneself or heal others.'

The rest, as they say, is history. These days Manning focuses his powers on healing, and by 2008 he has been consulted by tens of thousands of patients, including the likes of Prince Philip and Pope Paul VI. Despite many documented successes – from back pain to secondary cancer – Manning rejects any suggestion that he is special and describes himself as 'proudly irreligious'. He does not claim to understand how his powers work, only that they do. He has founded the Matthew Manning Centre in Bury St Edmonds, England, published books and issued audiotapes on the subject of psychic healing.

THE MESMERIC MONK

The story of Rasputin is a remarkable one, with the events of his life exceeded in peculiarity only by the truly inexplicable circumstances of his death. During his time he was a healer and self-proclaimed holy man, as well as the most unlikely of statesmen, enjoying incredible influence over the rulers of Russia.

The real name of the man who came to be known as Rasputin (the word means 'debauched' in Russian) was Grigory Yefimovich Novykh. Born in 1865 into a typical Siberian peasant family, he could never have envisaged, in his early years, how much he would go on to accomplish in his life. When he was about 18, Rasputin underwent a religious experience and decided to enter the monastery at Verkhoture, where he stayed for some months. Despite his famous soubriquet of 'the mad monk', however, Rasputin never actually became a genuine monk, perhaps because he was illiterate and unable to read the scriptures for himself. Whatever the reason, it is unlikely that any monastery would have

Right: Rasputin as he was in 1910

been able to contain for long such an unusual character as Rasputin.

While at this monastery, Rasputin became familiar with the Khlysty religious sect – which mixed its own brand of mysticism with a degree of sexual hedonism not often found in the church, and which had actually been banned in Russia on heretical grounds. In spite of the fact that he was married, Rasputin launched himself into this world of fornication with considerable enthusiasm, even holding orgies in the marital home. At this time he was beginning to be aware that he might possess some unusual powers, and believed that these could be directly attributed to his sexual indulgences – for this reason he took part in these excesses at every opportunity.

Rasputin gained a reputation as a healer and clairvoyant. He had developed an unusual ability to cure ailments without even having to make a diagnosis, almost as if he detected the nature of the problem through psychic means alone. He travelled as far as Mount Athos, in Greece, and Jerusalem, where he demonstrated his skills to the religious dignitaries, to great acclaim. And so he established his reputation as a 'staretz' (the term for a self-proclaimed holy man and faith healer). Needy people would travel great distances to meet him, rewarding him for his services with gifts or money.

After some time spent travelling, Rasputin returned to his village where he experienced the vision that was to alter not only the course of his own life, but arguably would have an enormous influence on the history of the whole world. While working in the fields one day, Rasputin apparently saw an apparition of the Holy Mother, who spoke to him and said it was his duty to help to save the life of the young Tsarevich Alexis, heir to the throne of Russia. The Tsarevich was suffering from haemophilia, which can cause fatal bleeding from even a small cut or bruise, as it prevents the blood from clotting. This hereditary disorder had no known cure, and the Tsarevich was in very grave medical danger.

Rasputin moved to St Petersburg, where he lived for two years before he came to meet the royal Romanov family. He had by now become famous for his lechery, and was extremely popular with Russian noblewomen, with whom he enjoyed many scandalous liaisons. Nonetheless, his success as a powerful religious healer became known to the Tsar and the Tsarina, and in 1906 they summoned him to see them, hoping that he might be able to cure their sickly son. They had to take Rasputin into their personal confidence, for the Tsarevich's illness was shrouded in secrecy because it might have threatened the prince's right to succession, if it ever became known to the public.

MIRACLE CURE

The decision by the Tsar and his wife to invite Rasputin into their lives cannot have been taken lightly, but was to prove fruitful. Through methods impossible to understand, Rasputin appears to have successfully brought to a halt the bleeding of the Tsarevich. This amazing feat rendered him indispensable to the royal family and it would eventually make Rasputin one of the most powerful men in Russia. The Tsarina Alexandra grew increasingly close to Rasputin, feeling indebted to him for the service he had performed in healing her young son. She was convinced that his power was a gift from God, and that he had been sent in answer to her prayers. Meanwhile, Rasputin's affiliation with the royal family was causing his influence within the church to grow. After a while, he came to enjoy such power that he was able to replace those who were against him with his own supporters, gradually eroding his opposition.

Yet Rasputin's support was far from universal. The predilection for alcohol and sexual deviancy that had earned him the name 'Rasputin' had also earned him enemies – since many church members and noblemen were absolutely appalled by his behaviour. They were also very concerned about the growing influence exerted by Rasputin over the Tsarina, and the rumours that the pair had become lovers – as was Tsar Nicholas himself.

Yet the Tsarina would hear nothing against Rasputin. As far as she was concerned, he was just an

illiterate peasant who had succeeded where everyone else, royal doctors, holy men and healers alike, had failed. Little is known about exactly how Rasputin healed the sick child, although many have surmised that it may have been through a form of hypnosis.

In 1915 Tsar Nicholas took personal control of the Russian armed forces that were fighting in the First World War. Tsarina Alexandra was left in sole

Tsar Nicolas II, his wife Tsarina Alexandra and their haemophiliac son, the Tsarevich Alexis

command of the country and she immediately appointed Rasputin as her personal advisor. This made Rasputin the effective leader of Russia, an incredible feat for a man who was born a Siberian peasant. Could this have been due simply to the magnetism of his personality, or was Rasputin in possession of psychic powers that enabled him to rise to power in this way?

POISONED CAKES

The evidence certainly seems to suggest that Rasputin had powers that were well beyond the abilities of most people. In addition to his well-documented and proven healing ability, there is evidence of his remarkably accurate predictions for the future. He even managed to successfully foresee his own murder, although he was unable to prevent it.

A group of disaffected aristocrats who deeply resented the power that Rasputin had acquired were intent on killing him and returning power to the nobility. The group of conspirators was led by Prince Felix Yossupov, who invited Rasputin to his home under the pretext of meeting his wife Irina, a woman famed for her beauty. Rasputin accepted the invitation and travelled to the palatial home of the prince, where he was warmly received. The conspirators planned to poison Rasputin with cyanide, which they concealed in some cakes and Madeira wine.

Prince Felix engaged Rasputin in conversation, and persuaded him to try some of the cakes. Although Rasputin's preference was for wine, out of politeness he ate a couple, washing them down with a good measure of Madeira. The prince watched in amazement as Rasputin appeared to shrug off the effects of enough poison to kill six men. At this point, the prince withdrew temporarily to confer with his fellow conspirators who were all mystified by Rasputin's apparent imperviousness to poison. Prince Felix was then presented with a pistol, and told to shoot his unsuspecting guest, whereupon he returned and shot Rasputin in the chest from point-blank range.

Believing Rasputin to be dead, the conspirators gathered over his body to observe their handiwork. At this point, Rasputin is said to have been roused from apparent death and forcefully grabbed hold of them. The men had to beat and stab him in order to free themselves. Amazingly, Rasputin is said to have

pushed them off and attempted an escape. He was then shot a second time before being bound with ropes. To be sure they had killed him this time, the assassins then dragged him to the icy Neva river and threw him in. A subsequent post mortem showed that he had drowned.

This kind of resilience seems beyond human comprehension. Rasputin was poisoned, shot, beaten, stabbed and drowned. Any one of these acts would have been enough to cause the death of a normal man. Surely this was irrefutable evidence of Rasputin's mysterious powers?

To further add to the intrigue and provide yet more proof of Rasputin's extraordinary abilities, it was discovered that he had predicted his own demise in a letter to the Tsarina, a communication that also contained a dire prophecy for the Romanov family.

FATEFUL PREDICTION

In the letter, dated 7 December 1916, Rasputin stated that he did not expect to live to see the New Year, a prediction that proved to be correct, for he was murdered only nine days later. The letter also specified that, should he be killed by a common man, then the family of the Tsar would survive, but – chillingly – should he die at the hands of a nobleman, the Tsar's family would all be dead within two years and, furthermore, that no nobleman would live in Russia for at least twenty-five years.

Only a few months after the death of Rasputin, the Bolshevik revolutionary forces overthrew the Romanov family and the entire system of Russian nobility. Within less than two years, the entire royal family had been assembled and killed, providing absolute and bloody proof that Rasputin's last chilling prediction had come true. The Bolsheviks also dug up and desecrated Rasputin's grave and burned his corpse, such was the strength of feeling he had generated in the country.

Although Rasputin is now famous only for his association with the Tsar and Tsarina, it should be remembered that he achieved that position as a result of his great success as a healer. He had spent several decades curing people who were sick and helping those who were uncertain about what the future held for them. What lay at the root of his amazing powers is still unclear – Rasputin himself claimed that his abilities were religious in origin, but his personal conduct would seem to suggest that they were simply an innate gift of his own. Whatever the explanation, this colourful Russian figure looks set to remain a source of intrigue to the world for the foreseeable future.

HEALER IMPRISONED

During his lifetime Jose Arigo became renowned for his inexplicable psychic talents, which he used to great effect in healing the sick and injured. Indeed, many of his actions were even proclaimed as miracles by his admirers. Sadly, however, his

attempts to use his amazing healing powers for the good of mankind were eventually cut short by his imprisonment, when the authorities ruled that his activities were contrary to the law.

Born in 1918 into the peasant class of Brazil, Arigo could never have anticipated the level of international fame he would eventually enjoy as a result of his unusual gifts. He first became aware of his abilities while visiting a dying relative; the whole family had assembled to bid their farewells to the woman who was suffering from a life-threatening tumour. However, as the priest read out the last rites, Arigo recounted how he felt strangely compelled to take action. Seizing a knife from the kitchen, he cut into the woman and removed the tumour on the spot.

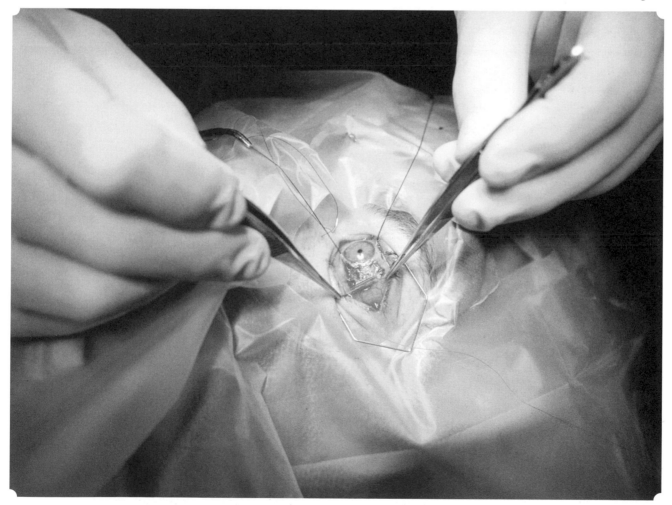

Conventional methods of modern eye surgery require specialized instruments and, above all, a sterile environment

Amazingly, she made a rapid recovery, and it was after this that Arigo's community realized that they were fortunate enough to have a remarkable psychic healer in their midst.

Such was the poverty in Arigo's neighbourhood that there was very limited access to doctors and medicine. It was not surprising, therefore, that the news of his healing ability spread rapidly, and soon he was being asked to treat large numbers of people. Although initially reluctant to put others at risk by operating on them, Arigo quickly discovered that he was able to repeat the success of his first operation on numerous occasions.

Arigo's explanation for his healing powers was an unusual one, as he attributed his skills to the fact that when he was operating he would become possessed by the spirit of a deceased German physician, Dr

Adolphus Fritz. It is difficult to find an alternative explanation for Arigo's remarkable abilities, since he was very poorly educated and certainly had no medical knowledge whatsoever.

The only other possibility is that Arigo invented the story of Dr Fritz in order to deflect attention away from the incredible powers that were actually entirely his own. Whatever the truth, Arigo continued to credit the success of his work to the spirit of Dr Fritz throughout his entire life.

Arigo had practised his healing on a large number of people before he came to the attention of the authorities. The medical establishment had serious concerns about the insanitary nature of his operations and his complete lack of any medical qualifications.

Eventually, in 1936, he was arrested for the illegal practice of medicine, after which he was fined and

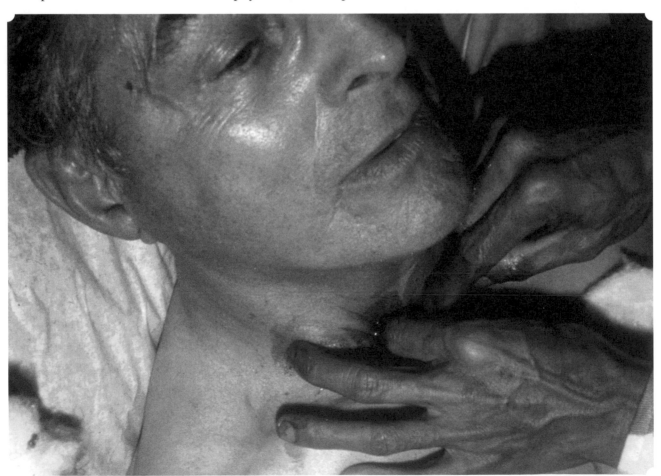

Psychic surgeon Feliciano Omilles, from the Philippines, working in Mexico in the early 1970s

sentenced to eight months in jail. The establishment was not prepared, however, for the huge level of public support for Arigo – the extent of which eventually caused the President of Brazil to step in and offer him an official pardon.

Almost thirty years later, however, in 1964, Arigo was not so lucky, and he was forced to face his sentence. Although the prosecuting judge, Filippe Immesi, was amazed by a demonstration of Arigo's powers, he was forced to conclude that Arigo was nevertheless breaking the law and sentenced him accordingly.

While in jail, Arigo still continued his healing practices, believing at this stage of his life that it was his mission to help as many people as possible.

Arigo died following a car accident in 1971. In the course of his lifetime, he had healed many thousands of people who, without his intervention, would surely have died.

PSYCHIC SURGERY

The career of Arigo was an early example of a phenomenon that was to become known as psychic surgery. Unlike psychic healers, psychic surgeons have claimed to undertake surgical procedures using paranormal means.

While many psychic healers say that they do not fully understand how their powers work, psychic surgeons are not so reticent. They say that they use their hands to penetrate the patient's body, removing diseased tissue or foreign bodies, and then close up the incision again using paranormal powers.

The discipline seems to have grown out of the spiritualist movement in the Philippines during the 1940s, with a noted spiritualist named Eleuterio Terte being the first man to perform psychic surgery on a major scale.

Terte trained others in the skills of psychic surgery and the practice spread to Brazil and other South American countries. Although the different practitioners used slightly different methods, they did tend to adhere to a set formula. The patient would be asked to lie down and relax partially unclothed.

The psychic surgeon would then go to work with his or her bare hands, sometimes aided by swabs and forceps.

Blood would flow and the surgeons fingers would seem to disappear into an incision made in the skin. Tissue or objects would be removed from the wound. The psychic surgeon would then close up the incision by psychic means before cleaning the area to reveal intact skin. The removed tissues or objects would be blamed for the patient's illness and disposed of.

FRAUD AND TRICKERY

The discipline remained largely the province of impoverished areas of Brazil, Paraguay and the Philippines until March 1984 when American comedian Andy Kaufman travelled to the Philippines to undergo a course of psychic surgery. Kaufman had been diagnosed with incurable lung cancer by his doctor and was seeking a cure. Tragically, he returned to the USA declaring that he had been cured, but just a few weeks later died of renal failure.

Despite Kaufman's death, the news of psychic surgery had spread and was taken up enthusiastically by many interested in the paranormal. Then came accusations of fraud.

In 1979 a leading psychic surgeon on a visit to Britain allowed herself to be filmed by the BBC performing an operation. When the film was slowed down and enlarged it clearly showed that the blood that had appeared to come from the patient's body had actually come from a small phial hidden inside the psychic surgeon's hand.

Soon other evidence of fraud and trickery was uncovered. This had serious consequences. Psychic surgery was discredited, at least in the West. But among the impoverished slums of South America and the Philippines it continues to exist.

As with psychic healing, psychic surgery continues to produce some evidence of cures and remission. Most conventional doctors hold that such evidence is proving only that the placebo effect is working well.

WITCHES

Sorcery is an age-old obsession. Humans seem irresistibly drawn to using supernatural powers against each other – whether it be in the form of issuing curses against places or people, or brewing up poisonous concoctions to seal the fate of another. The prospect that someone can manipulate natural or supernatural forces to their own ends is a frightening one, but when the practice of such ritual magic has been condemned, it has sometimes led to cruel and unjust punishment that seems to be the work of the Devil himself.

THE SALEM WITCH TRIALS

In 1692, seventy years after the arrival of the pilgrim fathers, Salem village in Massachusetts became the focus of a feverish witch-hunt that resulted in the death sentence for twenty residents and the imprisonment of dozens more. Salem remains a by-word for Satanic hysteria to this day.

It all began as child's play. The young people of Salem, constricted by overbearing Puritanism, were agog to hear vivid stories woven by Tituba, a Carib slave brought to the community from the West Indies. The tribal ritual and magic recounted by Tituba must have seemed a world away from the existence of grinding toil led by Salem residents.

But when 9-year-old Betty Parris fell ill and could not be cured by orthodox methods, the doctor said she was bewitched. The affliction quickly spread to her friends, who writhed and groaned and uttered fanciful accusations against adults.

The childrens' imagination was fired not only by the tales told by Tituba, but also by the words of self-appointed Satan expert Cotton Mather, author of a then recently published tome relating to the symptoms of witchcraft. Furthermore, they had been experimenting with fortune telling, and they knew their curiosity had led them into forbidden realms. The guilty children believed themselves to be bitten and pinched by devilish creatures or spectres and were soon seeing witches flying through the air.

Perhaps unsurprisingly, Tituba was swiftly arrested and faced the accusation of witchcraft. Two other women were also hauled before the authorities. One was Sarah Good, a pipe-smoking beggar, and the other was Sarah Osburne, a widow known to hold the church in contempt. Matters might have died down following their confinement, but for the admission by Tituba, implicating the other two women, of contact with Satan himself. When the child accusers were brought into their company, the youngsters fell into fits – proof, if any were needed, that these women were indeed witches.

Now the zealous village dignitaries led a witch-hunt, convinced that the Devil's agents were lurking in their midst. The first witch to hang was Bridget Bishop, a woman in her late fifties and a tavern owner of dubious reputation. A field hand claimed to have seen Bishop's image stealing eggs and then transforming into a cat to run off with her plunder. Another villager said she visited him at night in spectral form to torment him. Yet others maintained that she was responsible for numerous examples of bad luck in the community.

A short excerpt from the trial of Bridget Bishop reveals how pointless it was for supposed witches to try to prove their innocence in Salem at this time. When she was accused of being a witch, the luckless woman replied: 'I know nothing of it … I know not what a witch is.'

'How do you know then that you are not a witch?' was the response of the prosecutor. Her continuing protests were deemed unsatisfactory in law. Following her trial she was taken to Gallows Hill on 10 June 1692 and hanged.

Some of the unlucky women of Salem were brought to trial for witchcraft. Once denounced, they had little chance of survival

"THERE IS A FLOCK OF YELLOW BIRDS AROUND HER HEAD."

CHILDREN IN CHAINS

The plight of witch-hunt victims was heart-rending. Four-year-old Dorcas Good was arrested after Salem children claimed to have been attacked by her spectre. She spent months in jail in chains, weeping continually, and then watched her mother Sarah being carried off to the gallows.

Rebecca Nurse, a church-goer and a pillar of the community, was found not guilty at her trial. Judge William Stoughton was so irate at the decision that he sent the jury back to re-consider and they returned with a guilty verdict. On appeal, the state governor pardoned her, but prominent Salem men compelled him to reverse the decision. Eventually, Rebecca was excommunicated from the church and sent to hang.

Deputy Constable John Willard was brought before the court after he refused to make further arrests. His fate was the same as the convicted witches. Another tavern owner, John Proctor, was denounced as a witch after pouring scorn on the trials. Robust in his own defence, he asked for the trial to be moved to Boston. His request was denied and he was hanged, although his pregnant wife was spared the noose.

Former minister Reverend George Burroughs, it was decided, led young girls into witchcraft. Before he was hanged he recited the Lord's prayer, a feat supposedly impossible for a witch, and once again maintained his innocence. When the crowd hesitated, Cotton Mather himself stepped forward to remind them of the court's authority.

After Giles Corey refused to co-operate with the court he was pressed to death – pinned out in an open field with rocks piled upon his body until all life was crushed from it. This terrible punishment, probably illegal, was never used again in America.

Within a few months the lust for witch persecution in Salem was ebbing. A change in the judicial proceedings meant spectral evidence was no longer accepted. Given that firm facts were in short supply, this effectively put an end to the string of convictions. By May 1693, all prisoners awaiting trial or already convicted of witchcraft were released. Judges and jurors alike were largely filled with remorse and made public apologies. The notable exception was William Stoughton, one of the driving forces in the campaign, who maintained that the village had been riddled with witches. He went on to become governor of Massachusetts.

However, no fewer than twenty people had lost their lives during the witch-fever, all through public execution. A further four people died in jail where conditions were foul. Two unlucky dogs were executed as witch accomplices.

The terrible events that took place in Salem in 1692-93 were the result of a small community riven with feuds. Suspicion and distrust were rife amongst the villagers, and the witch-trials became an opportunity for them to settle long-standing scores. At the time there was an unshakeable belief in the existence of witches. The dangers of Satan and his faithful crones were expounded weekly from the pulpit to the God-fearing congregation. Witchcraft was an issue often hotly debated among adults, particularly after Cotton Mather's book appeared, and it was a constant worry to many.

WISE WOMEN AND CUNNING MEN

But what of Tituba, at the start of all the troubles? Ironically – having confessed her guilt – she walked free, and was ultimately sold on into another community. The effects of her story-telling there remain unknown.

There has been a tendency in recent years to dismiss the fears expressed at Salem as nonsense and to maintain that witches never existed – that they

> Before George Burroughs was hanged, he recited the Lord's prayer, a feat which was supposedly impossible for a witch

were harmless old women persecuted by their cruel neighbours. This is to overlook the well documented fact that in the days before the 20th century large numbers of men and women across Europe earned a living as witches, warlocks, wise women or cunning men. Some of these people were good-natured souls performing a valuable service in a pre-modern and largely agricultural society. But some were vindictive and spiteful folk who used their position to persecute those they did not like and to enrich themselves.

The witches, or cunning folk, had an important part to play in rural life. They knew the hundreds of herbs and plants that grew wild in the countryside – and fully understood the medicinal properties of those plants. They could prepare potions or poultices that could be highly effective, indeed chemicals extracted from those plants form the basis of many modern medicines. The witches and cunning men would be called in to tend to sick humans and animals alike. In an age that believed in fairies, goblins and ghosts more than we do today, the cunning men could devise amulets and charms to ward off such evil entities.

As with more modern psychic healers, there is no doubt that commonsense and the placebo effect went a long way to giving the witches their powers. Others relied on the magic of their names and the potency of their reputations. Cunning Jennings of 19th century Herefordshire was known for his ability to find stolen objects. His usual routine was to visit local pubs and other gathering places, telling everyone he met that on the following Sunday after church he would cast his spells to identify the thief and punish him with dire disasters. Almost invariably the missing object turned up before the Sunday, word having got back to the thief that Jennings was on the case. The fear induced by Jennings was enough to cause the thief to hand the item back.

Others had different powers. Wizard Wrightson of Yorkshire, who died in the 1840s, performed many tricks that were almost certainly achieved by hypnotism. He once came across a pair of malefactors sitting beside the fire at an inn. Wrightson began chatting to the men, while piling wood on to the fire. As the fire grew hotter, the men tried to move their chairs back but found that they were quite unable to move. Wrightson piled on the wood until the men were soaked with sweat and starting to suffer heat stroke. Only then did he broach the subject of their misdeeds and extract a confession.

Not all the people possessed of such powers used them for good. At Poynings in Sussex in the 1860s there lived an old witch who was greatly feared locally. She could cause illness among livestock with, it was said, a glance. The local folk were careful to always give her some meat when an animal was slaughtered, or a share of any crop gathered in. The local squire suspected the woman of putting poison into animal feed to cause the livestock to fall ill, but could not prove it.

There was no doubt that if a witch wanted to turn nasty, he or she had the means to do so. Whether their power was down to fear, hypnotism or herbs, the power was very real in the communities where they lived.

DEVIL WORSHIP

For the God-fearing men prosecuting the supposed witches of Salem, however, there was only one possible explanation for the source of the powers exercised by witches: they were devil worshippers. It was, in fact, the tales of demons and evil spirits that dominated the trials and which were responsible for the death penalties, not accusations of witchcraft as such.

According to many religions, the Devil is the opposite of God and an enemy of mankind. Known by different names, including Satan, Beelzebub and Old Scratch, he is a difficult figure to pin down. Just as some people have devoted their lives to searching for signs of God, there are others who seek affirmation of the Devil's existence.

The idea of a devil probably first evolved as a metaphor for the flawed side of man's character, the aspect that sought money, power and carnal pleasures. Ironically, the Devil was made larger than life by clergymen in the pulpit who sought to drive society that thrived through its twilight existence and elaborate rituals.

It was not until 1966 that the Church of Satan was unveiled in San Francisco, offering a belief system up to scrutiny. The founder of this unorthodox church was Dr Anton Szandor LaVey, who explained: 'Satan is a symbol, nothing more. He's a symbol of man's carnal nature – his lust, greed, vengeance but most of all his ego.'

THE CHURCH OF SATAN

Dr Edward Moody, an American social scientist, joined the Church of Satan to discover more. The churchgoers were, he discovered, society's least prepossessing members. 'The cult attracted them because it offered a simple explanation for their inadequacies: they were bewitched or under an unlucky star or not vibrating to the right rhythm. Their failure was supernatural; their remedy was supernatural. The rites and medicines of the church promised the success that had so far eluded them.'

Horrific crimes have been carried out in the name of Satan. The murders of pregnant movie actress Sharon Tate and others by the drug-addled followers of Charles Manson in the 1970s are the most notorious. Of course, these can hardly be taken as proof of the Devil's existence, since there have been other atrocities committed in the name of God. However, an incident that occurred more than 150 years ago in rural Devon, England, is still cited today as a mystery that perhaps points to an embodiment of the Devil at work on earth.

THE DEVIL WALKS IN DEVON

The bitter winter of 1855 turned southern Britain into an icy wasteland. The frail froze in their beds, thousands were laid off work and bread riots erupted in towns isolated by heavy snow. This was the 'Crimean Winter' – an uncertain, fearful time.

However, on the morning of 9 February, cold and hunger were briefly forgotten, when Devon villagers awoke to a new fall of snow bearing strange tear-drop shaped tracks. The tracks defied explanation, trod impossible paths and created a trail some hundred

Is the Devil a symbol of man's carnal nature, his lust, greed and ego? Or does he actually exist as a counterpoint to God?

their parishioners to God through fear. Naturally, some members of the congregation were intrigued and wanted to know more.

Worship of the Devil or Satanism ensued and was for centuries an underground movement or secret miles long. Soon there was talk of these being the Devil's footprints.

For weeks it dominated national newspaper letters columns. *The Times* referred to 'the marks of Satan' and added: '… that great excitement has been produced among all classes may be judged from the fact that the subject has been descanted on from the pulpit.'

On 24 February the *Illustrated London News* weighed in with an attempt to explain why the 'Great Devon Mystery' could not be attributed to farm or wild animals. The marks were 10cm x 5cm (2 x 3.9in), like a donkey's hoof, but whereas a donkey would have made double prints, the 'Devil's' appeared in a single line some 20cm (7.9in) apart. Every parish reported the same size print and stride. Struggling for a description, many witnesses said they seemed 'branded in the snow'.

The writer concluded: 'It is very easy for people to laugh at these appearances and account for them in an idle way … [but] no known animal could have traversed this extent of country in one night, beside having to cross an estuary of the sea 3km (1.86 miles) broad.'

By now south Devon was a cauldron of fear, rumour and wild speculation. Search parties armed with guns and bludgeons were dispatched from Dawlish to follow the trail. Fishermen spoke of prints emerging from the sea at Teignmouth. Doors were barricaded at night.

Some churchmen took advantage of the febrile mood, claiming that the Devil had singled out followers of the priest Edward Pusey. At the time, Pusey had been trying to re-introduce Catholic ritual into the Church of England and he controlled a handful of Devon parishes.

'Some people say it is sent as a warning to the Puseyites,' the *Western Times* gleefully reported, 'hence it is that the "phenomenon" has visited the Puseyite parishes of Woodbury, Topsham and Littleham-cum-Exmouth. In this place it has

The Illustrated London News *published a letter and an illustration showing how the prints appeared in a strange single line*

THE ILLUSTRATED LONDON NEWS

FOOT-MARKS ON THE SNOW, IN DEVON.

(From a Correspondent.)

As many of your readers have perused, I have no doubt, with much interest, the paragraph which appeared in several of the papers of last week, relative to the mysterious foot-marks left upon the snow during the night of Thursday, the 8th, in the parishes of Exmouth, Lympstone, and Woodbury, as also in Dawlish, Torquay, Totnes, and other places on the other side of the estuary of the Exe, in the county of Devon, extending over a tract of country of thirty or forty miles, or probably more; and as the paragraph I allude to does not fully detail the mysterious affair, it may probably be interesting to many to have a more particular account—which I think this unusual occurrence well deserves.

The marks which appeared on the snow (which lay very thinly on the ground at the time), and which were seen on the Friday morning, to all appearance were the perfect impression of a donkey's hoof—the length 4 inches by 2¾ inches; but, instead of progressing as that animal would have done (or indeed as any other would have done), feet right and left, it appeared that foot had followed foot, in a *single line;* the distance from each tread being eight inches, or rather more—the foot-marks in every parish being exactly the same size, and the steps the same length. This mysterious visitor generally only passed *once* down or across each garden or courtyard, and did so in nearly all the houses in many parts of the several towns above mentioned, as also in the farms scattered about; this regular track passing in some instances over the roofs of houses, and hayricks, and very high walls (one fourteen feet), without displacing the snow on either side or altering the distance between the feet, and passing on as if the wall had not been any impediment. The gardens with high fences or walls, and gates locked, were equally visited as those open and unprotected. Now, when we consider the distance that must have been gone over to have left these marks—I may say in almost every garden, on door-steps, through the extensive woods of Luscombe, upon commons, in enclosures and farms—the actual progress must have exceeded a hundred miles. It is very easy for people to laugh at these appearances, and account for them in an idle way.

At present no satisfactory solution has been given. No known animal could have traversed this extent of country in one night, besides having to cross an estuary of the sea two miles broad. Neither does any known animal walk in a *line* of single footsteps, not even man.

Birds could not have left these marks, as no bird's foot leaves the impression of a hoof, or, even were there a bird capable of doing so, could it proceed in the direct manner above stated—nor would birds, even had they donkeys' feet, confine themselves to one direct line, but hop here and there; but the nature of the mark at once sets aside its being the track of a bird. The effect of the atmosphere upon these marks is given by many as a solution; but how could it be possible for the atmosphere to affect one impression and not another? On the morning that the above was observed the snow bore the fresh marks of cats, dogs, rabbits, birds, and men clearly defined. Why, then, should a continuous track, far more clearly defined—so clearly, even, that the raising in the centre of the frog of the foot could be plainly seen—why then should this particular mark be the only one which was affected by the atmosphere, and all the others left as they were? Besides, the most singular circumstance connected with it was, that this particular mark removed the snow, wherever it appeared, clear, as if cut with a diamond or branded with a hot iron;—of course I am not alluding to its appearance after having been trampled on, or meddled with by the curious in and about the thoroughfares of the towns. In one instance this track entered a covered shed, and passed through it out of a broken part of the wall at the other end, where the atmosphere could not affect it.

The writer of the above has passed a five months' winter in the backwoods of Canada, and has had much experience in tracking wild animals and birds upon the snow, and can safely say, he has never seen a more clearly-defined track, or one that appeared to be less altered by the atmosphere than the one in question. Marks left upon thin snow especially may after a time blur a little, but never lose their distinctive character, as every one will know who has been accustomed to follow the track of the American partridge.

Should you think the above likely to interest your readers, or draw from any of them a better solution of this most singular occurrence than has at present been given, perhaps you will allow it a place in your most interesting journal. I send you a copy of the foot, taken from the snow, and also a succession of the steps, to show you the manner of progressing.　　SOUTH DEVON.

traversed the churchyard – and even to the very door of the vestibule.' Conveniently, the article ignores footprints in more conventional parishes.

BRANDED WITH A HOT IRON

The leading investigator of the prints was the Rev H T Ellacombe. He concluded the following: 'There is no doubt as to the facts – that thousands of these marks were seen on the snow on the morning of the 9th extending over many miles,' he wrote. It was 'as if the snow had been branded with a hot iron – ... tho' the snow in the middle part did not appear to be touched.'

The vicar sent various drawings of footprints (and a sample of 'white, grape-sized excrement') to the renowned naturalist Sir Richard Owen and the Oxford professor Dr I A Ogle. One of the sketches included claws, which Sir Richard believed might have belonged to a badger. The vicar's own theory was that birds' feet had become iced up, leaving single prints in the snow. But it seems unlikely that country folk would not have recognized common bird prints.

Bizarrely, a kangaroo had escaped from Mr Fisher's private zoo at nearby Sidmouth just before 8 February and was later shot at Teignmouth. But no reports relating to the footprints mentioned tail marks, so it seems the two events cannot have been linked.

There were attempts try to explain the prints, including the theory that they were in fact condensation marks, and claims that the cold and hungry population had become hysterical. In February 1855 the average temperature across southern England was minus 1.7 degrees and snow fell every day for six weeks.

In the later 20th century, Exeter University research fellow Theo Brown who unearthed Rev Ellacombe's notes, scoured the evidence. She came to the conclusion that a combination of events was probably responsible. She says the trail was not continuous, the prints were not all single file and neither were they identical. Crucially, she states that the prints were laid over several days rather than just

six hours. 'All the people concerned,' says Miss Brown, 'were quite content to leave the thing in the air, rather than spoil a good story.'

However, she concludes: 'To this day, no one has offered an explanation which takes account of all the available evidence ... even if the single-footed track only covered a part of the distance we still have no idea what creature could possibly have made it.'

Devon is an English county often associated with mysterious goings-on. On 3 January 2005, a walker stumbled across a gruesome scene near Sampford Spiney, just 32km (20 miles) west of the 1855 visitation. Six ewes and a ram had been herded together, strangled and laid out in what police believe may have been an occult ceremony. According to ancient belief, seven is a significant number for satanic rituals. A contract with the Devil had to contain seven paragraphs, was binding for seven years and needed seven signatures. It seems that the Devil had struck again.

WICCA

If the belief among medieval Christian clergy that witches were in league with the Devil and formed a trans-European network of malignant Devil-worship has served to muddle the general perception of witches, so has the rapid 20th century increase in the religion of Wicca, a faith that shows no signs of diminishing as the 21st century gets under way.

The exact origins of the Wicca religion are very much in dispute, but it is certain that the faith was publicized and expanded greatly by Gerald Gardiner in the 1950s and that this represents the start of the rapid growth in modern Wicca. Gardiner was a retired civil servant of the British Empire who returned home to Hampshire on his retirement. There, he claimed, he made contact with and was later initiated into a coven of witches. Later Gardiner came to fear that the Wicca faith was in danger of dying out in the modern world. He therefore set about collecting as much information as he could on the religion and published this in a series of books, of which *Witchcraft Today* published in 1954 was the first.

Gardiner also founded his own coven, initiating converts into it with enthusiasm. Some of these followers subsequently left to found their own covens, not all of which adopted the original rituals and beliefs laid down by Gardiner.

These daughter covens adopted aspects of pagan Celtic or English religion and developed their own forms of Wicca. The religion spread rapidly through Britain, then the USA and by the 1980s was beginning to be followed in a few non-English-speaking countries.

In the 2001 Census of the UK, 42,262 replied to the question on religion by stating that they were Pagan – the heading under which Wiccans registered themselves. Most authorities thought that many Wiccans preferred not to answer the question. By 2008 it was estimated that around 800,000 people around the world were involved in Wicca in some form or another. Not all Wiccans form part of a coven, though most rituals and activities do require more than one person to take part.

THE MOTHER GODDESS

Wiccans generally believe that their religion is a pre-Christian faith that somehow managed to survive the many centuries of Christian dominance in Europe. It is held to be pagan and to show great respect for females, indeed some follow a strictly matriarchal form of initiation and precedence.

It is for this reason that the female deity of Wicca is usually held to be superior to the male god. The goddess is usually depicted as a mother goddess, but sometimes appears in three forms: virgin, mother and crone. Some identify this great goddess with the Roman deity Selene, others insist that she is of Celtic origin. She is often symbolized by the moon.

The god of Wicca is a more shadowy figure. He is usually depicted wearing horns and so has come to be identified with the Celtic god of wild animals Cernunos. He is sometimes symbolized by the sun. He is thought to be the husband of the goddess, but his actual powers and role vary between covens. Some covens believe that these two figures are only the

Civil servant Gerald Gardiner (1894–1964) is known as the 'father of Wicca'; in the 1950s he was responsible for revitalizing what he claimed was a pre-Christian pagan witch cult

The best known and most widely celebrated rituals of the Wiccans are sabbats. There are eight of these spaced evenly throughout the year

supreme deities of a more expansive pantheon, while others prefer to hold that the two deities rule alone.

Gardiner's original book stated that there was only one overriding teaching of Wicca, which he expressed as 'As it harm none, do what ye will'. He later formulated what has become known as the Law of Threefold Return, a teaching that whether a person does good or ill the consequences will return to that person with triple force. Later Wiccans have taught that there are eight 'virtues', namely mirth, reverence, honour, humility, strength, beauty, power and compassion.

NAKED RITUALS

Wicca, like most religions, has its own rituals. These are varied but they usually take place within a sacred circle which is drawn on the ground to encompass an altar and those taking part. Ritual objects, such as knives or staves, are frequently employed.

Gardiner stated that some rituals were best conducted 'skyclad' or naked. Many covens employ nudity in at least some rituals and a few insist upon it for all participants in any ritual. Other covens favour ritual robes decorated with symbols of various kinds.

The best known and most widely celebrated rituals of the Wiccans are sabbats. There are eight of these spaced evenly through the year, of which the most important are the four 'quarter days'. These are Samhain (in the winter), Beltane (spring), Imbolc (summer) and Lughnasad (autumn). These derive from the pagan Celtic festivals held at about the same time and, so far as historians know much about them, seem to be similar in ritual content to those events. Samhain, for instance, involves the lighting of a ritual fire.

Although Wicca has no standard religious texts, those groups that derive from the coven set up by Gardiner do possess a *Book of Shadows*.

Each copy of the book is hand-written and passed on from one Wiccan to the next in a 'line of tradition'. The book is added to, edited and revised as time passes so that no two covens have identical copies. The contents are kept strictly secret within the coven to which it belongs and only initiated Wiccans are allowed to see it. Despite this secrecy, some Wiccans have revealed that the book contains theological content and instructions on carrying out rituals. Some non-Gardinerian covens have other books of unspecified origin.

While the history of Wicca since Gardiner is well known, its course before that time is unclear. Gardiner claimed that he was told by the Hampshire Coven that he joined that the religion had previously flourished in rural areas.

There had, he said, always been a minority of country folk in England who practise Wicca even though the vast majority of people were Christians. These covens had passed on the pagan heritage for over a thousand years, but by the mid-20th century the faith was in decline.

Scholars have, however, pointed out that there is little in Wiccan lore that can be shown to correspond to what is known about pagan English religion. Some of the most popular of English pagan deities – Tiw, Woden and Eostre – do not feature in Wicca at all. Nor do the rituals of Wicca seem to have much to do with the little that is known about pagan English ceremonies. It is true that there are some similarities between Wicca and pagan Celtic religion, but this would mean that the Wiccans not only kept their faith alive through some 1,300 years of Christianity, but also through two centuries of pagan English religious dominance.

THE 'WICKEDEST MAN ALIVE'

Others have pointed out that Wicca draws much inspiration from 19th and early 20th century occultists such as Aleister Crowley, who liked to boast that he was 'the wickedest man alive'. There are even hints in it of practices common in the lands where Gardiner served his time as an imperial administrator of the British Empire. It has been alleged that Gardiner concocted the Wicca faith himself out of his imagination and from what he had read and learned of assorted pagan faiths. Such an interpretation is, of course, vehemently denied by modern Wiccans.

SECTION 2

PARANORMAL NATURE

The world around us is – scientists tell us – fully explored and completely understood. But as anyone who has travelled the more remote regions of the planet will know, our world is not only stranger than we imagine, it is stranger than we can imagine. People see monsters swimming lakes or surfacing from fifty fathoms deep in the open ocean. Hairy man-apes stalk the remote forests of North America and the Himalayas, while bloodthirsty bear-like creatures make African nights even more terrifying. As if unknown animals were not enough, there are gigantic rogue waves big enough to swamp the largest modern ship that can strike without warning and paths of mysterious power criss-crossing the globe. Paranormal nature is all around us.

LAKE MONSTERS

Reaching to surprising depths, the great lakes of the world cover hundreds of square kilometres – plenty of space for even the largest of beasts to hide from humans. Reports of colossal serpentine creatures and prehistoric monsters have traditionally been dismissed as folklore and fantasy. Recently however, conjecture about the mind-boggling life forms that lie beneath the waves is at last getting scientific confirmation.

Gazing across a glassy Scottish Loch framed by rugged, stunning scenery, it is impossible to believe that such a tranquil scene could be shattered by the antics of a massive, possibly prehistoric, monster lurking in the depths of the lake. Yet this is precisely what has happened on numerous occasions, if hundreds of people who claim to have seen a serpent-style creature are to be believed.

This monster mania is not solely centred on Loch Ness, where the region's most famous and unusual inhabitant apparently resides. Curious beasts have been spotted in various lochs in Scotland and in other deep lakes around the world, and the testimony from witnesses about them has been as persuasive as accounts about Nessie, the Loch Ness monster.

LOCH NESS

For centuries, in Loch Ness, a creature has been oft seen and sometimes even photographed. The first recorded witness to Nessie's exploits was St Columba in the 6th century, who allegedly saved a man from its attack. Sightings have escalated since 1933, when a motor road was built along the shores of the loch for the first time. Before that time only locals had seen the monster, but after the road was

If the Loch Ness monster does exist, then perhaps it is rearing young in the depths of the loch, thus ensuring the legend will continue into the future...

constructed hundreds of people came to the loch shores every day – they now number in the thousands – and sightings increased.

The first sighting to hit the headlines was that of John McKay just weeks after the road was finished. He reported seeing 'an enormous animal rolling and plunging on the surface'. There have been photographs in abundance, most famously one taken by Dr Robert Wilson in 1934 that became known as the Surgeon's Photo – at first he preferred to remain anonymous though he gave his profession to reporters in an attempt to show that he was a reliable witness. The Surgeon's Photograph showed a small head atop a longish neck with a large, but indistinct body just below the surface. The photo caused a sensation, but later analysis revealed that the object was rather smaller than it at first appeared. There have been other photos, but most are rather indistinct and could be explained away by sceptics as uprooted trees drifting in the wind.

MYSTERY RIPPLES

Nevertheless sightings have continued to be made. In 1952 Nessie was accused of having claimed her first known human victim. On 29 September John Cobb attempted to break the world water speed record in his speedboat Crusader on Loch Ness. The loch was easily long enough to allow the boat to accelerate and slow down again either side of the measured mile course. All that was needed was a dead calm day, and that arrived on 29 September. Unfortunately, the speedboat hit a patch of ripples on the loch as it reached maximum speed and broke up, killing Cobb instantly. Later analysis of the film showed that the ripples were a low wake, like that caused by a small boat – but no boat had been present on the loch. It has been surmised that the wake was caused by Nessie swimming past submerged, but close to the surface.

In April 1960 a holiday maker, Tim Dinsdale, spotted just this sort of a wake created by a submerged object. Whipping out his movie camera, Dinsdale shot several seconds of film that clearly showed a wake being created, then dying away as whatever caused it dived down below the surface.

Subsequent analysis proved that some submerged object moving at around 6 knots had caused the wake. The hidden object was estimated to have had a width of about 150 cm (5ft).

In July 1963 two business men, who preferred to remain known only as Mr McI and Mr C, were in a small boat on the loch angling for salmon. Suddenly the boat rocked as it was hit by a wave, but no waves nor wakes were in sight. A few seconds later a long neck topped by a head rather like that of a dog reared up out of the water about 27 metres (30yd) away. The creature eyed the startled fishermen for around 10 seconds, then sank away out of sight amid a lot of froth and swirling water.

In 1970 the so-called 'Big Expedition', led by University of Chicago's Roy Mackal descended on Loch Ness with the very latest in sonar, hydrophones and underwater cameras. The results were impressive. The hydrophones picked up sounds that appeared to be a creature using echo-location pulses to home in on prey – much as dolphins do at sea. The noises always ceased when a boat drew close, only to restart as soon as the boat had gone. The hydrophones also picked up bird-like chirping noises coming from the deep central area of the loch. The sonar picked up what seemed to be an object being swept from side to side, which might have been a flipper or tail.

CAPTURING THE MONSTER

In 1975 a new expedition to Loch Ness used underwater cameras linked to sonar to capture several pictures that seemed to show the monster. One showed a rather indistinct head. Far more famous was a photo that showed a rhomboid-shaped flipper. Controversy has surrounded this photo as it has proved impossible to give a scale to the object – leaving open the possibility that it may be a fish fin.

In 2003 a BBC 'Nessie hunt' decided to test the waters using scientific expertise. The team sent 600 sonar beams into the loch without finding evidence of a deep-water creature. This result has fuelled the sceptics' cause, which assumes that Nessie has more to do with a buoyant tourist trade than any underwater phenomenon. There is insufficient food in the loch to support an animal of Nessie's dimensions sceptics argue and claim that the sightings are more likely to be of giant eels, catfish or sturgeons. However, they do not explain how the loch would provide enough food for these fish. One sturgeon was found to be 3.75 metres (4yd) long, weighed 400 kilos (880lb) and achieved an age of eighty years, so the idea may not be entirely far-fetched.

ELEPHANTS ON PARADE?

The latest attempt to debunk the Nessie story insists that the creatures spotted by witnesses were in fact elephants. During the 1930s, a travelling circus owned by Bertram Mills frequently fetched up on the banks of the loch and its elephants took a dip. The saga was stepped up by the sharp-witted impressario

Mills, who offered a vast reward for capture of the Loch Ness monster, having realized his elephants were the root cause of a rash of sightings.

Yet still there are regular reports that Nessie has surfaced from people who are neither tourist trade operators nor circus proprietors, who appear to have no vested interest in proving her existence.

MORAG

One venue for several famous sightings has been Loch Morar, where the monster is known as 'Morag'. Fishermen Duncan McDonnell and William Simpson were afloat on 16 August 1969, when they had a close-quarters experience with this being of gigantic proportions.

It was 9pm and the fishermen's boat was travelling at a speed of about seven knots when a splash in the loch nearby caught the men's attention. Natural

Loch Morar, 1988: the dark spot in the centre of the picture disappeared mysteriously just after this picture was taken: could it have been 'Morag'?

curiosity soon turned to terror as the thing churning the water made a bee-line straight for them. As McDonnell recounted: 'I looked up and saw about 18 metres [20yd] behind us this creature coming directly after us in our wake. It only took a matter of seconds to catch up with us. It grazed the side of the boat, I am quite certain this was unintentional. When it struck, the boat seemed to come to a halt or at least slow down. I grabbed the oar and was attempting to fend it off, my one fear being that if it got under the boat it might capsize it.'

Later, Simpson wrote of the terrible experience: 'We watched it catch us up then bump into the side of the boat, the impact sent a kettle of water I was heating on to the floor. I ran into the cabin to turn the gas off as the water had put the flame out. Then I came out of the cabin to see my mate trying to fend the beast off with an oar, to me he was wasting his time. Then when I saw the oar break I grabbed my rifle and, quickly putting a bullet in it, fired in the direction of the beast.'

The shot was enough to see off the marauder, although neither of the men believed the bullet had wounded it. They estimated that the creature measured about nine metres (10yd) in length and had a snake-like head extending some 0.5 metre (1.6ft) above the water. Its skin was rough and brown.

With a depth of 305 metres (1,000ft), Loch Morar is deeper than Loch Ness and its waters run clearer. If this were the home of a beast it would remain a private one, as there are no roads running around the loch. One rumour is that Morag is the ghost of a long-extinct dinosaur.

Very similar to Nessie and Morag is Selma, who lives on the other side of the North Sea at Lake Seljordsvatnet in Norway. Selma is said to be black, have flippers and measure somewhere between 3–12 metres (9–40ft) in length. Locals have reported sightings of their elusive neighbour since 1750.

THE CHAMP

Although Nessie is the best-known, there are monsters reported in other freshwater lakes in different parts of the globe. The creature that allegedly resides in Lake Champlain, lying between Vermont and New York in North America, has become fondly known as 'Champ'. A French explorer by the name of Samuel de Champlain recorded the first sighting of the creature in 1609, and since then reports have numbered in the hundreds. Native Americans in the region firmly believed in its existence and, in 1873, circus owner P T Barnum offered a $50,000 reward for its hide – though nobody claimed it.

In 1977, a photograph purportedly of 'Champ' stoked up the rumours and, as yet, the validity of the picture has not been entirely refuted. In 1979, sonar experiments on the lake apparently picked up evidence of a 5 metre-long (16ft) moving object beneath the surface, but even this failed to convince sceptics of a monster-type presence.

More recent sightings are just as convincing. On 9 August 2002 a creature with a thin neck rising some 20 cm (8in) from the water surface was watched by two people from a distance of around nine metres (30ft). They surmised it must be a young 'Champ'. Just two weeks later on 23 August, an adult 'Champ' was spotted in Bulwagga Bay. It was about six metres (20ft) long and seen from a distance of nine metres (30ft). A year earlier a Mr Drapes and his family spotted a detail that has been reported before, but is often missed. He said that the head of the 'Champ' he spotted had a pair of breathing tubes coming from its nostrils.

In the summer of 2005 came what some claim is the best piece of evidence for 'Champ' yet produced. Fishermen Dick Affolter and Pete Bodette were shooting a video of their boat when they saw a large, dark object approaching the craft from below. The video does indeed show a large submerged object moving across the screen. Some have claimed to be able to see a head and neck moving about, but others think that might be a mere shadow. Two retired FBI forensic image analysts reviewed the video and confirmed it had not been manipulated in any way.

Similar to 'Champ' is 'Chessie', a long, dark, snake-like creature, which has been sighted on numerous occasions since the 19th century in the lake at Chesapeake Bay in the USA. Evidence of its existence has been captured on film by tourists, who continue to flock to the region in the hope of catching a glimpse of the mysterious serpent.

Further reports of Chessie emanate from respected members of the community, with witnesses including an FBI agent, ex-CIA officials and coast guards. Although a fairly accurate description of the animal has been achieved – around 10 metres (33ft) long, about one third of a metre in diameter (1ft) and with a humped brown back – no-one has yet been able to establish exactly what kind of serpent it is. Some have suggested that it may even be an example of a dinosaur that has somehow survived to this day.

OGOPOGO AND FRIENDS

Meanwhile Canada, with its expansive wild terrain and deep lakes. has at least a trio of monsters to its name. In Lake Pohenegamook, Quebec, the reported resident is Ponik, a 12m-long (40ft) beast with a horse's head, humps and two flippers. The head is usually likened to that of a horse by those that see it, though a few say it has catfish-like whiskers.

In Newfoundland, the Crescent Lake is reputedly the home of Cressie, a snake-like creature with a fishy head. More detailed descriptions put the animal at over six metres (20ft) in length with a thickness similar to that of a human thigh. One witness, perhaps rather excitedly, said that 'it looked easily capable of eating four or five people.' The native peoples of the area have long told tales of the Woodum Haoot (Pond Devil) or Haoot Tuwedyee (Swimming Demon), which they say lives in the lake. During the winter, the frozen surface is frequently found to have holes smashed in it, apparently from underneath. The sheer remoteness of Crescent Lake means that few people venture out on to its waters, and so sightings are rare. On 14 August 2003, however, a local woman Vivian Short saw Cressie quite clearly.

Over in British Columbia, in Lake Okanagan, a creature called Ogopogo has been sighted on several

Ogopogo has been sighted in Lake Okanagan several times since 1850; the name means 'sacred creature of the water' in the language of local Native Americans

A sketch of Ogopogo drawn up from an eyewitness account

occasions since 1850. The local Native Americans knew the creature as 'Naitaka' or 'N'ha-aitk', which means 'sacred creature of the water'. White settlers, however, took little notice until 1926 when over a hundred people enjoying an organized picnic on the lake shore spotted the monster and reported it to the local newspaper, the *Vancouver Sun*. An editorial stated: 'Too many reputable people have seen [the monster] to ignore the seriousness of actual facts.'

A movie of the monster was shot in 1968 by Art Folden. It seems to show a dark object propelling itself through shallow water near the shore, but the object is so far distant that it is impossible to be certain of any real detail. A second film was shot in 1989 by Ken Chaplin, who was accompanied by his father Clem at the time. Again, clear detail is lacking but the film certainly shows a sinuous body moving in the water, followed by a large splash apparently caused by the creature's tail.

One night in 2000, a dozen witnesses watched as a 3.5m-long (12ft) Ogopogo swam over the lake surface, apparently using four flippers to propel itself along. On 9 September the same year, two fishermen who preferred to give their names to the press only as Andy and Vince were on board their boat when they watched a 12m-long (40ft) creature break into their fishing net full of shrimp. The notion that something lives in the lake is so much ingrained into Canadian culture that, should the monster surface, it would be against British Columbian law to harm it.

NOT SO EXTINCT

So can these really be supernatural beings or creatures isolated from a bygone age? The jury is still out on the exact identification of the creatures that reside in the lochs and lakes. Yet we do know that some things have survived in the deep for centuries, unknown to mankind.

The most prominent example is the coelacanth, the so-called 'fossil fish' that lived alongside the dinosaurs and was assumed to have become extinct millions of years ago. Then, in 1938, it was discovered alive and well and living in South African waters. Because of the extreme sensitivity of its eyes, the coelacanth is rarely caught by fishermen during the daytime or on nights with a full moon. If the coelacanth remained hidden from science – though it was well known to the local fishermen – then it is more than likely that other species reported by locals, but dismissed by scientists, may turn out to be every bit as real as the coelacanth.

Indeed, for all our technological advances, there are plenty of things about life in the murky depths of the world's vast inland waters that remain a mystery. It is tempting to believe that the Morag, Nessie and

There are many things about life in the murky depths of the world's vast inland waters that remain a mystery. It is tempting to believe that Morag, Nessie and other lake monsters are among them

the rest of the world's lake monsters are among them.

Certainly, many people have no doubt of the existence of creatures such as 'Nessie', 'Ogopogo' or 'Champ', but a number of questions still remain unanswered. Are these animals examples of the plesiosaur, a species of dinosaur long since believed to be extinct? If so, how many are there? How long do they live? And, if they are indeed survivors from the days of the dinosaurs, how did they manage to survive when so many other species have perished.

Perhaps, in light of these numerous reports, the time has come for a re-assessment of traditional theories concerning the extinction of the plesiosaur. With little information available on both the prehistoric and supposed modern-day version of this dinosaur, however, and the fact that sightings are fairly rare, scientists are faced with a daunting task. Unless a breakthrough discovery is made, it seems likely that the truth surrounding these dark creatures of the deep will continue to elude humankind.

SEA SERPENTS

L ake-residing creatures are not the only outsized serpents at large in the planet's waters. Given the size of the oceans, it is not surprising that unfamiliar creatures lurk in their depths. Heads, humps and tails of indeterminate origin have been spotted in the open waters off almost every continent.

It is sometimes said that with modern underwater cameras, probes and submarines criss-crossing the oceans it would be impossible for large animals of any kind to remain unknown to modern science. That is to go against the established facts. New species of fish, squid and molluscs are found every year. Even a new species of whale turned up in the 1990s. There

New species of fish, squid and mollusc are found every year. In the uncharted depths of the world's oceans there are surely many more big surprises awaiting the human race

is also the much overlooked fact that human intrusion into the oceans of the world has actually shrunk in the past 50 years.

STRANGE EVENTS AT SEA

Today merchant ships are much larger than they used to be, and fewer in number. They are also more likely to stay on recognized sea lanes than in the past when winds could drive ships off course with ease. Not only that, but modern ships need much smaller crews than did the older steamers, and fewer still than the sail-driven merchantmen of yore. And the crewmen that do sail the seas have videos and computer games to keep them occupied. Put simply, today there are only a fraction of the number of men that there used to be cruising the seas with nothing much to do other than gaze out over the waters. A whole pack of sea serpents could cruise past a modern merchant ship and there would be nobody idly gazing out at them. And entire populations could live in unfrequented areas of the oceans and encounter no ship from one year's end to the other.

It is no great surprise, therefore, that some of the best and most reliable testimony relating to sea serpents dates back to the days when there were hundreds of small ships plying the world's oceans – and each one carrying a number of off-duty seamen with little to do but look around them.

THE DAEDALUS SERPENT

A classic sighting of a sea serpent came at 5pm on 6 August 1848 in the South Atlantic 531 km (330 miles) off the coast of what is now Namibia. The warship HMS *Daedalus* was heading home from the East Indies under the command of Captain M'Quhae. The voyage had been uneventful and on this afternoon the ship was cruising easily to the northeast on the port tack through a long ocean swell running from the southwest.

Midshipman Sartoris spotted something unusual approaching the ship from the port beam. He hurried up to the quarterdeck to alert Lieutenant Edgar Drummond, officer of the watch. Captain M'Quhae was off duty, but happened to be on deck at the time. Seeing Sartoris pointing out to sea he walked up to find out the cause of the excitement.

M'Quhae wrote down what he saw: 'The object was discovered to be an enormous serpent, with head and shoulders kept about four feet (1.2m) constantly above the surface of the sea, and as nearly as we could approximate there was at very least 60 feet (18m) of the animal *a fleur d'eau*, no portion of which was to our perception used in propelling it through the water, either by vertical or horizontal

undulation. It passed rapidly, but so close under our lee quarter that had it been a man of my acquaintance I should have easily recognized his features with the naked eye. It did not, either in approaching the ship or after it had passed our wake deviate in the slightest degree from its course to the SW, which it held on at the pace of from 12 to 15 miles (20–24km) per hour apparently on some determined purpose. The diameter of the serpent was about 15 or 16 inches (39cm) behind the head, which was, without any doubt that of a snake, and it was never, during the 20 minutes that it continued in sight of our glasses, once below the surface of the water.

Its colour was a dark brown with yellowish white about the throat. It had no fins, but something like a mane of a horse, or rather a bunch of seaweed, washed about its back. It was seen by the quartermaster, the bosun's mate and the man at the wheel in addition to myself and the officers mentioned.'

[The phrase *a fleur d'eau* means partly visible above the waterline.]

IMAGE OF A MONSTER

As soon as the serpent was out of sight, M'Quhae and Drummond sat down to produce a sketch of what they had seen. They showed it to the other witnesses, made a few alterations to take their views into account and signed it as a true representation and pasted it into the ship's log. That sketch was later used as the basis for an engraving that appeared in the *Illustrated London News*. The artist put the *Daedalus* under full sail in the background. The same artist produced two other pictures of the serpent, based on conversations held with members of the crew.

An important point about the *Daedalus* serpent, as it has become known, is the number of witnesses of impeccable nature plus the close quarters and prolonged time that they saw the animal. It was within sight for 20 minutes and came to within about 45 metres (150ft) of the witnesses. Given that these were professional naval seamen whose lives might depend on accurate observations at sea it is unlikely that they were mistaken in what they saw, but what was it?

All the illustrations and written accounts agree that there was a head held clear of the water on a neck about 2.5 m-long (8ft). Behind that was what seemed to be the body of the creature that was half submerged, rising no more than about 60 cm (2ft) or so out of the water, but clearly having most of its bulk submerged. This section was up to 180m-long (60ft). Interestingly, the body did not weave or undulate as the body of a snake does when it is swimming. Clearly, something else was pushing it through the water. Mostly likely there were flippers thrashing at the water below the surface where the witnesses could not see them.

The great zoologist Sir Richard Owen entered the debate over the *Daedalus* serpent by writing a piece for the *Times* newspaper on 9 November. He dismissed any idea of a serpent and suggested instead that what the men had seen was a large seal. Of course, no seal is 60 feet long, so he suggested that the witnesses had mistaken the wake of the animal for a continuation of its body. Coming from such a highly respectable man as Owen – it was he who coined the word 'dinosaur' – the idea was quickly accepted by the majority of scientists.

Unfortunately for Owen, M'Quhae was still in London at the time. He was furious and stormed round to the offices of *The Times* to demand a right of reply. The resulting interview was published on 18 November. In forthright and direct language, M'Quhae demolished Owen's seal theory before going on to give his uncompromising views of scientists who prefer to dream up theories rather than confront evidence that is presented to them in good faith. It was a blistering piece, but sadly the scientists of the day chose to believe Owen rather than the sailor. A few days later M'Quhae left for another voyage that took him away from Britain for three years. The *Daedalus* serpent was forgotten.

In the years that followed the *Daedalus* serpent report, several other officers both in the Royal Navy and merchant marine came forward with reports of odd and unidentified animals that they had encountered. Most of these were seen in less clear conditions than those experienced by the *Daedalus* but so far as they add details the reports confirmed that the sea serpent was about 12 metres (40ft) or more long, had a snake-like head held on a long neck and swam without apparent movement of its body, which indicated underwater propulsion.

THE OSBORNE SERPENT

Then in 1877 came a sighting that could not possibly be dismissed as mere sea legend. The officer who made the report was none other than Commander H

The Osborne serpent: sighted off the coast of Sicily in 1877, various members of the crew saw a large animal swimming parallel with their vesssel but in the opposite direction

Pearson, the captain of the royal yacht *Osborne*. The command was one of the most prestigious in the Royal Navy and was given only to officers of proven ability and trustworthiness.

Unlike M'Quhae, Pearson did not go to the press but to the government's Inspector of Fisheries – one Mr F Buckland. Buckland consulted various naturalists, including Sir Richard Owen, as well as government officials. Having decided that the beast sighted by Pearson was not part of his responsibilities as Inspector of Fisheries, Buckland decided to publish his findings in the hope that somebody else could help provide an explanation.

COMMOTION ON THE WATER

According to Buckland's papers, the *Osborne* had been cruising off the coast of Sicily on 2 June when the crew went to supper and the officers began to prepare for the evening. Mr Moore, the engineer, was resting on deck when he saw a commotion in the water about 360 metres (400yd) away. Something large was moving about on the surface. Moore alerted Lieutenant Douglas Forsyth, who unlike Moore had a telescope. Moore used his telescope to see some large animal swimming parallel to the Osborne but in the opposite direction. Another lieutenant, Haynes, also used a telescope to study the animal. The two young men then called Pearson on deck to have a look.

The various witnesses gave detailed written accounts of what they had seen to Buckland – and Haynes added a sketch. Only that by Haynes has survived intact, though the others agreed in most particulars. Haynes wrote: 'The head was bullet-shaped and quite 6 feet (182cm) thick, the neck narrow and its head was occasionally thrown back out of the water remaining there for a few seconds at a time. It was very broad across the shoulders, about

'The head was bullet-shaped and quite 6 feet... the creature appeared to have a large, heavy body... powered by fins or flippers'

15 or 20 feet (4.5–6m), and the flappers appeared to have a semi-revolving motion which seemed to paddle the monster along.

They were about 15 feet in length. From the top of the head to the part of the back where it became immersed, I should consider 50 feet (15m), and that seemed about a third of the whole length. All this part was smooth, resembling a seal.'

Other than the fact that the fins – or 'paddles' were this time visible – the sighting again confirms the general appearance that can be deduced from other sightings. Although usually called a sea serpent, it is quite clear that the creature being seen was not snake-like in any way other than the shape of its head and neck. The creature appeared to have a large, heavy body that remained submerged and was powered through the water by fins or flippers that were likewise usually submerged. In his lost account, Pearson had apparently gone out of his way to report that the Osborne serpent did not blow or spout in the way that a whale did.

This would indicate either that the creature did not breathe air, or that it was not warm-blooded. Of the two the latter seems more likely, indicating that the creature might be a reptile of some sort, though the fact that it might be a fish could not be discounted.

UNUSUAL VISITOR

The best sighting of the body and flippers came in 1919 by Mr Mackintosh Bell who was on holiday on the Isle of Hoy, one of the Orkneys. Going out with fishermen for the day, Bell saw a sea serpent at very close quarters. Rising up from the sea only 27 metres (30yd) from the boat came a neck 182 cm (6ft) tall topped by a head 'like that of a dog, coming sharp to the nose. The eye was black and small, and the

Morgawr, as photographed in February 1976 from Rosemullion Head near Falmouth in Cornwall

whiskers were black. The animal was very shy, and kept pushing its head up then pulling it down, but never going quite out of sight. Then it disappeared. It swam close to the boat about three metres (10ft) down. We all saw it plainly. It was, seen below the water, dark brown, getting slightly lighter as it got to the outer edge, then at the edge appeared to be almost grey. It had two paddles or fins on its side and two at its stern. My friends thought it would weigh 2 or 3 tons, one said 4 to 6. The body from neck to the end of the tail flappers would be about 3.5 metres (12ft) long and circumference say three metres (10ft), but this I am not sure of as I never saw all round it. It would be 1.2 metres (4ft) across the back.'

MORGAWR

Off the coast of Cornwall, in England, a creature named Morgawr has been seen by several generations and is accepted by locals as an occasional part of the seascape. In two dramatic episodes, fishermen netted large and mysterious creatures that they could not name. The first occurred in 1876 and the second fifty years later, when the catch was described as 6.5 metres long (22ft) with a beaked head, scaly legs and hairy back. Unfortunately, the beasts were released, rather than being brought back to shore for investigation.

From the 1970s onwards, there have been a flurry of sightings and, intriguingly, witnesses were frequently in pairs. When more than one person is present at a sighting, the possibility that it was an imagined experience is eliminated. Several were also strangers to the area and probably unaware of local legends that might have influenced their interpretation of events.

In 1975, one couple walking along the coast saw a 'hideous hump-backed creature with stumpy horns and bristles down the back of its long neck.' Another pair in a motorboat saw two large, grey humps in the water before they submerged. The following year, a woman took photographs of an unknown beast which were published in a local newspaper. Although poor quality, the outline of a serpent is distinct. Choosing to remain anonymous, she nevertheless gave this account: 'It looked like an elephant waving its trunk, but the trunk was a long neck with a small head on the end, like a snake's head. It had humps on the back that moved in a funny way. The colour was black or very dark brown, and the skin seemed to be like a sealion's … the animal frightened me. I would not like to see it any closer.' When her description was published, the response from readers was astonishing, and scores more sightings were submitted by local people.

CLOSE ENCOUNTER

Following this, a fisherman who encountered Morgawr estimated it was twice the size of a horse. In 1999, John Holmes, who used to work at the British Museum's natural history unit, filmed a mysterious sea-borne creature in Gerrans Bay. Its head was raised a metre (3.2ft) above the water and it swam some 200m (650ft) from the shore. He kept the film under wraps for several years for fear of being ridiculed, but at least one expert has since examined the tape and found it to be genuine.

Later Mr Holmes told the BBC: 'I have gone through all the text books to try and work out what this may have been and my theory is that it could be a living fossil … It appeared bird-like at times, but was very uncharacteristic of any diving birds. I really do think there is some sort of zoological discovery around the coast of Cornwall.'

The legend of Morgawr was sufficiently strong to attract the interest of a television company. Documentary film-maker Tony White spoke to eight Morgawr witnesses. 'One of the people we spoke with was an elderly lady who saw the monster in the Helford River. And the most recent sighting was by some people out fishing … who said Morgawr reared up out of the water in front of their boat.'

Tony White continued: 'Descriptions of the creature vary, but many people describe it as looking a bit like the Loch Ness Monster, although an expert we consulted for the documentary believes that Morgawr could be some sort of primitive, prehistoric ancestor of a whale.' Morgawr differs from the Loch Ness monster, as one inhabits salt water while the other lives in fresh. There has been speculation that Morgawr is in fact some new species of seal. The stretch of coastline where most sightings occur is now locally known as 'Morgawr's Mile'.

FISHY CHARACTERS

Meanwhile, thousands of miles away, folk around Vancouver Island also insisted that something strange dwelt in the nearby seas. Their case was at least partly proven in 1937, at a whaling station, when a 3m-long (10ft) creature was discovered within a whale, with a serpent-head, fins and a tail. It has since been named as a Cadborsaurus and is known as Caddy for short.

Speculation about Caddy's existence began in the 1930s, after a couple boating near Victoria Island went public about their sighting. A greenish-brown creature coiled on the water surface before heading for the depths, close to the boat containing Mr and Mrs Langley. 'It took my fancy that it wasn't anything I had seen before,' Mrs Langley told reporters. After this encounter, more accounts came flooding in, and sightings have continued to the present day.

STRANGE CROSSBREED

On the south Georgia coast where the sea meets the land, there are creeks, inlets, marshes and rivers which, claim local residents, provide a home for Altamaha-Ha, named after the river Altamaha. This creature is said to look like a cross between an alligator and an eel, with dark skin and protruding eyes. Using its flat, horizontal tail, it reportedly undulates through the water, churning it up when it surfaces. Sightings in the vicinity have occurred with consistency.

PLESIOSAURS

The single suggestion continually surfacing about the true identity of the sea serpent, and sometimes of its freshwater loch and lake counterparts, is that they are plesiosaurs – or a close relative. Plesiosaurs were gigantic reptiles that swam in the seas while dinosaurs stalked the land. They had broad bodies

and would have weighed in at an estimated 150,000kg (150tn). Two years later, one of the best-preserved remains of a juvenile plesiosaur were found in Bridgwater Bay, off England's Somerset coast. It measured 1.5m (5ft).

The notion that plesiosaurs still lurk unseen in the oceans was reinforced in 1977, when a Japanese trawler dredged a bizarre rotting corpse from New Zealand waters that bore all the hallmarks of a

The coelacanth fish was thought to have gone the way of the dinosaurs, until a living specimen was discovered in 1938

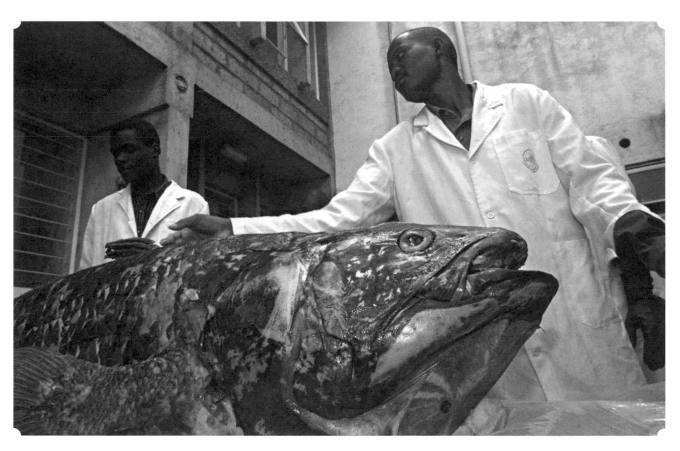

and short tails with small heads perched on the ends of long necks. They were distinguished by their flipper limbs, able to manoeuvre the huge creature with great delicacy and accuracy as well as considerable power.

In 2002, the fossilized remains of a plesiosaur were discovered in Mexico. Dubbed the 'Monster of Aramberri', it was a staggering 15 metres (50ft) long

prehistoric creature. The rotting corpse stank horribly, and the ship had nowhere to store it during the long voyage back to port. The body was dumped back in the sea, so precise evaluation was not possible. However, samples taken from it were analyzed and it seemed the odd body belonged to a basking shark.

At the moment, the existence of sea serpents is

still in doubt. There have been plenty of sightings across the world – sometimes accompanied by photos – but these accounts are not conclusive. A corpse or skeleton would excite both believers and sceptics alike. Presumably, though, when water-borne creatures like this perish, their bodies sink to the ocean floor, out of sight and beyond reach.

Sea serpents and lake monsters bear a likeness that encourages everyone with an interest in natural oddities to believe they are related. For the time being, all we can say with certainty is that they are cryptids, an animal species not yet recognized by scientists through insufficient evidence.

Reports of a similar creature continued to come in during the 1920s and 1930s. After the Second World War sightings have been much rarer, one of the last clear sightings at close range occurred on 17 May 1964 when a fishing boat searching for scallops – the Noreen out of New Bedford, Massachusetts – sighted a head perched atop a neck at a range of only 12 metres (40ft). By the 1980s sightings were almost non-existent. There are, of course, far fewer people idling around out at sea to be in a position to see a passing sea serpent so the lack of reports may simply reflect this fact. On the other hand, the seas are much more polluted than they used to be. Perhaps the sea serpent has declined in numbers in response. It may even be extinct. We can only hope that one day incontrovertible proof comes up.

THE KRAKEN

Sailors have long believed that gruesome beasts with a taste for blood lurk beneath the waves, occasionally surfacing to attack a passing ship and its unfortunate crew. On land, people have been swift to dismiss their tales as ludicrous exaggeration. But the latest scientific evidence says that they were right to be fearful of mighty creatures from the deep.

The monster most feared by Scandinavian sailors down the centuries was a gigantic squid-like beast known as the Kraken. Its flailing arms reached as high as the lookout nests in the masts of sailing ships, it had eyes the size of footballs and it was commonly depicted with the dimensions of a small island.

Probably seen over 2,000 years ago in classical times, the Kraken has been variously described as a squid, an octopus, a whale, a crab and a lobster.

Persuasive records of the Kraken exist in the *Speculum Reglae*, or *King's Mirror*, a Scandinavian text in the form of a conversation between a father and son dating from 1250. 'I can say nothing definite as to its length … for on those occasions when men have seen it, it has appeared more like an island than a fish. Nor have I heard that one has ever been caught or found dead. It seems likely that there are but two in all the ocean and that these beget no offspring, for I believe it is always the same ones that appear.'

When Erik Pontoppidan made records of the natural world in Norway in the 18th century, he also referred to the Kraken. And in 1802, an illustration of the monster by Pierre Denys de Montfort was circulated, who based his drawing on the recollections of sailors from a French vessel apparently attacked by the Kraken off the shores of Angola in Africa.

MONSTER OF THE DEEP

Speculation about a hitherto unidentified underwater beast was fuelled when a partly decayed body was discovered on a Florida beach in 1896. The body was 5.5m long (18ft) and some 3m wide 10ft). Detached tentacles were in the order of 11m (36ft) in length. Local naturalist De Witt Webb was sure it was an octopus, although other experts believed it could have been the remains of a whale. Either way, conventional scientists refused to accept the rotting body as evidence of an unknown monster in the deep.

But an octopus, even one of gigantic proportions, tends to be a shy creature and would be unlikely to attack ships. His cephalopod cousin the squid, with ten rather than eight tentacles, is far more aggressive and seems a more convincing candidate for Kraken. Two particular types of squid are in the frame but, until a short time ago, evidence for both was in short supply.

Until recently, mystery cloaked the activities of the giant squid (*Architeutis dux*), thanks to its secretive nature. The best indicator scientists had of

its existence was the presence of a few tentacles in the stomach of predator whales.

Scientists in Tasmania have, over the course of many years, collected the remains of huge sea beasts that have been washed ashore, and the rotting residue of tentacled creatures extracted from the stomachs of sperm whales by whalers. More recently, entire, smaller, juvenile specimens of these mysterious squid have been caught in deep-sea trawlers and brought to the Institute for Antarctic and Southern Ocean Studies in Tasmania, for examination.

While little is known about most species of giant squid, experts are now much better informed about one type in particular – the Architeuthis or 'chief squid'. This tentacled sea monster was identified back in 1856 by a Danish researcher, and numerous reliable reports exist of the creature being washed up on shores around the world. Despite all the horror

The Kraken was said to have flailing arms or tentacles that could reach as high as the top of a ship's mast

stories about the creature's ferocity, however, recent studies have concluded that, despite its mammoth proportions, it is in fact very slow and relatively weak. It is thought to drift in the cold currents of the deep ocean rather than dart to attack its prey, and its pincer action is believed to be clumsy and feeble.

Numerous questions about this giant squid have yet to be answered. For example, how many different populations exist in the oceans of the world? How long do these creatures live? What do they eat and how often? How many years do they take to reach maturity?

As far as the last question is concerned, it seems reasonable to assume that, in view of the animal's great size, the growth period is considerable.

GIANT SQUID

In 2001 a body was discovered off the coast of Spain, spurring scientists on to make fresh calculations about its lifestyle. It is believed that giant squid can reach up to 18m (60ft) in length and that their daily diet typically consists of 50 kilos (8 stone) of fish.

The year 2003 proved a pivotal time for squid-watchers. In January of that year, a French yacht taking part in the round-the-world race for the Jules Verne Trophy became enveloped in the arms of a giant squid. Yachtsman Olivier De Kersauson realized the creature was clamped to his boat's hull when he caught sight of a tentacle through a porthole.

'It was thicker than my leg and it was really pulling the boat hard,' said De Kersauson, who was close to the Portuguese island of Madeira when the incident happened. The squid, measuring an estimated 8.5m (28ft) in length, was jamming the rudder of the boat, effectively putting the vessel out of action. Giant squid can exert an amazing amount of strength by using the visible flaps of muscle at the top of their tentacles.

The suckers that help them to cling on to boats and other surfaces are the size of dinner plates. Fortunately for De Kerauson and his crew, the squid released its grip when the vessel stopped. 'We didn't have anything to scare off this beast, so I don't know what we would have done if it hadn't let go,' Mr De Kersauson said. 'We weren't going to attack it with our penknives. I've never seen anything like it in forty years of sailing.'

De Kerauson was one step ahead of marine scientists, who have never yet seen a giant squid alive. But, more significantly still, in April that year a colossal squid (*Mesonychoteuthis hamiltoni*) was retrieved almost intact from the Ross Sea in the Antarctic. Although it was dead, it gave scientists their first opportunity to study the species.

Its overall length could not be calculated due to damage to its tentacles, but its mantle (body) measured 2.3m (7.5ft), already exceeding the maximum body length of the giant squid. Startlingly, scientists believed it was not yet fully grown. One

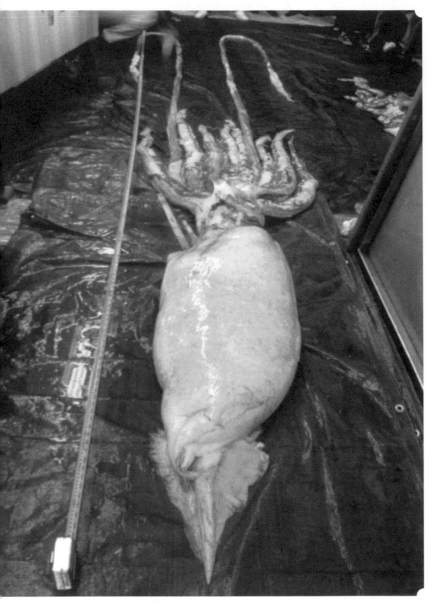

A giant squid has an extremely long, strong beak and it can exert a huge amount of pressure using the flaps of muscle on its tentacles

However, studies of other squid have revealed otherwise, and some naturalists believe that the total time taken to reach maturity could be as little as two years. This would make the creature one of the fastest-growing beasts in the entire animal kingdom. Scientists are working hard to try to understand more about this enormous sea-dweller, and in so doing, hope to be able to shed light on other species of giant squid at the same time.

feature that set it apart from other squid were swivelling hooks on the clubs at the end of its barbed tentacles. It also has the largest beak of any known squid. From studies carried out on the corpse, scientists have estimated that, had it reached maturity, it would have measured an astounding 15m (50ft) in length.

DEADLY TENTACLES

It would seem that this species is responsible for all the terrifying tales about tentacled sea monsters. The colossal squid is physiologically different from its feeble, drifting cousin, the Architeuthis, being armed and deadly. It possesses a powerful, muscular fin, and has rotating hooks along its arms and tentacles. These factors would seem to correlate with the scars and sucker wounds found on the whales that share the freezing habitat of this creature, which is thought to be capable of striking with speed and lethal accuracy.

Many of these postulations are based on theory and on the studies of other species of squid. From the work carried out, scientists are of the opinion that there could be many other similar species of giant squid awaiting discovery in other parts of the world. Perhaps future advances will one day enable researchers to see one of these living creatures for themselves and so help to solve this maritime mystery.

Both the giant and colossal squid usually stay well away from mankind at depths of between 60m (197ft) and 300m (984ft) in cold waters. Evidence of their sinister strength has been found on the washed-up bodies of mighty sperm whales that appear to have sustained deep cuts following squid attacks. A famous battle between these two ocean-going titans featured in Herman Melville's *Moby Dick*, and it seems that this is the stuff not just of fiction, but of reality.

Scientists now believe that the colossal squid is not only the biggest invertebrate known to mankind, but also one of the most aggressive predators on earth. Unexpectedly, their assertions have given credence to the stories of sailors from a bygone age.

THE KURANDA

Just as stories of enormous squid were once treated with disdain, so tales of giant jellyfish are also cautiously received. Jellyfish have been around for 650 million years, and so pre-date even the dinosaurs. They comprise 95 per cent water and have no heart, blood or brain. And giant forms are even rarer and harder to come by than the elusive gigantic squid. Yet there is conclusive evidence that at least one large, rogue jellyfish haunts the oceans.

In 1973, a ship called the *Kuranda*, travelling between Australia and the Fiji Islands, literally hooked up with a gigantic jellyfish. It is assumed that the jellyfish mistook the ship for prey before it latched on to the craft. One unfortunate seaman who came into contact with the jellyfish's stinging cells (nematocysts) experienced severely burned skin and later died from his injuries. The captain of the *Kuranda*, Langley Smith, said the tentacles of the lethal stinger measured some 60m (197ft) long.

GIANT JELLYFISH

Wedging itself on to the bow of the *Kuranda*, the weight of the enormous jellyfish began to push the vessel down. A swiftly-issued SOS brought another ship, the *Hercules*, to the extraordinary scene, whose crew managed to dislodge the jellyfish by using a high-pressure hose. Later, when the slime from the jellyfish was analyzed, it turned out to be from a species called Arctic Lion's Mane. The largest known Arctic Lion's Mane was washed up on a beach in Massachusetts in 1865, measuring 2.3m (7.5ft) across with tentacles 37m (120ft) long.

In 1969, two divers reported seeing a jellyfish measuring upwards of 46m (150ft). However, swimming at great depths in the remotest corners of the world's oceans have helped the jellyfish retain its largely obscure existence.

Safe on land, we tend to forget that two-thirds of the surface of the earth is taken up by the oceans, vast and mysterious watery territories that plummet to depths of several kilometres. Much of this ocean world remains unexplored by humans, and we have much to learn about the life forms that exist there.

What does seem clear is that the stories of seafarers, so often dismissed over the centuries, in fact provide a glimpse of sea monsters that are all too real …

MYSTERIOUS SOUNDS

The Earth's oceans are huge, unexplored underground kingdoms that have held mankind in their thrall for thousands of years. Today, these inaccessible areas remain as mysterious as the infinite expanses of space, although scientific advances have recently attempted to push back the boundaries of sub-aquatic understanding in order to cast some light on the black depths that cover our planet. This has produced several surprising results.

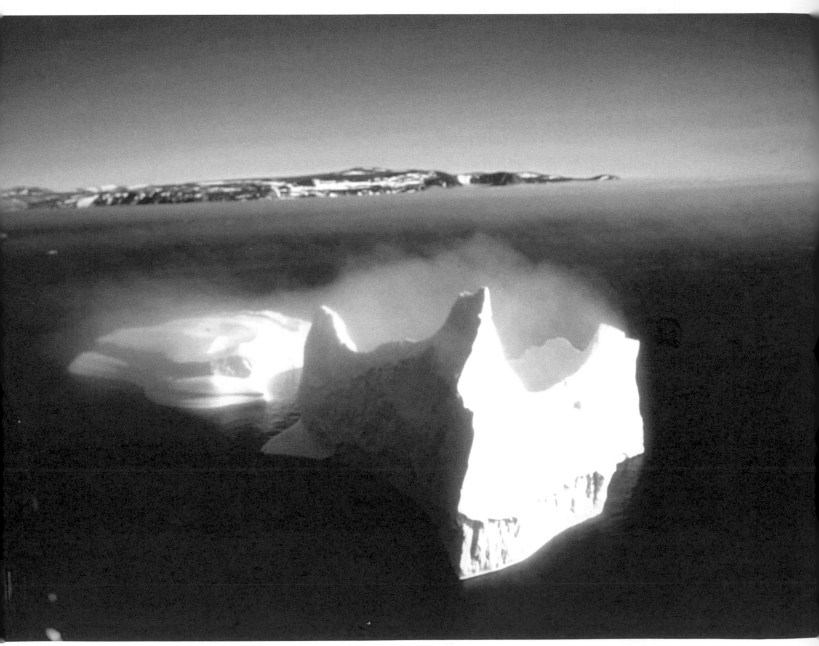

The bottom of an iceberg that has fallen away or 'calved' from the edge of a glacier. This event produces a tremendous amount of noise

SPOOKY SOUNDS

Scientists have established that one of the most effective methods of obtaining information about the underwater world is through the use of hydrophones. The origins of these underwater microphones can be traced back to the 1960s when they were utilized widely by the US Navy for the purpose of detecting the presence of Soviet submarines during the Cold War. Very quickly the naval men listening in realized that as well as hearing ship and submarine engines, they were hearing all sorts of other sounds and noises, some of them decidedly spooky. Most were soon identified as belonging to whales, dolphins and other sea creatures. Today, hydrophones have been found to be ideal for tracing, tracking and identifying many of the creatures travelling through the water.

The hydrophones, which are in essence a kind of listening station, are positioned hundreds of metres below the ocean surface. At this depth, factors such as pressure and temperature trap the sound waves within a layer known as the depth sound channel and, as a consequence, the waves can travel for many hundreds of kilometres without suffering distortion.

When the sound waves come into contact with hydrophones they produce a spectrogram, a visual representation of sound. This can be analyzed and compared to other, known, spectrogram patterns. Many ocean noises – such as those made by boats, submarines, whales and earth tremors, for example – occur frequently and are easily identifiable in this way, but there remains a large number of eerie echoes that evade explanation.

Most of these inexplicable noises occur at a low frequency and, therefore, have to be speeded up in order to be rendered audible to the human ear. While some sounds last for just a few seconds, others continue for days at a time, baffling researchers. Although underground volcanoes, icebergs and even enormous, undiscovered animals residing within the ocean depths have all been suggested as possible reasons for these peculiar sounds, the truth is still unknown.

One particularly mysterious noise picked up by hydrophone has been nicknamed 'Bloop'. While scientists suspect that this strange sound may emanate from an animal, since the spectrogram pattern showed the rapid variation in frequency characteristic of that produced by deep-sea creatures, there is one surprising factor in this case – the sheer volume of the noise.

BAFFLING BLEEPS

The fact that the Bloop signal has been detected simultaneously by sensors located more than 4,800km (3,000 miles) apart indicates that the noise produced is louder than that caused by any known animal. It has been suggested, therefore, that a giant squid, or some other type of undiscovered monster, could be roaming the depths of our oceans uttering the deafening Bleep for mysterious reasons of its own.

'Slowdown' is the name given to another signal that, again, raises more questions than it answers. The sound has been detected in the Pacific and Atlantic Oceans several times a year since 1997, and continues to baffle experts all over the world. One leading scientist, Christopher Fox, observed that the noise, which he likened to that of an aircraft, was coming from a southerly direction and so may have originated in the Antarctic. In order to rule out any obvious, man-made explanation, he consulted the US Navy. His suspicions that the sound could have been caused by top-secret military equipment were, however, unfounded.

Another theory which is currently being studied is that the noise could be caused by the shifting of Antarctic ice at the South Pole.

The spectrogram pattern produced by Slowdown is similar to that created in cases where friction is a factor, and might have arisen in this instance from the moving and shifting of huge masses of ice over land.

Many further tests will be necessary before the true origin of sounds such as Bloop and Slowdown can be confirmed. Whether they are indeed caused by the movements of mysterious alien creatures in the underwater depths, or whether there are other – purely geological – explanations, only time will tell.

BIGFOOT AND OTHER AMERICAN HOMINIDS

The Sasquatch, or Bigfoot, hit the world's headlines in 1958 when a construction crew building a road through the Bluff Creek area of remote northern California were thrown into panic when their worksite was visited at night by a beast that threw their tools about and left behind enormous footprints that looked very human – except for their enormous size. The local newspaper dubbed the unseen creature 'Bigfoot'.

But the encounter of 1958 was very far from being the first time that the Sasquatch or Bigfoot was encountered by humans. The oldest sources of stories about the Sasquatch are the native peoples of North America. As ever, scientists have tended to ignore tales told by local peoples and have demanded evidence.

The oldest contemporary account of a sighting by

Bigfoot and fellow hominids from around the world: (from left) the Yowie, the Orang-Pendek, the Yeren, Bigfoot, the Maricoxi, the Wildman

a European comes from the *Watchman* newspaper of New York state on 22 September 1818. This report states that a few days earlier, near Ellisburgh, a 'gentleman of unquestionable veracity' saw 'an animal resembling the Wild Man of the Woods'.

This would seem to indicate that the supposed Wild Man of the Woods was already a well-known figure of legend or rumour. The creature was described as being like a large man, but covered in hair. It walked out of the woods on to a road a few yards in front of the witness. Seeing the human, the creature turned and ran off, leaning forwards as it did so. The creature left behind footsteps that were human-like but very wide at the toes.

A photographer measures one of the footprints discovered at Bluff Creek – 'Bigfoot' was a nickname which stuck

Reports of similar hairy men continued to be made by frontiersmen and trappers throughout the 19th century. They caused a local stir, but were ignored by science and the national media alike. In 1924 the *Oregonian* newspaper from Portland carried a story that was quite unlike the others. The report began by mentioning the 'mountain gorillas' that had been leaving gigantic footprints around the Mount St Helens area of Washington State for some years and notes that 'Indians have told of the mountain devils

for sixty years'. It then went on to detail events that had happened to five gold prospectors who had been attacked by these 'gorillas' when panning for gold around the Lewis River, close to Mount St Helens.

The men were Fred Beck, Marion Smith, Roy Smith, Gabe Lafever and John Peterson. They had been working their claim for over two years by the time of the encounter. They had come across several footprints about 35.5cm (14in) long in that time but after the initial excitement that they caused, the men ignored them. One day in July 1924 Marion Smith and Beck were fetching water when they saw, about 100 yards away, one of the 'mountain gorillas'. It stood about 7 feet tall (213cm) on its hind legs and was watching the two men from behind a pine tree. Smith fired three shots and hit the tree, but the creature ran off uninjured. Smith and Beck ran back to the cabin to consult with the others. Faced by gigantic man-like creatures, the prospectors decided to flee. But because it was getting late in the day, they decided to stay the night rather than risk being caught in the woods in the dark with the 'mountain gorillas'.

HUGE CREATURES

At midnight the men were rudely woken by a terrific thump as something hit the cabin wall. The sounds of heavy footfalls came from outside the cabin. Smith peered out through a chink between the logs to see three of the huge creatures. It sounded as if there were others nearby. The creatures then picked up large rocks with which they began to pound at the walls. The men grabbed their guns and prepared to face the beasts if they should break in.

At least two of the apes got on to the roof and began jumping up and down. Another began pounding on the door, which Beck braced shut with a wooden pole. After several terrifying minutes the assault ended and the creatures slipped away into the darkness. Less than an hour later they were back. Again they attacked the cabin, trying to break in. Again and again the creatures retreated, only to return with redoubled fury to the assault. Finally, as dawn broke, the creatures left.

The terrified miners packed up and set off with as much as they could carry, they left behind over $200 worth of equipment – no small loss in those days when the dollar was worth far more than it is today. The newspaper reporters who covered the story dubbed the place where this amazing confrontation happened Ape Canyon, and is still known by that name to this day.

The sighting by William Roe in 1955 remains a classic for many reasons. Not only was Roe an unimpeachable witness who was widely known to be trustworthy and reliable, but his report included a wealth of detail that is rarely found. Most people who encounter a Sasquatch are so surprised by the sudden confrontation that they fail to note details – not so Roe.

Roe was a professional hunter who was investigating the area around Tete Jaune Cache, Alberta, in October 1955 to see if it might offer useful prey. Roe was alone and on foot as he approached an old abandoned mine which he knew was on the mountain. By his own account, Roe had decided to have a poke around the workings just to pass the time of day. It was about 3pm.

Roe was just stepping out into the clearing when he saw what he took to be a grizzly bear among the bushes on the far side. With the practised ease of a hunter, Roe silently stepped back into cover and squatted down to watch. At first he could see only the top of the creature's head, then a furry shoulder as it moved about under cover. Then the creature emerged into the clearing and stood up. It was immediately obvious that the creature was not a bear.

Roe at first took it to be a huge man in a fur coat. But as the creature ambled gently across the clearing toward him, Roe dismissed this idea. The creature was bigger than any man he had ever seen and moved in a peculiar way. The creature got to within 6m (20ft) of Roe before it stopped. It then squatted down on its haunches and began to eat leaves off a bush.

After a minute or two, the beast seemed to suddenly catch Roe's scent. It looked around, then fixed its eyes on Roe's. The creature shuffled back for four steps, then stood up. It walked off rapidly, glancing back over its shoulder at the bush where Roe sat hidden. Roe raised his rifle to shoot what he now realized would be a very valuable specimen. But as the creature looked back at him, Roe saw a spark of humanity in its eyes. He felt that killing this creature would be more like murder. He let it go.

The creature stopped on the far side of the clearing, tipped its head back and let rip with a call that sounded half-laugh and half-howl. Then it vanished into the woods. Roe saw it a few minutes later as it crossed a ridge about 200 yards distant. The creature again emitted its odd call, then was gone for good.

EYE WITNESS ACCOUNT

According to Roe's later written account, the Sasquatch had stood well over 182cm (6ft) tall and had shoulders about 91cm (3ft) across. He guessed its weight at around 180kg (400lb). He took the Sasquatch to be a female as it had a pair of large breasts and no obvious external penis. The body fell straight from the shoulders to the hips, not curving in and out again as does that of a human. The arms were heavily muscled and long in proportion, reaching almost to the knees. The feet were large, about 12.5cm (5in) across and had a grey-brown skin on their undersides. When it walked the creature put its heel down first, but seemed to glide along without the up and down bobbing of a human stride. The entire body was covered with a dark brown fur about an inch or so long.

The creature's head was higher at the back than at the front. The nose was broad and flat while the lips and chin jutted forward. It had ears the same shape as those of a human, but the eyes were small and black – more like those of a bear. The skin around the eyes and mouth was bare of hair. The face was capable of expression. When it saw Roe the creature looked so amazed that Roe could not help grinning.

All these physical features have been reported time and again by those who claim to have seen the Sasquatch.

Once the Bigfoot story broke in the national and international media in 1958, other people were encouraged to come forward more readily to talk to the newspapers, or to one or other of the new breed of researchers investigating tales about the Sasquatch. This contributed to the massive increase in the numbers of reports being made of the creature or its tracks.

An early instance came in 1961 when Larry Martin reported a dramatic confrontation with a Sasquatch in the wooded hills above Alpine, Oregon. He had gone into the woods early one evening to help a friend retrieve a deer that he had shot, but which had been too heavy for him to carry out. The two men drove up a dirt track to a spot close to the kill, then set off on foot. When they reached the spot where the deer should have been, it had gone. There was a clear drag mark leading away toward a patch of dense undergrowth. Intrigued, the two men followed. They were suddenly shaken with great violence by unseen hands.

Suddenly a Sasquatch came into view a few feet away. It was about seven feet tall (213cm) and stood upright. It had the head and face of a gorilla, Martin later reported. He did not stay to find out more, but screamed and fled, rapidly followed by his friend. The Sasquatch gave chase with long, loping strides that thumped the ground. The two men leaped into the car, started the engine and raced off. As he glanced in the rearview mirror, Martin saw the Sasquatch standing just a few yards behind the car watching them go.

Such sightings were interesting, but what was needed was more concrete proof. In 1967 that evidence appeared to arrive in the form of a movie shot by Roger Patterson near Bluff Creek on 20 October. Patterson and his companion that day, Bob Gimlin, were in the area looking for Sasquatch footprints that Patterson wanted to film for a TV station. As they rode around a pile of fallen trees and broken logs in the canyon they saw a Sasquatch beside the creek about 24m (80ft) from them. The creature saw them at the same time they saw it. It stood up abruptly and stared at them.

Patterson grabbed the cinecamera from the saddlebag, then sprang down from his horse and

The Sasquatch glances back in this famous still from the Patterson film; (below) the features are surprisingly human

began filming as the Sasquatch walked off along the creek bank, heading for the dense forests that lined the canyon. The creature turned to look at the two men, but did not break stride and soon passed around a bend in the canyon. That was when Patterson ran out of film, but the two men could hear the creature moving off. It seemed to be running quite fast.

GUARDED RESPONSE

When the movie was developed, it was shown to a panel of invited scientists at the University of British Columbia. The reaction of the dozen or so scientists who turned up was guarded. Conventional scientists have barely altered their view since. The general response to the movie, and to the handful of photos and videos to have emerged since, seems to be that it is not enough on its own to prove the existence of the Sasquatch.

Scientists inclined to consider that the Sasquatch does exist demand a body – or at least bones – before they will confirm the existence of a new species of ape. Those more sceptical consider the movie a hoax largely on the grounds that no Sasquatch has been proved to exist, so it does not exist, and therefore it follows that any movie of one must be a fake.

In the absence of a body, and with so many wolves

and bears around it is unlikely one will be found, researchers have presented other evidence. By far the most prolific evidence for the existence of the Sasquatch are the thousands of footprints that have been found in the forests where it is said to live. Some of these are isolated footprints in patches of mud, but others come from trackways that run over considerable distances. One track found in August 1967 ran along a dirt road in British Columbia for over half a mile and consisted of about a thousand footprints. Many hundreds of these tracks have been photographed or preserved as plaster casts, so it is possible to deduce what sort of a creature made them and if they are consistent with the sightings of the Sasquatch.

From studying the footprints of animals it is possible to deduce how many of them are living in a particular area, how large they are and, very often, what sex they are. The habits of the creatures in general can be worked out from the places the footprints are found. Individual actions, such as drinking, feeding or sleeping can be seen in the footprints.

GIANT STRIDES

Putting this evidence together gives a fairly clear picture of the type of animal that left the prints. Clearly the creature is bipedal for the marks of hands or front feet are reported only when the creature was scrambling up or down a steep slope. Secondly the flexing of the foot would give the walker an increased ability to grip the ground. In a human foot the stiff foot makes the toes the key feature of the push off part of a stride. Having a flexible foot, as indicated by the Sasquatch prints, puts the push off pressure on the front half of the foot and shin muscles. The toes are thus able to splay out or curl up depending on the surface being negotiated.

> By far the most prolific evidence for the existence of the Sasquatch are the thousands of footprints found in forests

A stride of around 120cm (4ft), a foot about 40cm (16in) long and a midtarsal break would indicate a height of around 213cm (7ft). This is, indeed, the sort of height reported for Sasquatches by witnesses. Moreover, the midtarsal break would give the Sasquatch a gait quite different from that of humans. Humans bob up and down as they walk due to the stiff foot, but Sasquatches would not show such an obvious vertical movement as they walk. Again, this is a feature that has been noted by witnesses who have seen a Sasquatch walking.

It is not only footprints and tracks that are evidence of the Sasquatch. Other marks left behind by what seem to be Sasquatch have been discovered and analyzed. In 1962 a passing Sasquatch lent against a house near Fort Bragg, California, and left behind its handprint. The handprint was 28cm (11in). Most of this length was taken up by the wide, flat palm. The fingers were relatively short and stubby, and of almost equal length. The thumb was nearer to the fingers than the wrist and was likewise rather stubby.

Studying droppings can tell you a lot about the creature that made them. It can reveal roughly how big it was and what sorts of food it had been eating. A few samples of droppings that seem most unlike those of known North American animals have been subjected to various tests. The contents have generally shown that the creature was eating mostly plants – including nuts and seeds – but also some meat. Interestingly, one sample contained the eggs of a parasitic worm that lived only in the guts of apes. Other samples could be proved not to belong to bear, humans, elk or other local animals large enough to deposit such droppings, but it was impossible to be any more definite.

Hairs are another potential source of evidence. Several researchers have collected hairs caught on branches or fences at the site of Sasquatch sightings or beside tracks. Mammal hairs can usually be firmly identified, so long as they are collected in good condition and have not suffered too much from weathering, trampling or other damage. It is sometimes possible to identify the group of animals from which a hair came, even if it is not possible to identify the precise species. The basic problem was stated fairly early on in the analysis of suspected Sasquatch hair by Ray Pinker, who analyzed hair for the California State College. Asked to analyze some hairs in 1968, Pinker said 'I could not identify these hairs as Sasquatch until I have a sample of authentic Sasquatch hair to match them to.'

He did, however, go on to state that the hairs in question did not come from any known North American animal.

ABSOLUTE PROOF?

In the final analysis, the evidence collected to date points strongly to the fact that there is a real upright-walking ape living wild in North America. But the evidence does not prove that this is the case. Sceptics are quite right to point out that it is inherently unlikely that thousands of seven-foot-tall apes are roaming about, but that nobody has yet been able to catch or kill one. The forested mountains of the northwestern areas of North America might be remote, but they are not that remote. Gorillas have been proved to exist in jungle areas every bit as remote as the suggested home range of the Sasquatch, so why is getting absolute proof of the Sasquatch proving to be so difficult? It would be thought that, one day, a Sasquatch would be found either dead or alive. Every year that slips by without such proof being found, the sceptics argue, is in itself proof that no such animal exists.

On the other hand, Sasquatch might well be a real species, perhaps more than one. If that is the case then humanity will have been guilty of an horrific ecological crime by not protecting its home range and not providing it with the means it needs to survive.

THE DE LOYS APE

It is among the most notorious images in the annals of natural history. Seated on a crate, and propped up grotesquely by a stick, the dead ape had been photographed in a mountainous forest district of Venezuela. The problem for early 20th-century zoologists was that no such animal was believed to exist in the continent of the Americas.

The photograph was taken in 1920 by François de Loys, a Swiss geologist on a three-year expedition to explore rivers and swamps southwest of Lake Maracaibo. Their aim was to identify lucrative oil reserves, but it was a mission that extracted a heavy price from de Loys and his men. Of the original twenty-strong party only four were still going by the end; the others had died or dropped out due to disease or attacks by hostile local tribes.

During the last year of the survey, the beleaguered group was camped beside the Tarra River when, according to de Loys, two red-haired creatures around 1.5m (5ft) tall emerged from the forest in an excitable state. De Loys thought at first they were bears, but as they moved closer he realized they were apes, probably male and female. The animals screamed, waved their arms, broke off branches (seemingly to use as weapons), defecated into their hands and threw their faeces at the camp.

This type of behaviour is a common aggressive response among spider monkeys and some apes and it suggested an attack was imminent. De Loys did what any self-respecting European explorer of the time would have done under the circumstances and shot them, to defend himself and his party. The female was killed and the injured male ran off into the jungle.

Gathering around the carcass, everyone in the party agreed that the species was unusual. De Loys, although not a zoologist, realized it might be of interest to science. Unfortunately, given the circumstances, the chances of getting the body back to Europe in a recognizable state were non-existent. De Loys decided to take a photograph as documentary evidence, and the picture was taken from a distance of about 3m (10ft) away.

The notorious photograph taken by de Loys shows the dead ape-like creature sitting on a crate, propped up by a stick

What happened next is by no means clear. Some reports suggest the flesh was cooked and eaten by de Loys' men; others that the remains were partly preserved and later lost in a battle with Motilones Indians. Either way, when de Loys finally returned home, his only evidence was the photo.

Curiously, it was nine years before the story of this unknown ape emerged. Even then, it was not de Loys who presented it to the scientific establishment but one of his close friends, George Montandon. A Swiss anthropologist, Montandon apparently chanced on the picture while inspecting some of de Loys' ageing files. Montandon published it in the *Illustrated London News*, naming the creature *Ameranthropides loysi*, meaning Loys' American ape, in honour of its intrepid discoverer.

LEAP IN THE DARK

Soon after this, the Academy of Science in Paris met to discuss the implications of the find. The cornerstone of primate evolution theory was that apes and humans emerged only in the Old World, and specifically Africa. If, after all, they were present in the Americas, then long-established rules would have to be re-written. It would be a leap in the dark and, unsurprisingly, the Academy did not take it. The scientists concluded that the animal was a sapajou, a fairly common New World monkey. The only evidence to the contrary, they argued, was its size and lack of a tail. Assessment of size was dependent on de Loys' word and the tail could have been either cut off or tucked out of shot.

The ape theory was further undermined when sceptics waded into the debate. Sir Arthur Keith – a noted British zoologist – implied that the animal was a spider monkey, while others went further, accusing de Loys of blatantly fabricating a crude hoax. Throughout the 20th century the same questions were asked: Why did de Loys not photograph a man beside the ape to provide size context? Why such an odd pose? Why wait nine years before allowing a friend to reveal such a major discovery? And so on.

As late as 1996, cryptozoologist Loren Coleman, writing in the *Anomalist Magazine*, argued that George Montandon had been working to a secret racist agenda. This theory held that different races of human were descended from different apes and consequently it could be argued that some were superior to others. Until the Venezuelan ape appeared, Montandon had struggled to explain which ape was the ancestor of Native American peoples.

In fact, the hoax argument is itself hardly watertight. For one thing why would de Loys, a serious geologist, wish to risk the wrath of the scientific establishment by pulling a silly stunt in an area outside his expertise? Secondly, in an expedition dogged by disease and violent deaths, he surely had more urgent priorities – such as getting home alive. And as for the nine-year delay, it would seem that de Loys simply did not appreciate the significance of what he had photographed.

Supporters point out that the size of the crate in the photo can be found in records of the time: It was 50cm (20in) high, putting the creature at 1.55m (5ft 1in), almost exactly the height de Loys claimed in his report. If so this would certainly rule out a spider monkey, which has an average height of between 38–68cm (15–27in). Other researchers say that while there are some likenesses to a spider monkey – the round ridges surrounding the eyes, the long hair and long fingers and toes – there are also several contradictory features. These include the shape of the face (oval rather than triangular) the lack of a prognathism (a protruding lower jaw) and a highly prominent forehead.

If Montandon had been alone in reporting a mysterious ape-like animal in this region of South America, his claim would be easier to dismiss. But in fact there are many accounts. A chronicle written in 1533 by the conquistador Pedro de Cieza refers to a Spaniard finding one dead in the woods. In the 18th century Edward Bancroft, doctor, naturalist and British spy, recounted Indian legends of a 1.5m-tall (5ft) creature which walked upright and was covered in hair.

Nineteenth century science writer Philip Gosse, in his *Essay on the Natural History of Guyana*, suggests the existence of 'a large anthropoid ape not yet recognized by zoologists', and in 1876 explorer Charles Barrington Brown wrote of a beast dubbed 'Didi' by Guyanese Indians – 'a powerful wild man whose body is covered in hair and who lives in the

forest'. More recently, in 1987, an American mycologist called Gary Samuels was working in Guyana, courtesy of a grant from the New York Botanical Gardens. Hearing footsteps, he looked up from his inspection of fungi to see a 1.5m-tall (5ft), bipedal, ape-like animal which bellowed at him before running away.

It is easy to dismiss the de Loys photograph as a hoax, perhaps because we are uncomfortable with the idea that such a significant species could exist without our knowledge. Yet natural history is littered with similar examples – the okapi, the Komodo dragon and the coelacanth were all 20th-century finds – and there remain surprisingly large swathes of the planet that have not been properly explored. De Loys may be a charlatan … but the jury is still out.

CURIOSITIES

Some of the strange creatures sighted by eye witnesses almost defy categorization. But reports of their existence continue, which suggests it might be inadvisable to write them off too quickly.

LIZARD PEOPLE

For example, the idea that a race of Lizard people could live covertly in North America sounds risible. Yet over the last century, frequent and credible eye-witness accounts of such creatures have attracted huge interest from cryptozoologists.

Reports of giant lizards roaming free are nothing new in the American Midwest. A traditional Shawnee Indian story tells of a Shawnahooc, or 'River Demon', living in the Little Miami River area of Ohio. As late as the 1950s, residents of the Ohio Valley related ancestral accounts of pink lizards up to 2.4m (7.9ft) long. In May 1955, an unidentified man driving home at 3.30am near Loveland, Ohio – close to the Little Miami – told police he had seen three bipedal lizard-like creatures standing by the roadside. He claimed to have pulled over and watched them for three minutes, recalling how one held a stick which spewed out sparks. The cops did a cursory search, found nothing, filed a report and quietly forgot the whole incident.

In some parts of the world, adult iguanas can reach gigantic proportions. The unaccustomed sight of a lizard such as this might well lead to speculation

In the freezing early hours of 3 March 1972 a policeman from Loveland was driving alone along Riverside Road when he spotted what looked like a large dog in the glare of his headlamps. As he got closer he saw a creature about 1m long with leathery skin and the head of a lizard or frog. It stared back for a few seconds, then jumped a fence and escaped down to the river. Later that day, the officer returned with a colleague and found what appeared to be slide marks on the embankment.

Two weeks later while driving on the same highway another policeman, Mark Matthews, spotted an animal lying motionless in the middle of the road. He assumed it had been struck by a car and pulled over to drag it clear, but as he approached it ran off. Realizing that it was a lizard, and anxious to prove his colleague had not fabricated the earlier sighting, Matthews squeezed off a shot. Although he

believed he hit the animal, it managed to flee the scene and its body was never found.

Neither officer filed an official report of their experience, but word of their encounters inevitably leaked to the press. When the story broke, a Loveland farmer came forward to say that he too had seen a frog-like creature in March 1972. Sceptics suggested the creature was either a Nile monitor lizard or a large iguana, although neither species is native to the area and exotic pets were very rare locally.

On 19 August 1972, the Royal Canadian Mounted Police received reports that a 1.5m (5ft) silver-coloured creature had emerged from Lake Thetis, near Cottonwood, British Columbia and attacked two young men. The location is close to Vancouver Island and Cadboro Bay, haunt of a legendary local sea monster nicknamed 'Cadborosaurus' by the media.

According to the men, Robin Flewellyn and Gordon Pike, the lizard appeared on the surface of the lake and chased them from the beach. Flewellyn claimed he had been cut on the hand by six razor-like spikes on its head and, to their credit, the RCMP took him seriously. 'The boys seem sincere,' said a spokesman.

Just four days later, the lake-based lizard revealed itself again – this time to two different male eye-witnesses, Mike Gold and Russell Van Nice. Both men ran as it emerged from the water, but Gold saw enough to give a detailed description. It was 'like a human being body but it had a monster face and it was all scaly [with] a point sticking out of its head [and] great big ears,' he said.

DRAGGED FROM HIS CAR

Back in the Ohio Valley, giant lizards were spotted in the Canip Creek area of Milton, Kentucky, where in 1975, junkyard owner Clarence Cable described a creature 4.5m (15ft) long with black and white markings, bulging eyes and a foot-long forked tongue. Isolated, single-witness sightings such as this were hard to corroborate, but in 1988 lizard-man investigators received a series of highly credible reports from the Scape Ore Swamp area of Bishopville, South Carolina. A 17-year-old called Chris Davis told how he fought off a reptilian creature trying to drag him from his car. Soon the local Sheriff was inundated with reports of encounters with a mysterious lizard-man.

According to one state trooper, Mike Hodge, officers checking the swamp area discovered 'humungous footprints' measuring 35cm x 18cm (14 x 7in). He and Lee County deputy Sheriff Wayne Atkinson followed these prints for 400m. They realized how close on the trail of the elusive beast they must have been, because when they returned they found fresh prints in their car tyre tracks. Analysis by biologists indicated that the prints matched no known species.

So what is the explanation? Even accounting for

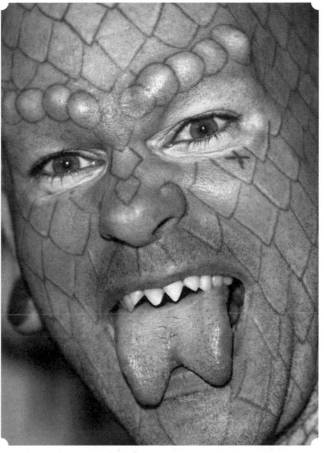

Some fanatics go to great lengths to turn themselves into human versions of animals. Could this be at the root of lizard-men sightings?

exaggeration, hoaxes and over-active imaginations, it is hard to see how so many solid eye-witnesses could be so wrong. In a country as vast as North America, is it possible that some unknown species survives in remote strongholds, occasionally venturing into urban regions for food?

WENDIGO

The state of Utah is home to numerous supernatural occurrences and strange beings. Of these, the so-called 'skinwalker', or 'Wendigo', is perhaps the most terrifying and the question of its existence continues to mystify and bewilder the inhabitants of this part of the USA.

According to Native American legend, the skinwalkers are a band of shape-shifting Navajo witches that roam the countryside terrorizing humans

specific animal renders the skinwalker a truly awe-inspiring and formidable foe. In addition to the possession of everyday human knowledge, these witches are blessed with powers that lie outside the realms of common wisdom. So a witch in the guise of a coyote will have amazing agility, strength and speed, combined with the dark powers of mind control and a knowledge of curses and other occult crafts.

Tradition relates that the skinwalkers have no choice about their metamorphoses, and that each change causes them much pain and torment.

Perhaps it is for this reason that they show such ferocity towards the creatures around them, jealous of their ability to maintain a fixed identity and so remain exempt from the perpetual torment of mutability.

As a result of the witches' constantly changing identity, very little is known about their origins or habits. One widespread belief holds that when the gods created humans they gave them to power to transform themselves. However, people began to abuse the power, so the gods came down to Earth to reclaim it. A few people hid the shapeshifting power, keeping it for evil purposes, and passed it on to their acolytes. It is generally thought that witches will be able to become fully fledged skinwalkers only if they murder a member of their immediate family – breaking one of the most powerful taboos of the Navajo.

Skinwalkers can take the form of any animal at any given moment

and animals alike. They can take on the form of any animal at any given moment, acquiring the inherent strengths and attributes of that particular creature while at the same time retaining their innate human cunning. This ability to maintain human intelligence while gaining the sensory or speed advantages of a

Many believe that they are linked to a region called 'Skinwalker Ridge' which, according to extra-terrestrial enthusiasts, is close to a region of intense UFO activity and which Native Americans studiously avoid. Could this region be a portal to another dimension from which the shape-shifters originate? Some people think so.

What is known about these eerie beings has been gleaned from the many reports in existence. Sightings by Navajos tell of the creature's glowing yellow eyes and ability to strike terror into even the bravest observer.

Encounters are not restricted to the Navajos, however, as the events of 1983 show. The isolated stretch of Route 163 that runs through the heart of the Monument Valley Navajo Tribal Park, although stunningly beautiful, is renowned for being the site of strange, otherworldly activities and local people warn outsiders that they should never venture into the region at night.

On this particular occasion, four members of a family were returning home from Wyoming, where they had been visiting friends. The most direct route was along Route 163, and having driven along this road without incident on the outward journey, they thought nothing of taking this course again on the way home.

The family reported that, on this pitch-black, moonless summer's evening, they had been driving for several hours without seeing another human being. They were making steady progress when the father, who was driving, mentioned that they were no longer alone. Looking behind them, the whole family saw headlights some distance behind the car. They continued on their journey, keeping the distant lights in their sights and afterwards said that they felt slightly comforted in the knowledge that there would be help at hand should their vehicle break down.

Suddenly, however, the lights from the other car disappeared. Disquieted by this fact, the daughter, Frances, asked her parents whether they should go back to see if the occupants of the vehicle required any assistance.

Her father was anxious not to prolong their journey, however, and instead insisted that they should keep going. Frances afterwards said that it was at this time that the atmosphere in and around the car changed ominously. Her sixth sense was proved to be justified a few minutes later. As they slowed to round a sharp bend in the road, the father saw something ahead on the road. Crying out in surprise, he struggled to maintain control of the car and it almost veered off the road.

The rest of the family, alarmed by the evident panic in his voice, pushed down the locks and held fast on to the door handles, even though at this point they had no idea what had caused him to yell out. Everything became all too clear when he slammed on the brakes to prevent the vehicle from careering over the edge of a steep drop.

ANGUISHED FACE

Leaping towards their vehicle was a creature unlike any the family had ever seen before. Although dressed in a man's clothing, the monstrous being could not be described, by any stretch of the imagination, as a normal human. Describing the course of events later to a Navajo friend, Frances recalled that the beast was black and very hairy, with long arms which clung on to the side of the car and an anguished face that stared in at them for a few seconds before they sped away along the road.

Having reached the relative civilization of the nearest town, the family felt able to discuss the terrifying sight that they had recently witnessed. Shaken by what had happened, they were keen to see some evidence that their imagination had not been responsible for the strange events, and so made a thorough inspection of the car. Incredibly, there was not one single mark or print to be seen in the thick dust that had inevitably accumulated on the vehicle during its long journey. Neither was there any sign in the town of the vehicle that had been following them until the time of its sudden disappearance.

Although reports of encounters with the skinwalkers in one form or another are not uncommon among the Navajo, what is notable about this occurrence is that this family was not of Native American origin. Among the many questions to be raised by these bizarre happenings are the following: why were these people chosen by the strange supernatural beings? And what did they want from them?

These curious shape-shifting witches have aroused great debate in this part of the USA and all over the world. Other beings that are said to possess a similar mutability are the werewolves of European renown, which also have the same ability to inspire awe and terror in the unlucky observer.

The provenance and purpose of these malevolent beings remain a matter of intense controversy and, until more clear evidence comes to light, the mystery is set to continue.

THE YETI AND OTHER ELUSIVE APES

THE YETI

The Yeti, or Abominable Snowman as the Press preferred to call it, hit the news headlines in the year 1951. Mountaineer Eric Shipton came back from an expedition to the Himalayas with photos of a series of footprints in the high Himalayan snows that ran for hundreds of yards across a snowfield. The footprints were roughly human in outline, but were enormous. The photos dominated British newspapers for days and later spread out to other countries.

HALF MAN, HALF APE

Although the general public were taken by surprise by these dramatic pictures, mountaineers and old India hands were less shocked. For decades they had been hearing stories about the strange half-man, half-ape beasts that lurked in the mountains. The only surprise was that somebody had finally managed to photograph a series of tracks.

The first outsider to hear tales of the strange beasts was the noted hill walker B H Hodgson. In northern Nepal in 1825 his march was interrupted when his porters saw a tall creature covered with long, dark hair that bounded off in apparent fear. Hodgson did not see the creature himself, but from the descriptions given by his excited porters thought that it must have been some sort of orangutan.

Other reports filtered out of the mountains over the years that followed. In 1889 Major L A Waddell found footprints in the mountains of Sikkim that looked like those of a gigantic man. About ten years later Mary MacDonald, daughter of a colonial

An encounter, in 1952, between Sherpa Anseering and his wife and a Yeti in the high pastures of the Himalayas

officer, heard a strange howling yelp when walking through the mountains close to the border with Tibet. Her local porter fled and refused to return. They told her that the cry had been made by a 'metoh kangmi'.

In September 1921 Colonel Howard-Bury was near Lhapka-la on his way to scout out Mount Everest for a climbing expedition when he saw three human-like figures walking across a large patch of snow. Some hours later the expedition reached the snowfield and Howard-Bury was able to study the tracks left by the figures. Each footprint was over 36cm (14in) long, but otherwise looked like that of a naked human foot. The porters told Howard-Bury that the figures were not men but 'metoh kangmi'.

It was Howard-Bury who translated the phrase 'metoh kangmi' to mean 'abominable snowman'. He passed it on to a Calcutta-based journalist named Henry Newman who wrote a few pieces about the mystery animal, calling it the Abominable Snowman, and it was under this name that tales of the mystery creature spread through the English-speaking communities of northern India.

It was in the postwar period that the name of Yeti began to be given to the strange creature. The word is not, in fact, very accurate as it is derived from 'yeh-the', a generic Nepalese term for any large animal that lives in the high mountains. This has led to some confusion over the years. Locals may refer to the Himalayan red bear, which they specifically call the dzu-the, as a 'yeh-the' since it is large and lives in the high mountains.

In 1954 the *Daily Mail* newspaper financed an expedition to the Himalayas to collect evidence for the Yeti and, if possible, catch one. The expedition hired 300 porters to carry the equipment up into the high mountains, contacted hundreds of locals and covered vast distances. No Yeti was captured, nor even seen, but the expedition did come back with a wealth of anecdotal evidence and a great boost in sales for the newspaper.

In 1970 Don Whillans was camping on an open slope at 13,000 feet. It was some time after dusk on a sparklingly clear moonlit night and Whillans was resting quietly when he saw something emerge from

A distant relative of Bigfoot, the Yeti is an ape-like creature about 1.5m (5ft) tall if it stands on its hind feet. It moves habitually on all fours, but can walk upright for a short distance

a patch of nearby woodland. He saw the creature distinctly and he estimated it to be about as tall as a human, but much bulkier. The beast went bounding across the turf on all fours, moving in a similar manner to a chimpanzee. In 1984, mountaineer David Sheppard was near the southern Col of Everest when he saw a large, hairy man-like creature following him for a while.

In December 2007, a new Yeti track was discovered and filmed by American television presenter Josh Gates. Each of the footprints was about 28cm (11in) long and 20cm (8in) wide.

The sightings by Whillans and Sheppard are the only times that a European has seen a Yeti in conditions when neither the witnesses' credibility was in question nor the visibility. There have, however, been numerous sightings by Sherpas and other hill peoples.

A typical sighting was made in March 1951 when Lakhpa Tensing went up to the hill pastures above Namche to search for a missing yak. He came across a Yeti about 1.5m (5ft) tall squatting on a rock eating a mousehare. The Yeti scampered off. A few years later Pasang Nima was leading a caravan over the Nepalese-Tibet border when he saw a Yeti sitting on the grass about 300 yards off the track. The creature was digging in the ground with its fingers, pulling up roots which it then chewed. The following year, in October, Anseering and his wife went up to the high pastures to look for medicinal roots. They emerged from some trees to see a Yeti apparently picking leaves off a bush. As soon as it became aware of them it bounded off on all four legs at high speed to disappear among a jumble of rocks.

The picture that emerges from these assorted sightings and other reports is that the Yeti is an ape-like creature about 1.5m (5ft) tall if it stands on its hind feet. It moves habitually on all fours, but can walk upright for a short distance. The Yeti seems to be mostly nocturnal, though it will occasionally come out in daylight. It seems to be omnivorous, feeding on plants and on small animals when it can catch them. Most sightings of Yeti or its footprints are of a solitary animal. It has been speculated that

these may be young males driven out of the family group to find a new territory, which would explain why they are seen at all. A creature in unfamiliar territory is more likely to be spotted than one on its home ground. It also seems to be the case that the usual home of these creatures is not on the high, snowy mountains, but in the densely forested valleys. This would make sense as that is where it would be most likely to find food.

Whatever the truth behind the Yeti might turn out to be, it is still a popular subject among cryptozoologists. On 26 September 2007 the original print of the Eric Shipton photos that launched the Yeti into the world's media sold at auction for £3,600.

THE ORANG-PENDEK

Tales of mysterious ape-like creatures are not as uncommon as most people imagine. If the majority of the public has heard of the Yeti or Bigfoot, there are a dozen other forms that have, at least to date, remained the preserve of specialists in cryptozoology. One such creature that has been the subject of increased interest in recent years is the Orang-Pendek or 'little man' of Sumatra.

SHY VEGETARIAN

Accounts of this animal come from a range of sources, most notably from the local people of the forested uplands of Sumatra, who have accepted it as a part of the diverse habitat in which they live. It is, they say, a shy creature that mostly feeds on vegetation, but may kill small animals for food – and in contrast to stories about other unknown apes – it has never attacked a human. It is, therefore, not regarded as a threat and is generally left alone by the natives.

The Orang-Pendek is described as short in stature, walking on its hind legs at a height of just 0.7m–1.5m (2ft 4in–5ft). Its pinkish-brown skin is covered with a coat of short, dark body hair and it has long, flowing hair around its face. Its arms, unlike those of most normal apes, are considerably shorter than its legs, and it appears more human than ape-like.

An Orang-Pendek sits eating fruit in a tree as a European walks by below. The average height of these animals is about 90cm (3ft) but some males are known to grow larger

Many footprints have been discovered over the years, and these have been put forward as proof of the animal's existence. Although these prints are said to resemble those made by a child of around seven years old, they are in fact much broader than a human's and some accounts actually describe the feet as pointing backwards.

To add to the natives' accounts of the Orang-Pendek, a number of sightings of the creature by

Western explorers have further corroborated the story. An early sighting of the Orang-Pendek by a Westerner occurred in 1910. The man described it as: 'a large creature, low on its feet, which ran like a man and was about to cross my path; it was very hairy and it was not an orangutan; but its face was not like an ordinary man's'. This description was echoed by that of a Dutch hunter 13 years later, who added that he felt unable to kill the beast because its physical appearance was so similar to that of a human being.

More recently, in the late 1980s, interest in the animal was re-ignited by the findings of the English travel writer, Deborah Matyr. Although initially sceptical that such a creature did in fact exist, after hearing of many sightings and studying its footprints on several occasions, she went on to become one of its most reliable and trusted witnesses

Following the emergence of poor-quality photographic evidence of the creature a decade later, it was decided that conclusive evidence of the Orang-Pendek was needed as the shadowy and blurred images that had been captured on film were deemed to be inadequate proof of its existence. Accordingly, a number of expeditions have set out lately to the Sumatran forests to try to gather definite proof. The discovery of hair and faecal samples, casts of footprints and a clear and incontrovertible photo, for example, would not only prove once and for all that this creature exists, but would enable scientists to determine if it is an example of a species of ape previously unknown to zoologists.

Scientists are, coincidentally, debating whether the Orang-Pendek might be linked in some way to the discovery, in a limestone cave on the Indonesian island of Flores, of a new species of miniature human. Evidence has been uncovered to show that these tiny people, nicknamed 'hobbits' on account of their diminutive stature, lived and hunted on the island 18,000 years ago. Perhaps this creature is not an ape at all, but, rather, an example of a sub-species of human being? It seems that further evidence will be needed before a definitive answer to the mystery of the Orang-Pendek is provided.

FAIRIES

THE LITTLE PEOPLE

Fairies have been a feature of folklore in many cultures through the centuries. Disney would have us believe they are all well-meaning, although other storytellers insist that they possess a malignant streak, stealing babies and blinding those who spy on them. One enduring question remains, do fairies really exist outside the realms of fantasy – and if they do, what exactly are these little people?

For centuries, the idea that humans shared the planet with small, shiny folk was beyond question. But with the spread of urban city life and a science that edged out religion in the West, faith in fairies fell into decline. By the later 20th century almost nobody in Europe took the fairies seriously any longer.

Even today, there are numerous parts of the world where talk of the 'little people' and their activities would not raise an eyebrow. The sceptical West mostly does not fall into this bracket, although there does seem to be a long-held desire for proof of their existence.

PRANCING FAIRIES

So when in November 1920 a London magazine proclaimed: 'An epoch-making event – fairies photographed', eager readers were fascinated. The writer was Sir Arthur Conan Doyle, creator of the archly logical detective Sherlock Holmes and – at the same time – a staunch advocate of the paranormal. He illustrated the feature with photographs taken in Cottingley, Yorkshire, by two young girls, Elsie Wright and Frances Griffiths, purporting to show fairies by a beck near to their rural home. And, at first glance, the photos did seem to show fairies prancing around the two girls.

Professional photographers failed to find evidence of a hoax when they inspected the negatives. To Conan Doyle's eye, it was the proof the world needed to endorse at last a widespread belief in fairies, especially as the girls initially refused the trappings of fame and fortune they might easily have seized upon in such extraordinary circumstances. Indeed, the photographs had lain undisturbed in a drawer at Elsie Wright's home for three years until her mother attended a Theosophy meeting in Harrogate, Yorkshire, where the subject of fairy folk was raised. Whenever Elsie wrote or spoke about seeing fairies, it was done so in passing and without any sense of drama. She seemed, to Conan Doyle's mind, a most convincing witness.

Not everyone was convinced, though, not least Elsie's father and the owner of the camera used in the episode. Critics were quick to point out the photographed fairies were wearing fashions akin to those of contemporary humans and that there was no sign of motion in the photographs, despite the fact that the fairies seemed to be airborne

Like many others, Conan Doyle invested greatly in the potency of the paranormal after losing a son and other close family members to the brutal fighting of the First World War. By the time the Cottingley fairy photos came along, he was considered ageing and eccentric by many. Some of the mediums he had championed were being exposed as fakes by campaigners like the eminent escapologist Houdini.

Despite their quality and apparent genuine features, the photographs were soon widely written off as being fraudulent. Decades later a fabrication was confirmed, although the belated confession left plenty of wriggle-room for believers.

Shortly before Elsie and Frances died, they

Left: Arthur Conan Doyle was a firm believer in fairies and was a vocal supporter of the Cottingley photographs; above: the Little Folk have been a part of folklore for hundreds of years

confessed to forging some photographs using cut-outs held in place by hat-pins. However, Elsie implied that she and Frances had only tried to reproduce what they had actually seen. The last photograph of five, called 'The Fairy Bower', was, they insisted, genuine. After seventy years of mockery, both went to their graves at great ages, still firmly believing in fairies.

Even if the girls had constructed the fairy scenes themselves, the publicity surrounding the Cottingley photographs brought forth numerous testimonies from other witnesses.

From the Isle of Man, Rev Arnold J Holmes wrote:

> '... my horse suddenly stopped dead and, looking ahead, I saw amid the obscure light and misty moonbeams what appeared to be a small army of indistinct figures – very small, clad in gossamer garments.'

On the other side of the world, in New Zealand, one Mrs Hardy saw 'eight or ten tiny figures on tiny ponies like dwarf Shetlands … The faces were quite brown, also the ponies were brown … They were like tiny dwarfs or children of about two years old.'

As the name of fairies has fallen into disuse, those who investigate sightings of such little people have come to prefer the word 'elementals'. Debate about whether these elementals are the souls of unbaptized children, ancestral ghosts, fallen angels or spirits of nature has made little headway and continues to dominate discussion – sometimes at the expense of actual research into sightings.

SECRET STRONGHOLDS

Fairy talk has continued since the Cottingley fairy era, and has gained momentum since the advent of the internet. But belief in fairies is still far from being considered 'the norm'. People like Sheila Jeffries in south-west England have become used to being mocked for maintaining an unflinching conviction in the existence of fairies.

A patch of ancient woodland on her Cornish smallholding – a place called Hallowglen on old maps – is, says Sheila Jeffries, among the last outposts of the fairy kingdom in Britain. She thinks they have fled to secret strongholds like this one in the face of environmental destruction wrought by humans on the countryside.

'If you wish to see them you must throw away your reasoning, sit very quietly and get rid of any resentment, stress or anger in your thoughts,' she says. 'They are very sensitive to people's vibes. You need to be totally relaxed.'

Mrs Jeffries has few explanations for her experiences. She thinks the fairies live 'in a separate dimension; not holes in trees'; that they were once regularly seen and accepted by country people and that advances in agriculture have driven them from all but Britain's wildest places. She flinches at the idea of photographing them and insists she would not even try. In the absence of such proof, she knows she will always be regarded as a crank.

She is not, however, alone. In 2005 in Scotland a developer was forced to re-think his plans when neighbours objected to him moving a rock widely believed to shelter fairies. The rock lies at St Fillans in Perthshire, on the banks of Loch Earn, and when builders moved in a local man was swiftly on the scene, shouting: 'Don't move that rock, you'll kill the fairies.'

Belief in fairies is interwoven with a strong superstition that moving ancient upstanding rocks like that at St Fillans will bring bad luck. In the face of the protest, the developer re-located his scheme to a nearby site. It was a small but significant victory for the minority that believes in the existence of fairy folk. They wholeheartedly share the sentiments once penned by Conan Doyle, that have a poignant appeal even for the sceptics:

> 'The recognition of [the fairies'] existence will jolt the material 20th century mind out of its heavy ruts in the mud and will make it admit that there is a glamour and a mystery to life.'

DINOSAUR SURVIVORS

onventional wisdom holds that all dinosaurs became extinct 65 million years ago. However, there is another school of thought that says at least one variety of these mighty beasts is alive and well, living in the dense and impenetrable jungle of equatorial Africa.

From an urban or Western perspective it seems inconceivable that there is a corner of the planet that remains obscure. Yet the part of the African continent most closely associated with dinosaur sightings is so remote and dense with undergrowth that it is impossible to explore it thoroughly.

Lake Tele is in the Congo Basin, an area recently torn by conflict and all too often rife with disease. It is fed by numerous tributaries, and it lies at the heart of some 142,450 square kilometres of swampland, only an estimated 80 per cent of which has been explored. Even in the 21st century, the number of visitors to the shores of the lake is startlingly few. If dinosaurs had survived largely unseen anywhere on earth, then it would be here.

MOK'ELE-MBEMBE

The evidence for the existence of a dinosaur is mostly anecdotal. However, thcsc are stories that have persisted for several centuries and are

Could mok'ele-mbembe be a form of the long-extinct dinosaur?

particularly potent among the indigenous population.

As long ago as 1776, before the existence of dinosaurs was even known about, the French missionary Abbé Proyart wrote a description of the clawed tracks he saw embedded in African mud. Their dimensions were 90cm (3ft) in width with about 2m (6.6ft) between steps.

In 1913, a German explorer revealed the name given by locals to the creature that left the mysterious tracks, 'mok'ele-mbeme'. The beast was, he claimed, 'of a brownish-grey colour with a smooth skin, approximately the size of an elephant, at least that of a hippopotamus. It is said to have a long and very flexible neck and only one tooth but a very long one, some described it as a horn. A few spoke about a long muscular tail 'like that of an alligator'. It sounded rather like a sauropod dinosaur, such as *Diplodocus* or *Brachiosaurus*.

In 1932, a British scientist roaming in the region heard some unidentifiable sounds and recorded gigantic tracks that belonged to no animal that he knew of.

The waters were muddied in the years following the Second World War by a hoax and by claims that creatures of similar dimensions were residing in the Congo River, the swamps of Gabon and also Lake Bangweulu in Zambia.

Nevertheless, a series of expeditions to the Congo from the UK, America and Japan was dispatched between 1972 and 1992 – with largely disappointing results. Most had difficulty reaching the shores of Lake Tele or even of the upper Congo River. Those that did often claimed that they heard noises that they presumed belonged to mok'ele-mbeme. Two men saw the monster, but in both cases film taken of the momentous event failed to come out.

In 1981 Herman Regusters took a number of pictures of a swamp beast but the film was apparently damaged by the extreme climatic conditions of the jungle. Two years later Congolese zoologist Dr Marcellin Agnagna was so awestruck when the creature reared up in front of him that he neglected to take the lens cap off his movie camera. The resulting footage was useless.

In 1992 the most convincing film was shot as a Japanese documentary crew flew over Lake Tele, not on the trail of the elusive monster, but in search of panoramic views of the region. As the plane sped over the lake the cameraman noticed a disturbance in the water. He struggled to maintain a focus on the object, which was creating a noticeable wake. By the time the plane banked around and returned the thing had vanished, although ripples in the surface of the water were still visible.

The film is indistinct. It could be the first genuine footage of mok'ele-mbeme or it might be an elephant on the move. The blurred shape in the frame mostly resembles two people travelling in a motorized canoe, although it is said that no people travel across this part of the lake. One inexplicably strange aspect of the film is that whatever is in the water ends up entirely submerged – unlikely for either an elephant or a canoe.

But the most irresistible evidence to date has come from people living in the vicinity. The swamp inhabitants are various pygmy tribes, all of whom appear to have some knowledge of mok'ele-mbeme. Shown pictures of gorillas, hippopotamuses and elephants they have quickly registered recognition and put a name to them all. When shown a picture of a sauropod dinosaur a consensus has also swiftly been reached. It is mok'ele-mbeme.

One hunter, Nicolas Mondongo, was a teenager when he encountered the monster. He said it had a head and neck some 2m (6.6ft) long, crowned by a frill like that of a cockerel. Its four legs were stout and its tail was greater in length than its neck.

Another persuasive tale was recorded among the people of the river villages who remembered when a monster was attacked and killed by fishermen. The corpse was cooked and eaten by selected tribespeople. All those who tasted the flesh died soon afterwards, although no one as yet knows why. The event apparently occurred in the later 1950s and there is still the hope that explorers will discover the bones discarded after the fatal feast.

From the villagers of the swamp, expedition members have discovered that mok'ele-mbeme is vegetarian but nonetheless ferocious, using its tail to lash out at anyone who gets too close. Tribespeople are also convinced there is enmity between mok'ele-mbeme and hippopotamuses as they do not cohabit the same stretches of water.

In November 2000, Adam Davies undertook one of the most recent expeditions to this inhospitable region and the following year he reported his findings in the Fortean Times, a journal that specializes in cryptozoology. Although Davies did not see or hear mok'ele-mbeme himself, he picked up two vital pieces of information. The first was a description from a village elder who claimed to have seen it many times.

> *'It has feet like an elephant and a neck like a giraffe. It does not live on the lake but in the forest. It travels across the lake for food.'*

The second fact that he gathered was from Dr Agnagna, who told him not to concentrate his search on Lake Tele but on other lakes close by that were even more remote.

At the end of the day, it must be admitted that the facts are maddeningly few. Something has been seen in the vicinity of Lake Tele – and at other locations – that has led a significant number of people to believe that dinosaurs still exist in the heart of Africa. A series of expeditions has brought various pieces of evidence to light, but these are mostly anecdotal and a definitive photograph has not yet been produced – still less any bones or other remains. Rather than an unknown beast, there is a possibility that the sightings were of unexpected activity by elephants – although local people well acquainted with wildlife might be expected to distinguish between elephants and other creatures. Testimony from local folk might be coloured by superstition or imagination.

The density of the jungle works both for and against sceptics. While hostile terrain makes the dinosaur idea difficult to prove, it likewise means the notion is perhaps feasible, as this is uncharted territory and no one can say with certainty what does, or does not, reside there.

SURVIVING PTEROSAURS

Whether or not the mok'ele-mbeme actually exists – and if it does what it turns out to be – a strange tale emanating from local people in Zambia might indicate that a quite different prehistoric reptile has survived to the present day. Over the centuries there have been numerous reports of ferocious flying reptiles that bear an uncanny resemblance to a supposedly extinct group of ancient reptiles known as pterosaurs.

CERTAIN DEATH

These claims have inspired such curiosity that, in 1932, the traveller Frank H Welland ventured into the Jiundu swamps in the Mwinilunga district of western Zambia to investigate the story. The locals gave him detailed accounts of monstrous, reddish birds, with a wingspan of two metres (6.6ft), long beaks full of teeth and leathery skin in place of feathers. They called these creatures 'kongamato', which translates as 'overwhelmer of boats', due to the fact that the huge birds would often overturn small vessels, attacking and sometimes killing the occupants. So terrified were the locals of the kongamato that it was thought that just one look at it would result in certain death. Welland wrote an account of the natives' descriptions in his book, In *Witchbound Africa*, which received great publicity for it also revealed that, when Welland showed the Zambians drawings of the prehistoric pterosaur, they unanimously and unhesitatingly agreed that these sketches identified precisely the creature they knew as the kongamato.

Many people were sceptical of these claims. They argued instead that the Zambian people had in fact obtained the description of the pterosaur from those natives who had worked on excavations in Tanzania where the fossilized bones of pterosaurs had been discovered some years earlier.

There are several problems with this theory, however. First, was it possible for descriptions of the dinosaur bones to have travelled from Tanzania to Zambia, a distance of 900km (560 miles)? Second, even if this had been the case, and the Zambians had heard about the skeletal structure of the pterosaur,

how would they have known about the creature's leathery skin and lack of feathers? Finally, if the sightings were nothing more than the product of fervent imaginings, why was it that they did not come directly from the excavation site in Tanzania, rather than from as far away as Zambia?

LONG-BEAKED BIRD

Sightings of the mysterious creature continued, one story being told to the English newspaper correspondent, Mr G Price, by a civil servant living in Africa. The expatriate recounted how he had met a native who had suffered an almost fatal wound to the chest while exploring the much-feared swampland. The man claimed that he had received his injury in an attack by a huge long-beaked bird.

Such stories were not limited to the inhabitants of the Zambian swamps, however. One account came from the famous zoologist and writer Ivan Sanderson who, in 1933, was leading an expedition to the Assumbo Mountains in the Cameroons on behalf of the British Museum.

He described how, while out hunting one day, he had shot a fruit bat over the fast-flowing river. Wading out into the water to retrieve the fallen animal, Sanderson lost his balance and fell. Having regained his footing, he heard a warning yell from one of his colleagues and to his horror saw a monstrous black creature bearing down upon him from the sky at great speed.

Sanderson ducked into the river to escape the huge bird and then made for the riverbank. At this point, the creature renewed its attack, diving down on him again and both he and his companion threw themselves on the ground, conscious only of the sound of the beating of the creature's powerful wings.

Fortunately, the animal then flew off into the night, leaving the two men to return to the safety of their camp. Here, they related their story to their guides, asking them if they knew what their attacker might have been. The locals fled in terror without answering the question.

An artist's impression of a pterodactyl, a type of pterosaur known to have existed in prehistoric times

Sanderson reflected on what he had seen – fortunately, he had had sufficient time to note the physical appearance of the creature and, due to his zoological expertise, was able to give a precise description of the animal. He described it as having been about the size of an eagle, with a semicircle of sharp white teeth in its lower jaw. This report matched not only those of other sightings, but also corresponded with what is known of the pterosaur. Sanderson also remarked that the beast, like the pterosaur, resembled a bat. However, he discounted the possibility that it was only a fruit bat on the basis that these creatures are not known to attack humans.

Some years later, in 1942, similar stories from other areas in Africa, such as Mount Kilimanjaro and Mount Kenya, were related to the author, Captain C Pitman. They described the existence of a large bat-like bird, which produced tracks suggesting that it had a large tail that dragged along the ground behind the creature.

In his book, *A Game Warden Takes Stock*, Captain Pitman went on to describe how the animals were alleged to feed on rotting human flesh if corpses were not buried to a sufficient depth. Further accounts of the birds were contained in another publication, Old Fourlegs, in which fossil expert Dr J L B Smith described 'flying dragons' in the region of Mount Kilimanjaro.

ALIVE AND KICKING

Today the sightings continue in remote areas of Africa. In 1998, a Kenyan exchange student, Steve Romando-Menya, declared that the existence of the kongamato is common knowledge among the bush dwellers in his country. Moreover, all witnesses, when asked to draw what they have seen, are repeatedly reported to draw a pterosaur.

What are these mysterious creatures? Sceptics claim that it is impossible for the prehistoric pterosaur to be in existence today, and yet the number of confirmed reports from reliable sources would seem to indicate otherwise. The controversy and debate continue to this day.

THE NANDI BEAR AND OTHER CREATURES

It comes as something of a surprise to most people to learn that around eight per cent of the land surface of Earth is unexplored. It has been mapped, of course, and that tends to confuse the issue. But mapping rivers, mountains and lakes using satellite photos or aerial surveys reveals nothing about the animals and plants that live there. To learn about wildlife in an area, it is necessary to go there. That is when the problems start.

There are vast areas of swamp, forest and mountain that offer no real inducement for humans to investigate them. There are no valuable mineral deposits, no profitable logging to be had and no lands that could be turned to productive agricultural use. Such areas have long been shunned by humans. A few are penetrated by the odd hunter or fisherman who hopes to make a small profit, but they have never been properly explored by anyone likely to write down what he or she has found.

It is in these remote, but substantial areas of the world where the mysterious animals studied by cryptozoologists are most often said to lurk. Cryptozoology means the study of hidden animals, but increasingly often it turns out that the animals are not so much hidden as ignored.

People living in the Vietnamese forests have for years been telling Europeans of a large antelope-like creature that is very rare, very shy and lives in the dense mountain forests of the Nghe An and Ha Tinh provinces. Nobody took the tales seriously until 1992 when a zoologist was handed a pair of horns that he could not identify. With hard evidence of some unknown animal, an expedition was organized and sent into the mountains. Within a very short time they had been shown one of the mystery creatures by local huntsmen. The saola has been accepted as a known animal ever since. There are thought to be only a few hundred of them browsing on leaves in the forests. Whether it is a type of cattle, antelope or goat is as yet unclear.

What is clear is that it really does exist. What other animals really do exist, but are currently being ignored by conventional science is the business of cryptozoology.

THE NANDI BEAR

Of all Africa's unexplained animals, the Nandi bear is said to be the most ferocious and is consequently the most feared. It is renowned across much of East Africa, where it strikes terror into the hearts of both local people and Westerners alike. The nature of its existence is a mystery – is it really a bear, or could it be some other kind of animal? And how has it managed to avoid categorization by scientists?

A modern-day grizzly bear in the USA: the Nandi bear is said to be a vicious killer and about the
same size as a lion, with hind quarters like those of a bear

There would certainly appear to be a strange, unidentified killer animal prowling around the villages of East Africa. Numerous eyewitness reports from both indigenous and Western inhabitants describe the beast as resembling a large hyena, being about the same size as a lion and having a dark, possibly reddish-brown, coat. It is said to be a nocturnal creature, and there are numerous reports of vicious attacks on humans.

Several accounts of this animal have been publicized in the Kenyan press, and one article in particular thrust it into the limelight. The report described the experiences of two of Kenya's most famous citizens, who were outside one moonlit night when they spotted what they believed, at first, to be a lioness. This initial identification was quickly proved to be inaccurate, however. As the animal became more visible, it could be seen to have a snout and a back which sloped down to its hind quarters, just like those of a bear. It also had the thick, dark fur and shuffling gait commonly associated with members of the bear family.

PREHISTORIC LEFTOVER?

Although it is known, from the ancient writings of Pliny and other authorities, that bears did once roam North Africa, according to official animal demographic statistics, there are no native, wild bears living in Africa today – and certainly not south of the Sahara. Moreover, there is no evidence of the creature that might provide further, vital information. Although locals claim to have killed several of the beasts by setting fire to them and Westerners report having taken shots at the creature, the fact remains that no-one has yet been able to make a positive identification.

It is known that one type of bear did once roam the continent, but this species is thought to have become extinct during the Paleolithic period. With so many factors – such as the animal's shape, behaviour, appearance and ability to stand on its hind legs – suggesting that this creature might be a type of bear, it has been asked whether some of this supposedly extinct species could have managed to survive, and evade detection by scientists.

Although this so-called Atlas bear matches the descriptions of the modern-day Nandi bear, the identification raises a number of significant problems. Not least of these issues is the fact that fossil records of the Atlas bear have been found solely in northern Africa, whereas the Nandi bear is located only in the east of the country. It is unlikely that the Nandi bear is a different species of bear altogether for, apart from the fact that the Atlas bear is the only type known to have inhabited Africa, not one single fossil record of the Nandi has been discovered.

Perhaps, then, this mysterious beast is not a bear at all? Many people believe instead that it is some sort of huge, lumbering hyena, which could either be a previously undiscovered species, or else a remnant from prehistoric times.

In support of this argument is the fact that palaeontologists have found evidence of the existence on the continent of a short-faced hyena, similar in size to a lion which lived until the Paleolithic era.

Others suggest that the creature could be a Chalicothere, a sloped-back animal related to the horse, but having claws instead of hooves. Like the hyena, this species is also believed to have become extinct in the Paleolithic era. Although this description matches that of the Nandi bear, there is one crucial factor which makes the proposition less likely: the Chalicothere, in common with all horses, was a herbivore, whereas the Nandi bear is known to be a vicious killer.

The Nandi tribe, from which the beast derives its most commonly used name, describe the bear as a primate, resembling a large baboon. Baboons are omnivores, known to make savage attacks on animals such as smaller monkeys and sheep, and are also able to stand on two feet.

Differences in behaviour between the baboon and the mysterious animal – such as the fact that the baboon hunts in packs and is not nocturnal – have been noted, but can possibly be ascribed to the fact that the two creatures could have a slightly different genetic make-up.

On the evidence provided by the fossils of giant baboons and the description of the Nandi tribe, researchers are seriously considering the possibility that the Nandi bear could be some sort of hitherto unknown species of baboon. Alternatively, it might be a survivor from prehistoric times.

Until more thorough research is carried out, however, or a specimen has been caught, scientists and cryptozoologists are unable to verify exactly what kind of animal this is. Only once this is known can they start to solve the riddle of its origins.

THE SPOTTED LION

As well as being told about the Nandi bear, early Europeans visiting East Africa were assured that a spotted species of lion lived in the inland mountains. As so often with 'native tales', the local Europeans were inclined to believe them but scientific experts dismissed them out of hand.

In 1923 the first report of a Spotted Lion sighting by a European was made. Big game hunter G Hamilton-Snowball reported that he had come across two small, but distinctly spotted lions in forests at an altitude of 11,500 feet in the Mau Forest. The Spotted Lions had bounded under cover before he could get a shot off. Puzzled that lions should be seen so high, Hamilton-Snowball questioned his guides. They told him that the animals were not lions but 'marozi'. These were lion-like creatures that lived only in the mountains and hunted in pairs of one male and one female, not as prides like the lions of the plains. Hamilton-Snowball inspected the pugmarks left by the strange cats and thought that they were identical to those of a young adult lion.

Other hunters have reported similar encounters, while in the 1920s a farmer named Powys Cobb complained that a small spotted lion was preying on his cattle. Cobb mounted guard around his herd and found that the Spotted Lion fled whenever it saw him. After a few weeks the predator left the area.

In 1923 the first sighting of a spotted lion was made by a European when big game hunter
G Hamilton-Snowball came across two of them in the Mau Forest

Then, in 1931, a hunter named Michael Trent shot two Spotted Lions 10,000 feet up in the Aberdare Mountains. He was unable to carry the carcasses out of the forests, but did skin the beasts and carry the pelts back to show them to naturalists. The scientists of the time dismissed the pelts as those of juveniles that had kept their cub spots for longer than was usual. Trent photographed the skins, then sold them and now only the photos remain.

It is true that on rare occasions, some animals will retain the markings of babies into adolescence. If Trent's skins had been produced in isolation this might well be the explanation for them. However, many other people have reported coming across lions in dense mountain forest. These lions are invariably said to be smaller than normal lions and to have distinct spots on their coats. Almost always they are seen in pairs. That there is a rare form of Spotted Lion seems beyond doubt. Whether it is a separate type of big cat, or merely a sub-species of lion adapted to life in the forests we do not know and will not discover until some scientist takes the animal seriously.

THE MOA

There is no doubt at all that Moas have been seen by humans, indeed they were once a favourite food source for the Maoris of New Zealand. The question that is almost impossible to answer is when did the Moa go extinct – if indeed it ever has.

The largest of the Moa is known to science as the *Dinornis*, from old bones that have been found. It stood around 3.6m (12ft) tall – half as tall again as an ostrich and much more massive. The smallest was the *Anomalopteryx* which was about as big as a good-sized Christmas turkey. When Captain Cook reached New Zealand from Britain in 1773 none of the Maori told him anything about any giant birds. None of the explorers that followed him were told about them either, so when the first fossilized bones turned up in 1839 they were assumed to have come from a bird that went extinct long before humans arrived.

As so often, however, that was to ignore the stories and beliefs of the local people. Earlier in the 1830s

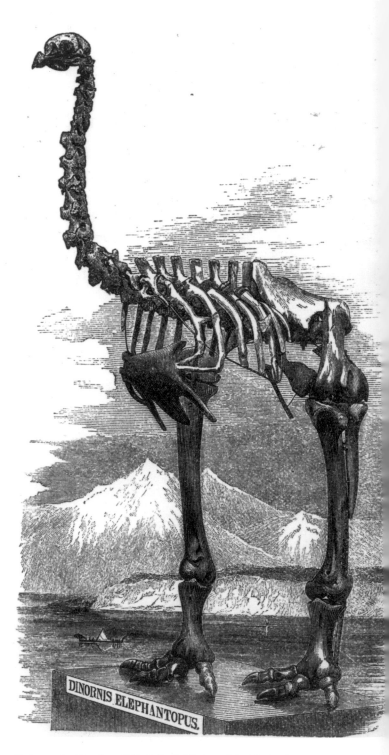

Skeleton of a Moa from W L Buller's History of the Birds of New Zealand *(1887–8): an adult bird stood about 12ft tall*

J Polack spent some time trading with the Maori of North Island and, as a hobby, collected their oral history. He recorded: 'The natives hold that in times long past very large birds had existed, but the scarcity of animal food as well as the easy method of entrapping them has caused their extermination in this area. I feel assured, from many reports I received from natives, that a species of this bird still exists on that island in parts which have never yet been trodden by man.'

About the same time a missionary, Rev W Williams, active on South Island recorded: 'I heard from the natives of a certain monstrous animal or bird that in general appearance somewhat resembles an immense domestic cock, with the difference however of its having a face like a man. It dwells in a cavern in the mountains and that if any human ventures to approach the dwelling of this wonderful creature he would be invariably trampled on and killed by it.'

MAN KILLERS

Once the Moa bones had been found and identified, several Maoris came forward with tales of encounters with the giant birds. In 1850 a very old man named Haumatangi said that his father had taken part in Moa hunts as a young man – probably around 1770. The birds, Haumatangi said, had been rounded up by being driven into stockades and then killed with special, heavyweight spears. The birds were said to be quite capable of killing a man with a single kick of their clawed feet, but were slow-moving and dull-witted.

That these large, grassland-living forms of Moa are extinct there is now little doubt. However, the smaller varieties of Moa have always been said to have lived in forests and to have been active at night. Reports from Maori hunters record the last successful hunts for these birds to have taken place in the 1880s. That was about the time that the Maori were abandoning their traditional lifestyles for a more European style of life farming or working in towns. Some cryptozoologists believe that the smaller Moa stopped being caught not because they

went extinct, but because they stopped being hunted.

That the smaller Moa may still be alive and well is indicated by the story of the goose-sized flightless bird known as the takahe. It was first found by Europeans in 1849 living around lakes in the mountains of South Island. By 1862 it was declared extinct, all known breeding grounds having been exterminated by hungry settlers and their dogs. Thereafter Maoris said that the bird was alive and well among the high mountains. Some European settlers saw footprints and heard calls. In 1879 one European even claimed to have seen the bird itself. Nobody believed him.

In 1948 naturalist Geoffrey Orbell was on an expedition to the high mountains of South Island when he stumbled across a colony of breeding takahe. He estimated that there were about 200 birds. He photographed them to prove they existed, then left and kept the location a secret. So far as is known the takahe are still there. Perhaps the Moa are as well.

THE BUNYIP

According to the Australian Aboriginal myth of creation – usually referred to as Dreamtime – deep in the heart of the Australian outback there lurks a mysterious creature known as the Bunyip. This beast is said to inhabit and defend lakes, swamps and billabongs, leaving its territory at night to venture into human dwellings to prey upon vulnerable women and children. Stories abound of its spine-chilling bellowing as it moves in search of its prey in and around the Australian waterways. But is this creature purely a fictional, symbolic warning about the very real dangers presented by the inland waters of this vast continent? Or is there some truth behind the tales?

Among the Aborigines, there are varied descriptions of the Bunyip. Some say it is covered in feathers, others that it has scales like an alligator. Almost all describe the animal as having an equine tail, flippers and walrus-like tusks. These reports run counter, however, to the stories of the Bunyip related shaggy coat and small, wing-like flippers. The second species, the Long-necked Bunyip, apparently possessed a similar coat to the Dog-faced Bunyip, but with a longer neck, a horse-like mane, tusks and flippers.

There are numerous written and spoken accounts of encounters with Dog-faced Bunyips during the 19th and early 20th centuries. The creature was sighted in lakes, rivers and billabongs all over Australia and Tasmania. By contrast, reports of the rarer Long-necked Bunyip seem to be restricted to the state of New South Wales.

The sheer number and collaboratory nature of the stories seems to negate the possibility that these strange hybrid creatures belong purely to the realms of fantasy. But if they do exist in reality, what type of animal are they and where did they come from? And, most importantly from a conservational and cryptozoological perspective, what has become of them?

HERBIVOROUS MARSUPIAL?

Of the various theories in existence about the Bunyip's origins, one in particular seems to have excited researchers, although many remain sceptical. The Bunyip bears a strong resemblance, both in its appearance and behaviour, to a supposedly extinct creature known as the *Diprotodon*, a large rhinoceros-sized herbivorous marsupial that roamed the land more than 10,000 years ago. Some experts believe that the *Diprotodon* was, like the Bunyip, equally at home on the land and in the water. Perhaps, then, in a land rich in marsupial diversity, the *Diprotodon* evolved over the course of thousands of years into a sort of marsupial hippo – the Bunyip? Although there are those who maintain that this might be possible, in general scientists have dismissed the notion that a small population of these ancient animals may have somehow survived until the 20th century.

Another theory is that the Bunyip was, in fact, a seal and that the mystery is a simple case of repeated misidentification by inland locals who have never

Illustration of an Aboriginal hunter from the nineteenth century: in the lore of native Australians, deep in the heart of the Outback lurks a mysterious creature called the Bunyip

by the first Western settlers. Far from being a savage creature, these people describe the Bunyip as a kind of aquatic herbivore that lived in the waterways and peacefully grazed on the abundant grasses of the riverbanks and marshland.

These reports suggest that there were, in fact, two main species of Bunyip. The most often sighted of the two was the Dog-faced Bunyip, which, as its name suggests, possessed a canine face, a long, seen sea-dwelling seals. Similarly, it has been suggested that Bunyips might have been seals that migrated inland along the waterways, evolving to fit into their new surroundings by shedding their blubber and replacing it with thick fur.

These possibilities are also a matter of fierce debate, however. If the Bunyips were no more than seals, how could they have been observed grazing on land? Seals are aquatic mammals that feed on fish, not herbivorous grazers that are capable of living on land as well as in water. Moreover, the physical attributes of the Long-necked Bunyip do not match those of a seal.

There are many unanswered questions on the subject of the Bunyip, but it seems the truth will never be known. The Bunyip has not been seen for almost a century so if it really did exist, it may have perished as a result of environmental changes in the waterways and the effects of pollution. The only place in which it would seem to live on is in the imaginations and traditions of the local people in the areas in which this enigmatic creature was seen.

THE JERSEY DEVIL

Could a corner of North America really be haunted by a devilish beast from a species unknown to mankind? It certainly seems unlikely, yet, in the early years of the twentieth century, a cluster of appearances by a grotesque winged creature paralyzed villages across the state of New Jersey.

A string of sightings of this mysterious beast, which came to be known as the Jersey Devil, led to panic amongst local people. Schools were closed and factories barricaded. Small town streets were deserted as residents retreated behind closed doors for fear of meeting the monster.

Policemen, postmasters, trappers and vicars were among those who reported sightings of the devil in and around New Jersey during January 1909. Although the descriptions sometimes differed in detail, the beast was unquestionably one and the same. After spotting it outside his Gloucester house on 19 January, Nelson Evans gave the following detailed description:

'It was about 3½ft (1m) high, with a head like a collie dog and a face like a horse. It had a long neck, wings about 2ft (60cm) long, and its back legs were like those of a crane, and it had horse's hooves. It walked on its back legs and held up two short front legs with paws on them. It didn't use the front legs at all while we were watching. My wife and I were scared, I tell you, but I managed to open the window and say, "Shoo", and it turned around, barked at me, and flew away.'

MASS HALLUCINATION

During the month-long episode, witnesses of the Jersey Devil numbered in the hundreds. Could they all have been subject to some manner of mass hallucination? The creature has frequently been described as being similar to a traditional horned Satan, and perhaps the news of an extraordinary beast at large infected the fertile imaginations of local people and led them to believe the devil was roaming in their midst. Yet the communities where sightings occurred were scattered far and wide, so it was highly unlikely that the panic and rumours rife in one village should spread to the next.

If it did exist, the Jersey Devil made its home in the Jersey Pine Barrens, some 5,180 square kilometres of forested wilderness once inhabited by gangs of thieves. The area had a fearsome reputation for being dangerous and lawless, so the devil might well feel at home there.

Over time, various explanations have been proffered for the Devil's existence in New Jersey. One of these holds that a local woman, frustrated at falling pregnant again, cried out that the devil should take her next child away. Although it was born normally, her baby then sprouted wings and flew away up the chimney. Another version of the story maintains that when a local woman fell in love with a British soldier during the American Revolutionary War, people cursed her, swearing that her offspring would be a devil.

Other explanations are that the Jersey Devil is the product of a local liaison between a witch and Satan, or that a devil was installed in the region to punish a community after they mistreated a minister. Mysteriously, the people involved in the mythology often have the surname Leeds or live at Leeds Point. For this reason, the beast is sometimes alternatively known as the Leeds devil.

Sometimes the appearance of the Jersey Devil is taken as a sign that things are about to take a turn for the worse, although there is no immediate evidence to back up this theory. Sightings have been an occasional feature of the region for several hundred years. Among the most notable witnesses are Commodore Stephen Decatur (1779–1820), who allegedly shot at the beast although failed to harm it, and Joseph Bonaparte (1768–1844), one-time king of Spain and brother of the French emperor Napoleon Bonaparte, who saw the devil when he was living in America.

But the number of accounts that came pouring forth in during one week in January 1909 was unprecedented. The Jersey Devil was seen in flight and on the ground. The fire department of West Collingwood allegedly trained its hoses on the beast, but it escaped uninjured. Its bizarre tracks were to be found everywhere – even on rooftops – in the snow that blanketed the district. Two trappers who tried to follow a trail discovered the owner of the prints leapt over fences 1.5m (5ft) high – and also squeezed through 20cm (8in) gaps. Many people, although they did not see it in the flesh, heard its barks and piercing screams. It left behind a trail of farm animal corpses and even pet dogs suffering bad wounds.

With good reason, the small communities scattered around the Pine Barrens were rivetted by the stories and limp with fear. No one could explain the oddities surrounding the Jersey Devil. Some hoaxers took advantage of the fevered atmosphere to play tricks on the public, including planting tracks with a stuffed bear's paw. Two men, Jacob Hope and Norman Jefferies, even claimed they had captured it. They covered a kangaroo with green paint and feathers, placed deer antlers on its head and charged gullible punters a fee for a peek. However, even when the pranksters had been discovered, there was

Could a corner of North America really be haunted by a devilish beast of a species unknown to mankind? In the early years of the last century, a cluster of appearances by a grotesque winged creature paralyzed villages across the state of New Jersey

still plenty of evidence that defied explanation.

Clearly it has not been a kangaroo causing a stir in New Jersey, but the precise identity of the flying fiend remains unknown. Some people think it is a prehistoric relic that has lived – and may still be living – hidden in a subterranean cavern. The evidence for this theory is based on the proportions of the footprints, recorded in 1909 and at other times, that are similar to those of a pterodactyl.

Others are convinced that a large bird, such as a crane, is to blame, and another alternative is that the creature is of supernatural origin. Since 1909 sightings have diminished in number, although they do still occur. Some locals believe the advent of street lighting, wide roads and fast cars is keeping the creature at bay.

In 1957 the Department of Conservation is believed to have discovered a corpse of an unknown beast, with prominent hind legs and feathers. Could this have been the remains of the Jersey Devil? If so, could it be that the beast has finally been laid to rest, or will he continue to haunt the residents of New Jersey? At the moment there is little to indicate exactly what struck terror into the hearts of witnesses almost a century ago. It is hard to believe that their collective imagination was the only thing fuelling the whole episode. Yet until another body is discovered and undergoes analysis, imagination is all that underpins the story of the Jersey Devil.

EL CHUPACABRAS

In the 1990s the world was gripped by a cryptozoological mystery that has yet to be solved. Across the Americas, attacks in the dead of night left farm animals dead, their bodies drained of blood. But just who or what was responsible for the vampiric assaults, no one could say.

At first the attacks occurred solely in Puerto Rico, a Caribbean island lying some 1,600km (990 miles) off the Florida coast. Then the focus switched to Mexico, where a cluster of similar events made the news headlines. Before long there were reports of farm animals with single puncture wounds in their lifeless necks or chests in countries as diverse as Brazil, the Dominican Republic, Argentina, Bolivia, Chile, Columbia, El Salvador, Panama, Peru and the United States. Conspicuously, the flesh of the dead animal was left intact.

A suspect came to the fore, dubbed El Chupacabras which, translated from Spanish, means 'goat-sucker'. There were numerous sightings of it, and these appear to fall into three different categories.

The first is an upright lizard standing some 1.25–1.75m (4–5.8ft), with scaly green-grey skin and sharp spines on its back. The horrific picture is completed with a forked tongue and fangs. Alternatively, the chupacabras has been described as a wallaby- or kangaroo-style creature with a dog's face covered by coarse fur. The last of the trio of descriptions is a hairless dog with a pronounced spinal ridge. All of the above have in common red eyes, three-toed tracks and a distinctive screeching or hissing sound. Sometimes witnesses detected a sulphurous odour in the vicinity of a chupacabras. More tantalizing still are the reports that the goat-suckers have been seen at the same time that UFOs were spotted cruising in an area.

The first chupacabras attack is generally recognized as being in Orocovis in Puerto Rico in 1995 when eight sheep were found dead. Allegedly, their bodies were entirely drained of blood. In August the same year at least 150 barnyard animals were slaughtered in the same ghoulish manner. Three months later came another spate of deaths and the first sightings of the creature deemed responsible.

CRIMSON-EYED BEAST

A hairy, crimson-eyed beast came through the window of an urban home to rip a child's teddy bear to pieces. In its wake there was a slime puddle and a piece of rancid meat. Another witness claimed the chupacabras disappeared before his eyes, while a third decided it was a member of the monkey family. Unsurprisingly, the population of Puerto Rico was terrified by events. Mobs several hundred strong roamed the countryside at night on the trail of the monster but failed to capture it.

Could the chupacabra be a kind of vampire bat? The creature has frequently been compared to a horned Satan

In the early months of 1996 there was a lull in the killings, coinciding with some unseasonably cold weather. Observers came to the conclusion that the goat-sucker had hibernated to escape the chill. In March it was back, though, having killed thirty cocks and hens belonging to farmer Arturo Rodriguez. Shortly afterwards a strange creature walking on two legs, with red eyes, pointy ears, fangs and claws was spotted by a boy called Ovidio Mendez. The creature made no threatening moves towards young Ovidio before it finally bolted. Police were called to the scene, but they failed to find any further clues about the beast's identity. Scientists on the island stuck to their theory that dogs or perhaps even rhesus monkeys were to blame.

STARVING BATS

By 1996, when chupacabras activity was focused on the United States, the response from the population was similarly fearful. In Florida, a police department spokesman commented: 'People here are hysterical.' Meanwhile in San Salvador, attacks of the same nature were firmly blamed on vampire bats. The bats were starving, the government minister elaborated, for vampire bats rarely, if ever, kill their food source. By the end of 1996, one Mexican newspaper reported that there had been forty-six domestic attacks involving more than 300 animals and four people.

Since then, chupacabras killings have diminished, but are certainly still in evidence. Farming folk in affected areas remain cautious or even terrified. Different national authorities are united in their dismissal of events as being the work of wild animals or the product of fertile imaginations, fatally combined with sensationalism in the press.

Were chupacabras around before the 1990s? There are sporadic reports of bizarre animal slayings in the Americas before this date, which some observers now believe fit the modus operandi of the beast. Cattle deaths in one area of the United States in the 1970s were thought to have been the work of a rogue condor, but perhaps the truth was more sinister.

Speculation that chupacabras existed years ago is mainly based on their apparent facial likeness to the gargoyles that adorn old European buildings. If we accept that this string of farm animal killings is more than a bizarre coincidence that can be blamed on various starving predators, then what is the explanation? The hypotheses are fascinating, even if some are barely credible.

Biblical scholars pointed to the fact that demonic creatures of this type were forecast as a precursor to the apocalypse in the Book of Revelation. Elsewhere, a clairvoyant monk claimed the chupacabras were representative of a race of vampires that could only be countered with a laser beam or silver bullet. Another group decided these were creatures from space almost certainly infected with deadly diseases, whose intention was to cripple the human race. Failing that, they could be alien pets given some freedom on the planet after a long space voyage, with the mother ship hovering nearby.

Thinking along similar though not identical lines, there were those who felt the chupacabras were the horrible results of a genetic experiment that had gone badly awry. Humans or aliens could have carried out such experiments, and then let loose the hideous spawn of their research. This would explain why the governments of afflicted countries were slow with a response at times of crisis, unwilling to admit to clandestine or unethical experimentation.

There is, of course, the suggestion that chupacabras is a supernatural beast. The paranormal argument is given credence by the few examples of animals attacked by the beast and killed within cages that have remained intact. As in the case of the child whose teddy was ripped to pieces by an unknown beast, there are often traces of slime among the animal corpses. There is no firm evidence yet as to what this substance might be.

The mysterious chupacabras looms large for those faced with the consequences of its actions, but there is no consensus about what it actually is. For now its activities provoke more questions than answers. The prospect of this cryptozoo-conundrum being resolved in the near future appears remote.

CROP CIRCLES

While some crop circles are just circular indentations, others appear to show complex mathematical equations and scientific symbols, leading people to believe that intelligent beings constructed them

The inexplicable formation of flattened circles in fields of crops has gripped our imagination since the first recorded evidence in a seventeenth-century woodcut. They range from complex geometric patterns and DNA symbols to more delicate versions that look like snowflakes and spiders' webs. While enthusiastic hoaxers may be responsible for many crop circles and patterns, not all can be dismissed so easily.

ROLLING HEDGEHOGS

In the mid-1980s, the crop circle phenomenon gained momentum, as hundreds of patterns began appearing in the fields of southern England. More outlandish explanations – flying saucers, fairies, field sprites and the Devil himself – were quickly laughed off by a sceptical media. But 'natural' explanations, such as rolling hedgehogs, mating foxes, plasma clouds, whirlwinds and changes in the earth's magnetic field hardly seemed more credible. Within a few years, many commentators had agreed that the circles were all just a big hoax.

Soon newspapers were revealing how gangs of tricksters armed with ropes, planks, surveyors' tape, stakes and plastic garden rollers were touring the shires to make their mark in the dead of night. These groups of hoaxers even gained a measure of notoriety and were given names – Merlin & Co, The Snake, Spiderman, The Bill Bailey Gang – but the undisputed grand old men of British 'cereology' were known simply as Doug and Dave. In 1992, Doug Bower and Dave Chorley admitted to devoting more than twenty-five years to making crop circles. This seemed ample proof for the sceptics that all circles were hoaxes. And yet a couple of successful pranksters working for a few years in southern England could not explain historical and worldwide

reports of crop circles. This was certainly not the end of the story …

There is nothing new about crop circles. One of the earliest documented reports appeared in 1686, in *The Natural History of Staffordshire* by Robert Plot, a Professor of Chemistry at Oxford University. Professor Plot was seeking to discover a 'higher principle' behind the formation of crop circles. He set out to debunk the then popular theories (rutting deer, urinating cattle and, perhaps inevitably, fairies) and decided that electrical storms were to blame.

'They must needs be the effects of lightning exploded from the clouds most times in a circular manner,' he wrote. The energy would emerge from the cloud 'so as at due distance to become a circle and in that forme to strike the earth.' Occasionally, he believed, the energy would form rectangular shapes – reflected in the more unusual crop patterns.

UFO NEST

While southern England remains a hot-spot for crop circles, they are by no means unique to this corner of the world. Similar markings have been reported in Japan and North America, and perhaps the most celebrated link between a circle site and a UFO came in 1966 with Australia's 'saucer nest' case at Tully, north Queensland. On 19 January of that year, George Pedley, a 28-year-old banana farmer, was driving his tractor past Horseshoe Lagoon when he saw a dull, blue-grey UFO, roughly 8m x 3m (26ft x 10ft) and shaped like 'two saucers face to face'. The UFO apparently rose out of the swamp grass, dipped slightly and accelerated away at extraordinary speed. Pedley could hear a hissing sound above the noise of his engine.

When Pedley ran to look in the lagoon he found a circular area about 9m (30ft) across where the reeds

> A banana farmer was driving his tractor past Horseshoe Lagoon when he saw a blue-grey UFO shaped like 'two saucers face to face'

had been flattened. Three hours later, the reeds had floated back to form a clockwise radial pattern – similar to some 'basic' crop circles. Investigations by the police and Royal Australian Air Force were inconclusive, but the most likely explanation was said to be a 'willy willy' – a peculiar type of small whirlwind that occurs in warmer parts of Australia and is known to create a hissing sound.

If this was indeed the explanation, then the UFO shape witnessed by Pedley was simply a huge mass of debris sucked up by the twister as it moved off. However it does not fit with Pedley's clear description of the craft (he was standing just 30m away) and fails to account for a distinct lack of debris left on the ground. Neither does it explain why a 'willy willy', which is associated with thunderstorms, should strike Horseshoe Lagoon on a windless, sunny day.

WHIRLWIND VORTEX

Nonetheless, the whirlwind theory is held by many experts to be at least feasible. In 1988, British consultant meteorologist Dr Terence Meaden of the Tornado and Storm Research Organisation, went so

Some experts believe that simple crop circles could be formed by a whirlwind vortex touching down into a crop, flattening it and then moving on

far as to claim the mystery had been solved. He told an Oxford conference that most genuine crop circles were formed near hills where wind, gusting on one side, caused a vortex of gyrating air to suddenly spiral downwards.

'EYE' OF THE CIRCLE

Three years later, he seemed to have eye-witness confirmation of his theory. Gary and Vivienne Tomlinson of Guildford, Surrey, told how they were caught in the 'eye' of a circle as it was being made in a Hampshire cornfield. Mrs Tomlinson recalled:

'There was a tremendous noise. We looked up to see if it was caused by a helicopter, but there was nothing. We felt a strong wind pushing us from the side and above. It was forcing down on our heads – yet incredibly my husband's hair was standing on end.

'Then the whirling air seemed to branch into two and zig-zag off into the distance. We could still see it, like a light mist or fog, shimmering as it moved. As it disappeared we were left standing in a corn circle with the corn flattened all around us. Everything became very still again and we were left with a tingly feeling.'

ELECTRIC ATMOSPHERE

Other scientists believe that electrically super-charged air plays a key role in the formation of crop circles. Professor Yoshihiko Ohtsuki of Tokyo's Waseda University stated: 'The circles are caused by an elastic plasma, which is a very strong form of ionized air. In an experiment … we created a plasma fireball which, if it touched a plate covered in aluminium powder, created beautiful circles and rings just like the ones seen in fields.'

This theory of naturally occurring bodies of plasma has been used to explain other apparently anomalous phenomena. Ball lightning is a mysterious feature that takes the form of a ball of fire or glowing air about 60cm or so across. It will bob

about, sometimes bouncing off objects without so much as touching them, but at other times will explode with a deafening bang and considerable force when it approaches a solid object. Unfortunately it has yet to be proved that such a plasma can actually form naturally.

Some years bring more circles than others, and 1991 has long been regarded as the best of several vintage crops, so to speak, by British cereologists. Apart from the Tomlinsons' bizarre encounter, southern England seemed to be alive with furtive circle-makers, including one formation on farmland right next to the British Prime Minister's country retreat, Chequers.

Further west, near Bristol, Eddie Wise spent four nights in a Wiltshire field which had been the site of previous crop circle activity. He was not disappointed in his vigil, and claimed to have witnessed an enormous alien spaceship land. 'There were no lights but I could see what appeared to be windows,' he said. 'A long object was lowered from the base of the craft and when it touched down in the field everything became quite still.'

UFO LINK

Even some of the crop circle hoaxers believe in a UFO link. No less an authority than Doug Bower, the godfather of circle pranksters, swore he had seen UFOs – reminding onlookers that just because some formations are obvious hoaxes, this does not mean that they all are. As Ray Cox, chairman of the UK Centre for Crop Circle Studies, put it in a 2005 interview with the *Guardian* newspaper: 'Crop circles are an ongoing enigma unfortunately coloured by people who want to believe extraordinary things, and hoaxers. They make some very beautiful things, but I wish they'd leave it alone so that science can get on with trying to evaluate the real thing.'

The fact is that the formation of genuine crop circles remains a mystery to baffle even the world's best scientists. Whether they are formed by the atmospheric conditions on earth, or by extraterrestrials touching down for a visit, the forces at work in our fields lie far beyond human comprehension.

LEY LINES

In 1921, an English mill owner called Alfred Watkins discovered a strange feature of the British landscape – the alignment of ancient sites and natural features across many miles. He called these connections 'ley lines' after the Saxon word ley, meaning 'clearing'. Today the debate over their purpose and origins still rages.

THE REAL ISSUE

Most open-minded archaeologists accept that ley lines exist. True, it is possible to quibble over detail – a burial mound may be bisected at one edge rather than the centre, for instance – yet given the effects of agriculture and land management over several thousand years such imprecisions must be expected. The real issue lies not in proving the leys are there, but in interpreting them.

Watkins built up knowledge of his subject over many years travelling the rolling hills of his native Herefordshire. During visits to mills and farms he would note familiar landmarks, photograph them and plot their locations on a map. Combined with his expertise in local history, folklore and place names he soon had an unrivalled insight into the county's geography. When he eventually realized what he had discovered, he likened the feeling to 'a flood of ancestral memory'.

In his first short book, *Early British Trackways*, Watkins describes how the flash of insight occurred one summer's day: 'I had no theory when, out of what appeared to be a tangle, I got hold of the one right end of this string of facts and found to my amazement that it unwound in an orderly fashion and complete logical sequence,' he wrote.

An ancient trackway typical of the ley lines discovered by Alfred Watkins. The network of trails extends across the whole of the British landscape

'A visit to Blackwardine led me to note on the map a straight line starting from Croft Ambury, lying on parts of Croft Lane past the Broad, over hill points, through Blackwardine, over Risbury Camp, and through the high ground at Stretton Grandison, where I surmised a Roman station. I followed up the clue of sighting from hilltop, unhampered by other theories, found it yielding astounding results in all districts, the straight lines to my amazement passing over and over again through the same class of objects ...'

LEY LOGIC

In his main book on the subject, *The Old Straight Track* – published in 1925 and still the definitive work on leys – Watkins explains his theory in depth. He believed he had uncovered an ancient system of trackways, initially laid out as far back as the Stone Age. These would then have been adopted by subsequent cultures and preserved, some of them right up to the present day. The tracks were marked by obvious reference points to assist travellers, and they might bisect man-made landmarks such as castles, churches, burial mounds, standing stones and stone circles, as well as natural features like hilltops, 'notches' on a ridge, ponds and even prominent groups of trees.

There were some obvious flaws in Watkins' argument, not least that many castles and churches were constructed long after the neolithic period when he believed leys were created. However, it is generally accepted by historians that these structures were often built on sites that were already occupied or had some ancient significance. It follows that certain ley markers are original and others evolved from their predecessors. As for trees, while it is true that a few British species date back thousands of years, it is also quite possible for their descendants to occupy the same spot. Very often, clumps of trees are found atop the sites of their forebears.

As mentioned earlier, some sceptics accuse ley hunters of being too 'flexible' in their enthusiasm to plot lines through map landmarks. They argue that a ley is either straight or not, and that a few metres out is not good enough. Watkins himself was more relaxed about these measurements, noting that

'ancient methods of alignment ... tended to pass through the edges of circles, not taking their centres as is now the case.'

But how would the ancient inhabitants of Britain have planned straight tracks, without modern methods of measurement and navigation? Watkins believed the 'straight-sighted track' would have been planned using fire beacons at strategic points and a team of men with staves. (He even suspected that these surveyors were the inspiration for the chalk figure of the Long Man of Wilmington in Sussex.) Once the ley was plotted, scrub and woodland along the line would be cleared and additional markers added.

COLOUR DETECTIVE

Place names formed a key component of Watkin's theory. He pinpointed fields called ley or lea as possible sites. Place names containing references to the colours red and white suggested pottery or salt trade routes respectively. It followed that a place name referring to the colour gold was linked to the transport of precious metals, but Watkins later postulated that the answer was more mystical: a 'gold ley' was aligned to the midsummer sunrise.

Black was harder to explain, until Watkins realized that in Anglo-Saxon times the word meant something quite different. Black could mean shining, white or pale – perhaps a reference either to the signal fires or reflective ponds. Watkins decoded many ley names, tracing their symbolism back into the mists of the past.

THE DOUBTERS

But however mysterious and captivating this might be, a key question remained. What was the motivation for constructing leys? To our knowledge, there were almost no straight roads and paths in the

ancient British landscape, apart from the Roman legacy. Are we expected to believe that a tradition of straight track-building simply died out, and that ley lines are all that remain? Isn't it just as likely that landmarks form purely chance alignments and that ley followers are all wishful thinkers? Over the years, leading mathematicians have attempted to illustrate this, with varying degrees of success.

CRUDE EXPERIMENT

Watkins answered his critics with a crude, though intriguing, experiment using a map of the Andover district. He noted the positioning of 51 churches on the map and counted the number of alignments between them. He found that there were 38 alignments of three churches, eight alignments of four churches and one of five churches. He then marked 51 random crosses on an identically-sized piece of plain paper.

This produced 34 three-cross alignments, one of four crosses and none of five crosses. Watkins concluded that the number of four-church alignments in Andover was 'exceedingly strong evidence of deliberate alignment'.

If this sounds unscientific, remember that dozens of known leys bisect considerably more than four landmarks. For example, at Glastonbury there are at least seven landmarks aligned over 34km (21 miles), at Stonehenge there are eight over 35.5km (22 miles), and one ley line bisecting Cambridge has ten landmarks aligned across just 22km (13.5 miles). Nor are 'old straight tracks' unique to the British Isles. In the western Cordillera of the Andes one track stretches for 32km (20 miles) across a hilly landscape at a height of 3,960m (13,000ft).

The Long Man of Wilmington in Sussex: could this be a depiction of one of the ancient surveyors who plotted the ley lines?

MYSTERIOUS PURPOSE

The question of what leys were for remains a tantalizing mystery. It could be they were simply a neolithic version of motorways, allowing travellers to take the straightest, clearest, safest route irrespective of whether this meant climbing a hill or traversing a river. In the busy, urbanized world of today, we generally prefer to take the easiest path between two points, avoiding hills and obstacles even if it is longer as the crow flies. But it does not follow that Stone Age humans would have done the same. Given their active, outdoor lifestyle, striding up a hill or two would hardly have counted as strenuous.

Modern research has vindicated one aspect of Watkins's original theory: we now know that stone-age humans did travel long distances. Scientists can study the chemical composition of teeth to deduce where a human was living when his or her teeth were forming in childhood. The skeleton of a man found near Stonehenge proved to have been brought up in southern Germany, while a body in Italy was that of a woman who had spent her childhood in the Balkans. If humans were travelling such long distances they would have needed routemarkers of just the type Watkins postulated.

Leys may have had other practical or religious purposes – perhaps they were used for astronomical alignment (see Stonehenge on page 274). Inevitably they have taken their place in New Age thinking, and some pagans believe they were intended to channel an undefined 'earth energy' between sacred sites. Others claim they are linked to UFOs.

Our landscape is criss-crossed with these mysterious lines, but the truth is, we still do not know why they are there. More than eighty years after Watkins' breakthrough discovery, their presence in the British countryside remains as enigmatic as ever.

> Some pagans believe ley lines were intended to channel 'earth energy' between sacred sites. Others claim they are linked to UFOs

ROGUE WAVES

An 1867 illustration of the effects of a tsunami, which unlike rogue waves are caused by shifts on the ocean floor and volcanic eruptions

The notion of giant waves higher than ten-storey buildings looming up from the earth's oceans was once dismissed as the fantasy of melodramatic sailors. Now science has stepped in to prove that not only do rogue waves like this actually occur, they are even fairly commonplace.

The sight of a voluminous wall of water inspires awe and terror. Mighty ships that seem invincible on shore look miniature and vulnerable when dwarfed by such a vast amount of water, rearing into the air. Many have simply been swamped and sunk within seconds, leaving little trace of their existence.

In 1995 the luxury liner *Queen Elizabeth II* encountered a 30m (100ft) wave during a voyage across the North Atlantic. Captain Ronald Warwick said: 'It looked as if we were going into the white cliffs of Dover.' It was this encounter, reported and recorded by impeccable witnesses and the most modern of devices that forced scientists to take the old sailors' tales seriously. They soon realized that waves like these are not tsunamis. Those gigantic waves are otherwise known as tidal waves as their impact when they strike land is much like a vast tidal surge rushing inland. Like the tsunami that happened in the Indian Ocean on 26 December 2004, these waves appear to be quite small out at sea, being only a few feet tall though hundreds of feet across. They become dangerous only when they reach the shallow waters around coasts. Instead the rogue waves, measuring some 25–30m (80–100ft) tall are most dangerous at sea. Their hazardous nature is made far worse by the fact that they seem to happen randomly and nobody knows when or where they are going to occur next.

OFFICIAL INVESTIGATION

Film footage of the phenomenon is rare and sailors' stories were generally thought to be subject to exaggeration. After the *Queen Elizabeth II* incident a film shot in 1980 by a lucky survivor of a rogue wave was re-examined. It showed a great mass of water rising out of the sea and crashing down on the deck of his ship. This rare film image shows the wave in question towering above other waves in the water at that time. Calculations, using the known height of the ship's mast as a guide, estimate its height to have been as much as 20m (65ft) – this figure could, in fact, be increased to 30m (100ft) because a huge trough of water usually precedes this type of wave, increasing its height substantially.

DANGER AT SEA

In 2000, by which time it was calculated that severe weather had sent 200 supertankers and container ships exceeding 200m (650ft) in length to the sea floor over a period of just two decades, an official investigation into major wave activity was launched, orchestrated by the European Commission.

The investigators used satellite information from the European Space Agency about the state of the oceans during three weeks spanning February and March 2001. They proved that during that short snapshot of time, there were more than ten giant waves around the globe measuring over 23m (75ft).

'Two large ships sink every week on average, but the cause is never studied to the same detail as an air crash. It simply gets put down to "bad weather",' explained senior scientist Wolfgang Rosenthal, of GKSS Forschungszentrum in Germany, one of the major partners of the probe. 'Having proved they [rogue waves] existed in higher numbers than anyone expected, the next step is to analyze if they can be forecasted.'

Of course, it is not only ships that are at risk. Oil platforms are also vulnerable to these giant waves and in twelve years, no fewer than 466 were recorded to have unleashed their power over the North Sea's Goma oilfield. Appearing seemingly out of nowhere, these huge walls of water are terrifying in their power and wreak havoc on anything in their path, but they then disappear as suddenly as they arose.

If, then, the rogue wave is now an accepted and ever-increasing phenomenon, what is believed to be its cause? Oceanographers remain baffled, as the three factors that are key to the development and size of normal waves – wind speed, the amount of open water and the length of time the wind blows across the sea – would seem not to apply in this case. If all waves are subject to the same conditions, why is it that one wave grows to a height of 34m (111ft), for example, while its neighbours might be only 10m (33ft) high?

One theory is that each rogue wave is the result of smaller waves joining together to form one huge mass of water. This could be caused when fast-flowing currents collide with opposing strong winds, slowing the waves down and allowing them to unite. As many rogue waves seem to occur in areas which are prone to exactly these conditions – such as the Gulf Stream, the Kuro Shio current to the south of Japan and around the legendary Cape Horn – this would appear to be a plausible explanation of some of the giant waves. However, it fails to shed any light on why such waves occur in waters where there are no fast-flowing currents.

Another explanation of this phenomenon is based on the chaos theory, a mathematical model that is applied more frequently to financial markets and the weather. With this rationale stating that tiny changes can lead to disproportionate results, it is possible that the slightest change in wave height, wind speed or direction could result in the creation of a colossal column of water. The mathematical equations that are being used to test this theory would appear to show that there might be some truth behind this hypothesis, although further tests will be necessary before any definitive conclusions can be drawn.

The fact remains that the cause of the rogue wave is still far from clear. Perhaps as the science of oceanography progresses, an explanation will present itself before long, giving human beings more understanding and awareness of the complexity of the world in which they live.

THE SS WARATAH

With broad acceptance of rogue waves in the scientific community now established, it seems likely that at least one enduring ship mystery has been solved. This concerns one dramatic episode which gained a place in history for bizarre circumstances surrounding the disappearance of a ship.

In 1909, the SS *Waratah*, flagship of the Blue Anchor Line, vanished in broad daylight after setting sail from Durban, heading for Cape Town, taking with her 211 passengers and crew. Subsequent generations have been fascinated by this sudden disappearance, not least since several passengers displayed a strong sense of foreboding about the ship's fate.

In 1910, the Board of Trade carried out an inquiry into the disaster in London, where company director Claude Sawyer, a first-class passenger travelling on the *Waratah*, related his lucky escape. Together with fears about the ship's listing, he suffered from troubling dreams. 'I saw a man with a long sword in a peculiar dress. He was holding the sword in his right hand and it was covered with blood. I saw this vision three times.

'The second time it came I thought, "I will know it again," and the third time I looked at it so intently that I could almost design it, sword and all, even now.

'Next day I mentioned the dream to a gentleman and he said, "It's a warning." Then I began to think why I should be warned and I was anxious to leave the ship.' The fortunate Sawyer took heed of his warning dreams and decided to remain in Durban, while his fellow passengers boarded the ship again.

On the night the three-year-old *Waratah* disappeared, Sawyer was once again subject to a vision. 'That night I had another dream. I saw the *Waratah* in big waves, one went over her bows and pressed her down. She rolled over on her starboard side and disappeared.'

He was not the only passenger to have qualms. But he was luckier than one girl, known only as Evelyn, who confided to a friend that on three consecutive nights before embarking she had dreamt the *Waratah* would sink. In the aftermath of the disaster, this friend wrote to a British newspaper saying that the last time she saw 15-year-old Evelyn she had been 'frantically clutching the handrail as she was led weeping up the gangway'.

Another passenger, Nicholas Sharp, declared the

life-saving apparatus on board was inadequate. The ship's chief officer had advised him to secure passage on another vessel as 'this one will be a coffin for somebody'.

RAISING THE ALARM

The *Waratah* was sighted out at sea on the morning of 27 July by another steamship. Only when she failed to turn up in Cape Town was the alarm raised. Despite a widespread search, no wreckage or bodies were found.

It was known that bad weather swept across the ship's route on 28 July. That same day a mounted rifleman on shore reported a ship foundering at the mouth of the Xora River. Nearly a month later crew from a steamer called the *Tottenham* may have spotted wreckage and corpses in the water, but the captain refused to deviate from his course. The Board of Trade inquiry did not conclude that either of these sightings definitely related to the missing vessel. A lifebelt belonging to the ill-starred ship finally washed up on the shores of New Zealand in 1912, a poignant symbol of the fate of those on board.

Could the Waratah *have been hit by a rogue wave? A steamer called the* Tottenham *may have spotted wreckage and corpses in the water but the captain refused to deviate from his course*

Speculation about the Waratah came to the attention of Sir Arthur Conan Doyle, author and spiritualist, who decided to hold a séance to determine what had happened to the doomed ship. Spirits of the passengers told him the *Waratah* had been hit by a giant wave, which sent it immediately to the ocean floor.

Ninety years after the *Waratah* vanished, marine historian Emlyn Brown thought that he had located its wreckage using sonar and filmed it with closed-circuit television cameras during a deep-water dive. He had been financed by Adrian White, whose grandfather, a ship's steward, perished in the tragedy. The ship in fact turned out to be the *Nailsea Meadow*, a cargo ship carrying British Honey tanks torpedoed in the Second World War by a German U-Boat.

The *Waratah* may well be one of the untold thousands of ships to be claimed by rogue waves, its loss remains remarkable for the psychic sub-text now firmly attached to the story. For those embarking on subsequent voyages, it is spine-chilling to think that the incredible sight of a rogue wave was the last thing those unfortunate passengers ever witnessed.

Arthur Conan Doyle, author and spiritualist, who decided to hold a séance to determine what happened to the Waratah

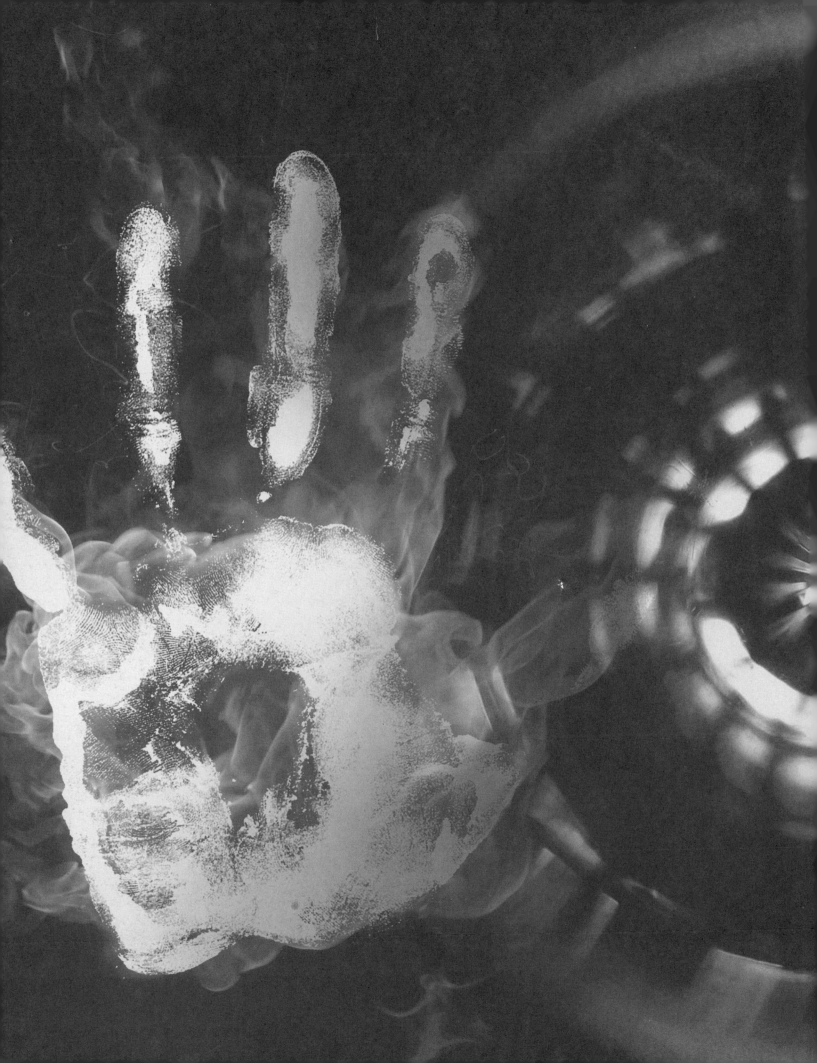

SECTION 3
PARANORMAL EVENTS

The paranormal is no respector of time or place. It can intrude into our world of safe assumptions and apparent normality without warning. Nobody knows when a poltergeist will take up residence in a home or workplace, hurling furniture around and stealing objects, only to return them days later. Nor can it be predicted when a UFO will come down to land, a curse strike down an apparently wealthy family, nor when a human being will spontaneously burst into flames. Such paranormal events occur without warning, and end just as suddenly, leaving behind dramatic and often fatal signs of their passing.

REINCARNATION

Most of us are kept busy enjoying or enduring our everyday lives, too frantic to hear the quiet inner voice that speaks of another place, another time. But for a minority of people, details of a previous existence encroach on the present, making a strong case for the principles of reincarnation.

Several major faiths, including Hinduism, Sikhism, Jainism and others give credence to life after death. Buddhists have a similar but not identical philosophy of re-birth, although Tibetan Buddhists invest heavily in the idea of reincarnation in order to identify legitimate heirs to the role of Dalai Lama.

SEARCH FOR THE DALAI LAMA

Tenzin Gyatso, today's Dalai Lama (pictured left), is believed to be the reincarnation of his predecessor. Indeed, he was born in the same year his predecessor died (1935), to a peasant family in north-eastern Tibet. A Buddhist dignitary trying to divine the identity of the new Dalai Lama had a vision in which he saw a monastery. Aides were given detailed descriptions of the monastery and dispatched across the region to find it.

They discovered one that fitted the description in Taktser. There they encountered a two-year-old boy who demanded the rosary being worn by one of the party that had once belonged to the deceased Dalai Lama. When he correctly identified the men in the deputation by name and rank, it was deemed that he was the embodiment of the Dalai Lama. He was finally enthroned in 1940.

There is a growing body of evidence in the West to say that earthly life after death is a reality. Two methods have been used to gather examples of past lives: regression through hypnosis in adults and the spontaneous recollections of young children, whose previous lives remain fresh in their memories.

Psychologist Helen Wambach carried out a ten-year survey of past-life recollections among 1,088 subjects. With the exception of only 11 people, the descriptions given about minute details of past lives, including kitchen utensils, clothing and footwear, were uncannily accurate.

She found that the majority of the lives described were in the lower classes, reflecting the appropriate historical distribution. She also discovered that 49.4 per cent of the past lives were female and 50.6 per cent were male, reflecting the correct biological balance. Although she started out as a sceptic, Wambach became convinced by the evidence in front of her. In 1978 she declared: 'I don't believe in reincarnation — I know it!'

CELEBRITY REINCARNATION

Among the celebrities of today are several who are convinced they have lived before. These include Sylvester Stallone, who thinks he has been here no less than four times in the past, and was on one occasion guillotined during the French Revolution. He also claims to have been a boxer who was killed by a knockout punch in the 1930s. Actor Martin Sheen talked of being a cruel US cavalry soldier who was trampled to death by a horse.

Today he has a loathing of horses, which might be linked to his past-life experiences. Singer Englebert Humperdinck thought he once ruled the Roman Empire, while pop goddess Tina Turner has been told she is a reincarnation of the Egyptian queen Hatshepsut.

Shirley MacLaine also claims numerous past lives, among them a Moorish girl living along a pilgrim trail in Spain. Under hypnosis, movie star Glenn Ford was able to speak fluent French, since one of his past lives was spent as a French cavalryman in the reign of Louis XIV.

HYPNOSIS

The fact that hypnosis subjects are suddenly able to speak in a foreign language is one of the oddest and most compelling pieces of evidence about past lives. Other positive benefits such as the relief of long-term illnesses, nightmares or phobias have been felt when the harm supposedly caused by past-life injuries or experiences was addressed.

Opponents to hypnosis believe it is perilous and that beneficial results are unproven. They believe that symptoms people put down to past existences are more likely to be caused by inherited or suppressed memories. Hypnosis might even be making the problem worse by creating a multitude of personalities in a subject, rather than pinpointing true past-life experiences.

The experience of a Colorado housewife who regressed into a supposed past life as Bridey Murphy of 19th-century Ireland was documented in a book. But the account was swiftly debunked when it was proved that no woman of that name was born in the year she had claimed. Nor was her death on record anywhere. Her command of the old Irish language and lifestyle was later deemed to have been learned through a close relationship with an Irish woman in her early years.

Still, the stories relating to hypnotherapy remain intriguing. In 1983, psychologist and former sceptic Peter Ramster featured in a documentary with four women who recounted their past-life experiences. One woman remembered a life in Somerset, England, in the second half of the 18th century. When she was taken to the rural village in question – a place she had never visited before – she was able to find her way around and identify local landmarks, some of which had been long forgotten. Furthermore, it became clear that she had a thorough knowledge of local legends, dialect and families.

> One woman remembered life in rural Somerset in the 18th century. When she was taken there for the first time, she knew her way around

A CHILD'S HISTORY

For many, the coherent and cohesive descriptions of different environments recounted by very small children are altogether more persuasive. One benchmark case is that of Shanti Deva. In 1930, aged 4, Shanti told her parents that she had once lived in a place called Muttra, that she had been a mother of three who died in childbirth and that her previous name had been Ludgi.

Only when they were continually pressed by the youngster did the bewildered family from Delhi investigate. They discovered there was indeed a village called Muttra and that a woman named Ludgi had recently died there. When Shanti was taken to the village, she lapsed into local dialect and recognized her previous-life husband and children. She even gave 24 accurate statements that matched confirmed facts, an impressive feat for such a young child, and one that it would be impossible to hoax.

Since 1967, psychiatrist Dr Ian Stevenson has pioneered the scientific study of spontaneous past-life recollections among infants. Usually a youngster is aged between two and five years old when they describe what went on in a previous existence. In most cases, although not all, recall has faded by the age of seven.

Having interviewed thousands of children from all over the world, Dr Stevenson has discovered some interesting facets to the phenomenon. In some cases, the mother had experienced a prophetic dream, announcing or implying the past-life identity of the child in her womb. Meanwhile, a number of children claiming a previous existence bore birthmarks that corresponded to wounds inflicted on them when they lived before. For example, a boy in India who was born without fingers on one hand remembered that in a prior existence he had put his hand into the blades of a fodder-chopping machine, amputating the digits.

Dr Stevenson aimed to corroborate the verbal evidence of a child with relevant death certificates and interviews with witnesses to both existences.

Critics think the prophetic dreams are no more than wishful thinking. They credit Dr Stevenson with collecting anecdotal rather than scientific evidence.

SHARED RECOLLECTIONS

Yet some of his cases are compelling and strangely thought-provoking. On one occasion, Dr Stevenson made an unannounced visit to a Druze village in Lebanon to see if any children there were subject to past life statements. He was immediately dispatched to the home of 5-year-old Imad Elawar, who had for several years been talking about another life in a different village some 40km distant. Young Imad had even stopped a former neighbour in the street to share recollections about the life he once lived. His first words as a child were Jamileh and Mahmoud, the names of his mistress and uncle in his previous life. Stevenson noted more than 57 separate claims by the child about his past life, the majority of which could be supported with evidence from elsewhere.

While the study of reincarnation has leapt ahead recently, it is a subject that is by no means the preserve of the modern age. In 1824, a Japanese boy called Kastugoro recounted details of a village where he had once lived and the family that was once his own. Despite his tender age, the minutiae he recalled were sufficient to persuade investigators of the day that past lives were a reality.

Throughout the ages, belief in reincarnation has been powerful and widespread. Perhaps we are closer to history than we imagine …

THE CATHOLIC DAUGHTERS

In post-war Britain the concept of reincarnation was considered to be an alien idea peculiar to the exotic Eastern philosophies of Hinduism, Shintoism and Buddhism. So when, in 1962, a Catholic father announced that his daughters were living proof of the existence of reincarnation it was seen as a challenge to the authority of the Church which had declared the concept heretical.

John Pollock had lost his first two daughters, Joanna, 11, and Jacqueline, 6, in May 1957 when a driver lost control of her car and careered into the children near their home in Hexham, Northumberland. Pollock assumed that God had taken his girls to punish him for believing in reincarnation, but a year later, when his wife learnt that she was pregnant, Pollock became convinced that the souls of the two girls would be reborn in order to demonstrate that the church was wrong to deny the natural process of death and rebirth. When his wife's gynaecologist informed the couple that they were to expect a single child Pollock assured him he was wrong – there would be twins, both girls. On 4 October 1958, he was proved correct.

The twins were monozygotic (meaning they developed from a single egg) yet the second twin, Jennifer, was born with a thin white line on her forehead in the same place that her dead sister Jacqueline had sustained a wound while falling from her bicycle. Her parents were also puzzled by the appearance of a distinctive birth mark on her left hip, identical to the one that Jacqueline had.

The girls grew up in Whitley Bay, but when they were three and a half their father took them back to Hexham and was astonished to hear the girls point out places they had never seen in this life and talk about where they had played, even though they had left the town before they could walk. They knew when they were approaching their school although it was out of sight, and they recognized their old home as they passed it although their father had said nothing.

Six months later, they were given Joanna and Jacqueline's toy box. They identified all their dead sisters' dolls by name. They were also observed playing a game that their mother, Florence Pollock, found disturbing. Jennifer lay on the floor with her head in Gillian's lap, play-acting that she was dying and her sister would say, 'The blood's coming out of your eyes. That's where the car hit you.' Neither parent had discussed the accident with the children. On another occasion their mother heard them screaming in the street. When she came out she saw

them clutching each other and looking terrified in the direction of a stationary car with its motor running. The girls were crying, 'The car! It's coming at us!'

The possibility that they might be the reincarnation of their elder, deceased sisters brought no comfort to their mother who could not reconcile the evidence of her own eyes with the Church's edict that belief in reincarnation was a mortal sin. For this reason she made an excellent impartial witness. To Florence Pollock's relief, however, the incident with the car marked the end of the affair. At the age of five the girls abruptly ceased to seem conscious of the

The girls pointed out places they had never seen before in this life

connection with their former lives and developed into normal, healthy children.

This is consistent with a belief that at the age of five all children lose their link with the other world. At this point, to borrow an expression from the esoteric tradition, 'the veil comes down'. Children cease to play with imaginary friends and become grounded in the 'real' world. And perhaps something of the magic of childhood and worldly innocence dies with it.

SPONTANEOUS HUMAN COMBUSTION

It is beyond doubt that some unfortunate people are found to have dropped dead from unexplained causes, but what makes their demise enter the realms of the paranormal is the fact that their bodies are reduced to ashes by a fire the causes of which cannot be identified and which seems to have affected nothing around the body. To all appearances, the body seems to have ignited spontaneously and to have been consumed without setting fire to anything else. The phenomenon is rare, but has been given the name of Spontaneous Human Combustion by those who research it.

THE UNFORTUNATE COUNTESS

Perhaps the earliest known case of Spontaneous Human Combustion is that of the Countess Cornelia Bandi who met a grisly end in Verona on 4 April 1731. The details of the case were recorded by the local magistrate, Bianchini, who ruled out foul play but was unable to explain what had killed the countess.

On the evening of 3 April Countess Bandi had retired to bed as usual. Her maid had helped her to undress and put her jewellery back in its boxes. She had then sat chatting to the countess for some time before leaving for her own chamber. Nothing had appeared to be amiss. Next morning the maid returned to awaken her mistress. Even before

Spontaneous human combustion has been recorded over many centuries: it occurs when the human body is reduced to ashes by causes which can not be explained

entering the room she could smell the pungent stench of burned clothing, but it was not until she opened the door that she realized the full horror of the situation.

The bedclothes where turned back and rumpled as if the countess had thrown them off in a hurry. Four feet from the bed lay what was left of the countess's body. 'There was a heap of ashes, two legs untouched with stockings on, between which lay the head, the brains half of the back part of the skull and of the whole chin burned to ashes, among which were found three fingers, blackened but intact. All the rest was ashes which had this quality, that they left in the hand a greasy and stinking moisture.'

Nor was that all. A thin layer of soot was spread across the chamber, like several days worth of dust in an abandoned room. The floor had pools of a thick goo which stank and had the texture of glue. Another patch of the same offensive liquid was smeared down one wall underneath a window.

Unsurprisingly the maid fled to call the forces of law and order. They arrived promptly, but very quickly found that the lady's jewels and money were untouched, ruling out the theory that she had been murdered by robbers and the body then burned. There was, in fact, no sign of a forced entry and no indication of how the body had been set alight. The mystery was abandoned as being inexplicable.

A similar case took place on 22 March 1908 in Whitley Bay in northern England. Wilhelmina Dewar shared a house with her sister Margaret, but the two ladies slept in separate rooms. That night the two ladies went to bed as normal. Just after midnight something awoke Margaret.

She checked that there were no prowlers in the house, then smelled smoke and traced the smell to her sister's room. Opening the door, Margaret found that Wilhelmina was dead and her body below the chest had been reduced to a pile of ashes in her bed. The blankets and sheets immediately touching the

Picking up the pieces: the emergency services comb through Mary Reeser's apartment in the wake of her mysterious death in July 1951

body had also been burned, but the bed had not caught fire and the room was untouched by the flames. The body above the chest was intact and the face showed no signs of pain or distress.

Whatever had happened had killed Wilhelmina very quickly.

Margaret Dewar ran out of the house screaming to pound on the door of her neighbour. When the neighbour had gone to look at Wilhelmina's body he sent for the police. The first policeman to arrive found Margaret a gibbering wreck quite unable to answer any questions. The house was sealed off and a doctor summoned. He was unable to find a cause of death and had no explanation for the odd burn pattern of the fire.

REDUCED TO ASHES
The case went to the local coroner as an unexplained death. After listening to the evidence, the coroner declared that the tale was impossible and ordered an adjournment so that everyone involved could go away and think again. Quite what happened during the adjournment is unknown, but it seems that pressure was brought to bear on Margaret Dewar and her neighbours. When the court reconvened the evidence had changed. Now it was said that the unfortunate Wilhelmina had died of a stroke and the body set on fire by a tumbled candle. The coroner recorded a natural death.

Modern interest in the phenomenon was set off by the death of Mrs Mary Reeser of Petersburg, Florida, on 1 July 1951. Neighbours found the body of Mrs Reeser when they could get no reply at her door. With the exception of limb extremities, the body had been reduced to ashes.

Mrs Reeser had been sitting in an armchair when she died. The upholstery and padding of the chair seat had been burned down to the wire springs, but the sides and back of the chair were only singed. The local police told the coroner that the elderly Mrs Reeser was a smoker and theorized that she had fallen asleep when smoking and so had set herself alight.

The idea might have been accepted were it not for

the fact that Dr Wilton Krogman, a forensic scientist who specialized in deaths by fire, happened to be in town and heard of the unusual death in time to carry out his own investigations.

After reviewing the facts of the case, Krogman ended up totally baffled. To reduce bone to ashes needs a temperature of around 3,000 degrees Fahrenheit. If Mrs Reeser's body had been subjected to such temperatures the resulting radiated heat would have set fire to not only the chair, but the carpet, the furniture and everything else in the room. And yet nothing had been so much as charred. 'Were I living in the Middle Ages, I would mutter something about black magic,' concluded Dr Krogman.

With the specialist baffled, the Florida coroner opted for the police's cigarette theory and recorded the incident as 'accidental death'.

The Reeser case brought the phenomenon to the attention of researchers into the paranormal and unusual, but it remained an apparently isolated case until the death of Dr J Irving Bentley, a retired doctor living in Coudersport, Pennsylvania. Dr Bentley lived alone and could walk only with the aid of a zimmer frame. He was, however, in good health and spoke to neighbours on the afternoon of 4 December 1966 when nothing seemed to be wrong. Early on the morning of the 5 December a gas company employee named Don Gosnell arrived to read the meter. He got no reply, but found that Dr Bentley's door was ajar. He went into the home and was immediately aware of a pale blue smoke and an unusual odour hanging around. Gosnell traced the smoke to the bathroom and found himself confronted by an astonishing sight.

On the bathroom floor was a tumbled zimmer frame covered with a pile of ashes from which projected a human leg intact from the knee down. There was a large hole in the floor, where the

> On the floor was a tumbled zimmer frame covered with a pile of ashes from which projected a human leg intact from the knee down

floorboards had burned through, but otherwise the room was untouched by flames or heat. A thin layer of greasy soot covered most surfaces. Gosnell fled to call the fire brigade and the police. When the firemen arrived they found a small burn on the bath, but no sign of how the fire had started.

It was known that Bentley was a heavy smoker, and there were some burn marks around the house apparently caused by carelessly discarded cigarettes. The coroner accepted the idea that Bentley had fallen asleep while smoking, set himself alight and woken up. He had then gone to the bathroom in search of water, but had died and collapsed allowing the fire to consume his body. No attempt was made to explain how the fire could have consumed his body so completely, but left the room virtually untouched. Nor was it explained why his singed dressing gown was in the bathtub. As with the Dewar and Reeser cases it seems the coroner was keen to get some official explanation down so that the case could be filed rather than the coroner being faced by a long and time-consuming inquiry into a possibly paranormal event.

Despite the coroner's finding, the death of Bentley made Spontaneous Human Combustion a major topic among paranormal investigators. Theories began to emerge to account for the phenomenon. These theories took as their starting point the features that seemed to be shared by the cases so far known. The fires took place suddenly and were over relatively quickly. The temperatures attained were very high, but of short duration. There was no obvious source of fire to be found.

One early idea was that the body somehow ignited itself, a theory that gave rise to the phrase of Spontaneous Human Combustion. This theory suggested that each and every cell in the body exploded into flames at the same moment, thus reducing the body to ashes in seconds. This would account for the high temperatures and short duration, and why nearby objects were not burned. However, no mechanism other than supernatural causes could explain this, so some researchers dismissed the idea.

Some suggested that ball lightning might be to blame. This very rare natural phenomenon occurs when electrically charged air forms a plasma ball which heats to extremely high temperatures, then floats through the surrounding air.

It may disperse harmlessly after a few seconds, but if it makes contact with an object able to conduct electricity will explode with a blinding flash. One witness saw ball lightning near Mrs Reeser's house about the time she died. The theory is still held by some, but was dismissed by others due to the lack of other sightings of ball lightning to coincide with instances of Spontaneous Human Combustion.

Another cause of a fire starting might be static electricity. It has long been known that some shoes when worn to walk over some types of carpet can cause a build-up of static electricity.

In extreme cases this can lead to a charge of over 3,000 volts, which when discharged is enough to start a fire if a highly combustible material is close at hand. It now seems that a very few people are susceptible to even higher charges of static electricity – and that they can build up these charges even when not wearing the plastic-soled shoes that cause the charges in others. Such a massive build-up could, it is theorized, set fire to clothing or even human flesh when discharged as a hugely powerful spark.

Sceptics argued that there was always a perfectly normal source of fire, but that it was simply missed by the first people on the scene. A badly burned cigarette end can be missed amid the heaps of ash, while an overturned candle will burn away to nothing. This might be true, but does nothing to explain the strange fact that objects around the body do not catch fire.

The usual explanation for this is the so-called 'wick effect'. This occurs when a smouldering fabric is in contact with oil or fat. The fat melts and is drawn up into the fabric where it burns with a small flame or smoulder, but often at very high temperature.

This is how a candle works. For a wick effect fire to burn for a prolonged period of time it needs to have ready access to large amounts of fat or oil. It has been argued that a human body contains plenty of fat, especially if the person is overweight, and that normal clothing could act as a wick. If a person died suddenly, say of a massive heart attack, and fell so that their clothing came into contact with a candle, cigarette or other source of fire a wick effect fire might be started that would consume the body.

It is an attractive idea, but one that is almost impossible to test. An attempt was made in August 1998 by the BBC TV programme *QED*, which sought to explain the phenomenon in terms of a wick effect fire. Obviously a human body could not be used, so a pig carcass was wrapped in fabric and set alight.

The resulting fire did settle down to a slow wick effect burn that over the period of about eight hours did consume a large part of the pig's body. Pieces of wooden furniture placed close to the burning pig did not catch fire, though one did scorch.

Sceptics hailed the BBC test as an explanation of Spontaneous Human Combustion. Others pointed out flaws. First, the fire did not catch first time and had to be started by soaking a portion of the fabric in petrol. Second, the fire took eight hours to burn part of the pig, while at least some cases of Spontaneous Human Combustion are known to have consumed a body in as little as an hour.

Finally, a pig has thick layers of fat just under the skin, which is ideal for a wick-effect fire, but a human body generally does not.

The explanation for Spontaneous Human Combustion is still to be found but many people swear that it is a natural phenomenon which they have witnessed with their own eyes.

OUT OF BODY EXPERIENCES

*An Out of Body Experience occurs when a person has the sensation
that they are moving outside their body*

As its name suggests, an Out of Body Experience (OOBE) occurs when a person has the sensation that they are moving outside their body. Sometimes they can see their body, apparently left behind while they float off elsewhere, but just as often the person senses that they are in a different place entirely. OOBEs generally occur unprompted, though many occur at times of great stress and some people claim the ability to initiate them almost at will.

Some researchers refer to that part of the person that leaves the body as the 'astral projection', 'astral self' or simply 'astral'. This phrase is employed to try to avoid a discussion of the subject of OOBEs getting bogged down in quasi-religious debates that might be prompted should a word such as 'soul' or 'self' be used, as it has been in the past.

ANCIENT CASES

It is quite clear that many pagan societies believed that it was possible for the astral of a priest or holy man to leave his body to converse with the gods. The ancient Egyptians referred to the astral as the ba, and usually showed it in art as a bird with a human head. Shamans in traditional Asian societies, such as the pre-Buddhist Mongols or modern Siberians, believe that to commune with the spirit world the shaman must enter a trance-like state so that he can leave his body and wander into the realms of the invisible beings.

One of the earliest documented cases of OOBE occurred in 1226, but the event was viewed as being a gift from God rather than a paranormal experience. A Franciscan friar named Anthony of Padua – later to be canonized as a leading thinker of the Franciscan movement – was preaching a sermon at a church in Limoges, France, when the church bell rang. He suddenly remembered that he had promised to read the lesson at a different church in the town at that time. Excusing himself from his congregation, Anthony knelt down and pulled the hood of his robe up to hide his face. He knelt in apparent silent prayer for a few minutes, then stood up and resumed his sermon.

Meanwhile, in the second church the priest had been wondering where Anthony had got to. Suddenly the side door opened and in walked Anthony. Without glancing to left or right or paying any attention to the priest, the friar strode up to the lectern. He delivered his reading faultlessly, then turned and stalked out again without a word. He had been seen in two places at once, and had seemingly been fully aware of what he was doing throughout.

BACK FROM THE DEAD

Some centuries later the writer Ernest Hemingway was hit by shrapnel from an exploding artillery shell while fighting in the First World War. His comrades took him for dead, and so did Hemingway. He later described what happened next. 'My soul or something like it came right out of my body, like you'd pull a silk handkerchief out of a pocket by one corner. It flew around and then came back and went in again. And I wasn't dead any more.' His comrades

Ernest Hemingway during World War I

saw Hemingway's body twitch, so they sent him to hospital where he recovered.

In 1937 Sir Auckland Geddes, a noted Scottish doctor, had a similar OOBE when he suffered a life-threatening injury. In Sir Auckland's case the injury took the form of inadvertently taking a dose of deadly poison. As he slumped forward he tried to grab a phone, but failed and next thing he knew he was standing beside his body looking at the prostrate form. He wandered in astral form out of the room and into the garden. He then saw a friend of his enter the house and returned to the room where his body was. Sir Auckland saw his friend grab a phone, and a few minutes later a doctor arrived. He heard the conversation that followed quite clearly, but was unable to make himself heard. As Sir Auckland watched with detached curiosity, he saw the doctor inspect the poison, then grab a syringe and plunge it into his body. Sir Auckland felt himself being dragged back into his own body as a wave of searing pain engulfed him. Then he blacked out to come round again back inside his body a few hours later.

SPECTRAL DOOR

Not all OOBEs occur during a crisis of this sort. Pat, a florist in Canterbury, England was dozing in her living room when she opened her eyes to find herself floating near the ceiling. Glancing down, she saw her body on the sofa, apparently asleep. A spectral door then appeared floating in mid-air, and the woman was aware that she would gain knowledge if she passed through. Still as an astral, the woman opened the door and stepped through to find herself now floating in mid-air outside the house. She could see quite clearly the surrounding buildings and people walking about. She then suddenly got worried and felt the need to return. Within an instant she was back in her body.

Most people who experience an OOBE do so only once, and are as surprised and taken aback by the experience as one might expect. A few people, however, have the experience more than once. One man who did was named Robert Monroe. After several OOBEs he decided to carry out some form of

test next time one occurrred to see if he could prove that he had, indeed, travelled outside his body rather than just imagining the whole thing.

When he next experienced an OOBE, Monroe walked out of his house in astral form and found a female friend of his chatting to two other women. After trying to attract his friend's attention by shouting and waving, Monroe pinched her on the waist. When he came out of his OOBE state, Monroe called his friend to ask her if she had been aware of anything. He found that she had met the two women he had seen when in astral form, and that she had felt a pinch or scratch on her waist when chatting to them.

SPATIAL AWARENESS

In August 2007 the Swiss neurology researcher Olaf Blanke published a paper that summarized a huge number of experiments on the part of the brain known as the right temporal parietal junction (right TPJ). This showed that in some cases a strong magnetic field applied to the right TPJ would result in the subject viewing the room as if from a point some distance away from where their body actually was. The percipient was able to describe the scene very accurately from their 'new' position, but significantly could not describe anything that was out of sight from where their body was located. It was surmised that disruption of the brain activity in the right TPJ resulted in the loss of spatial awareness to an extreme degree and that in a few cases this manifested itself as the person imagining themselves to be somewhere other than where they were.

Some have speculated that these experiments have shown that OOBEs are nothing more than a similar effect taking place spontaneously. This may well explain some cases, but cannot account for cases where the percipient could, in fact, see things out of sight of his body. Sir Auckland Geddes, for instance, was slumped unconscious with his eyes shut, and yet 'saw' exactly what was going on around him. Monroe, meanwhile, was able to see quite clearly things taking place outside his house and several hundred metres away.

Sir Auckland Geddes

NEAR DEATH EXPERIENCES (NDES)

One type of OOBE that seems to be quite different from the others is that which occurs when a person is on the point of death. These have become known as Near Death Experiences and have been the subject of much research and interest. It is hoped by some researchers that the NDE will offer humans some hint of what may await us after death.

What has proved to be most interesting about NDEs is that they generally conform to a set pattern, no matter the religious views of the person who experiences them. It would, therefore, seem likely that the experience, whatever it is, is real and not completely imaginary. If the followers of each religion had seen images that corresponded to their faith, then researchers might conclude that the experience had been invented by the person's brain. A Christian, for instance, might imagine meeting angels and saints, while a Buddhist would find himself preparing to reincarnate. The very

consistency of NDEs indicates that they are the result of a real and shared cause.

Although every NDE is different in detail, the typical experience tends to move through a number of stages. Although an NDE will usually end at some point in the sequence it is highly unusual for a percipient to experience the stages out of order.

First there comes the realization that the percipient has died, often accompanied by a noise that is described as being unpleasant or deeply distracting. There then follows a feeling of calmness and serenity as any worries or unpleasant emotions seem to slip away. After this the person experiences something akin to an OOBE as he feels that he is leaving his body. Sometimes the percipient is able to look back at their body as if standing close to it. There then opens up a dark tunnel or doorway which has a light at the far end. The person is drawn irresistibly toward this doorway or tunnel. The person usually feels that they are floating upward at this point, though some report a sinking feeling. At some point along the tunnel the person might meet friends or relatives who have died some time previously.

Sometimes, but not always, a conversation follows during which the percipient is assured that everything will be fine and that there is nothing to worry about. A very few people report that the conversation is not at all reassuring, but includes threats of punishment and pain. A number say that the conversation takes place not with somebody they know but with a stranger, often described as being benevolent or holy in some way. Those who progress through the doorway or to the far end of the tunnel may then find themselves confronted by a succession of scenes from their life, often replaying as if on a movie screen incidents of great emotional importance. Finally the percipient comes to a second doorway or gateway. If they have not already done so, the percipient at this point experiences a feeling of awkwardness, followed by a strong sense that they are in the wrong place and need to return. They then experience a sense of sudden and very swift movement after which they return to their bodies.

'ASCENT OF THE BLESSED'

These sorts of NDEs have been experienced by critically ill people for centuries. A famous painting by the 15th century Dutch painter Hieronymous Bosch entitled 'Ascent of the Blessed' depicts a view that could come from many NDEs. The souls of the righteous dead are shown floating up toward a long, circular tunnel at the far end of which stands a silhouetted figure bathed in a bright light. The piece was commissioned for a church, so Bosch has added some suitably Christian angels to the scene, but the similarity to modern NDEs remains unmistakable.

It was not until the 1970s, however, that anyone noticed that patients who had almost died – and in many cases been declared clinically dead only to be later revived – reported similar experiences. It was the researcher Raymond Moody who coined the phrase NDE and popularized the topic in his book Life after Life, published in 1975. Moody and others, including Kenneth Ring and Michael Sabon, have sought to investigate the subject further on a scientific basis. Unfortunately most medical authorities have proved to be uninterested and funds for research have been few and far between.

LACK OF FUNDS

In part the lack of research funds has been caused by the link established between the NDE and the paranormal. Many people believe that an NDE actually reveals what happens to a human soul when the body dies. The progression through the various stages is believed to show that after death a soul passes through a gateway to meet the souls of those already dead before reaching a 'point of no return'. Those who experience an NDE are turned back at this point to continue their lives on Earth, while those who pass beyond die and begin their next life in whatever form that may take.

As usual with scientific bodies, there is a great reluctance to get involved with anything religious or paranormal, so funds for research have traditionally been scarce to the point of non-existence. Scientists, who like everyone else have to earn a living, therefore spend their time on other research. Some manage to conduct research in their spare time or as an adjunct to other work.

In 2001 a heart doctor in the Netherlands named van Lommel, for instance, conducted a study of patients who had suffered severe cardiac arrests and who had been revived artificially. Among much other information, he found that 18 per cent of them had had an NDE, the remaining 82 per cent could recall nothing from the period when they were unconscious.

In the 1990s Dr Rick Strassman was conducting research into users of the drug DMT, which has known hallucinatory side-effects. He found that 2 per cent of his patients reported having visions very similar to those of the NDE although they had been in no danger of dying at all. He postulated that the NDE was caused by the brain producing a self-induced hallucination to cover up the hideous experience of dying with an altogether more consoling vision.

Other researchers have followed a similar line, with some suggesting that the tunnel leading to a light is in fact caused by the extremities of the brain closing down as the heart stops and the flow of oxygenated blood is cut off. In the absence of any funds for detailed research, however, these theories remain untested.

The vast majority of those who undergo an NDE, however, are in no doubt about what they have witnessed. They are almost unanimous in believing that they have experienced evidence that the human soul does survive physical death.

> Many people believe that an NDE reveals what happens to a human soul when the body dies... before it reaches a 'point of no return'

GHOSTS

I f there is one aspect of the paranormal that is to be found almost everywhere on Earth, it is ghosts. These insubstantial phantoms flit about in eerie ruined abbeys, pop up in the most modern of hotels and seat themselves in aircraft. Some ghosts return time after time to the same place, others are seen only once or twice before disappearing for ever.

Very often the story behind the ghost is known, for the person whose spectre returns can be recognized. Very often the person led a life of high drama, deep tragedy or died in violent circumstances. Other ghosts are anonymous, going by names such as the Brown Lady, Man in Green or Old Man. Nobody knows whose phantoms these are, though their date can often be fixed by the fashions they wear. And very few ghosts are transparent or float in the air. Most appear as solid as a perfectly normal human – until they vanish into thin air.

By and large these ghosts are quite content to wander about pursuing whatever business they have among us mortals without bothering us too much. The typical ghost will appear in the same place every time they are seen, and go through the same actions time after time. Some suspect that this means that the ghost is not so much the soul of the returning dead so much as some sort of recorded playback of an incident in the past.

But whatever ghosts really are, one thing is certain: you never know when you are going to meet one.

MARILYN MONROE

Hollywood may seem like a place of glamour and easy living, but behind the bright façade lie dark secrets. Many of the stars lured to Hollywood by fame and fortune have died untimely and mysterious deaths, and continue to haunt the luxurious settings of their success.

Marilyn Monroe: is she still with us?

Perhaps the most famous of these Hollywood haunters is celluloid sensation Marilyn Monroe. In life, she was a tormented soul whose poignant pursuit of personal happiness touched a generation. So perhaps it is hardly surprising that she has remained a restless figure in death.

Monroe's career started at the Roosevelt Hotel on Hollywood Boulevard. It was here that she posed on a diving board for her first advertisement, for sun-tan lotion, brimming with aspiration. The starlet, blessed with stunning looks and a voluptuous figure, appeared to have the world at her feet. But later she became embroiled in studio politics and struggled through many doomed love affairs. She even developed a draining drug dependency. On 5 August 1962, she was found dead at her Brentwood home, aged just 36. She is believed to have died from a self-administered drug overdose, although some people doubt this explanation, and conspiracy theorists have since claimed she was murdered.

RESTLESS SOUL

Since her death, Monroe's reflection has been seen in a full-length mirror that once hung in her favourite poolside suite at the Roosevelt Hotel, where she started out years before. Could it be that her restless soul is seeking to recapture youth and happiness? The dark-framed mirror that has captured her ghostly image has been moved to the hotel basement.

HAUNTED HOTEL

And Marilyn is not the only A-list celebrity making unscheduled appearances at the 320-roomed Roosevelt. Montgomery Clift – her co-star in the 1961 film *The Misfits* – can be heard up in room 928 labouring over his lines for the 1953 movie *From Here to Eternity*.

After becoming a star, Clift, like Monroe, led a tortured existence. He became an alcoholic and a drug addict. He was also homosexual, a fact he felt compelled to hide from the public for fear of people's response. He was found dead in his New York home at the age of 45, apparently suffering from heart disease.

Staff at the Roosevelt have been alarmed after hearing loud noises while standing outside Room 928. Sometimes the telephone is found off the hook. One member of staff claimed a ghostly hand brushed her skin. It seems Clift never really checked out.

The last spooky site in the hotel lies in the Blossom Ballroom where a sizeable 'cold spot' has been noted by some visitors, management and staff. This room was the setting for the first ever Academy Awards in 1929. Perhaps the phenomenon is the result of some bitter disappointment suffered by an early Hollywood hopeful.

THE SIDEWALK CAFÉ

Comedy actress Thelma Todd starred in more than forty films before her death in 1935, aged 29. She had appeared alongside the Marx brothers and Laurel and Hardy to great acclaim, and she also ran a restaurant called Thelma Todd's Sidewalk Café (situated on what is now known as the Pacific Coast Highway).

Her body was discovered in a car, in a garage above the café, still wearing evening clothes and a mink stole. The cause of death was presumed to be suicide through carbon monoxide poisoning. Yet there has long been speculation that it was murder, by a jealous former husband, an angry lover or perhaps even the Mafia.

If there was indeed an undetected murder, this might explain why Todd's ghost would want to return to earth. She has been seen descending a staircase at her old café, now owned by the religiously inclined TV and film company Paulist Productions. Employees have also smelled fumes in the building.

SPOOKY CEMETERY

Clifton Webb is another wandering soul, witnessed close to his burial place in the Hollywood Memorial Park Cemetery. His spirit also reportedly appears from time to time at his old home in Retford Drive, Beverley Hills. Webb was famous for his roles as 'Mr Belvedere' and for an enduring friendship with playwright Noel Coward. However, nothing in his life took precedence over his beloved mother

Hollywood Memorial Park Cemetery is the final resting place of many big-screen stars, not that all of them are resting. There are reports of several returning to old haunts and past glories

Mabelle. The pair lived together until her death aged 91. Frustrated by Webb's excessive grief, Coward remarked with characteristic humour: 'It must be tough to be orphaned at 71.'

Another ghost has been heard in the same graveyard, that of Virginia Rappe. This ill-fated starlet died after apparently being shut in a hotel bedroom with outsized comedian 'Fatty' Arbuckle during a debauched party. Later she was discovered weeping and in pain. She died later from peritonitis brought about by a ruptured kidney. The ensuing scandal engulfed Hollywood and Arbuckle's career was ruined by it, although he was eventually cleared of wrong-doing.

STILL AT THE STUDIO

The cemetery is also the last resting place of Douglas Fairbanks and Rudolph Valentino. Although Valentino's spectre has not been seen in the cemetery itself, it is thought to haunt the costume department of the Paramount Studios on Marathon Avenue.

Not to be outdone, Universal Studios has its own celebrity ghost, since the actor Lon Chaney is alleged to be haunting Sound Stage 28. But this does not seem to be his favourite haunt, since he was most often seen on a bus stop bench at the intersection of Hollywood and Vine. The son of deaf-mutes, Chaney learned to communicate with facial expressions. During his career he acted mostly in horror films and was heavily made up, becoming known as 'the man of a thousand faces'. He died in 1930 of throat cancer, aged 47. It is not known which

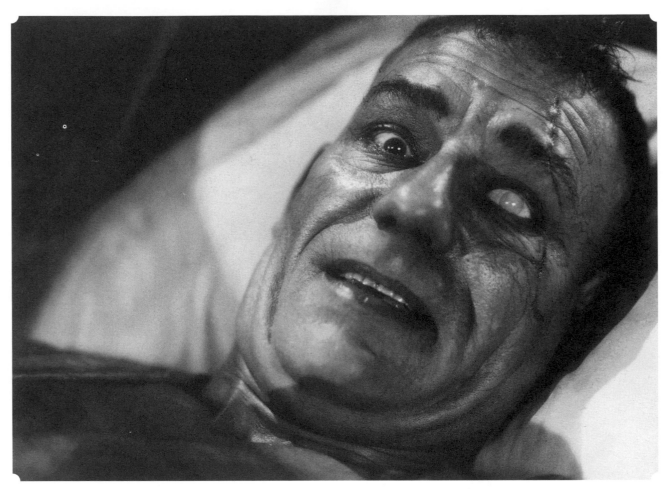

of the thousand faces the ghost at the bus stop used to wear. When the bus stop seat was removed the ghost moved on.

Actor Lon Chaney, 'the man of a thousand faces', in the 1926 film The Road to Mandalay. *Chaney's ghost divided its time between Universal Studios and a bus stop*

HARD TO LEAVE

Another man who has struggled to leave Hollywood behind is former bull-fighter and *War of the Worlds* broadcaster Orson Welles. Since his death in 1985 aged 70, he has been glimpsed at his favourite restaurant, Sweet Lady Jane's in Melrose Avenue. Not only do staff occasionally see his corpulent, caped frame, but they smell the cigars he was fond of smoking and the brandy he loved to swig.

GHOSTLY EXPERIENCE

In 1934 Wing Commander Victor Goddard was flying a Hawker Hart biplane from Scotland to Andover in Hampshire. During turbulent weather,

Goddard went into a spin and only narrowly avoided crashing. As soon as he regained control of the rudimentary aircraft, he suddenly found himself in radically different conditions. The clouds had parted, and the sun was beating down. Below him he recognized Drem airfield, which he had visited the day previously. It had been abandoned after the First World War and was now derelict.

Yet the airfield was a hive of activity. Three biplanes were there, just like his own but painted yellow, and there was a fourth plane of a type he had never seen before. Goddard saw ground crew dressed in blue overalls, although as far as he knew all Royal

A squadron of British monoplane fighters of the type Goddard saw at Drem airfield. During the Second World War, these were said to be the fastest warplanes anywhere in the world

Air Force uniforms were brown. The men failed to notice Goddard's plane above them, and when Drem airfield was out of sight he found himself once more in the teeth of the storm.

Goddard put this strange incident to the back of his mind. But in 1939 as Britain geared up for war, he was astonished to see biplanes being painted yellow and mechanics' uniforms switching from brown to blue. Monoplanes, like the fourth plane he had seen at Drem, were finally being flown by the RAF. And after the outbreak of the Second World War, the airfield was put into use again. When Goddard finally wrote about this eerie experience in 1966, he came to a bizarre conclusion about this incident: he must have flown into the future.

SPIRIT IN FLIGHT

One of the most striking examples of a ghost photo is that featuring a flight unit of the Royal Air Force based at HMS *Daedalus* in Cranwell, Lincolnshire in 1919. Servicemen and women gathered together and formally posed in full uniform for the photograph before they all scattered to new postings.

The close-knit flight unit had been devastated when, three days prior to the photograph being taken, one of their number had died in a horrific and tragic accident. Freddy Jackson perished on the tarmac when he stumbled into a whirling propeller. Some of those in the official picture, taken by Bassano's Photographic Company, even marched behind the coffin of their friend and colleague during the military funeral.

Yet when the photograph was pinned up alongside an order form for reprints, there was an audible gasp. The face of Freddy Jackson was clearly seen peeping out from the back row. The photograph became a cherished possession of a Wren driver at the base, Bobbie Capel. Australian-born Capel saw Jackson regularly in the course of her duties, driving to and from the *Daedalus* vehicle maintenance yard. She clearly recalled his death occurring shortly before the photograph was taken. 'When we lined up for that photograph to commemorate the disbanding of the transport yard, we all knew one familiar face would not be with us. Only later did we discover that, actually, he was.'

SUPERNATURAL EVENT

Capel met her first husband, Royal Flying Corps pilot Flt Lt Henry Moody MC, while serving at HMS *Daedalus*. He died 12 years later in a flying accident. In 1934 she married her second husband, Air Vice Marshal Arthur Capel. Like both men, she believed those present on the day of the photograph

Scrutiny of the back row of the flight unit photograph shows the face of Freddy Jackson, fourth from the left, peeping out from behind his colleagues

witnessed a supernatural event. 'I cannot entertain the idea that this was a deliberate fake. For one thing the photographer came from outside the base. He didn't know any of us and once he'd taken his picture he left immediately. He just would not have known about the accident. Neither can I understand how the face could have appeared by some mishap. I have thought and puzzled over it for years, but I can think of no explanation other than that it is the picture of a ghost.'

Her view is supported by Air Marshal Sir Victor Goddard. As a navy Flight Lieutenant at the time, Goddard also saw the photograph and wrote about it in his memoirs, *Flight Towards Reality*. 'There [Jackson] was, and no mistake, although a little fainter than the rest ... Indeed he looked as though he was not altogether there, not really with that group, for he alone was capless, smiling ... Not only would Bassano's not have dared to fake it; the negative was scrutinized for faking and was found to be untouched.'

FACES OF THE DEAD

In 1924, another curious photograph was taken by Keith Tracy, captain of the oil tanker SS *Watertown*, following the death of two crew members. James Courtney and Michael Meehan were overcome by fumes while they were cleaning a cargo tank as the vessel sailed from New York towards the Panama Canal. Both were duly buried at sea.

Yet for several days afterwards both fellow crew members and the captain himself saw phantom faces resembling the dead men in the ship's Pacific wake. The tale might have been dismissed as a sailor's yarn, had Tracy not photographed the phenomenon to provide proof to those on land. When the pictures were developed, the faces of the dead men were distinct in the murky waters.

Another remarkable image was captured in November 1995, while an English town hall was burning down. Local man Tony O'Rahilly took photographs intended to record the momentous event. In fact, he discovered later, in doing so he had captured the image of a small, partially transparent girl standing in a doorway. At the time of the fire neither O'Rahilly, other onlookers or firefighters had seen any trace of the girl. After the photograph was submitted for analysis, Dr Vernon Harrison, a former president of the Royal Photographic Society, decided the negative appeared genuine. Delving into the past to explain the mystery, it was found that much of the Shropshire town had been destroyed by fire in 1677. The blaze had been accidentally started by a young girl called Jane Churm. Could it be that Jane's spirit had been roused when the town hall was once more engulfed in flames?

HAMPTON COURT MYSTERY

If legend is to be believed, Hampton Court Palace just outside London, once home to the larger-than-life character King Henry VIII, is swarming with

The image of one of Henry VIII's unfortunate wives haunting the corridors of Hampton Court Palace: could this be Catherine Howard, his fifth wife, who was beheaded on a charge of adultery?

ghosts. Only one, though, has been caught on closed-circuit television cameras.

In winter 2003, security staff at the palace were alerted when alarms sounded, indicating that the fire doors of the exhibition hall had been opened. On investigation, the guards found the doors were closed, so they viewed security film to determine what had occurred. The film revealed a white-faced man in flowing clothes shutting the open doors from the inside. The alarm was set off at the same time on three consecutive days, but the figure was only caught on camera once. Although the palace does employ guides dressed in Tudor garb, it was quickly established that the figure was no ordinary employee. Although some observers claim the figure looks altogether too earthly to be a ghost, inspection of the digital film by independent experts implied it was genuine.

But the ghost did not fit the description of the usual suspects. It did not appear to be that of Jane Seymour, Henry VIII's third wife, who died giving birth to their son Edward. She is said to haunt a cobbled courtyard clutching a lighted taper. Nor was it the oft-reported screaming white lady, thought to be the ghost of Catherine Howard, Henry's fifth wife who was beheaded on a charge of adultery. Indeed the ghost has never been identified, despite choosing to haunt such grand surroundings.

THE FLYING DUTCHMAN

The creaking timbers of a swaying ghost ship looming through swirling mists, with red warning lights on its bow, is sufficient to strike fear into the stoutest heart. For the phantom crew of the vessel the threat is past, but for unfortunate observers it lies just ahead.

So runs the tale of the *Flying Dutchman*, a ship that foundered on the tip of Africa after being lashed by a ferocious storm more than three centuries ago. The ship's captain, Hendrick Vanderdecken, refused either to seek shelter or to drop anchor despite the raging tempest. Following curses made either to God or the devil, he was allegedly condemned to sail around the region forever with, quite literally, a

The Queen Mary *in dry dock. This vast and sumptuous liner is said to be the portal to another realm, teeming with ghostly passengers from a long-gone era*

skeleton crew. Moreover, anyone who sights the phantom vessel is also doomed.

Since the dawn of the seafaring age, sailors have been notoriously superstitious. They are quite likely to interpret cloud formations and naturally forming prismatic effects as ghost ships haunting the high seas. Curiously, though, there have been numerous reports about the *Flying Dutchman*, some from highly reliable sources.

On 11 July 1881, a lookout on the HMS *Bacchante* rounding the Cape of Good Hope was the first to see what he believed to be the *Flying Dutchman*. Before the phantom ship vanished, no fewer than 13 men had witnessed it first hand. In the ship's log, the midshipman recorded: 'During the middle watch the so-called *Flying Dutchman* crossed our bows. She first appeared as a strange red light, as if a ship all aglow, in the midst of which light her spars, masts and sails, seemingly those of a normal brig, some 200 yards [183m] distant from us, stood out in strong relief as she came up.

'Our lookout man on the forecastle reported her close to our port bow, where also the officer of the watch from the bridge clearly saw her, as did our quarter-deck midshipman, who was sent forward at once to the forecastle to report back. But on reaching there, no vestige, nor any sign of the ship, was to be seen either near or away on the horizon.'

The writer went on to become George V of England – and he fared notably better than the lookout, who fell from the rigging and died later in the voyage.

Among other definitive sightings of the *Flying Dutchman* was one off South African shores in 1939. Bathers on Glencairn beach were united in their description of the sailing ship heading towards the sands, although few can have known details about merchant vessels of the 17th century. According to the British South Africa Annual of that year: 'Just as the excitement reached its climax, however, the mystery ship vanished into thin air as strangely as it had come.'

THE QUEEN MARY

Once one of the most prestigious liners afloat, the *Queen Mary* now has the reputation of being the most haunted. The spirits that frolic in the ship's first-class swimming pool area are so prolific that a 'ghost cam' is trained on it at all times. Staff have seen child-sized wet footprints appear around the pool when no accompanying body is visible. Sounds of water-borne high jinks are heard from outside when the pool is empty. A medium invited aboard to investigate the sights and sounds believed one of the changing cubicles to be 'a portal to another realm'. If there are ghosts in the pool, they appear to belong to the years between the maiden voyage of the *Queen Mary* in 1936 and its war service, which began in 1940.

THE WHITE LADY

From the same era come accounts of the ghost of a white lady who, once spotted, disappears behind a pillar. However, some of the unearthly sounds that emanate from the ship are thought to be later in origin, stemming from the death of 17-year-old John Pedder, who perished trying to escape a fire onboard in 1966, just a year before the liner ended its service. Loud and frantic knocking sounds have been heard from behind Door 13, and sometimes it feels hot to the touch. Could Pedder's ghost still be haunting the liner, condemned to relive his terrible last moments to the end of time? The *Queen Mary* is now a permanent fixture in Long Beach, California, where she is a major tourist attraction, not least for the paranormal activity rumoured to take place aboard.

THE LADY LOVIBOND

Another ghostly vessel spotted off the English coast is the *Lady Lovibond*. During her last voyage, she was bound from London to Portugal, carrying not only cargo but also Captain Simon Peel's bride and fifty of their wedding guests.

On deck, first mate John Rivers was contorted with jealousy. He had hoped to make Peel's bride his own wife, but his hopes had been dashed. By way of desperate revenge, he drove the three-masted barquetine in full sail on to the treacherous Goodwin Sands. All on board were killed as the ship's woodwork splintered and smashed down.

The incident happened in February 1748, on an unlucky Friday the 13th. However, that particular superstition is rooted in 20th-century lore, so it would not have resonated with audiences of the time.

But this was not the last of the ill-fated *Lady Lovibond*. In 1798, exactly fifty years after the vessel foundered, Captain James Westlake of the *Edenbridge* reported seeing its apparition across his bow. The *Lady Lovibond* resurrected itself from that ship's graveyard again in 1848 and in 1898. On both occasions, it was seen in full sail by Kent fishermen. However, nothing was reported in either 1948 or 1998, despite the best efforts of ghosthunters from across Britain. They might have been thwarted because an 18th-century calendar switch (when England adopted the Gregorian calendar) would have the ghost ship sailing some 11 days earlier than expected.

THE GREAT LAKES

Ghost ships are not only found on the open sea but also in lakes and even rivers. There are two similar stories from the great lakes of North America that have fascinated seafarers and public alike. The first dates back to September 1678 when the *Griffon* vanished from Lake Michigan. Although no trace of the vessel was ever found, several sailors in ensuing years reported seeing the ship sailing on the lake. Much later, in 1975, the *Edmund Fitzgerald* sank into the waters of Lake Superior, taking 26 crew members with her. Once again, sailors in the region have spotted the ship afloat and untouched by disaster.

Mention should also be made of the SS *Iron Mountain*, which was not so much a ghost ship as a vanished vessel. In June 1872 it left Vicksburg, Mississippi, with its cotton and molasses cargo, towing a line of barges. Later that day, another steamship by the name of *Iroquois Chief* came across the barges floating freely down the river with the tow line apparently cut. Crew secured the barges and waited for the arrival of the SS *Iron Mountain*.

In 1975, the Edmund Fitzgerald *sank during a storm on Lake Superior, killing twenty-six crew members. But the ship has refused to sink into obscurity, and its ghost lingers on...*

It never came. Indeed, no one ever saw the ship, its crew or its cargo again. Nor was there a trace of wreckage along the river banks. The fate of the SS *Iron Mountain* remains unknown.

No one knows just how many ghost ships may be sailing the oceans and great lakes, lost in time and space. Whilst the sea swallows up some vessels and their crews without a trace, others seem condemned to return as haunting reminders of their watery fate.

THE TOWER OF LONDON

If any site deserves its formidable reputation for spectral sightings it is the Tower of London whose weathered stones are soaked in the blood of countless executed martyrs and traitors. It is said that the walls still echo with the screams of those who were tortured there during the most violent chapters of English history and with the muffled sobbing of those innocents who were put to death for displeasing the monarchy. It is a place of pain where the unquiet souls of those who were imprisoned relive their suffering seemingly for eternity with no prospect of finding peace.

Its long and bloody history began almost 1,000 years ago in 1078 when William the Conqueror built the White Tower in a strategically significant location on the River Thames. Over the next 500 years, the 18-acre site was developed into a formidable fortress within which a succession of kings exercised their divine right over the lives and deaths of their subjects: former friends, wives and enemies alike.

By the dawn of the 17th century, English royalty had moved to more palatial quarters and the Tower became a soldier's garrison and prison. On the morning of their execution, condemned prisoners were ceremoniously paraded past jeering crowds to the scaffold erected on nearby Tower Hill where they would be beheaded, or hanged, drawn and quartered, and then their bodies would be brought back for burial within the walls of the Tower. These processions of sombre figures have been seen in modern times by sentries who were able to describe accurately the uniforms worn by the burial party.

Among the Tower's most illustrious residents were the young princes Edward and Richard who were declared illegitimate and imprisoned in the so-called Bloody Tower by their ambitious uncle the Duke of Gloucester. It is believed by some that he ordered their murder so that he could be crowned King Richard III. The princes have been sighted several times walking hand in hand through the chilly corridors after dusk, possibly in search of their murderous uncle. Their alleged murderer has not been seen skulking around the scene of his hideous

The four-turreted White Tower was the first structure to be built on the site of the Tower of London and has a long history of hauntings. It has been the site of numerous murders and executions

Singular Execution of the Countess of Salisbury in 1541.

Cruikshanks. del.

ordered the death of his Lancastrian rival Henry VI on 21 May 1471 at the end of the War of the Roses, but it is not Edward who haunts the oratory in the Wakefield Tower where the killing took place, but Henry who has been seen seated outside the oratory praying that his soul might find peace.

Anne Boleyn, the second wife of Henry VIII, is said to still walk in the Tower Chapel where she made her peace with her God before she was despatched to his heavenly kingdom in 1536. She is reported to have been seen leading a spectral procession through the chapel both with and without her head.

CONDEMNED TO DEATH

One of the most gruesome episodes in the Tower's history was the botched execution of Margaret Pole, Countess of Salisbury (pictured left). Margaret was 70 years old when she was condemned to death in 1541 by Henry VIII, even though she posed no threat to his dynasty.

Standing resolutely regal on the scaffold, she refused to submit to the hooded executioner who waited for her to rest her head on the block, but instead she commanded him to sever her head from her neck where she stood. When he refused she fled, forcing him to pursue her around Tower Green swinging the axe like a serial killer in a modern splatter movie. Within minutes the hideous spectacle was at an end; the last female Plantagenet had been hacked to pieces. If you find that too gruesome to be true, you only have to ask permission to remain in the

crimes which may suggest that his conscience was clear. Given the murdered princes' sense of injustice or revenge, ghosts appear to be an emotional residue rather than a conscious presence.

This is borne out by the nature of the other ghosts which haunt the Tower – they are all victims, not the perpetrators, of the many crimes which took place there. Edward IV, father to the murdered princes,

Tower after dark on 27 May, the anniversary of her execution, to see the scene re-enacted by the principal players themselves as Margaret's ghost tries once again to outrun her executioner.

Other apparitions are less active. The headless ghost of James Crofts Scott, the illegitimate son of King Charles II, for example, is said to do little more than walk the battlements connecting the Bell and Beauchamp Towers dressed in cavalier attire. Apparently, James was not satisfied with being made Duke of Monmouth as compensation for losing the crown to his uncle, James II, in 1685, and chose to assert his claim by force of arms. His rebellion was shortlived and he paid for his disloyalty by forfeiting his head.

TRAGIC FIGURE

Arguably the most tragic figure to haunt the site of her untimely death is Lady Jane Grey who was a pawn in the Duke of Northumberland's stratagem to usurp the English crown from the rightful heir, Mary Tudor. Lady Jane, who was only 15, ruled for less than two weeks before she was arrested and condemned to death together with her young husband and his father in February 1554. Her grieving ghost has been sighted by reliable witnesses on several occasions. In 1957, two sentries swore they witnessed the apparition of the young queen form from a ball of light on the roof of the Salt Tower, while others have reported seeing the spirit of the Duke sobbing at the window of the Beauchamp Tower as he had done on the morning of his execution.

One would imagine that a spell in the Tower would be sufficient to bring even the most rebellious subjects to their senses, but Sir Walter Raleigh incurred the monarch's displeasure more than once. In 1592, Queen Elizabeth I ordered him to be thrown into the Tower, but upon his release he continued to bait the Queen in the belief that he was too popular

LADY JANE GREY.

Lady Jane Grey was put on the throne by scheming guardians

to be executed. After Elizabeth's death, James I lost patience with Raleigh's preening and boasting and had him convicted on a trumped up charge of treason. He was eventually freed in 1616 on condition that he journeyed to the New World in search of gold to fill the royal coffers, but he ignored the King's express orders not to plunder from England's Spanish allies and was beheaded on his return. His ghost still walks the battlements near what were once his apartments in the Bloody Tower.

Not all of the Tower's non-corporeal residents have returned because they cannot rest or because they desire revenge. The ghost of Henry Percy, 9th Earl of Northumberland, has been sighted strolling amiably on the roof of the Martin Tower where he enjoyed walks during his enforced incarceration which began in 1605. Percy, who had been implicated in the Gunpowder Plot, was one of the few prisoners to have been allowed to keep his head and he whiled away the days debating the latest advances in science and other subjects with other educated nobles until his release 16 years later. Percy owed his freedom to his willingness to pay a fine of £30,000. Since he is clearly reluctant to leave the Tower centuries after his death, perhaps he feels he hasn't had his money's worth.

The forbidding exterior of Glamis Castle

THE GHOSTS OF GLAMIS

If the typical collection of 'true' ghost stories is to be believed, every castle in the British Isles has its own resident ghost. Whether there is any truth in that or not, Glamis Castle in Scotland certainly claims to have more than its share.

Glamis is the oldest inhabited castle north of the border and is renowned for being both the setting for the tragedy of *Macbeth* and also the ancestral home of the late Queen Mother, Elizabeth Bowes-Lyon. It also has an unenviable reputation as the most haunted castle in the world. Not all the ghosts are tortured souls. In the Queen Mother's sitting room the ghost of a cheeky negro servant boy has been sighted playing hide and seek. There is no doubt that the legends of Glamis provide more gruesome thrills than an old-fashioned Gothic thriller. However, fact and fiction are so creatively intertwined that it is now impossible to know which is which.

Several visitors and guests have been distressed by the apparition of a pale and frightened young girl who has been seen pleading in mute terror at a barred window. Legend has it that she was imprisoned after having had her tongue cut out to keep her from betraying a family secret – but what that secret might be remains a mystery. In the 1920s, a workman was said to have accidentally uncovered a hidden passage and to have been driven to the edge of insanity by what he found there. Allegedly, the family bought his silence by paying for his passage to another country. There are also tales of a hideously deformed heir who was locked in the attic and an ancient family curse about which the 15th Earl is reputed to have said: 'If you could only guess the nature of the secret, you would go down on your knees and thank God that it was not yours.'

The family's troubles are believed to date from 1537 when the widow of the 6th Lord Glamis was accused of witchcraft and burned at the stake. From that day to this her ghost has been seen on the anniversary of her death on the roof of the clock tower, bathed in a smouldering red glow. Several of the castle's 90 rooms have a dark and bloody history. King Malcolm II of Scotland was murdered in one of

them and the floor was boarded because the bloodstains could not be scrubbed clean. It is thought that this may have been the inspiration for the murder of King Duncan, Thane of Glamis, in Shakespeare's play *Macbeth*.

During the years of inter-clan warfare, the castle acquired an entire chamber of vengeful spirits when men from the Ogilvy clan were given refuge from their enemies in the dungeon, but were then betrayed by their host who walled them up alive. When the wall was torn down a century later, it is said that their skeletons were found in positions which suggested that they had been gnawing on their own flesh. The Scottish novelist Sir Walter Scott, who considered himself a hardy adventurer, braved a night there in 1793 and lived to regret it. 'I must own, that when I heard door after door shut, after my conductor had retired, I began to consider myself as too far from the living, and somewhat too near the dead.'

THE WHITE HOUSE

When the tour guides in Washington, DC, talk of the White House being haunted by the ghosts of former US presidents they are not speaking metaphorically, nor are they being melodramatic. It is known that Eleanor Roosevelt held séances in the White House during the Second World War and she claimed to be in contact with the spirit of Abraham Lincoln. During the Roosevelt residency their guest Queen Wilhelmina of the Netherlands was awoken in the night by a knock on her bedroom door. Thinking that it might be Eleanor Roosevelt she got out of bed, put on her nightgown and opened the door. There, framed in the doorway and looking as large as life, was the ghost of Abe Lincoln. Queen Wilhelmina's reaction is not recorded.

Winston Churchill was a frequent visitor to the White House during the Second World War and he often indulged in a hot bath, together with a cigar and a glass of whisky. One evening he climbed out of the bath and went into the adjoining bedroom to look for a towel when he noticed a man standing by the fireplace. It was Abraham Lincoln. Unperturbed, Churchill apologized for his state of undress: 'Good had a premonition of his own death. He dreamt that he was walking through the White House when he heard the sound of weeping coming from the East Room. When he entered he saw an open coffin surrounded by mourners and guarded by a detachment of Union soldiers. He asked one of the guards who it was who lay in the coffin, to be told, 'The President. He was killed by an assassin.' Lincoln then approached the coffin and saw his own corpse.

President Harry Truman often complained that he was prevented from working by Lincoln's ghost who would repeatedly knock on his door when he was attempting to draft an important speech. Truman wasn't known for his sense of humour and no one would have thought of playing practical jokes during his tenure in the Oval Office so it is assumed he was in earnest.

In the 1960s, Jacqueline Kennedy admitted that she had sensed Lincoln's presence on more than one occasion and 'took great comfort in it'. It is thought that Lincoln's ghost might be drawn to the White House because his son Willie died there and it is reported that the son has himself been seen wandering the corridors in search of his father.

TOYS "R" US

It is a common misconception that ghosts only inhabit crumbling castles and mouldering mansions. The modern Toys "R" Us superstore in Sunnyvale, California occupies a substantial plot on what had been a ranch and an apple orchard back in the 19th century. It is assumed that the poltergeist activity that has been witnessed there is connected with the previous owner John Murphy who, it appears, disliked children, as well as the commercial development of his former home.

Each morning, employees arrive to find stock scattered across the floor and items placed on the wrong shelves. Turnover in staff increased when sensitive staff members heard a voice calling their name and were then touched by invisible hands. The fragrant scent of fresh flowers has unsettled several employees, but it was the unwanted attentions of a phantom who assaulted female staff

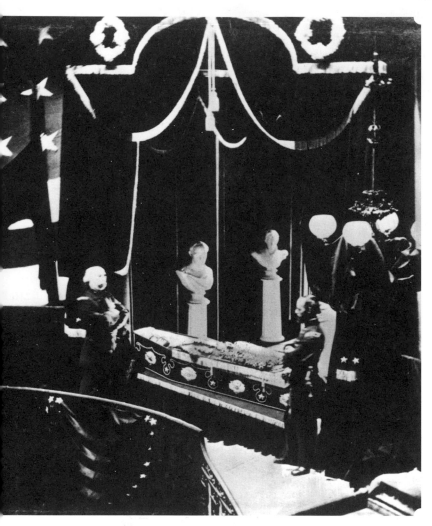

Lying in state, but not apparently resting: the ghost of Abraham Lincoln is a reassuring presence in the White House, on hand to meet and greet many visitors over the decades

evening, Mr President. You seem to have me at a disadvantage.' Lincoln is said to have smiled and tactfully withdrawn.

The wife of President Calvin Coolidge entertained guests at the White House with her recollections of the day she entered the Oval Office and saw Lincoln looking out across the Potomac with his hands clasped behind his back – a habit he acquired during the Civil War. Lincoln himself was a firm believer in the afterlife and enthusiastically participated in séances during his tenure in office prior to his assassination in 1865. He confided to his wife that he in the ladies' washroom which brought the matter to the attention of the local press and ghost buffs around the globe in 1978.

As a result, local journalist Antoinette May and psychic Sylvia Brown camped out in the store overnight with a photographer and a number of ghost catchers. Once the staff had left for the night and the lights were dimmed, Sylvia began to sense a male presence approaching the group. In her mind's eye she 'saw' a tall, thin man striding down the aisle towards her with his hands in his pockets. In her head she heard him speak with a Swedish accent, identifying himself as Johnny Johnson and warning her that she would get wet if she stayed where she was. It later emerged that a well had existed on that spot. Sylvia established such a strong connection

'Each morning, employees arrive to find stock scattered across the floor and items placed on the wrong shelves... staff members heard a voice calling their name and were then touched by invisible hands'

with Johnson that she was able to draw out his life history. He had come to California in the mid-1800s from Pennsylvania where he had worked as a preacher before succumbing to an inflammation of the brain which affected his behaviour. This appears to account for his antics in the aisles and the ladies' washroom, as well as the nickname 'Crazy Johnny', given to him by locals at the time.

Johnny lived out his later years working as a ranch hand for John Murphy, pining for a woman named Elizabeth Tafee who broke his heart when she left him to marry a lawyer. Johnny was 80 when he died from loss of blood after an accident with an axe while chopping wood.

Infra-red photographs taken for Arthur Myers' book on the haunting, *The Ghostly Register*, appear to show the figure of a man in the aisles of the store. Surprisingly, the publicity surrounding the haunting hasn't put off the customers, and it has allayed the fears of the employees who are no

longer upset by the disturbances – they now know it's only 'Crazy Johnny'.

The bodies of the slain on the battlefield of Gettysburg, July 1863: 53,000 men lost their lives in a slaughter that surpassed even the bloodiest battles of World War One

BATTLEFIELD PHANTOMS

In three days of fighting at the battle of Gettysburg in July 1863, a battle that was to mark the turning point in the American Civil War, 53,000 men lost their lives. The scale of the slaughter surpassed even that of the bloodiest days on the Somme during the First World War. No wonder then that visitors to the site have sworn that they have seen spectral soldiers wandering the battlefield as disoriented as the day they were killed. Some say it is the most haunted place in America.

On the first day of the battle rebel snipers were able to pick off retreating Union soldiers from their vantage point in the Farnsworth House on Baltimore Pike. The house, still pockmarked with bullet holes, is now a small hotel where guests have awoken in the

night to find an indistinct figure at the end of their bed. Odder still was the occasion when a local radio station set up an outside broadcast from the Farnsworth House only to have the power and telephone lines cut out. A local psychic, who was on site to give impressions to the listeners, heard disembodied voices warning their comrades that 'traitors' were around and he suddenly realized that the sound engineers were dressed in blue shirts and blue jeans – the same colour as the Union uniforms of the Civil War.

Several tourists have approached the park rangers over the years to ask the identity of a ragged, barefooted man dressed in a butternut shirt and trousers with a large floppy hat who appears at the rock formation known as the Devil's Den. He always says the same thing, 'What you're looking for is over there,' while pointing north-east towards the Plum Run, then promptly vanishes. The description fits that of the Texans who were a rag-bag unit feared for their fighting spirit.

At the wooded end of the Triangular Field, site of Colonel Chamberlain's heroic bayonet charge which drove Confederate troops off the hill known as Little Round Top, visitors have documented chaotic paranormal activity including phantom musket fire and drum rolls. Shadowy rebel sharpshooters have been seen taking cover among the trees, but whenever the ghost hunters enter the field to record these phantom figures their cameras malfunction. There appears to be some form of electromagnetic disturbance hanging like a pall over the field; even photographs of the area taken from the outside looking in are either fogged or fail to develop. One possible explanation is that it is a mass of residual personal energy discharged into the atmosphere following the violent death of so many soldiers.

Several visitors have regaled their fellow travellers with tales of having heard musket fire from Little Round Top and even having smelt acrid clouds of cordite and cannon smoke. In fact, it is known that on the third day of the battle the sound of the massed cannons was so loud that it could be heard in Washington, 80 miles away. But the most unearthly episode must have been that experienced by a group of volunteer re-enactors who worked as extras on the epic recreation of the battle for the movie *Gettysburg* in 1993. During a break in filming the group were admiring the sunset from Little Round Top when a grizzled old man approached them in the uniform of a Union private. He smelt of sulphur which was used in gunpowder of the period and his uniform was threadbare and scorched, unlike those of the extras. The man handed out spare rounds and commented on the fury of the battle. It was only later when they

Confederate General Lewis Armistead at Pickett's Charge at the battle of Gettysburg. His forces were virtually annihilated

showed the rounds to the armourer that they learnt these were authentic musket rounds from the period.

The battle was finally decided by a single suicidal assault, the infamous attack known as Pickett's Charge, in which 12,000 Confederate infantry marched shoulder to shoulder across an open field only to be massacred by massed cannons and musket fire. In that single, fatal hour 10,000 were killed and with them died General Robert E Lee's hopes of victory. Park rangers have witnessed many apparitions in the field after visiting hours including an unidentified mounted officer and another who was the image of General Lee. Local residents have maintained that on warm summer evenings they have encountered cold spots while out walking which transformed their breath to mist.

HIGHLAND BLOODBATH

One of the most famous battlefields in British history is Culloden Moor in the Scottish Highlands, the site of the last battle to be fought on mainland British soil. The ferocious and bloody fighting that took place on that sodden day in April 1746 lasted a mere forty minutes, but the effects of the slaughter abide to this day.

The battle was between the Jacobites, under Bonnie Prince Charlie, who were seeking to restore the Stuart monarchy to the throne and Government troops, led by Prince William, the Duke of Cumberland. The Jacobites were exhausted, having spent many days marching back from an ineffectual mission to gather more troops and a failed surprise attack on the Duke's men. They were also vastly outnumbered and not suited to fighting on boggy moorland.

The battle commenced with an artillery exchange that decimated the Jacobite forces. Bonnie Prince Charlie was notably absent from the front line, so the men were left leaderless and hesitant, with no real battle plan. The slaughter intensified when they finally decided to charge, as those troops who had managed to survive the bombardment were then slain by a new, and highly successful, strategy employed by Prince William's troops.

Cunningly, this involved stabbing the highlander to the right of the man directly faced, and took the Jacobites totally by surprise. It meant that the government troops were able to inflict wounds on their enemy under the right sword arm, an area left unprotected due to the fact that the small shield that they carried, known as a targe, was borne on the left arm.

Those who were not mortally wounded were cruelly slaughtered as they lay on the blood-soaked ground, and those who fled were hunted down and murdered without pity. Bonnie Prince Charlie managed to escape to Italy, but was never able to return to his native land.

Those who have visited the scene of this battle speak of numerous mysterious happenings, particularly on the anniversary of the action on 16 April. For example, they see the ghostly soldiers and hear the clamour of carnage and the clash of steel. Specific sightings of a tall, gaunt Highlander who utters the word 'Defeated' under his breath are described. Others report coming across the spectre of a dead Highland soldier lying beneath a tartan cloth on one of the many burial mounds of the battle site. Birds are said to fall silent in the region of these mounds, and there are also numerous wells strewn across the area that are said to abound with the spirits of the dead, most notably St Mary's Well.

THE GHOSTS OF GLASTONBURY

Glastonbury is one of the most sacred and mysterious sites in Britain, and of great spiritual significance to mystically minded Christians and pagans alike. Legend has it that King Arthur and Queen Guinevere are buried within the ruins of Glastonbury Abbey and that the Holy Grail, the chalice from which Jesus is said to have drunk on the night before his crucifixion, is hidden nearby. But of all the legends associated with Glastonbury the most extraordinary and controversial is that concerning the discovery of the ruins of the abbey itself.

In 1907, architect and archaeologist Frederick Bligh Bond (1864–1945) was appointed director of

The ruins of Glastonbury Abbey where Bligh Blond and Bartlett uncovered secrets from the past

excavations by the Church of England and charged with the task of unearthing the abbey ruins which several previous incumbents had spent their lives searching for in vain. The work was unpaid, but Bligh had a thriving architectural practice in Bristol and he viewed the search for the abbey as an almost mystical mission. He was confident that he would succeed where the others had failed for he believed that he had an uncommon advantage over his predecessors.

GHOSTS OF LONG DEAD MONKS

His interest in paranormal phenomena had led him to join the Society for Psychical Research through which he had met Captain John Allen Bartlett, an eager advocate of automatic writing. Together the two men took up pen and paper in the hope of pinpointing the location of the ruins by tapping into what Jung had called the Collective Unconscious. The quality of the messages they received swiftly persuaded them that they were in communication with separate discarnate personalities, quite possibly the ghosts of long dead monks who had lived in the monastery.

At the first session, which took place in November 1907, the two men sat opposite each other across an empty table in reverent expectation. Bartlett took the part of the medium and Bond the 'sitter'. This involved Bond asking the questions while placing two fingers on the back of Bartlett's hand to make a connection with the spirits.

'Can you tell us anything about Glastonbury,' asked the architect, to which an invisible force answered in a legible scrawl by animating Bartlett's hand: 'All knowledge is eternal and is available to mental sympathy.'

The connection had been made and information as to the location of the chapels and other buried structures was freely given in a mixture of Latin and English by a disembodied spirit who identified himself as a 15th-century monk named Brother William (possibly William of Malmesbury).

To Bond and Bartlett's delight the 'monk' and his

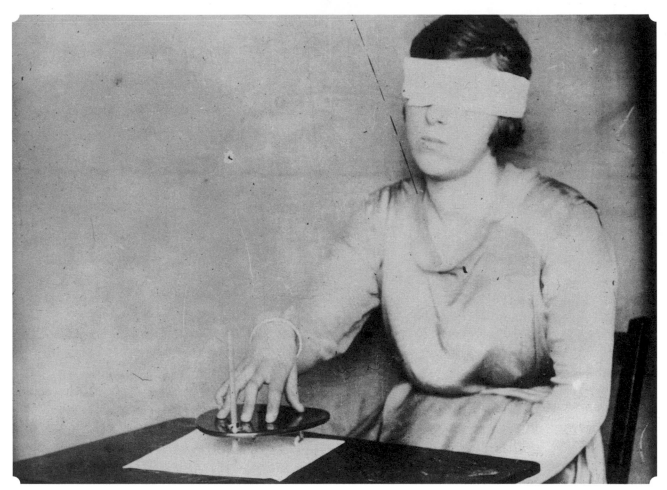

A girl using a planchette – a wheeled platform with a pencil attached – another 'automatic' way of receiving messages from spirits

companions, known as 'The Watchers', supplied very detailed information regarding the location of the abbey's foundations. When the excavations started, often the workmen would simply have to dig a few feet down to hit the precise spot, after which the archaeologists would move in and begin sifting the soil for artefacts.

Needless to say, Bond's benefactors were beside themselves and the full extent of the ancient site was revealed over dozens of sessions during the next five years

By 1917, Bond felt justly proud in having uncovered one of Britain's most sacred sites and decided to tell his story in print. But when *The Gates of Remembrance* was published in 1918, the Church condemned it and strenuously denied that anything other than conventional methods had been used to unearth the abbey. In an effort to distance themselves

from Bond they terminated his employment, banned him from ever setting foot within the grounds again and ordered that his guidebook to Glastonbury be removed from the shelves of the gift shop.

Since that time the occult significance of the abbey's location has been argued over by scholars who believe that it was intentionally built on an ancient pagan site to conform to an alignment of stars. Bond's communications with 'Brother William' appear to confirm this.

'... *our Abbey was a message in ye stones. In ye foundations and ye distances be a mystery – the mystery of our faith, which ye have forgotten and we also in ye latter days.*

'All ye measurements were marked plain on ye slabbes in Mary's Chappel, and ye have destroyed them. So it was recorded, as they who builded and they who came after knew aforehand where they should build. But these things are overpast and of no value now. The spirit was lost and with the loss of the spirit the body decayed and was of no use to (us).

'There was the Body of Christ, and round him would have been the Four Ways. Two were builded and no more. In ye floor of ye Mary Chappel was ye Zodiac, that all might see and understand the mystery. In ye midst of ye chappel he was laid; and the Cross of Hym who was our Example and Exemplar.'

GHOST FLIGHT

Executives of American carrier Eastern Airlines were literally haunted by their past when they decided to reuse parts salvaged from a crashed Tristar Lockheed L-1011 to repair other planes in their fleet. Their troubles began in December 1972 when Flight 401 fell out of the sky over the Florida Everglades claiming more than 100 lives including the pilot, Bob Loft, and flight engineer, Don Repo.

Within months of the crash, members of the cabin crew were reporting sightings of both men on their flights and these were augmented by sightings from passengers who had been disturbed by faint but full-length figures, subsequently identified as Loft and Repo from their photographs. One female passenger became hysterical when she saw the man in the seat next to her disappear. He had looked so pale and listless that she had called an attendant to see if he was ill. The attendant arrived just in time to see the man disappear before her eyes. He had been dressed in an Eastern Airlines uniform and was later identified from photographs as Don Repo.

On several occasions the pair have taken an active interest in the flight. A flight engineer was halfway through a pre-flight check when Repo appeared and assured him that the inspection had already been carried out. One particularly persuasive account was recorded by a vice president of Eastern Airlines who had been enjoying a conversation with the captain of his Miami-bound flight from JFK until he recognized the man as Bob Loft. Needless to say, the apparitions played havoc with the schedules. When the captain and two flight attendants saw Loft fade before their eyes they hastily cancelled the flight.

Usually the pair appear simply to check that all is well but on one particular flight they intervened to prevent a potentially fatal accident. Flight attendant Faye Merryweather swore she saw Repo looking inside an infrared oven in the galley and called the flight engineer and the co-pilot for assistance. The engineer immediately recognized Repo's face, then they heard him say, 'Watch out for fire on this airplane.' The warning proved timely. During the flight the aeroplane developed serious engine trouble and was forced to land short of its destination. The oven was subsequently replaced to appease the cabin crew who were becoming increasingly unsettled by such incidents.

This and other episodes are a matter of record in the files of the Flight Safety Foundation and the Federal Aviation Agency. The former investigated several incidents and concluded: 'The reports were given by experienced and trustworthy pilots and crew. We consider them significant. The appearance of the dead flight engineer [Repo] ... was confirmed by the flight engineer.'

The airline responded to the intensifying interest in their planes by refusing to co-operate with anyone other than the airline authorities. It appears they have learnt the true meaning of 'false economy'. The story inspired a bestselling book, *The Ghost of Flight 401*, by John G Fuller and a 1978 TV movie of the same name starring Ernest Borgnine and the then unknown Kim Basinger.

TEMPLE NEWSAM HOUSE

In Leeds, West Yorkshire, is an imposing Tudor-Jacobean house named Temple Newsam House. It is set in 1,200 acres of lush, rolling parkland. Dwellings on this site were listed in the Domesday Book of 1086, and in the 12th century the house became the property of the Templar Knights. In the 15th century, it passed to the family of Thomas, Lord

A commemorative effigy of Lord Darnley: he grew up surrounded by political intrigue, which eventually culminated in his fateful and turbulent marriage to Mary Queen of Scots

Following this, the house was requisitioned by Queen Elizabeth I and since then has passed through many royal hands, undergoing several transformations along the way. It has remained a centre of political strife, and Darnley's murder has not been the only one carried out within its walls. Perhaps it is not surprising, then, that 'the Hampton Court of the North' seems to be home to more than just the living.

Numerous spirits have been seen in various parts of the house over the ages, most notably in the Darnley Room, located in the south-west corner of the early Tudor part of the building. Frequent sightings are made of the spirit of a Knight Templar, still on guard after 900 years, and the disturbing spectre of a small boy who is said to appear from inside a cupboard and cross the room, screaming in pain and anguish.

THE BLUE LADY

Another ghost to haunt this property on a regular basis is the 'Blue Lady', the spirit of Mary Ingram, whose portrait hangs in the Green Damask Room, and who lived in the property during the 17th century. One night, while returning home in her carriage, the unfortunate woman was attacked and robbed by highwaymen. Although not physically harmed, the incident seems to have damaged her psychologically, for from that point on she became obsessed with concealing her possessions. She roams the house to this day, dressed in a long blue dress and lacy shawl, hunting for her long-lost treasures.

Another former royal residence to see more than its fair share of scandal and intrigue is Cumnor House in Oxfordshire. During the 16th century it was home to Lord Robert Dudley and his wife Amy Robsart. Dudley was a close friend of Queen Elizabeth I and barely left the side of the young monarch during the early years of her reign.

Rumour was rife about an impending royal marriage, seemingly hindered only by the fact that Dudley was already married.

In the pursuit of power and royal favour, Dudley abandoned Amy, who was only too aware that she

Darcy, a friend of Cardinal Wolsey, who became the first of a number of people to build parts of the house that still stand today. Following Darcy's brutal beheading for his involvement in the Pilgrimage of Grace revolt, the house was seized by Henry VIII and given to his niece, the Countess of Lennox.

It was in these spectacular historical surroundings that Henry, Lord Darnley, after whom the most famous room in the existing house was named, was born. Darnley grew up surrounded by political intrigue, eventually culminating in his fateful and turbulent marriage to Mary Queen of Scots, which ended with his mysterious murder.

remained the only obstacle to her husband becoming king.

Fearing for her life, she retreated inside Cumnor with just a few trusted servants for company. She became paranoid about her safety, taking great care over what she ate for fear of poisoning and not even venturing out into the beautiful grounds that she loved so dearly.

Despite these extreme precautions, however, Amy could not cheat her destiny. One day, when her staff had left her alone in order to attend the annual fair, she met with tragedy, and when her servants returned from their day out they found her broken body lying at the bottom of the stairs. Slander and calumny ensued, with Queen Elizabeth and Lord Dudley as the prime suspects. The scandal forced the queen to abandon her plans to marry Dudley, as this would have seemed to confirm the rumours. Instead, she made him the Earl of Leicester, and they remained close friends until his death in 1564.

The truth of the mystery surrounding Amy Robsart's death has never been established. Perhaps it is for this reason that there were so many sightings of her restless soul drifting around the stairs where she met her unfortunate end. Eventually, in 1810, the owners decided to demolish the staircase. This had little effect since her sad spirit simply transferred its lonely wanderings to the gardens and parkland surrounding the house. Despite further attempts at exorcism by clergymen, locals to this day claim they see Amy in the vicinity.

RAYNHAM HALL

Another haunted English residence is Raynham Hall in Norfolk. This ancestral home of the Marquess of Townsend is inhabited by a restless spirit called 'The Brown Lady', whose presence has, over the last 170 years, been felt, seen and even captured on film.

This famous ghost is thought to be the spirit of Dorothy Walpole, sister of Sir Robert Walpole, the first Prime Minister to live at 10 Downing Street. Dorothy, like Amy Robsart before her, suffered at the hands of a cruel husband, who took custody of her

The famous picture of 'The Brown Lady' descending the stairs where she met her death at Raynham Hall: she is thought to be the spirit of Dorothy Walpole

children when she started to show symptoms of mental health problems.

The unfortunate woman was then incarcerated in a first-floor bedroom and, again like Amy Robsart, died mysteriously after falling headlong down a flight of stairs.

This house became the site of one of the most famous photographs to be taken of any supernatural entity. While shooting the property for a feature in Country Life magazine, a photographer made an astonishing discovery – one of his pictures clearly showed the outline of a woman descending the main stairway where Dorothy had met her death. Despite rigorous scientific testing, sceptics have been unable to label the picture a forgery. In fact, on the contrary, it seems to prove the existence of the ghost of a tortured soul who continues to haunt her former abode in the endless search for justice.

AUSTRALIA'S MOST HAUNTED HOUSE

Further evidence of ghostly activity can be found many thousands of miles away, on the other side of the world in Australia. The Monte Cristo Homestead in Junee, New South Wales was built in 1884 by Christopher Crawley, a local farmer. Today, it is known as the most haunted house in Australia.

Crawley was an intelligent man, who showed immense foresight in building the Railway Hotel at the same time as he built his home. With the Great Southern Railway Line having arrived in the area in 1878, he was able to take advantage of the sudden explosion in the town's growth, and thus his future was assured.

Crawley lived with his wife and family at the Monte Christo Homestead for many happy years, during which time he made improvements to the already impressive structure. Tragedy, however,

struck this once happy home in 1910, when Crawley died as a result of infection. His wife spent the remaining 23 years of her life in mourning, reportedly so devastated by her husband's death that she only left the house on two occasions following the funeral.

In 1948 the last member of the family left the house and it stood empty and desolate until it was bought and restored in the early 1960s. Since that time, its many occupants have borne witness to an extraordinary amount of supernatural activity. Some witnesses have seen the spirit of a small boy playing in the gardens, and others have observed a woman dressed in period costume pacing the balcony. The most frequent sightings, however, are of the Crawleys themselves, in particular the long-suffering Mrs Crawley. She is reported to roam around her former home, barring some from entering the property, and has also been seen in the chapel, wearing her mourning dress and a large silver cross.

Of the many visitors to the house over the years, the vast majority claim to be aware of a mysterious presence there. People speak of feeling uneasy, or of being watched, and report an inexplicable drop in temperature in certain areas of the building. Its current inhabitants say that strange incidents, such as the banging shut of the doors of empty rooms or the sound of footsteps on the carpeted floor of an unoccupied room, are so frequent that they no longer find them strange.

The number and similarity of these accounts lend them real credibility. As a result, the house has recently been the subject of a paranormal investigation, and was filmed as part of a documentary. The publicization of this investigation and the residence's ensuing widespread reputation have made this old house famous throughout Australia.

> Some witnesses have seen the spirit of a small boy playing in the gardens, and others observed a woman in period costume pacing the balcony

POLTERGEISTS

While the vast majority of hauntings take the form of apparitions moving around properties, usually taking the form of a person known to be dead, there is a whole class of hauntings where the manifestations are altogether more physical and frightening. These are known today as poltergeists, a German word meaning 'noisy ghost'. It is these hauntings that see objects thrown about, fires started and other disturbing events. Typically a poltergeist seems to be centred on a person rather than a place. The person is usually a teenager who is undergoing stress of some kind – perhaps difficult exams, a new job or difficult family relationships. Poltergeist hauntings include some of the most famous in history.

BORLEY RECTORY

During the 1930s and 1940s, Borley Rectory acquired a sinister reputation as 'The Most Haunted House in England'. This unimposing vicarage near Sudbury, Essex, was built in 1863 on the site of a Benedictine monastery which had a dark and unholy history. It was said that a Borley monk had seduced a local nun and the pair had planned to elope. They

Bones were found in the cellar of the rectory and, in an effort to quieten the ghost, given a decent burial in Liston churchyard in 1945, attended by the Rev. AC Henning, two local residents and Harry Price

A ruined Borley Rectory after the blaze of 1939: this unimposing vicarage was built on the site of a Benedictine monastery

were caught and the monk was executed and the nun was walled up alive in the cellar.

The first incumbent of the new rectory was the Reverend Bull who built a summerhouse overlooking a path known as the Nun's Walk. From there he sometimes observed the materializations of the weeping woman as she wandered the gardens searching for her murdered lover. Bull often invited guests to join him on his ghost watch but few stayed long enough to share his vigil. Once they had caught the nun peering in through their groundfloor bedroom window they made their excuses and cut their visit short. Bull's four daughters and his son Harry resigned themselves to regular sightings of the forlorn spirit drifting across the lawn in broad daylight, but when it was joined by a spectral coach and horses galloping up the drive, the Bull children decided to move on. Their father had died in the Blue Room in 1892 and his son Harry in the same room in 1927.

SOBBING NUNS

At the end of the 1920s, the Reverend Eric Smith and his wife took up residence, shrugging off stories of phantom carriages and sobbing nuns. They had barely had time to unpack their belongings before a burst of poltergeist activity encouraged them to move out. However, during their two-year tenure they took the unusual step of calling in the man who was to ensure Borley a place in paranormal history – ghost hunter extraordinaire Harry Price.

Price was a notorious self-publicist and one-time music hall conjurer who had hoped to make a name for himself by exposing fake mediums and debunking the whole spiritualist movement as mere charlatanism. The more he saw at first hand, however, the more convinced he became that some of it was genuine.

Eventually, he came to the conclusion that he was more likely to fulfil his ambition of becoming rich and famous if he could find proof of life after death than if he merely unmasked a few fraudulent mediums.

PHANTOM FOOTSTEPS

At the invitation of the Reverend Smith, and later with the encouragement of the next tenants Mr and Mrs Foyster, Price recorded incidents involving phantom footsteps, flying objects and even physical attacks: on one notable occasion Mrs Foyster was even turned out of bed by an invisible assailant. She was also the subject of near-unintelligible messages scrawled on the walls.

Her husband had the house exorcized but the spirits persisted. The servants' bells rang of their own accord and music could be heard coming from the chapel even though no one was in the building. The Foysters admitted defeat and left the spooks in peace. Subsequent owners fared little better.

Eventually, the house burned down in a mysterious fire in 1939 as predicted by a spirit 11 months earlier during a séance conducted on the site by Price. Witnesses stated that they saw phantoms moving among the flames and the face of a nun staring from a window.

THE GHOST-HUNTER'S BOOK

Price published his findings in 1940 under the title *The Most Haunted House in England*, boasting that it presented 'the best authenticated case of haunting in the annals of psychical research'. The book was an instant bestseller providing as it did some escapism in the first anxious months of the Second World War and quickly established a non-fiction genre of its own – the haunted house mystery. Its success generated a slew of similar books by self-proclaimed experts and sufficient interest in Price to spawn several biographies. Price revelled in his newfound fame, but it was shortlived. He died in 1948 having spent the last 40 years of his life providing what he believed to be irrefutable evidence of the paranormal. But he was not allowed to rest in peace.

In the decade after his death there were spiteful personal attacks on his reputation by rival ghost hunters alleging that Price had faked certain phenomena. Mrs Smith wrote to the Church Times denying that she and her husband had claimed that the rectory was haunted, although it is thought that she may have done this to ingratiate herself with the Church authorities who had been embarrassed by the whole affair.

An investigation by the SPR, conducted by members who were openly hostile to Harry Price, concluded that he had manipulated certain facts to substantiate his claims and that other incidents probably had a 'natural explanation'.

Price's reputation had been seriously undermined, but the fact remains that the Reverend Bull and his family had said that they had seen spirits before Price arrived on the scene. (Miss Ethel Bull had reported seeing a phantom figure at the end of her bed and of sensing another sitting on the end of the bed on more than one occasion.) Also Mrs Foyster appears to have provoked an outbreak of genuine poltergeist activity. Price himself suspected that she augmented it with some phenomena of her own creation, perhaps because she craved attention, or at least so as not to disappoint his expectations.

Either way, questions remain. If Price had faked phenomena, why did he rent the rectory for a year

The ruins of Borley Rectory at the start of its demolition: a brick (circled) flies through the air. Paranormal event or staged trick?

after Mrs Foyster moved out, only to admit that there was nothing anomalous to report? He would have had more than enough time and opportunity to stage something truly astounding to substantiate his claims. The inactivity during that period suggests that the spirits might have been attracted by the presence of the Reverend Bull and Mrs Foyster who perhaps possessed mediumistic abilities.

A subsequent investigation by the SPR under R J

Hastings unearthed previously unpublished letters from the Reverend Smith and his wife to Price, written in 1929, in which Smith states emphatically that 'Borley is undoubtedly haunted'. This discovery forced the SPR to revise its earlier findings. Price had been vindicated.

Whatever shortcuts Price may have taken to enhance his reputation as Britain's foremost ghost hunter, it cannot be denied that there was something out of the ordinary occurring at Borley.

A footnote to the Borley investigation was added in the 1950s by the novelist Dennis Wheatley, author of *The Devil Rides Out* and dozens of occult thrillers:

> 'Kenneth Allsop, the book reviewer of the *Daily Mail*, told me that when Borley was in the news he was sent down to do an article on it, and with him he took a photographer. Borley was then being debunked so that had to be the tone of the article. But when the photographer developed his photos the figure of a nun could be quite clearly seen on one of them. He took it to Allsop, who took it to his editor, but the editor said, "No, I just daren't print it."'

A curious postscript to the Borley saga occurred on 28 August 1977 when ley line expert Stephen Jenkins visited the area with a view to seeing if there was anything to the theory that the curious manifestations might be linked to a spider's web of ley line alignments.

> 'The time was precisely 12.52 pm and we were driving south-west along the minor road which marks the north end of the hall ground, when on the road in front in the act of turning left into a hedge (I mean our left across the path of the car), instantaneously appeared four men in black – I thought them hooded and cloaked – carrying a black, old-fashioned coffin, ornately trimmed with silver. The impression made on both of us was one of absolute physical presence, of complete material reality. Thelma and I at once agreed to make separate notes without comparing impressions. We did so and the descriptions tallied exactly, except that she noted the near left bearer turned his face towards her. I did not see this as I was abruptly braking at the time. What I had seen as a hood, she described as a soft tall hat with a kind of scarf falling to the left shoulder, thrown across the cloak body to the right. The face was that of a skull.
>
> 'The next day we returned to the spot at precisely the same time and took a picture. It is a Kodak colour slide. In the hedge near the gap where the funeral party vanished (there's a path there leading to Belchamp Walter churchyard) is a short figure apparently cloaked, his face lowered with a skull-like dome to the head ... I hazard a guess that the dress of the coffin bearer is that of the late 14th century. There seems to be no local legend of a phantom funeral.'

WEIRD NIGHT IN A HAUNTED HOUSE

While Harry Price was accused of having falsified some of his evidence and having made fraudulent claims in order to boost his reputation as Britain's foremost ghost hunter, the following article from the *Daily Mirror* of 14 June 1929 suggests that Harry's first visit to Borley was lively enough without the need for artificial aids or exaggeration:

'WEIRD NIGHT IN "HAUNTED" HOUSE
From our Special Correspondent'

> 'There can no longer be any doubt that Borley Rectory, near here, is the scene of some remarkable incidents. Last night Mr Harry Price, Director of the National Laboratory For Psychical Research, his secretary Miss Lucy Kaye, the Reverend G F

Harry Price, ghost hunter extraordinaire with his trusty camera: he was a member of the Magic Circle and his autobiography was called The Search for Truth

Smith, Rector of Borley, Mrs Smith and myself were witnesses to a series of remarkable happenings. All these things occurred without the assistance of a medium or any kind of apparatus. And Mr Price, who is a research expert only and not a spiritualist, expressed himself puzzled and astonished at the results. To give the phenomena a thorough test however, he is arranging for a séance to be held in the rectory with the aid of a prominent London medium.

'The first remarkable happening was the dark figure that I saw in the garden. We were standing in the Summer House at dusk watching the lawn when I saw the "apparition" which so many claim to have seen, but owing to the deep shadows it was impossible for one to discern any definite shape or attire.

'But something certainly moved along the path on the other side of the lawn and although I quickly ran across to investigate it had vanished when I reached the spot.

'Then as we strolled towards the rectory discussing the figure there came a terrific crash and a pane of glass from the roof of a porch hurtled to the ground. We ran inside and upstairs to inspect the room immediately over the porch but found nobody.

'A few seconds later we were descending the stairs, Miss Kaye leading, and Mr Price behind me when something flew past my head, hit an iron stove in the hall and shattered. With our flash lamps we inspected

'**Behind me something flew past my head, hit an iron stove in the hall and shattered. With our flash lamps we inspected the broken pieces**'

the broken pieces and found them to be sections of a red vase which, with its companion, had been standing on the mantelpiece of what is known as the Blue Room which we had just searched. Mr Price was the only person behind me and he could not have thrown the vase at such an angle as to pass my head and hit the stove below.

'We sat on the stairs in darkness for a few minutes and just as I turned to Mr Price to ask him whether we had waited long enough something hit my hand. This turned out to be a common moth ball and had apparently dropped from the same place as the vase. I laughed at the idea of a spirit throwing moth balls about, but Mr Price said that such methods of attracting attention were not unfamiliar to investigators.

'Finally came the most astonishing event of the night. From one o'clock till nearly four this morning all of us, including the rector and his wife, actually questioned the spirit or whoever it was and received at times the most emphatic answers.

'A cake of soap on the washstand was lifted and thrown heavily on to a china jug standing on the floor with such force that the soap was deeply marked. All of us were at the other side of the room when this happened. Our questions which we asked out loud were answered by raps apparently made on the back of a mirror in the room and it must be remembered though that no medium or spiritualist was present.'

THE EDGAR ALLEN POE HOUSE

The spirit of Edgar Allen Poe, author of *The Fall of the House of Usher* and other tales of terror, haunts both American fiction and the house in Baltimore where he lived as a young man in the 1830s. The narrow two and a half-storey brick house at 203 North Amity Street in an impoverished area is said to be so spooky that even local gangs are scared to break in. When the police arrived to investigate a reported burglary in 1968 they saw a phantom light in the groundfloor window floating up to reappear on the second floor and then in the attic, but when they entered the property there was no one to be seen.

Even in daylight the house is unsettling. An eerie portrait of Poe's wife, painted as she lay in her coffin, hangs in one room, her melancholic gaze following visitors around the room. Local residents have also reported seeing a shadowy figure working at a desk at a second floor window, although Poe, whose morbid obsession with premature burial led to his incarceration in an asylum, worked in the attic.

POLTERGEIST ACTIVITY

The curator has recorded many incidents of poltergeist activity and this appears to originate in the bedroom that belonged to Poe's grandmother. Here, doors and windows have opened and closed by themselves, visitors have been tapped on the shoulder and disembodied voices have been heard. Psychic investigators have also reported seeing a stout, grey-haired old woman dressed in clothing of the period gliding through the rooms.

In a twist of which the master of the macabre might have been perversely proud, local parents still use the spectre of the horror writer to terrify their children into doing what they are told. Poe has become the bogeyman of Baltimore.

'There did stand the enshrouded figure of the Lady Madeleine... there was blood upon her white robes' from The Fall of the House of Usher *by Edgar Allen Poe*

CURSES

Can the utterance of a few malicious words really change someone's destiny? Those who believe in the power of a curse are convinced that catastrophe will follow in its wake. And sometimes ensuing mishaps and disasters are so bizarre and numerous that all the evidence points to a jinx.

CURSE OF THE BOY KING

Perhaps the most infamous curse of all was one that protected the tomb of King Tutankhamun. When Egyptologist Howard Carter discovered the tomb in 1922, it was the culmination of a career spent scouring the desert for riches. The honour of opening the inner door, revealing the treasures of the king in

Lord Carnarvon and Howard Carter with Lady Evelyn Herbert at Tutankhamen's tomb

all their splendour, fell to Lord Carnarvon (financier of the expedition) on 17 February 1923. Within weeks after that fateful day Carnarvon was dead, apparently from an infected mosquito bite. The bite mark on his cheek was said to resemble one borne by the boy king himself.

When Carnarvon died, the lights in Cairo flickered and failed, while miles away at home his dog fell into a fit and passed away. Tales of other expedition members dying suddenly abounded.

Even the pilots who took the royal artefacts as cargo on their planes apparently met unexpected deaths. For several years the string of terrible ill fortune continued, as museum curators associated with the exhibition of Tutankhamen's treasures keeled over.

LETHAL SPORES

The curse that protected the tomb was written in hieroglyphics on a clay tablet. When deciphered, it read: 'Death will slay with its wings whoever disturbs the peace of the Pharaoh.' Yet, despite careful cataloguing of all the tomb's contents, the dire warning has vanished. Perhaps it never existed in the first place, being the product of some sun-affected imagination. However, there is another explanation. Carter may well have hidden the tablet bearing the curse to prevent a walk-out by superstitious local workers, on whom he was reliant for his work.

Cynics have poured scorn over the curse claims, pointing out that mosquito bites were and still are frequently fatal. They say that the lights in Cairo often blacked out, and that the story of the death of Carnarvon's dog is only anecdotal. Much has recently been made of the theory that the tomb contained lethal spores that afflicted those who went inside, giving weight to the sceptics' argument. Yet when Carter died a decade later it was from natural causes. The debate on the curse continues.

Unluckiest of all, of course, was King Tutankhamun himself, who died when he was still a teenager and whose memorial was all but erased by subsequent royals.

A HISTORY OF CURSES

Belief in curses stretches back into the mists of time. Ancient verbal curses may seem comical today, but in the past they would strike terror into the heart: 'May the seven terriers of hell sit on the spool of your breast and bark in at your soul-case,' says an old Irish curse. 'She should have stones and not children,' according to a Yiddish one.

In the past people have made a profitable business out of issuing curses. The philosopher Plato (427–347BC) wrote in *The Republic*, 'If anyone wishes to injure an enemy; for a small fee they (sorcerers) will bring harm on good or bad alike, binding the gods to serve their purposes by spells and curses.'

Curses are a common Biblical theme, perhaps the most famous being issued by God against Adam and Eve in the Garden of Eden.

THE HOPE DIAMOND

A wrathful god appears to have orchestrated fearful vengeance after the Hope diamond was plundered from a temple in Mandala, Burma in the 17th century. Mined in India, it was a fabulous violet-coloured specimen of the very highest quality. No one knows what happened to the thief, but it fell into the possession of a French trader, Jean-Baptiste Tavernier. Tavernier sold the diamond to French king Louis XIV, who had it made into a heart before giving it to his mistress Madame de Montespan. Shortly afterwards she was publicly disgraced in a black magic scandal. The luckless trader Tavernier met a grisly end on a trip to Russia and dogs were discovered gnawing on his bones.

The gem remained in the royal collection, and it was worn by Marie Antoinette before she was beheaded in the French Revolution. In the chaos that enveloped Paris it was stolen and its whereabouts were unknown for some three decades. Could it be that the curse of the Hope Diamond had finally lost its power?

The diamond turned up in the 1830s, in the possession of Dutch diamond cutter Wilhelm Fals. Its exquisite beauty bewitched his son Hendrick, and the hapless boy ultimately committed suicide.

Evelyn Walsh McLean who bought the Hope Diamond for $180,000

The dangerous gem was then bought by the banker Henry Philip Hope, who gave it his name, but suffered no harm from it. Afterwards, though, the curse appears to have gained some momentum. It was bequeathed to a relative, Lord Francis Hope, whose marriage collapsed.

By 1904 a certain Jacques Colot was the owner, until he lost his mind and committed suicide. Russian nobleman Prince Kanilovsky presented it to his lover, whom he later shot and killed before being bludgeoned to death himself. Diamond dealer Habib Bey drowned and Greek merchant Simon Montharides plunged to his death with his wife and child when their horse and carriage went over a cliff top. The Hope diamond then went to the Ottoman ruler, Abdul Hamid III, shortly before an uprising usurped the Sultanate. His favourite wife, often seen wearing the jewel, was stabbed to death.

The last ill-fated owner was wealthy Evelyn Walsh McLean. Within a year of purchasing the diamond from jewellery impresario Pierre Cartier for $180,000, her son Vinson was killed in a car accident. Her husband Ned began drinking, left her for another woman and finally lost his mind. Then, in 1946, their daughter took an overdose of sleeping pills. After Evelyn died in 1947 the gem finally went into the Smithsonian Institute in Washington, a move that appears to have neutered its potency.

Evelyn had received numerous warnings about the curse of the Hope diamond, many in unsolicited letters from strangers. But she maintained that the bad luck attached to its ownership was pure chance. 'What tragedies have befallen me might have occurred had I never seen or touched the Hope Diamond. My observations have persuaded me that tragedies, for anyone who lives, are not escapable.'

From treading the sacred corridors of Tutankhamen's tomb, to plundering the exquisite jewels of Burma, many of the most potent curses seem to be released when humans tread too far into forbidden territory. And where some curses seem to lose potency over time, others retain their venom, wreaking havoc down hapless generations…

THE KENNEDY CURSE

A family rich in fame, fortune and political power often arouses envy, but could anyone be so jealous as to invoke terrible curses, designed to bring a dynasty to its knees? Many people believe that the appalling misfortunes that befall a few well-known clans occur at a rate far beyond what could be expected under

Joe and Rose Kennedy, unaware of the calamities that were to befall their children, pose for a family portrait in 1934

normal circumstances – and that a jinx is the obvious explanation.

Although no known curse has been sworn against the Kennedy family, a prominent political clan in the

United States, the number of tragedies they have suffered far exceeds the average, and seems almost unnatural.

For Joe Kennedy, the adage that 'money can't buy happiness' must have left a sour taste. A multi-millionaire by the age of 30, and the father of nine children, Joe appeared to have the Midas touch. But although he and his wife Rose lived long, comfortable lives, their children were famously ill-starred.

SUCCESSION OF DEATHS

In 1944 their eldest son, also called Joe, died aged 29, when the bomber aircraft he was piloting exploded above the English Channel. He was fighting in the Second World War – a war which Joe Senior had publicly advised the US against joining. His son's body was never found.

His daughter Kathleen's husband, the Marquis of Hartington, died in the same year, and Kathleen herself perished in an aircraft accident aged 28, in 1948. Another daughter, Rosemary, was institutionalized in 1941.

In 1960, second son John Fitzgerald Kennedy became the thirty-fifth president of the US, fulfilling Joe Senior's dearest ambitions. But just three years later, the 46-year-old was shot in the head by an assassin as his motor cavalcade crawled through Dallas, Texas. He and his wife Jackie Kennedy had already lost their son Patrick, who died at just two days old.

Now the political aspirations of the grieving Joe Kennedy lay with his son Robert. But within five years he was also dead, killed in Los Angeles while campaigning for the presidency.

If all these deaths in the family were not hard enough to bear, the tragedy was compounded when youngest brother Teddy, a senator, was in a near-fatal car accident in 1969. His car plunged from a bridge and sank into the waterway at Chappaquiddick Island, and although he struggled to safety his passenger, Mary Jo Kopechne, 29, was drowned. Questions were raised about the reasons for the crash, and why Teddy had been unable to rescue his passenger. It seemed the trouble would never end.

Daughters Eunice, Patricia and Jean emerged largely unscathed from these troubled times. But the curse regained momentum with the next generation of Kennedys. John Junior died in a light plane crash in 1999. One of Robert's sons, David, died of a drugs overdose in 1984, while another was killed in a skiing accident at Aspen in 1997. Meanwhile Teddy Junior, son of Edward, was struck down with cancer and had to have a leg amputated.

Joe Kennedy senior saw only a portion of the disasters that fate had in store for his family. He died in 1969, aged 81. Were his children the pawns of a cursed fate, or were they simply the victims of aberrant behaviour or poor judgement? Perhaps the real victim of the string of tragedies was Rose, who lived until the age of 104, scarred by the misfortunes that piled upon her children and grandchildren.

MONACO MISFORTUNE

The royal family that rules the small principality of Monaco has often hit the headlines through a succession of calamities. In 1956, a union between Monaco's Prince Rainier III and Hollywood film beauty Grace Kelly seemed to augur well for the dynasty. Together they had three children and were the picture of happiness.

Unfortunately, all that ended in 1982, when a car driven by Princess Grace with her daughter Stephanie as passenger plunged down a cliff. Grace was immediately killed, aged just 52, while 17-year-old Stephanie suffered neck injuries and was emotionally scarred.

After this tragic incident, the ties that bound the close-knit family began to unravel. Stephanie had a succession of doomed relationships – she even ran away with the circus in pursuit of love. Her sister Caroline's first marriage ended after two tumultuous years, and she eventually found happiness with Italian businessman Stefano Casiraghi and had three children. But they were still infants at the time of Stefano's tragic death in a powerboat crash in 1990.

Prince Albert II of Monaco, who inherited the throne when Prince Rainier died in 2005, has shown

a marked reluctance to marry and produce an heir. Perhaps he is mindful of the curse reputedly laid upon the family when one of his ancestors, Prince Rainier I, kidnapped and raped a witch. Her revenge was to curse the family with the words: 'Never will a Grimaldi find true happiness in marriage'.

And if that were not sufficient, there is talk of another curse laid in 1297, the year the first Grimaldi, Francesco the Spiteful, conquered the world's second smallest state. After he tricked his way into a fortress by dressing as a monk, he was cursed by its defeated defenders.

NOBLE DEATHS

Problems have beset the Craven family in England, since 17th-century baron William Craven made a servant girl pregnant and refused to wed her. She used her Romany heritage to summon a curse that seems to have had lasting effects.

Since then, the family history has been fraught with calamity. The eighth Earl, Simon Craven, died

Bruce Lee in Enter the Dragon *(1973)*

in a car crash in 1990. He had inherited the title from his older brother Thomas who, morbidly obsessed with the curse and depressed following a drugs incident, shot himself aged 26. Their father, the sixth Earl, had died of leukemia aged 47. His father had drowned after falling from a boat following a party. Indeed, from the creation of the peerage in 1801, none of the incumbents have reached the age of 60. Could the curse of the servant girl all those years ago really still have the power to cause so many untimely deaths?

A PERSONAL CURSE?

The efficacy of curses is often psychological, and has much to do with the victim's state of mind. If someone feels like a victim, in many cases they will become one. Indeed, in many parts of the world, an effigy speared with pins, such as a voodoo doll, is still a powerful and disturbing symbol of a curse.

This practice has long been used in India, Iran, Egypt, Africa and Europe to provoke profound fear when witnessed by the intended victim.

This psychological aspect of curses seems to have sealed the fate of Kung Fu fighter Bruce Lee, who achieved international stardom with his films. Yet his success could not shield him from his dreadful personal conviction that demons were lying in wait for him. His greatest fear was that the curse he believed was intended for him would pass to his offspring.

In 1973, Lee collapsed in convulsions on a film set. Within two months, aged 32, he died after apparently suffering a brain haemorrhage. His son Brandon grew up in the same mould as his father, loving Kung Fu and fearing its spiritual powers. In 1993, aged just 27, he was killed following a film stunt calamity. Lee was shot by a gun that should have contained blanks, but was in fact inexplicably loaded with live bullets.

Logically, it seems impossible that supernatural forces could emanate from oaths uttered centuries ago, or from dolls pierced with pins, to blight the lives of a dynasty. Yet curses, like superstitions, have a habit of proving themselves. However ancient their origins, belief in curses stays firm even in the twenty-first century.

THE LITTLE BASTARD

James Dean, the iconic Hollywood film star, died tragically young, at a point in his life when his acting career was going from strength to strength. Although he had starred in only a few films, he had earned himself much acclaim and a sizeable fortune.

With his new-found riches, Dean had bought a sports car, a Porsche Spyder, one of only ninety in the world at that time. He nicknamed the car 'The Little Bastard', and had this name painted on the machine along with a racing stripe.

Dean had intended to race his beloved car himself, but sadly was never given the chance. On 30 September 1955, only two weeks after he had bought the car, he died in it, following a head-on collision with another vehicle. The driver of the other

James Dean, as he appeared in the film Giant

car survived, having sustained only cuts and bruises.

In the weeks preceding his death, Dean had been seen driving his car everywhere, proudly displaying it to all of his friends, although he was surprised to find that many of them failed to share his enthusiasm for the powerful machine.

Several of them apparently felt a sense of horror when they saw the vehicle – some out of concern for the dangers that such a fast car might pose to Dean's reckless nature, others simply because of an innate sense of foreboding about the machine.

PATTERN OF MISFORTUNE

At the time, Dean would not have been aware that a number of strange happenings had already been linked with the car since its arrival at the Competition Motors showroom. Several mechanics had hurt themselves on the car shortly after it was delivered, one breaking his thumb after trapping it in one of the doors and another cutting himself as he adjusted the engine. At the time, these events seemed to be no more than accidents, but later they would be seen as part of a much larger pattern of misfortune, or even something altogether more sinister.

After the fatal crash, the car wreckage was bought for salvage by the motor mechanic George Barris, the very man who had customized the machine for Dean several weeks earlier. It was only when he began to re-use parts of the car that he started to suspect that some form of terrible curse might be attached to the vehicle, a curse that had not only claimed the life of the young film star, but was also causing numerous other disasters in the lives of those unlucky enough to have acquired a piece of the car.

The engine of 'The Little Bastard' had been largely undamaged by the crash, so Barris had reconditioned it and sold it to a racing enthusiast, Dr William F Eschrich.

One of the doctor's friends and fellow racer, Dr Carl McHenry, learned of the sale and decided to buy the transaxle of the car. Barris also sold several other vehicle parts, including the two back tyres.

In the first race in which the two doctors tested their new equipment, both men were involved in

The twisted wreckage of the 'The Little Bastard' being lifted away after James Dean's fatal crash in September 1955

serious accidents. Dr Eschrich's car turned over after locking up on entering a bend. Fortunately he survived the crash, although he was left paralyzed. Dr McHenry was not so lucky: he was killed after losing control of the car and hitting a tree. As if this were not enough, before the week was out, the driver who had bought the two back tyres narrowly escaped death after both tyres blew out simultaneously during another race.

Learning of the multiple disasters, Barris decided that he would try to put the car to some kind of beneficial use. Accordingly, he lent the crumpled machine to the California Highway Safety Patrol for publicity purposes, thinking that Dean's fame would greatly enhance their campaign on accident prevention. Unfortunately, at that point he did not realize that the car was actually a source of accidents in itself.

The car was taken into the possession of the Highway Patrol and stored in a garage with a large number of other cars. While it was there, a mysterious fire broke out – many cars were completely destroyed and almost all incurred serious damage. Curiously, 'The Little Bastard' emerged from the fire remarkably unscathed.

A short time later, while the car was being taken to a display area for demonstration purposes, a strange accident took place. Dean's car was being transported on the back of a flat-bed truck, driven by an experienced driver named George Barhuis, when it skidded on a wet road, and the truck's rig crashed into a ditch. Barhuis was thrown from the cab by the impact, but is believed to have survived the crash. However, in a bewildering tragedy, he was then killed when the wreck of 'The Little Bastard' fell from the back of the truck and landed on top of him, crushing him to death.

Yet the litany of disasters was still not complete. On the fourth anniversary of Dean's fatal crash, a teenager in Detroit was viewing the car, which was on a large display. Without warning, the structure on which the car was resting collapsed, and the car toppled forward crushing the boy's legs. It seems inconceivable that, following this, the car

The grave of James Dean in Fairmount, USA, is still visited by fans from all over the world, who leave quirky tributes to their hero

was still put out on display to the public.

A few weeks after this accident, the car was once again being transported by truck, when it fell from the back of the vehicle, smashing into the road and causing the serious injury of yet more people.

DOOMED

Fortunately, the cursed car was doomed itself. Shortly after this final accident, the vehicle spontaneously fell apart while on show in New Orleans. Attempts were made to put it back together, but George Barris stepped in and arranged to have the remains of the car transported back to his garage in California. When the delivery arrived, the container was opened and, to their astonishment, the car had disappeared.

It is not known if it had been stolen by an obsessive admirer of the film star, but no trace of it has ever been found. Certainly, if anyone had been foolish enough to take the vehicle into their own possession, they would have been very fortunate to escape the curse that had randomly struck at those connected with the car. Nevertheless, the fact that it is now missing can only add to the sense of mystery that surrounds not only this jinxed machine, but also the tragic, doomed figure of James Dean.

This enclosed area is a preserved part of the original

African Burial Ground

...d in 1794, the African Burial Ground once covered more than f... ...timated that as many as 20,000 or more African men, wor... ...l cemetery. Unearthed during building construction in... ...ark and within the New York City African Burial Grou... ...ng remnant of the burial ground is dedicated to the peopl... ...slaved in the city's early history from 1626 until July 4, 1827

BLACK HOPE CEMETERY

Some curses are so general that they are feared by large numbers of people or entire populations. Trinkets and lucky charms are often worn as a means of self-protection. Other curses are more specific, directed at a particular person, group or place – often these individual stories become woven into the very fabric of superstition, reinforcing the notion that such malevolent powers do, in fact, exist.

This type of personal experience was certainly the case as far as the Haney and Williams families were concerned, when they bought their brand-new homes near Houston, Texas, in 1982. Moving into the neighbourhood was the culmination of their family dreams, as their houses were set in large gardens on an attractive new estate.

One year after the move, Sam and Judith Haney appeared to have settled well into their new home.

Reverend Jesse Jackson speaking at the New York African Burial Ground which was unearthed in 1991 during building works

This was all to change, however, when they decided to have a swimming pool built in their garden. Digging commenced, whereupon an elderly man living in the area knocked on their door and brought them some unsettling news.

He informed them that their new house was built on the site of an old African-American burial ground and that, in excavating part of the garden for the swimming pool, they were digging precisely over some of the graves.

He even gave the Haneys the names of some black families who used to live in the area so that they could corroborate his story. The Haneys, however, were sceptical and continued work on the pool.

After a short while, two crude coffins were unearthed, containing the remains of a man and a woman. Appalled by their discovery, the Haneys realized that the old man had been right. Once the shock had settled, they decided that it was imperative that the bodies should be returned to their resting place with a proper burial.

So they set about trying to establish the identity of the bodies. Their search culminated in the discovery of an elderly man, Jasper Norton, who had worked as a gravedigger within the former black community. He informed the Haneys that the housing estate on which they lived was indeed built on the site of a former cemetery which had been named Black Hope, and contained mainly the graves of slaves. He identified the exhumed bodies as belonging to two slaves, Charlie and Betty Thomas, who had died when he was a young man.

The Haneys continued their search, this time for descendants of the buried couple. When this proved fruitless, they decided to return the remains to the spot from which they had come. They were troubled at having disturbed a grave, and hoped that, by reburial, they could lay the whole episode to rest – as events were to reveal, however, they were very much mistaken.

Not long after they had reburied the bodies, the Haneys' lives began to be affected by strange happenings. At first, this took the form of disembodied voices that disturbed their nightly sleep, but soon there were other incidents such as appliances and lights spontaneously turning on and off, further unnatural noises and the discovery of a pair of Judith Haney's shoes on the very spot where Betty Thomas lay buried.

After a while, the Haneys' fear and bewilderment grew to such an extent that they confided in their neighbours, Ben and Jean Williams. To their amazement, they discovered that they were not the only family to have suffered from paranormal interventions – at least a dozen of the households had experienced some kind of unexplained activity, ranging from doors opening and closing to strange apparitions.

STRANGE DEEP HOLES

Like the Haneys, the Williams family also believed that they were being persecuted by a curse from beyond the grave. Although they had not themselves actually found any corpses on their land, they had been astonished to find that nothing seemed to grow in their garden, and that strange, deep holes would continually appear, forming afresh even after they had been filled in. This belief turned to outright conviction when six members of the Williams family were diagnosed with cancer in the same year – sadly, for three of them, this was fatal. As far as the Williams were concerned, this was a direct intervention from beyond the grave.

Events took an even more tragic turn when Jean Williams decided to find out whether there were any graves in her garden, such as there were on the Haneys' land. So one day she and her daughter, Tina, started to dig up the garden. After a short while, Tina collapsed.

Two days later, she died from a heart attack, aged just 30.

CURSED LAND

Could it be that these two families were right and that the dead had objected so strongly to the desecration of their graves that they had managed to bridge the gap between their world and ours? For the residents of the former Black Hope cemetery, there was no question. They believed that the land was cursed, and that they had activated this curse by disturbing the graves.

Events proved too much for the Haney and Williams families, who decided to sell up and move on. Whatever force had been acting upon them, whether it was the workings of their own subconscious or the 'Black Hope Curse' itself, several lives had been lost and many families had been driven from their homes in fear.

Curiously, subsequent tenants of their former homes did not report any problems at all. Had the spirits' anger been satisfied, or had the unpleasant knowledge that they lived above a graveyard just been too much for the 'cursed' families? If events had been restricted solely to the occasional strange happening within the households, then perhaps they could have been accused of paranoia. The extent of the illnesses and deaths involved, however, seem to make the case for a curse a rather convincing one.

POINT PLEASANT

For many years the area of West Virginia known as Point Pleasant has been beset by a series of disasters

A Shawnee warrior of the Chillocothe tribe

and misfortunes. Although these could be attributed to nothing more than bad luck, some ascribe the events to the ancient curse of a betrayed Indian chief.

In order to understand the nature and power of a curse, it is necessary to know the background to the events – only then can it be judged whether there could have been sufficient cause for such a potent force of revenge. The story in this particular case dates back more than 200 years, to the 1770s, when the American frontiersmen were battling against the native Indians in their attempts to push west, and later fighting the British for their independence.

As the American settlers found their way to the land around the Ohio River, now West Virginia, they encountered strong resistance from the Indian tribes, some of whom had joined together to form a powerful confederacy. This was led by the chieftain of the Shawnee tribe, a man called Keigh-tugh-gua (Cornstalk).

A battle between the American settlers and the Indians took place in 1774, and both sides sustained heavy losses. The Indians were forced to retreat westwards as the settlers took over the land and fortified it. Cornstalk, recognizing that he would have trouble defeating such heavily armed men, decided to make peace with them.

A few years later, trouble was to erupt again, as the British began to stir up feeling against the rebellious settlers. They tried to bring as many Indians on to their side as possible and several tribes from Cornstalk's old confederacy joined them to prepare an attack on the settlements. Cornstalk chose instead to honour his peace and he and another chief, Red Hawk of the Delaware tribe, went to the American fort to discuss the situation.

On their arrival, the chieftains were taken hostage by the Americans, as it was believed that the Indians would not attack while their chiefs were being held. While in captivity, Cornstalk was well treated, and even assisted the American settlers in planning their tactics against the British. After a few days, Cornstalk's young son, Ellinipisco, came to the fort with news for his father, whereupon he was also taken hostage.

TURN FOR THE WORSE

Shortly after this, events took a dramatic turn for the worse after a number of American soldiers who had gone out to hunt deer were ambushed and killed by Indians. When this was discovered, discipline inside the fort broke down and an angry mob broke into the prisoners' quarters with murder in mind. They showed no mercy to Cornstalk or his young son, who was shot before his very eyes. It was this act of murder and betrayal that prompted Cornstalk to utter his mighty curse, words that, it seems, have affected the area for hundreds of years.

According to legend, he declared 'I came to this fort as your friend and you murdered me. You have murdered by my side my young son. For this may the curse of the Great Spirit rest upon this land. May it be blighted by nature. May it be blighted in its hopes.'

After these tragic events had taken place, Cornstalk was afforded a proper burial, and he was interred near the fort where he had been killed. He was not allowed to rest in peace, however, since his remains were dug up and moved twice for the sake of new buildings and monuments – first in 1840, and then again in 1950. If the original act of betrayal had not been sufficient to secure the power of the curse, then the desecration of his grave surely was.

This area became known as Point Pleasant and, almost in defiance of the curse, residents decided to erect a monument in honour of the soldiers who had defeated Cornstalk in the first battle of 1774. Strangely, this monument was to be struck twice by lightning, first in 1909, delaying its unveiling ceremony, and then once again in 1921, causing serious damage.

These happenings were nothing, however, compared to the catalogue of disasters that was to befall this relatively small community. In 1880 a huge fire ravaged an entire block in the centre of town, while in 1907 America's worst mining disaster was responsible for the deaths of 310 men. In 1967, the Silver Bridge disaster killed 46 people.

This coincided with strange local sightings such as lights in the sky and the regular appearance of the mysterious stalker known as 'Mothman'.

Shortly after this, in 1968 and 1970, a number of aircraft crashed in the area, killing more than 100 passengers. In 1978 a derailed freight train caused an immense spill of toxic chemicals that poisoned that land and the water basin of the area, destroying all the local wells.

It is thought that this environmental catastrophe could be the blight of nature mentioned in Cornstalk's curse, while the blighting of hope appears to have been manifest in the depressed economy of Point Pleasant.

There are many who would maintain that when disaster befalls a person or community, it is just a matter of misfortune. To suggest that it is as a result of a curse, they say, is to resort to ancient superstitions which have no place in the modern world. When, however, such a huge chain of catastrophes occurs, as has been the case with Point Pleasant, it is difficult not to admit that a curse might have been responsible after all.

THE EARLS OF MAR

The ruins of Alloa Tower in Scotland are now all that remains of a vast manor, the hereditary seat of the Erskine family, the Earls of Mar. The fate of the place was interwoven with that of the family who lived there, not just because they had lived there for generations, but because of the curse that predicted, and assured, the doom of the family and the seat of their power.

It is believed that this curse was uttered against the Earl of Mar by the Abbot of CambusKenneth during the 16th century. In destroying the Abbey at CambusKenneth, the Earl had unwittingly sealed the fate of his lineage for years to come, for many of the predicted details of the curse, although cryptic when uttered, were to come shockingly true.

Remarkably, it was not unusual at that time for Scottish curses to predict suffering that would last for several generations, but this particular curse was very specific about certain matters. Most importantly, and typically for a curse of this kind, it was foretold that the Erskine family would become extinct – a fate which was the ultimate disaster for any hereditary aristocratic lineage. The curse elaborated further: before the family died out, all its estates and property would fall into the hands of strangers – again, this would have been a horrifying concept to a family of landed gentry. At this point it might have been expected that even the Abbot's rage would have been satisfied, but the curse did not stop there.

It predicted that a future Erskine would later live to see his home consumed by flames while his wife burned inside it and three of his children would never see the light of day. Moreover, adding further disgrace to the name of Erksine, the great hall of the family seat would be used to stable horses and a lowly weaver would work in the grand chamber of state. The curse was predicted to end only after all this had passed and an ash sapling had taken root at the top of the tower. Although the curse must have worried the Earl of Mar, he managed to live his entire life without seeing any of the predicted events come true and, on his deathbed, he must have reflected that the family had escaped from the Abbot's wrathful utterings. In this, he was greatly mistaken.

This seems to have been a patient curse because it was a while before certain events began to show the truth behind the predictions. In 1715 a subsequent Earl of Mar declared his allegiance to James Stuart, the son of James VII of Scotland, who was known as 'the Old Pretender'. The Earl led a failed Jacobite rebellion against the crown in an attempt to install

A contemporary portrait of James Stuart

James Stuart as king. He was defeated and, in retribution, the family were stripped of their land and titles – in this way, one part of the curse had come true. Whether the Earl actually attributed this to the curse is unknown, as he might have merely viewed events as a punishment for his own actions. However, more of the predictions were to be borne out within a few generations.

PAYING THE PRICE

Almost a century later, in 1801, it was John Francis Erskine who was unlucky enough to bear the brunt of the prophecy, and so pay the price for his ancestor's mistakes. To begin with, three of his children were born completely blind – thus, as the curse had foretold, they would 'never see the light of day'. Then Alloa Tower, all that remained of the family's former glory, was devastated by fire and Erskine's wife perished in the flames.

The main body of the curse had now come true and only the details were left to be completed. Sure enough, a troop of cavalry used the half-ruined hall as shelter for their horses while they were moving around the country. Subsequently, a homeless weaver took up residence in the ruins of the building and plied his trade in the nearby town. In 1820 a small ash tree was seen to have taken root in the ruins of Alloa Tower. The curse had now been fulfilled in every detail.

Of all the questions that spring to mind in this case, the first revolves around the existence of the curse. Was it ever really uttered or could it have been made up after the events to explain and justify the demise of the Erskines and serve as a useful warning to other potentially rebellious landowners? Certainly, both historical fact and local folklore indicate that the curse was a reality, but there is always the possibility that, rather than having the ability to bring about such terrible events, the Abbot was simply in possession of astonishing visionary powers.

Either possibility could apply in this case. Perhaps the Abbot did have the power to seal the destiny of the Erskine family through a curse, or maybe his powers of divination were comparable to those of a prophet, although this would appear to be the only instance of such a prediction from the Abbot. Whatever the truth of the matter, it seems that the mystical powers of the Abbot of CambusKenneth were so great that they are remembered to this very day.

THE EVIL EYE

The 'evil eye' is one of the world's oldest superstitions, with many examples dating back to the time of the Ancient Egyptians. It is also one of the most unusual curses, for it can be cast only by those who themselves possess the evil eye and, remarkably, it is usually cast unintentionally. The evil eye can place a curse on almost anything, from children and livestock to crops and property.

This curse seems to have resonance with a large sector of humanity as it is known all over the world. The Scottish term for it is *droch shuil*, the Italian *mal occhio*, the Arabic *ayin harsha* and the Hebrew *ayin horeh*. Belief in its power is most concentrated around the Mediterranean and Aegean seas, but extends into Northern Europe, North Africa and the Middle East.

Those who possess the evil eye cannot simply acquire it – rather, they have to be born with it. Moreover, they may not have any malicious intent towards the object of the curse, but they can just be unlucky enough to spread misfortune with a simple glance. Such a person was Pope Pius IX, who was said to possess the evil eye as catastrophe seemed to follow wherever he went.

Generally, however, the evil eye is possessed by women and, more specifically in Mediterranean countries, women with blue eyes. Those women unfortunate enough to fall into this category may be treated with fear and suspicion, or even as a witch in some societies, particularly if any form of misfortune befalls a community.

In many cultures, belief in the evil eye revolves around the perceived sin of envy, with the offending look depicted as being envious in its intent, although often accompanied by praise. Children brought up in such societies will be taught not to covet their neighbour's possessions or envy their success, for fear of the evil eye. The malevolent powers of the curse are believed to act upon those who possess the evil eye just as much as upon those on whom the curse is cast.

The evil eye seems to have been most powerful in matters connected with fertility, no doubt due to the fact that the lives of our ancestors were dominated by the fertility of the land. Thus, likely results of such a curse might be the illness of an infant, infertility, a failed crop or diseased livestock.

In an effort to counter such malevolence, therefore, fertility charms have commonly been worn. These charms, usually made out of horn or shell, were often representative of the sexual organs.

If these were not available, various hand gestures could be made instead for the purposes of protection. Some of these gestures stay with us, although for most they have lost their ancient

Singer Ben Folds makes the sign of the bull's head, a gesture from European folklore which has taken over the world of rock music

cultural connotations. For example, the middle finger that is extended from a clenched fist represents a penis, while the sign of the bull's head is a representation of the womb and fallopian tubes.

PROTECTIVE DEVICES

Even today, in the Mediterranean region, amulets and talismans are worn by many. The most common of these is a simple blue representation of the eye to return the stare to anyone who may issue the curse. Similarly, the eyes painted on the bows of fishing boats are intended to return the stare of the evil eye. Further east, in India, small mirrors and shiny surfaces are used to reflect the power of the evil eye back whence it came. Strings of mirrors may be hung over or across doorways to protect the households within, and animals and vehicles are often adorned in this way.

Other attempts to neutralize the curse involve soiling whatever has just been praised or stared at. For example, in some cultures, it may be necessary to spit on one's child if it is thought that it has been cursed. In other cultures, boys may be dressed as girls, to prevent the envious evil eye being cast over any highly prized sons.

THE EVIL EYE

Many, particularly those in modern Western society, are sceptical of the existence of the evil eye, dismissing it as unscientific. Yet it is true to say that many people speak of picking up 'bad vibes' from another person, and would confess to feeling uncomfortable when confronted with a display of envy or jealousy. Perhaps it is possible for these emotions to manifest themselves in a physical way, the power of the curse depending in effect on the belief placed in it? Whatever the explanation – whether the curse is due to nothing more than the power of superstition or whether the evil eye really does have malevolent powers – there are certainly large numbers of people all over the world today who would not take kindly to being the object of the evil eye.

VAMPIRES

Vlad the Impaler, aka Dracoyle Wayda, sates his appetites – he was the inspiration behind Bram Stoker's Dracula

Most people are familiar with the image of a vampire. These horrific undead are humans whose souls have been sucked out and sent to eternity by a demon that then inhabits their bodies. Once the bodies are buried, the demon reactivates it to return to the surface of the Earth, stalking the world to seek humans on whom to feast, sucking them dry of blood to assuage its endless lust for the rich, red fluid of life. Most people are aware that a vampire can be killed by 'staking' it, that is driving a wooden stake through its heart.

These terrifying denizens of the night have featured in numerous movies, TV shows and books over the years. A prominent recent appearance was in the hit American TV show *Buffy the Vampire Slayer*, which ran to seven series of action-packed episodes. In such modern fictional incarnations, vampires are often shown as being part of a wide demonic world that lives alongside our human dimension, intruding from time to time with horrific consequences.

DRACULA

Nearly all these modern vampires of fiction derive from the book *Dracula* written by the British novelist Bram Stoker in 1897. Stoker was a hugely successful theatre owner and producer in late Victorian London, and many of the elements in the Dracula book show clear theatrical influence. It is almost as if the book was written to be staged, and indeed it has been made into plays and movies many times.

The vampire in Stoker's novel is a Transylvanian nobleman who has, for some unexplained reasons, become a vampire. The fictional vampire is descended from Vlad Dracul, a real-life prince who led the Christian Transylvanians in wars against the Moslem Turks in the 15th century – he famously slaughtered 30,000 Turks in a single battle. Stoker's Dracula established the genre with his flowing black cape, impeccable manners, suave good looks, brilliant intellect and deadly tastes of pure evil.

Although Stoker's fictional monster spends most of the book sucking blood in England – the main market for the novel – he came from Transylvania and Stoker had a very real reason for making that

distant area of the Balkans the home territory of Dracula. It was from the Balkans that legends of vampires had originally come, indeed belief in the reality of blood-sucking undead has long been widespread in that area. News of this belief had been filtering out of the Balkans to the rest of Europe since the later decades of the 18th century. Details were, however, few and far between. Only the bare outlines of the legend of the vampires were known in Britain in Stoker's day, so he was free to reinvent the legend in a guise of his own choosing to suit the horrific nature of his novel.

THE REAL VAMPIRES

So what of those real beliefs that lay behind the image of Count Dracula that today dominates our views of vampires? What were these real vampires supposed to be like and, crucially, did they ever actually exist?

The first disappointment for an aficionado of modern vampire literature is to learn that the vampires believed in so firmly by Balkan locals were not suave aristocrats of charm and intelligence. Anyone could become a vampire, no matter what social class they came from nor how virtuous their lives had been. All that was necessary to become a vampire was for a person to be feasted upon by a vampire at some point. The mingling of human blood with vampire lusts could, in some circumstances, be enough to condemn a perfectly normal peasant or merchant to an eternal afterlife as a vampire.

Most victims of vampirism, however, did not become vampires. They simply fell ill with a mysterious illness that featured extreme fatigue and pale skin – both thought to be caused by loss of blood to the vampire's fangs. A number of people going down with such symptoms in an area would be enough to convince locals that a vampire was about, coming out at night to suck blood and incapacitate its victims.

Dismissing vampires as mere superstition might be convenient, but there are a number of documented cases of vampires that simply cannot be pushed aside. One such occurred in 1732 when a rural area near Belgrade was afflicted by an alleged vampire. The public prosecutor was of the opinion that some criminal or madman might be on the loose and sent a team of officials to investigate and bring the culprit to justice.

The officials found a village in a state of terror. Over the previous few months three girls and a young man from the same family had all died overnight from no obvious cause. Then a fourth girl had awoken in the middle of the night to find a human-like figure bending over her. The intruder stank with the stench of the dead. The girl screamed, bringing her family running to her aid. The stranger fled, but not before the girl's brother had got a good look at him. To the boy's astonishment, the attacker was his own grandfather – a man who had died three years earlier.

STAKE THROUGH THE HEART

It was at this point that the officials arrived from Belgrade. Determined to settle the issue, the officials marched the terrified family up to the local graveyard and ordered them to dig up the grave of the long dead grandfather. What was discovered was not the expected skeleton, but an apparently healthy body that seemed to be merely sleeping. Convinced that they had unmasked a vampire, the locals swiftly despatched it in time-honoured fashion by driving a stake through its heart. The body poured forth a foul fluid that seemed to be blood mixed with a whitish pus. Quicklime was poured into the grave to make sure, and then the body was reburied. The officials went back to Belgrade to lodge their report with the Prosecutor's Office.

This is only the most famous and detailed of dozens of similar court and official records relating to vampires. The mass of evidence does point to nocturnal attacks taking place on people across the Balkans. Such attacks were frequently blamed on vampires and when coffins of alleged culprits were opened they frequently revealed bodies apparently immune from corruption. When staked those bodies often gave forth a disgusting stench and blood – evidence of their vampiric status.

With so many reports, many completed by government officials and highly educated men, testifying to the fact that something was going on, the researchers had to reach for some sort of explanation. Those involved at the time seem to have been convinced that vampires were to blame. More modern researchers have looked for a more normal cause.

It is certain that the outbreaks of symptoms commonly blamed on vampire attacks might be nothing more than some form of contagious disease. Given the poor state of medical knowledge in medieval times it may well be that local peasants were completely incapable of identifying the true cause, and instead blamed a vampire for the death and illness around them.

As for the corpses that are undecayed by time, there are two possible explanations. The first is that some soil conditions cause the normal processes of decomposition to be slowed down so that a body will appear to be undecayed some weeks or months after it is buried. The rotting of the body has not, however, ceased merely been slowed down so that if a stake is driven into such a corpse the foul smell of decay will burst forth. Rather more horrific is the theory that the person was not actually dead when buried. Instances are known of people who slip into a coma-like state that is very close to death. Some have been mistakenly thought to have died and taken to morgues before the mistake was realized. In times past perhaps some such unfortunate folk were actually buried when still alive.

The last word on vampires should go to the actor Hamilton Deane who starred in the first stage version of *Dracula* in 1924. As the final curtain fell, Deane appeared on stage and called out, 'Just a moment, ladies and gentlemen, before you leave. We hope that memories of Dracula won't give you bad dreams, so just a word of reassurance. When you get home tonight and the lights have been turned out and you are afraid to look behind the curtain and you dread to see a face appear at the window – why pull yourself together! And remember that, after all, there are no such things.'

ZOMBIES

In the early 21st century, most Westerners think of zombies as the dreadful, decomposing creatures with a taste for human flesh that have featured in numerous horror films. These are, of course, the products of fertile imaginations and talented make-up artists in the movie studios. The revolting appearance was developed to frighten viewers, while the craving for human flesh was invented by a writer seeking a hideous story line. These Living Dead have nothing in common with the allegedly real zombies of Haiti apart from their name.

HAITIAN ZOMBIES

The true zombie is a very different creature from that seen in Hollywood movies, but it is no less disturbing for that. The true zombie of Haitian legend is a person who has been killed by a voodoo sorcerer using magical means. Once the soul has departed, the dead body is then reactivated by the sorcerer to serve him as a willing, but mindless slave. Such a tale stretches credulity, but there is evidence to show that zombies really do exist. Sapped of their personalities, perhaps by a cocktail of drugs, they are lowly slaves rendered incapable of independent action.

The phenomenon of zombies is associated with the voodoo faith in Haiti, and there are several well-documented examples, including that of Clairvius Narcisse.

Clairvius Narcisse died at the Albert Schweitzer Hospital in Haiti in 1962. After his death had been certified, he was buried. Eighteen years later, a shambling tramp turned up at the home of Clairvius' sister and announced that he was Clairvius. At first the sister was incredulous, but the tramp was able to recount stories from their childhood that only Clairvius could know.

He told how his brothers had been angry about his refusal to sell family land, and how they had sought revenge by ordering his zombification.

According to Clairvius his 'death' had been merely a deep trance-like coma induced by drugs given him by a voodoo practitioner hired by his brothers. After his burial, during which he lay conscious but inert in his coffin, Clairvius was taken from the graveyard and became the subject of spells by a voodoo witch doctor (known as a *bokor*) that turned him into an empty vessel. He was able to move, but he could not communicate properly and had lost his free will. Voodoo worshippers see a zombie as a body without a soul, and this is what he seemed to have become. For two years he worked in the fields alongside other zombies. After the death of his master Clairvius wandered off to live rough for 18 years, during which time he gradually recovered his memory of his past life. He returned home only when he was sure that the brothers who engineered his zombification were themselves dead.

Clairvius' story matched with the hospital records. His cheek bore a scar that, he said, was inflicted when a nail was driven into his coffin. So just what happened to Clairvius after his apparent death in hospital?

For years the assumption was that zombies – if they existed – were literally raised from the dead through the supernatural powers of the *bokor*. Today it seems more likely that a poison is administered to a living victim. This poison slows down bodily functions so much that they become imperceptible and the body seems corpse-like. Following burial, the barely-breathing body is then retrieved and further drugs are given that bring about a controlled recovery. So while the victim might regain physical strength, his mind remains feeble, his memory is all but erased and he is effectively powerless.

Much of the mystery was revealed by anthropologist Dr E Wade Davis, who, following extensive research, assured the world: 'Zombiism

Felicia Felix-Mentor from Haiti who died and was buried in 1907. She was found wandering about the countryside in a zombified state in 1937

actually exists. There are Haitians who have been raised from their graves and returned to life.'

TOAD SKIN AND PUFFER FISH

Davis analyzed some of the poisons used by *bokors* and found toad skin and puffer fish (illustrated above) were two of the most significant ingredients in the poison used to induce a coma.

Toad venom is known as a potent painkiller, while the puffer fish contains tetrodotoxin that affects the nervous system. Thereafter, different drugs, including Jimson's Weed (a poisonous type of nightshade plant), are used to keep the victims of zombification stupefied.

Davis paid tribute to the macabre talents of the voodoo *bokors*. 'A Witch doctor in Haiti is very skilled in administering just the right dose of poison. Too much poison will kill the victim completely and resuscitation will not be possible. Too little and the victim will not be a convincing corpse.'

Davis acknowledges that the deep religious beliefs prevailing in Haiti are vital to the process carried out by the *bokor*. Because people believe in zombiism, it is more likely to become a reality. The voodoo religion is intense and ritualistic, although not inevitably sinister. Broadly speaking, voodoo is a cross between native African beliefs and the Catholic faith once forced upon slaves when they were

transported to destinations like Haiti. Davis believes that zombiism is carried out as a punishment and the mindset of the Haitian people permits *bokors* to do their worst.

Certainly this unquestioning and fearful faith would explain how the dictator Francois 'Papa Doc' Duvalier (1907–71) maintained his grip on the reins of power in Haiti. After coming to power in 1957, Duvalier posed as a witch doctor to encourage the belief that he possessed unearthly powers. His henchmen were called the Tonton Macoute, taking their name from the Haitian word for 'bogeymen'. The conviction that transgressors would be turned into zombies – or that the Tonton Macoute were themselves zombies – loomed large. Political opponents were murdered and poverty became endemic as Duvalier inflated his personal bank account. Only long after his death did the population realize they had been duped. But Duvalier's death did not rid them of their folk superstition, and they hauled his corpse from its grave and ritually beat it.

Some commentators remain unconvinced, and question whether zombies exist at all. One piece of research found that the vast majority of Haitians said they knew of a zombie. On further examination, however, it was always a distant cousin or friend of a friend that was the zombie rather than someone they knew well. This is also a feature of urban legends in Western society, when outrageous events occur to someone known only by reputation to the storyteller.

Another theory is that the zombies are in fact people suffering from mental illness who, in the absence of an effective healthcare system, were compelled to wander the countryside begging or undertaking menial labouring jobs to survive. Bereaved relatives identify the so-called zombies as family members through the distortion of grief and because of a desire to see the dead person once more.

But the existence of zombies among Haitians is beyond question, and there is even legislation on the issue. According to the penal code it is illegal to induce a lethargic coma in another person. If proved, the perpetrator is treated in the same way as a murderer.

POSSESSION

Possession has decidedly negative connotations, but there have been incidents in which the uninvited spirit proved to have a benign purpose. In the summer of 1877, Mary Lurancy Vennum, a 13-year-old girl from Watseka, Illinois, suffered a series of convulsions, falling into a trance-like state for hours at a time. All efforts to awaken her failed.

THE VENNUM CASE

While she was in this state she spoke of seeing angels and a brother and sister who had died some years earlier. Shortly after this, Lurancy was subdued by a succession of dominant personalities who spoke through her, including a crotchety old woman called Katrina Hogan. The family finally resigned themselves to having their daughter committed to an asylum, but then a neighbouring family named Roff intervened. They persuaded Lurancy's parents to consult a doctor from Wisconsin who had treated their own daughter, also with the name of Mary, in the months before she died. Mary Roff had suffered similar 'fits' in which she demonstrated clairvoyant abilities such as being able to read through a blindfold. These episodes had been witnessed by several eminent and respectable citizens of Watseka who were prepared to swear to what they had seen.

When Dr Stevens visited the Vennum house on 1 February 1878, Katrina Hogan was in control. At first she was cold and aloof, gazing abstractedly into space and ordering Dr Stevens to leave her be whenever he attempted to come near. But his persistence paid off and by and by Dr Stevens was able to draw out 'Katrina's' personal history. Soon another personality appeared, a young man named Willie Canning whose hold on Lurancy was erratic and offered little of value that the doctor could verify. With the parent's permission Dr Stevens tried hypnosis and Lurancy reasserted herself but remained in a trance. She spoke of having been possessed by evil spirits, but that may have been her interpretation conditioned by her strict religious upbringing. Then events took an even more interesting turn.

Lurancy announced that she could see other spirits around her, one of whom was Mary Roff. Lurancy did not know Mary Roff, who had died when Lurancy was just a year old, nor had she visited the Roff home up to that point.

Mrs Roff was present when her 'Mary' came through, speaking through Lurancy, but there is no suggestion that Lurancy was faking to impress or ingratiate herself with the dead girl's mother. The next morning 'Mary' calmly announced her intention to go 'home' by which she meant the Roff household. This naturally created some embarrassment for Mr and Mrs Vennum who were reluctant to have their daughter 'adopted' by a neighbour, but in her present state of mind it could have been argued that Lurancy was no longer their daughter. On 11 February, after much soul searching the Vennums agreed to let their daughter have her way.

En route they passed the Roff's old house where their daughter had died and 'Mary' insisted on being taken there, but she was eventually persuaded that it was no longer the family home. When she arrived at the new house she expressed delight at seeing her old piano and appeared to recognize the relatives who greeted her.

Of course, none of this proves anything. Lurancy could have been shamming in order to secure attention. There was little risk in claiming to recognize the Roff's previous home as in those days everyone knew their neighbours and the history of the town. As for the piano, it was a fair assumption that it would have been in the family for some years and presumably had occupied pride of place in the previous house.

BENIGN POSSESSION

But even the most cynical witnesses were astonished to hear 'Mary' greet her old Sunday School teacher using her maiden name which Lurancy could not have known. Intrigued, the family subjected 'Mary' to a barrage of probing personal questions relating to seemingly insignificant incidents in her childhood which even the most imaginative impostor could not have faked. She satisfied them on all counts. She even remembered details of a family holiday and could name the spot where her pet dog had died. Most remarkably of all, she recalled the exact words written many years earlier by a medium during a séance who claimed to be channelling Mary's spirit communications.

Over the following weeks she recognized personal items that she had owned which Mr and Mrs Roff left unobtrusively in the hope of them being identified, but 'Mary' did more than acknowledge them. She would snatch them up in delight and offer some minor detail related to the item that her parents could verify. Clearly this was something more than a remarkable performance. It was a phenomenon, a rare example of benign possession which was similar in many ways to recorded cases of reincarnation, except that Mary Roff died when Lurancy was a small child. It could not be explained as a multiple personality disorder since 'Mary Roff' evidently had intimate personal knowledge of the Roff family and her previous life.

On her arrival at the Roff house 'Mary' had predicted that she would be using Lurancy for three months after which she would return to the spirit world and allow Lurancy to continue with her life. She kept her word. On the morning of 21 May, 'Mary Roff' vacated the body of her host and Lurancy returned to her parents. She later married and lived a normal happy life, but from time to time Mr and Mrs Roff would pay a visit at which time their daughter would make an appearance to reassure them that all was well. In gratitude for

'The next morning "Mary" calmly announced her intention to go "home"'

being allowed to say goodbye to her family, the benign spirit even intervened during the birth of Lurancy's first child, putting her into a trance to alleviate the pains of childbirth.

SOUL MUSIC

Not all cases of possession are as inconvenient for their host as the Mary Lurancy Vennum case, or as unpleasant as that portrayed in *The Exorcist*. The following is a case in point.

On New Year's Day 1970, the musicologist Sir Donald Tovey gave his expert opinion on the authenticity of certain compositions by Beethoven and Liszt which had reputedly been 'channelled' through London medium Mrs Rosemary Brown. He then took the opportunity to share his insights into why the world was now ready to receive these gifts from heaven.

'To understand himself fully [Man] should become aware of the fact that he does not consist merely of a temporary form which is doomed to age and die. He has an immortal soul which is housed in an immortal body and endowed with a mind that is independent of a physical brain. In communication through music and conversation, an organized group of musicians who have departed from your world are attempting to establish a precept for humanity; i.e. that physical death is a transition from one state of consciousness to another wherein one retains one's individuality. The realization of this fact should assist man to a greater insight into his own nature and potential super-terrestrial activities.'

This was profound and revealing stuff. The only problem was that Sir Donald Tovey had been dead for some years when he gave this 'lecture' through the auspices of Mrs Brown. Sceptics might say that it was extremely convenient that Mrs Brown was able to channel both the great composers and a respected music critic to verify their work, but there was no

disputing the fact that the music was of a very high quality and that its complexity was way beyond Mrs Brown's humble talents. By all accounts she was a pianist of moderate ability and her knowledge of music was rudimentary at best. Yet for the last five years she had been taking dictation from Liszt, Beethoven, Chopin, Schubert, Brahms and Debussy at a speed she could barely keep up with and, according to a number of influential musicologists, in their distinctive style.

There was one problem, however, and this appears to be the key to the whole mystery. The music was 'first class' according to one critic, but it was not music of genius. If the great composers were active again on the other side, why then did they not produce masterworks rather than highly proficient imitations which any serious music student could

By all accounts, Mrs Brown was a pianist of moderate ability who was producing music way beyond her modest talents

conceivably have created to impress their professor? And why choose Mrs Brown? Admittedly she was a practising medium, but surely they would have attempted to commune with a serious musician who would have done their new compositions justice and with whom they would have had a greater empathy.

Although this appears to be a clear case of possession, there is a distinct possibility that it might be an example of split personality disorder, albeit a highly productive one. Word association tests carried out by researcher Whately Carrington in 1935 with the mediums Osborne Leonard and Eileen Garrett suggest that the 'controls' which mediums claim are the mediators between themselves and the spirits

In the same way that Mrs Brown channelled long-gone composers, some artists claim to have been similarly inspired. The top picture is by F Thompson and it was later found to resemble a painting by the dead artist RS Gifford (see below), who is supposed to have 'drawn through Thompson'

might actually be their own sub-personalities and that these sink back into the unconscious when the dominant personality reclaims control (when the medium wakes from their trance). In comparing their responses to key words Carrington discovered that the controls were mirror images of the mediums – a characteristic of multiple personalities. This would account for the mediums' inability to remember what they had channelled and also for the mysterious appearance of their phenomenal latent talents. At the same time it might also explain why the music was

technically impressive, but not of the quality that such men of genius would be expected to produce if they had been given a chance to continue working from the 'other side'.

This theory does not explain incidents of genuine mediumship in which the medium has communicated personal information that he or she could not have had access to, unconsciously or otherwise, and which was subsequently verified as correct by the bereaved. But it could be significant that subjects have exhibited telepathic abilities under hypnosis, such as sharing physical sensations with the hypnotist, which might suggest that when the left side of the brain (the objective or ordinary mind) is put to sleep, the right side of the brain (also known as the subjective or subliminal mind) might then be receptive to spirit communications.

THE ARTIST WITHIN

Automatic art, or automatism to give it its clinical name, is not a recent phenomenon. In the 1930s, the American psychiatrist Dr Anita Muhl experimented with the technique to see if she could connect with her mentally ill patients. Against all the laws of logic and the expectations of her medical colleagues, many of Dr Muhl's patients produced impressive prose, paintings, sketches and musical compositions with their passive hand (the one they did not normally use to write with), with both hands simultaneously, and occasionally writing and drawing upside down or even backwards. A number of patients were even able to draw 'blind', without looking at the paper. All of this was done fluidly, at great speed and without error. Dr Muhl believed that these latent talents originated in the unconscious, but there are those on the fringes of the scientific community who suspect that there might be spirits or a past-life personality at work. What other explanation, they say, can account for the feats of former antiques dealer John Tuckey who can complete epic Dickensian novels in a distinctive 19th-century copperplate script in a matter of weeks? Or what about the remarkable achievements of the Brazilian automatic artist Luiz Gasparetto who can produce two paintings in the style of different great masters simultaneously, one working upright and the other created upside down? Often Gasparetto will take less than a minute to produce a sketch worthy of Cézanne or Manet – and he doesn't even use brushes. He will employ his

fingers and even his toes to create a one-minute masterpiece.

There is another theory to account for such accomplishments and this is that each of us contains more than one personality. These extra personalities are normally controlled by the dominant persona that has, effectively, taken the driving seat.

Often Gasparetto will take less than a minute to produce a sketch worthy of Cézanne or Manet – and he doesn't even use brushes

THE THREE CLARAS

When psychiatrist Morton Prince placed patient Clara Fowler under hypnosis he unwittingly freed two contrasting personalities, each unaware of the other. Clara had been morose, subdued and suffered from depression while her two alter egos could not have been more different. One was considerably more mature and self-assured while the second, which identified herself as 'Sally', was a lively and mischievous little girl who would 'possess' Clara at inconvenient moments. Without warning 'Sally' would take over for hours at a time and when Clara regained control she would find herself in another part of town, bewildered as to how she got there. At the height of her influence, 'Sally' moved to another town, secured a job as a waitress for two weeks and then vacated her host who consequently had to talk her way out of a job she hadn't applied for and find her own way back home.

Spiritualists might interpret these experiences as evidence of possession, while a psychiatrist would regard them as sub-personalities, but if they are merely aspects of our unconscious why then do they create a separate personal history for themselves, speak in another voice and exhibit talents which the dominant personality does not possess? Could it be that they are, in fact, transitory memories and talents from that person's former lives which have been reawakened?

PARANORMAL SKY FALLS

The sky above our heads is a strange and bizarre place. Aircraft may fly through the air with great regularity and rapidity, but there is still much about the sky that remains a complete mystery. The strangest things can fall out of it without warning.

STRANGE DOWNPOURS

In 1844 a short, sharp thunderstorm hit the town of Selby, Yorkshire. The local residents scattered for cover, huddling in shop doorways and under porches to escape the rain. Then they noticed something very odd about the rain, it was made up not only of falling water but also of falling frogs. Several men held their hats out into the shower to make sure, and they quickly filled with wriggling amphibians. Each frog was about 15mm (0.6in) long, making them fairly young specimens. Other than the fact that the frogs fell from the sky, they were perfectly normal common frogs. One man estimated that around 10,000 frogs fell in the space of about 20 minutes.

In June 1979 another thunderstorm that dumped frogs on England struck, this time just outside Bedford. This time tadpoles came down as well as juvenile frogs. Another similar shower of frogs fell just outside Montreal, Canada, in 1941.

FALLING FISH

It is not only frogs that fall from the sky. Around 20,000 fish fell on Calcutta in 1837, while in 1808 a column of marching troops outside Delhi was hit by a short storm that battered the men with around 500 fish as well as rain. On 16 June 1954 a man in upstate New York noticed the gutters of his house were blocked during an isolated downpour. As soon as the rain had passed he went up a ladder to investigate only to find the roof, gutters and downpipes chocked with young trout.

On 25 August 1969 some 500 rats fell on the Indonesian village of Batudjai, near Lombok. In 1680 a downpour of mice fell on southern Norway. More mice fell just outside Inverness in May 1832.

SHOWER OF HAZELNUTS

On 9 May 1867 several streets in Dublin were bombarded with thousands of dried berries. On 13 March 1977 Mr Alfred Osborne was walking home from church when he and his wife were suddenly subjected to a shower of hazelnuts that fell from a clear sky. After the bombardment ended, he collected several hundred of the nuts, which he afterward ate

saying that they were 'fresh and sweet'. In April 1980 Trevor Williams of Tonna, Wales, was sitting in his garden when around 5,000 peas fell from the heavens. In February 1979 the Hampshire garden of Roland Moody was blanketed by cress seeds that fell from a dark cloud. He counted one 6 inch square area and found it contained 500 seeds, which worked out at around 40,000 seeds in all.

The usual explanation given by scientists for such odd showers from the sky is that they are caused by whirlwinds or waterspouts that suck up the objects, then dump them some distance away. As theories go, it is perfectly good until it is inspected.

NO EXPLANATION

Leaving aside the rather obvious point that witnesses do not report a whirlwind or waterspout in the area at the time, there are practical difficulties. Where would a whirlwind get more than a thousand hazelnuts in England in March? And if several hundred frogs were sucked up from a pond, why did only the frogs fall and not the waterweed, snails, fish and other contents of the pond? In any case there are several instances on record of witnesses seeing a whirlwind strike a body of water. The result is not that water and other objects are sucked up to be suspended in mid-air and then dropped a distance away. What happens is that the contents of the pond or river are scattered about randomly close to where they are sucked up.

Things do fall from the sky without explanation. It is odd enough when apparently normal things such as seeds, nuts and fish fall, but even more bizarre when the objects themselves appear to be paranormal.

ANGEL HAIR

Angel hair is a rare and perplexing phenomenon that has so far defied explanation. It is a delight to behold, made up of silken threads that rain down on to the earth and look startling against a cloudless blue sky. But reach out to touch it and it will almost certainly vanish before your eyes.

In September 1741, one corner of Hampshire, England, became remarkable for a blizzard of gossamer that continued for hours. Residents from three small towns – Bradley, Selbourne and Alresford – saw the downpour, which indicates that the fall covered a considerable area. One witness related what he had seen in a letter written four years after the astonishing event:

'As the morning advanced the sun became bright and warm, and the day turned out one of those most lovely ones which no season but the autumn produces: cloudless, calm, serene, and worthy of the South of France itself.

'About nine [in the morning] a very unusual appearance began to demand our attention, a shower of cobwebs falling from very elevated regions, and continuing, without any interruption, till the close of the day. These webs were not single filmy threads, floating in the air in all directions, but perfect flakes or rags; some near an inch broad [2.5cm], and five or six long

[13–15cm], which fell with a degree of velocity which showed they were considerably heavier than the atmosphere.

'On every side as the observer turned his eyes might he behold a continual succession of fresh flakes falling into his sight, and twinkling like stars as they turned their sides towards the sun … Neither before nor after was any such fall observed; but on this day the flakes hung in the trees and hedges so thick, that a diligent person sent out might have gathered basketsfull.'

WORLDWIDE PHENOMENON

This account is one of the best-known stories of an angel hair shower, but by no means was it an isolated incident. Since then, there have been reports of this strange occurrence from all over the world, although the greatest number are from North America, Australia, New Zealand and western Europe.

In 1914, soon after the first winter rains arrived in South Australia, there were accounts of angel hair

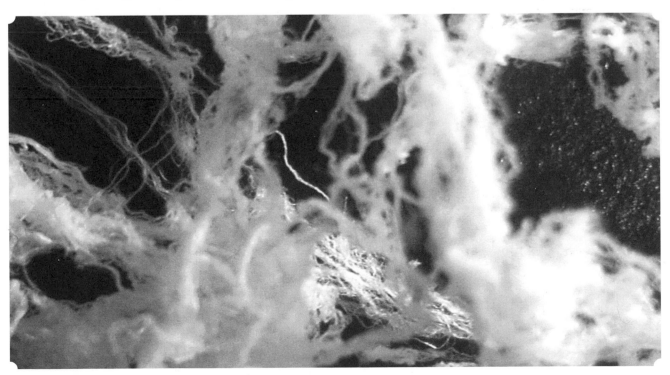

Angel hair is described as being similar in substance to spider's web, made of gossamer-like intertwined fibres

falling in pieces between 15cm and 23cm (6–9in) long, and then swiftly dissolving on the ground. Three weeks later another shower, lasting for an hour, was reported.

According to a 1950 edition of the *Philadelphia Inquirer*, two police officers in South Philadelphia in the United States were on evening patrol when they saw what they thought must be a parachute falling to earth. When the 1.8m-long (6ft) object finally landed, the officers saw it glow in purple and crystalline colours. As one of the men reached down to touch the substance, 'the mass on which he laid his hands dissolved, leaving nothing but a slight, odourless, sticky residue.' Within 25 minutes it had all disappeared.

Two years later, a school headmaster in Oloron-Sainte-Marie in south-west France saw objects in the sky that he could not identify. In their wake came trails of an unknown substance, which was described as gelatinous at first, but that quickly turned into vapour.

Global reports about angel hair have continued to appear with surprising frequency, sometimes detailing that it arrives in balls rather than flakes. Indeed, descriptions vary from fluorescent filaments, through to flecks and strands and even to jelly and goo.

One conclusion is that the substance has come from spiders or perhaps another silk-spinning insect. Spiders do sometimes migrate by flying in wind currents, but there is a marked absence of spiders in the material described as 'angel hair' and, as yet, a link to arachnids has not been proven.

The mystical qualities of this substance are enhanced by the fact that some – although not all – accounts of angel hair are associated with the sighting of an unidentified flying object (UFO).

At Oloron, in southwest France, a head teacher saw UFOs trailing strands of angel hair. Could this bizarre substance be ET exhaust?

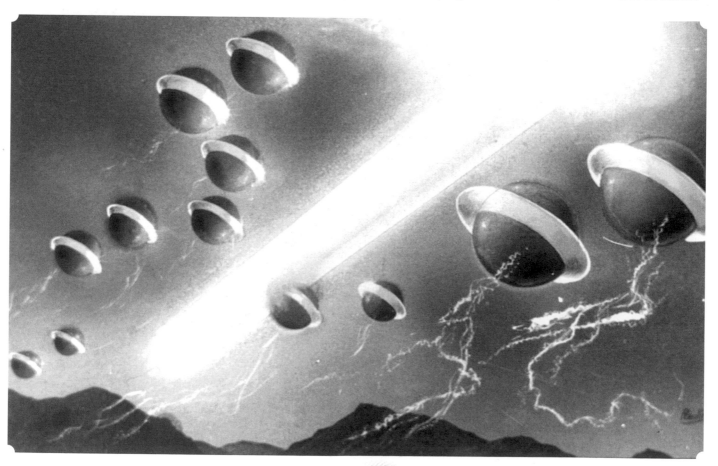

THE RESEARCH

So far, there has been little orchestrated research into the qualities of angel hair. This is primarily due to a lack of reliable data, as it tends to disappear after coming into contact with human flesh. However, one woman is trying to change this. Analytical scientist Phyllis Budinger, from Ohio, has used the restricted number of angel hair samples available to draw some conclusions about its chemical content.

She investigated four samples, drawn from across North America. Incredibly, the first dated from 1977 and had been stored in two air-tight glass jars for more than twenty years before being analyzed. It fell in Los Gatos, California, and the samples lay forgotten until 1998.

In 1999, a bemused driver who had driven for some 24km (15 miles) through a fall of angel hair near Sacramento, California, collected the second sample. Some strands were just a few centimetres long, while others measured up to 17m (56ft) long.

SLIMEY GOO

The third sample came from Burlington, West Virginia, in 2000, and was discovered after the householder heard a mysterious droning noise lingering outside her home the previous night. It was only in this case that the substance was described as transforming into a slimy goo. Inexplicably, both the householder and her dog fell ill after finding the angel hair, although it is not known if the events were linked.

Shenandoah in Iowa was the location of the fourth angel hair sample. The fall occurred in 1981 and lasted for nearly six hours. This case was notable for being concurrent with the sighting of a UFO.

Budinger was able to scrutinize the Los Gatos samples through an extremely powerful microscope and saw bundles of fibres rather than single strands. They were even thinner than spiders' silk, and the droplets often seen with arachnid webs were not apparent. However, while it is true that spiders' silk is frequently characterized by the presence of droplets, this may not always be the case. Only further research into the nature of spiders' webs will clarify this.

Unfortunately, access to the powerful microscope was no longer available when the other samples reached Budinger's laboratory. Nevertheless, she was able to determine that all four specimens had similar molecular structure. She defined this as 'a polymer containing protein-amide type linkages'. A polymer is formed from repeated units of smaller molecules, while amides are ammonia-based compounds.

WEB OF MYSTERY

Budinger's findings indicate that angel hair originates from a biological source. But to date, she has been unable to identify this source. There are similarities between angel hair and spider or caterpillar silk, but they do not seem to be identical.

Angel hair is not only difficult to collect, but it is also highly sensitive. It is subject to contamination from car exhaust fumes, or even from the human hand, which might skew the chemical results of analysis.

The two most compelling samples of angel hair are those collected at Burlington and Shenandoah, where there is a strong suspicion of UFO activity. Indeed, a different analysis of information about angel hair falls in Australia discovered that in eleven cases there were no reports of UFO sighting, while in eight there were. It is this extraterrestrial aspect of angel hair that both baffles and intrigues investigators today.

Budinger is in no doubt as to what is now needed to resolve the mystery of angel hair. 'Clearly a broader database is required. Most important is the need for angel hair from events coinciding with witnessed UFO activity.

'More samples are needed from a variety of locations and from falls at different times of the year. Unfortunately, a predominance of data is from falls in the United States and in the month of October … Proper sampling is needed. It should be done as soon as possible after the event … Proper analytical testing is required.'

Until such a thorough scientific approach is adopted, the unusual sight of a fall of angel hair can be valued as one of today's enduring mysteries.

UFOS

T he notion that extraterrestrials have visited earth and abducted humans for close-quarters examination has been around for some fifty years. More recently it has come to light that those who believe they have had close encounters may be marked out forever by an intravenous implant.

Alone and helpless, the abductees are reportedly taken to a brightly lit clinical room on board the spacecraft where the aliens proceed to examine them

THE START OF AN ERA

Kenneth Arnold was an experienced pilot who had been in Chehalis, Washington State, on business. On the morning of 24 June he set off to fly home to Oregon in his single-engined Callier light aircraft. With both time and fuel to spare he decided to first spend an hour or so over the Mount Rainier area searching for a US military transport aircraft that had been reported missing and was presumed to have crashed.

It was while turning on to a new leg of his search pattern at an altitude of 9,200 feet that Arnold saw a bright flash of light sweep over his aircraft. Such a thing usually happened when sun reflected off the surfaces of another aircraft close by. Fearing a collision with an aircraft he had not seen, Arnold hurriedly levelled his aircraft and scanned the skies desperately seeking another aircraft. He quickly saw a DC4 airliner some miles distant and flying away from him. Discounting this as the source of the flash he saw a second flash far to the north.

Staring at the location of the flash, Arnold saw a line of nine aircraft flying towards him at an angle. As the aircraft came closer he saw that they were flying in echelon, a usual military formation, but arranged with the lead aircraft above the others contrary to the standard military practice. Arnold at this point assumed that the fast-approaching aircraft were military jets of some kind and relaxed.

But as the nine aircraft got closer, Arnold was able to see them in detail and at once realized that he was seeing something very strange indeed. Each aircraft was shaped like a wide crescent with neither fuselage

A flight of PT-21 USAF training aircraft in echelon formation: Arnold at first thought the UFOs were military aircraft

The Flying Saucer as I
Saw it... by Kenneth Arnold
Per copy 50¢

nor tail. Moreover the aircraft were flying with a strange undulating motion quite unlike the straight line flight of all known aircraft. They also fluttered or dipped from side to side at times, sending off bright flashes as the sun reflected from their highly polished silver-blue surfaces. There were no markings that Arnold could see, though he was now concentrating hard on the mysterious aircraft.

STRANGE AIRCRAFT OVERHEAD

The formation of strange aircraft was moving fast, Arnold timed them passing over landmarks on the ground and later estimated the speed at around 1,300mph (2,092kph). This was much faster than any known aircraft of the time, even military fast jets flew at only around 700mph (1,126kph). The aircraft were soon out of sight.

Arnold headed for Yakima Airfield and went to see Al Baxter the general manager of Central Aircraft. The two men discussed the strange aircraft, and Arnold drew pictures of what he had seen. Other pilots and air crew joined the conversation, but none could explain what Arnold had seen other than to guess that the strange aircraft were some kind of secret military project. Still confused, Arnold then resumed his interrupted flight home to Oregon.

By the time he arrived, Arnold had begun to worry that he had seen some sort of highly advanced Soviet war machine. He decided to inform the FBI, but their office was closed so he dropped in at the offices of the *East Oregonian* newspaper. He told the reporters there all about his experience. One of them, Bill Bacquette, queried the way the strange aircraft moved. Arnold elaborated on the undulating motion by saying: 'They flew like a saucer would if you skipped it across water.'

Bacquette filed his report with a national news agency, writing about 'flying saucers'. It was repeated across America and soon the public was agog at news of these flying saucers.

Signed by Kenneth Arnold, this artwork shows the kind of aircraft Arnold witnessed during his famous sighting

Meanwhile, Arnold had returned to the FBI to tell them about the strange aircraft. The local FBI man passed the details on to head office in Washington concluding his report with the words 'It is the personal opinion of the interviewer that Arnold actually saw what he states he saw in the attached report.' Already concerned about Russian intentions and military technology, the US military pounced on Arnold's report.

An era was born.

NEW REPORTS

It is generally believed that the entire Alien Encounter phenomenon began with this startling sighting of 'flying saucers' or Unidentified Flying Objects (UFOs) by Kenneth Arnold, but in fact this is very much a matter of using the wisdom of hindsight. At the time, neither Arnold nor anyone else even thought about aliens or UFOs. It was assumed that what he had seen was some kind of top secret military aircraft of revolutionary design. Nor was Arnold's the first sighting of such objects. It was merely the first to make it into the national and international press. For that we must thank the reporter who took Arnold's description of the mysterious aircraft he had seen and dubbed them 'flying saucers'. The name caught the public imagination and made good newspaper copy.

The story took a dramatic new twist when it became clear that whatever Arnold had seen, it was not a secret weapon being developed by the United States Air Force (USAF). The speed, design and motion of Arnold's aircraft were utterly unlike anything being developed. The first thought that most people in aviation had was that the Soviets had developed some startling new technology – though Arnold's aircraft seemed so far in advance of anything the Russians had used during World War II, which had ended only two years earlier, that this seemed rather unlikely.

It was not long before people across the USA started coming forward with their own sightings of mysterious aircraft. These people had been reluctant to speak publicly before either because they feared ridicule or because they had not realized that they had seen anything particularly odd – like Arnold they had assumed that they were seeing some new secret type of aircraft.

SAUCER-SHAPED OBJECT

It must be remembered that at this time jets, rockets and helicopters were all new inventions shrouded in secrecy and mystery. There seemed to be no limit to the inventiveness of aircraft engineers.

At this early stage the reports that were made to the press or the military were usually fairly vague. People reported seeing saucer-shaped objects flying very fast, or bright lights at night moving in unusual ways.

On 19 August 1947, for instance, a Mr and Mrs Busby were sitting on the porch of their house in Butte, Montana, with a neighbour enjoying the warm evening. A large bright object flew overhead, heading northeast at a tremendous speed. Ten minutes later another ten objects came over flying rather slower, but again heading northeast. As the startled witnesses watched, three of the objects peeled off from the triangular formation and headed due north.

The Busbys did not give any clear description of these objects as regards size, shape or colour. Merely that they were bright and moved fast.

Rather more detailed, but not much, was the report made by Major Jones of the USAF. This report had great credibility as Jones was the Chief Intelligence Officer of the 28th Bombardment Wing based at Rapid City Air Force Base in South Dakota. If an air force intelligence officer was unable to report accurately what he saw in the sky, nobody could.

Jones said that he was walking across the parking lot at the air base when he saw 12 strange aircraft diving down toward the base from the northwest. The aircraft were in a tight, diamond-shaped formation, indicating to Jones that they were military aircraft. He stopped to watch, wondering what type of aircraft these were.

When the formation was about four miles away, the aircraft began a slow turn at an altitude of about 1,520m (5,000ft). Jones could now see that the strange craft were shaped like an elliptical disk and each was about 30m (100ft) across. Having turned to face southwest, the craft accelerated to a speed estimated to be around 400mph (644kph) and climbed out of sight.

THE EXETER INCIDENT

The Exeter Incident, as it became known, gained fame largely because the two policemen involved refused to be fobbed with anodyne 'official explanations' issued by the United States Air Force through its official UFO investigation unit, Project Blue Book.

The incident began at 1am when Patrolman Eugene Bertrand was driving along Route 108. He saw a car parked by the side of the road in a remote rural spot and pulled over to investigate. Inside the car Bertrand found a woman driver in a state of some distress.

She said that her car had been followed by a bright white light in the sky that had dived down to hover over the vehicle. She had then stopped and the light seemed to fly off as Bertrand approached. After a quarter of an hour the light had not returned, so the woman drove off while Bertrand continued his patrol.

Bertrand reported back to Exeter Police Station at about 2.30am. There he found Norman Muscarello who was shaking with fear and almost unable to talk. After a few minutes Bertrand and desk sergeant Reginald Towland got Muscarello calmed down and managed to get his story from him.

PULSATING RED LIGHTS

Muscarello said he had been hitchhiking on Route 150, but unable to get a lift was walking to Exeter. He had reached Carl Dining Field Farm when a group of five red lights came swooping down from the sky to hover over a house about 100 feet from where

A time-lapse photo enhances the stars over rural America – the Exeter Incident took place in just this sort of landscape

Muscarello was standing. The red lights began to pulsate in a pattern that repeated itself. As the startled Muscarello stood watching, the lights suddenly darted toward him. Muscarello dived into a ditch, when he peered back over the edge of his hiding place, the lights were diving down behind a line of trees as if landing in the field beyond.

Bertrand drove Muscarello back to the site of his encounter. The pair got out of the parked patrol car and looked about. There was nothing to be seen, so Bertrand radioed back that all seemed quiet. Towland

suggested that the field where the lights were seen to land should be investigated. Bertrand switched on his flashlight and began advancing. He was about 15m (50ft) from the car when cattle at the nearby farm began to call out loudly as if in alarm, then mill about in excitement. Suddenly the red lights rose up from the ground behind the trees.

THE LIGHTS GET NEARER

Bertrand drew his pistol and Muscarello began shouting, 'Shoot it, shoot it'. But as the lights came closer Bertrand thought better of opening fire and instead raced back to the patrol car. The two men hid behind the car as the lights approached to within about 30m (100ft). So bright were the lights that Bertrand began to fear that he might get burnt. He scrabbled inside his car to find the radio and called for back-up.

Patrolman David Hunt took the radio call at 2.55am. By the time he arrived at Bertrand's parked car the red lights had retreated. Hunt saw them clearly enough about half a mile away. A minute or two later the lights rose higher into the sky and headed off in a southeasterly direction, accelerating rapidly as they went.

All three men were considerably shaken by the experience. When word got out they came in for a fair degree of teasing from colleagues and friends, but both Hunt and Bertrand felt that they should make a formal report. They accordingly wrote out and signed statements that they sent to Project Blue Book.

The local press took up the story, prompting the Pentagon to issue a dismissive statement that the men must

Confronted by a UFO, patrolman Bertrand drew his gun, but perhaps wisely chose not to fire

A B47 heavy bomber: the USAF at first tried to pass off the Exeter Incident as the sighting of a B47 by untrained witnesses

have failed to recognize a flight of B47 military aircraft that was overflying the area.

Bertrand and Hunt were indignant at the suggestion. Both men had spent long hours driving the lonely highways at night when aircraft of all types were flying about overhead. They felt that they knew what a B47 looked and sounded like, as well as other aircraft, and were adamant that what they had seen that night was entirely different. Moreover, Bertrand had spent some years in the USAF before joining the police and was even more accustomed to seeing aircraft under all sorts of conditions. In any case the B47 flight had passed over at around 1.30am, and the sighting had continued until past 3am.

In the centre of the clearing was a dark grey object about 6m across. The object seemed to be hovering above the ground

The two men wrote to Blue Book restating the facts and demanding that the USAF formally absolve them either of making the story up or of being incompetent witnesses, a charge that might well damage their careers. After some weeks, and the sending of a formal second letter, the two policemen got the reply they wanted. The sighting had been reclassified by Blue Book as 'unidentified' and the competence of the officers accepted.

The Exeter Incident is interesting not just for the details of the UFO itself but also for the reactions of those involved. The cattle at the farm were clearly aware of something unusual, while both the unknown woman motorist and Muscarello were terrified. The two policemen reacted on the night with commendable courage, especially Bertrand, but did not really know how to respond to a situation outside their experience.

The USAF and Pentagon ridiculed the idea of a UFO even before they had had a chance to study the information, which prompted the townsfolk of Exeter to ridicule their policemen. Bertrand and Hunt then stuck to their story absolutely until they received a partial vindication. Thereafter both Exeter and the patrolmen dropped out of the UFO story as nothing further of a UFO variety happened.

It is indeed as if something utterly bizarre and inexplicable fell out of the sky over Exeter that night, then vanished.

TERROR IN THE FOREST

When Scottish forestry worker Robert Taylor walked into a clearing in a wood outside Livingston, west of Edinburgh, he expected to see nothing more exciting than his pet dog chasing rabbits. What he really did see changed his life. It was 9 November 1979.

It was 10am when Taylor left his pick-up truck to walk through the dense stands of conifers. His task was to check the fences and gates surrounding the forest and ensure that no sheep from neighbouring farmland had got in. His dog, an Irish setter named Lara, had run ahead of Taylor but was nowhere to be seen. Presumably it was somewhere in the forest searching for rabbits.

TWO SPHERES

In the centre of the clearing was a dark grey object about 6m (20ft) across. It was round with a high-domed top and a narrow rim projecting out from its base. Standing up from the rim were a number of poles topped by what looked like small propellers. At intervals around the base of the dome were darker round patches that were almost black in colour. The object seemed to be hovering slightly above the ground, but was emitting no noise. It was, however, giving off a strong smell akin to burning rubber.

Understandably, Taylor came to a sudden halt as he stared in some surprise and no little alarm at the object. Almost at once he realized that he was being approached by two small round black balls that came from the direction of the grey object. Each ball was a little under a yard in diameter and had half a dozen straight legs sticking out from it. The balls rolled toward him on the legs, there being a soft sucking noise as each leg touched the ground.

Things were happening fast. Before he could back off the two spheres had reached him and each pushed

Before he could back off, Taylor was approached and attacked by two black spheres which
seized him by the legs and started dragging him off

out a leg to grab hold of his leg with another soft sucking sound. The balls began to move back toward the object, dragging Taylor with them. Now alarmed, Taylor struggled to get free. The burning stench increased in intensity to the point where Taylor found he could barely breathe. Gasping for breath and trying to fight off the black spheres, Taylor felt himself growing dizzy and losing consciousness.

STRANGE MARKS IN THE GRASS

The next thing Taylor knew he came to some 20 minutes later lying face down on the grass with Lara trembling and whimpering nearby. The strange objects had all gone. Taylor's trousers were torn where the spheres had grabbed him. One of his legs was badly bruised and his chin was cut and bleeding. Taylor tried to stand, but his legs were weak so he began to crawl back toward his truck. When he tried to talk to Lara he found he could not utter a sound. Reaching the truck, Taylor tried to radio his base, but was still unable to speak. He headed home, his house being closer than the forestry base.

When he staggered through the door, Taylor was at last able to talk. He gasped out his tale to his wife, who phoned Taylor's boss, Malcolm Drummond, who in turn called a local doctor, Gordon Adams. Drummond arrived first with a team of workmen and headed into the forest to investigate.

When the men reached the clearing they could not at first see anything. Then one of the men spotted some strange marks in the grass. Drummond ordered the men out of the clearing so that they did not disturb the ground and called in the police.

Dr Adams had meanwhile arrived and examined Taylor. All the tests came up normal, though Taylor by this time had a pounding headache to add to his minor bruises and cuts. Adams suggested an X-ray, but the local hospital was too busy and by the time the X-ray machine was available the headache had gone so Taylor never bothered having the test.

The police then called and took away Taylor's clothing for forensic tests, while other officers studied the marks in the clearing. There were two different sorts of marks to be found. The first consisted of two parallel tracks some 2.4m (8ft) long and 30cm (1ft) wide. These were formed of crushed grass as if an enormously heavy weight had rested on them. Around these tracks were two circles of holes driven into the soil. Each hole was circular, about 10 cm (4in) across and 15cm (6in) deep. There were 40 holes in all, each of them driven down at an angle away from the tracks.

Checks with forestry workers revealed that no heavy machinery had been in use in the clearing for months. The marks must have been left by the object encountered by Taylor. Police forensic checks showed nothing unusual about the soil samples taken from the holes or beneath the tracks. Taylor's clothing likewise had nothing unusual about it. The tears to the trousers were consistent with them being tugged violently by blunt hooks rather than being cut.

Everything the police found was entirely consistent with Taylor's story. But what the object was and why it was in the forest the police could not explain at all.

THE SOCORRO INCIDENT

The Socorro Incident of 24 April 1964 for the first time brought together a credible witness, solid evidence and the sighting of humanoids linked to a UFO. It quickly became, and remains, a classic UFO Close Encounter of the Third Kind.

On 24 April 1964 at around 5.45pm Patrolman Lonnie Zamora was heading south from Socorro in his Pontiac police car in pursuit of a speeding motorist across the semi-desert landscape of the area. Another car was heading in the opposite direction but had not yet passed Zamora when an object flew overhead.

The motorist heading north took it to be an aircraft in trouble as it was moving rather erratically. Seeing a police car apparently investigating, the motorist did not report the sighting as a UFO, but merely mentioned the incident when he stopped to refuel his car in Socorro.

Zamora, meanwhile, had not seen the UFO as it passed overhead. He did, however, notice a sudden flash of blue-orange flame in the sky to the west. The bright light was followed by the sound of a roaring explosion. Knowing that a dynamite shack lay in that direction, Zamora feared either that it had exploded or was about to do so. He gave up his chase of the speeding motorist and decided to investigate the apparent explosion.

Zamora turned off the road on to a rough gravel track used only by off-road mining vehicles. As he dipped down into a shallow gully the flame came again. This time Zamora got a better view. It was shaped like a cone with the top narrower than the bottom and was some four times taller than it was wide. There was a plume of dust kicked up from around the base of the flame. The roar came again and lasted for 10 seconds, sounding a bit like a jet but descending from a high to a low pitch.

The police car had trouble getting out of the gully on to the top of a low hill. Zamora had to try three times before his Pontiac managed to get a grip on the gravel and ascend the steep slope. As he crested the hill Zamora saw an object standing on the ground some distance from the dynamite shack, which was intact.

Zamora at first took the object to be an overturned car and the two figures standing beside it to be a pair of youths who had crashed. The figures were wearing white overalls of some kind and may have had rounded caps or helmets on. They had been apparently talking to each other, but one turned round to look at Zamora as the police car crested the hill.

Zamora then radioed back to his police station 'Socorro Two to Socorro. Possible 10-40 (motor accident). I'll be 10-6 (busy).' The station logged the call, then radioed Patrolman Sam Chavez and sent him out to assist Zamora.

ROUGH TRACK

Meanwhile, Zamora had given up trying to drive any further on the rough track. He got out and walked toward the object. The two figures had vanished. He could now see that the object was not an upturned car at all, though it was about the same size as one. It was a whitish-silver colour and shaped like an oval

Patrolman Lonnie Zamora suspected a traffic violation

standing on one end. There were four legs projecting down on which the object rested. It was about four feet across and perhaps 20 feet tall. On one side was a red marking that resembled an upright arrow within an arch with a horizontal line underneath. There then came two loud thumps as if somebody had slammed a door. Zamora later assumed that this was the sound of the two humanoids shutting their door after they got into the craft.

By this time Zamora was within about 23m (75ft) of the object. The roar then began again, getting gradually louder, and the blue-orange flame erupted from the base of the craft. Zamora turned and ran,

fearing that the object might explode or the flames engulf him. He struck his leg on his car's fender and fell headlong, then got back to his feet and ran further trying to keep the patrol car between himself and the object.

Having covered about 7m (25ft), Zamora glanced back. The object was now hovering on its flame some 4.5m (15ft) above the ground. Zamora leapt over the edge of the hill, then turned to look back, thinking that he could duck down into cover at a moment's notice. The flames and the roaring sound had by now stopped and the strange object was hanging eerily motionless. The object then began to move silently off toward the southwest, gathering speed as it went. It stayed only 45m (155ft) or so off the ground and vanished behind some hills.

As Zamora was climbing back to his car, Chavez arrived in his patrol car. Together the two policemen went to check the dynamite shack, then turned to investigate the spot where the object had been seen. The greasewood scrub that dotted the area was burnt and smouldering, smoke still curling up by charred twigs. Four prominent marks were seen in the ground where heavy objects had pushed down into the dry soil. Each mark was about 5cm (2in) deep and rectangular in shape. Given the soil composition in the area the object that made the marks must have weighed between three and five tons. Nearby were smaller, indistinct marks that might have been footprints.

Later analysis showed that the four marks were arranged as if on the circumference of a circle, as they would have been if they were four legs supporting a round object as Zamora had reported. Moreover the centre of the burned area of ground was underneath where the centre of gravity of an object supported on the four legs would have been.

The key importance of the Socorro sighting was that Zamora was an excellent witness who was highly respected by his colleagues. Dr Hynek of Project Blue Book was on the scene just two days

later, and returned several times to check up on measurements, cross-examine Zamora and investigate further. His conclusion that a real, physical event of an unexplained nature had taken place lifted the reports of ufonauts out of the margins and into the mainstream.

ALIEN RAY GUN

The encounter with aliens experienced by French farmer Maurice Masse on 1 July 1965 did not attract a huge amount of attention at the time, at least not outside the area where he lived. However it has since been recognized as one of the most crucial early sightings of aliens as it established a number of patterns that were to be repeated time and again.

The day of the encounter began normally enough for Masse. As a farmer he was used to working long hours, so he rose at 5am, ate a quick breakfast and climbed into his tractor to start work in his lavender fields. Despite the isolated position of Masse's farm he had been suffering strange attacks of vandalism

An investigator scrapes up soil samples from the site of the UFO landing in France. Nothing unusual showed up in the lab

Artwork based on Zamora's description: this 1964 sighting was the first clear sighting of ufonauts by an impeccable witness

with lavender bushes being torn up. Masse assumed that some local youths were to blame. He was a former fighter in the French Resistance and had decided that if he ever caught the culprits, he would teach them a stern lesson.

About 6am Masse stopped his tractor for a cigarette break. He heard a strange whistling noise that came from the other side of a small hillock. Jumping down from his tractor, Masse trotted around the hillock to investigate.

He saw an egg-shaped object of gleaming silver metal mounted on six thin metal legs and thick central support. It was about the size of a small van. Of more immediate interest to Masse were what he took to be two boys aged about eight years old who

were nearby pulling at a lavender plant. They had their backs to him.

Thinking he had finally caught the vandals who had been plaguing him, Masse crept towards them. When he was about 5m (16ft) from the 'boys' one of them seemed to hear him. The figure stood up and turned around, then quickly whipped out a small gun-shaped object and pointed it at Masse. The farmer stopped in alarm, but his alarm turned to fear when he realized that he had been paralyzed and could not move.

While Masse watched, the second figure also stood up. Masse could now see that they were not boys at all, but bizarre entities. Each figure stood about 120cm (4ft) tall with thin, slender bodies and

Based on the descriptions given by French lavender farmer Maurice Masse, this reconstruction shows the UFO and its crew that Masse encountered in 1965

limbs. The feet seemed to be wearing boots and there were shorts of some kind around the groin. Otherwise the figures were dressed in tight-fitting green overalls. The heads were oval, with a pointy chin and small ears. The eyes were large and oval in shape, slanting up to the side of the face. The mouths were thin slits without lips.

EGG-SHAPED OBJECT

The figures made strange grunting noises, which Masse took to be their speech. Strangely the mouths did not move, the sounds seeming to come from the throat area. The figure who had first seen Masse returned the gun-shaped object to a pouch attached to the side of his belt. With a final look at the lavender, the two figures moved toward the egg-shaped object. A sliding door opened in the side of the object and the two figures entered. They did not climb in, but seemed to float up from the ground.

The door slid shut and the object began to emit the whistling noise that had first attracted Masse's attention. There was a dome on top of the object. A window appeared in this and Masse saw one of the figures peering out of it at him. Then the window closed.

The object rose vertically into the air to a height of about 18m (60ft). The whistling noise then stopped and the craft disappeared off into the distance toward the nearby village of Manosque.

Still Masse was paralysed. He now began to become seriously concerned, worried that he was permanently disabled and might die. It was not until some 20 minutes later that he regained use of his body, though only slowly even then. Once he felt confident of moving, he began walking, then running for the village of Valensole. There he met the owner of the local cafe, who was just opening up for business, and blurted out his story. The cafe owner called the police.

Later that day Captain Valnet of the gendarmerie arrived uncertain as to quite what had happened, but determined to get to the bottom of the trouble. The official investigation that followed collected evidence competently, including details of damage to the lavender and drawings of the marks left by the craft. It was noted that the plants around the landing site itself died over the following days. Those further from the spot where the craft had landed recovered, but those that had been under the craft did not. Masse himself was very tired for several days, sleeping much longer than was usual and being unable to undertake the more strenuous jobs around the farm.

Despite collecting a mass of evidence of various kinds, it is unsurprising that Valnet failed to reach a firm conclusion of any kind.

What makes the Valensole case so interesting is that the features reported by Masse were to crop up again and again in the years that followed, and remain typical in modern cases.

The aliens themselves fit the category that is now referred to as 'Tricksters'. Their pallid skin, slanting eyes and pointed chins are typical, as are the rounded, bald heads and tight-fitting costumes. Their behaviour would also become typical. The interest of the aliens in plants, particularly crops, is something that is reported time and again. The strange floating movement of the aliens as they boarded their craft is another feature that was thought bizarre at the time, but which has since become an almost routine element in reports of aliens.

PROMPT ACTION

Likewise the fact that they were neither hostile nor friendly to the human that saw them is a striking feature of this case. Quite clearly they did not want to be disturbed and took prompt action to disable Masse as soon as they realized that a human was nearby, but were otherwise unconcerned. They did not attack, however, and no lasting damage was done. Compared to some other types of aliens, which may attack on sight or flee, this behaviour is typical of the 'Tricksters'.

All of these features were reported by a French farmer who lived in an area about as rural as it is possible to get in western Europe who had never taken any previous interest in UFOs, nor had ever read or seen any of the science fiction books or movies then being made. It would seem that the only explanation for this is that Masse did in fact have a real experience.

There is one final fact that is worth recording. Some years after the incident at Valensole a French UFO investigator sent Masse a drawing of the UFO that had landed at Socorro in New Mexico, USA, as he thought it sounded similar to that seen by Masse. Masse's reaction was immediate and emphatic.

'That is what I saw,' he replied. 'You see, I was not dreaming and I was not mad.'

CALLING CARD

For over a decade, implants have been reported in the hands, feet, abdomen and nasal cavities of abductees. Only X-ray technology can discern whether aliens have left their extraordinary calling card, as there are no obvious indications remaining on the skin. However, those afflicted are frequently dogged by illness, even before any suggestion of an implant is made.

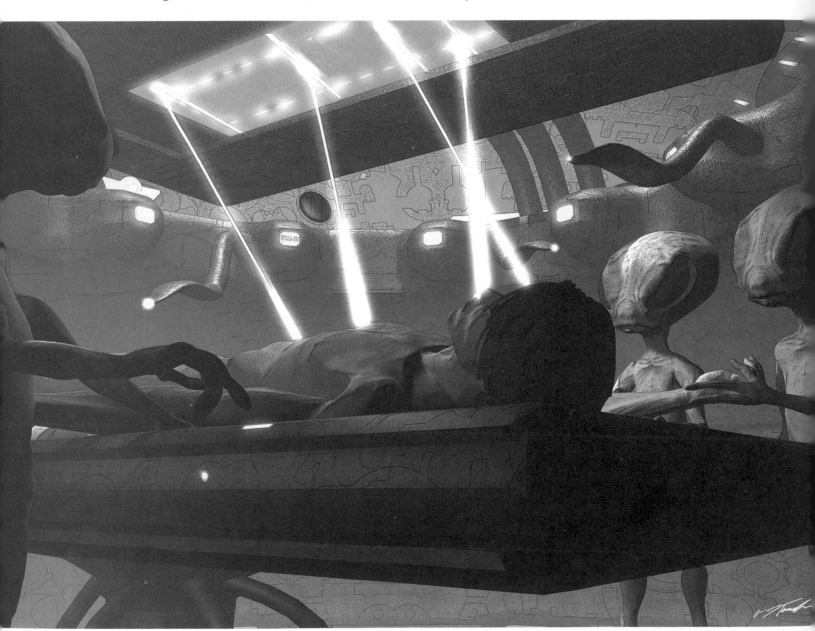

Many people have reported being abducted by aliens and then subjected to medical examination before an implant is inserted to part of the body

A woman undergoes hypnotic regression in an attempt to discover what happened when her conscious memory went blank

So why would aliens implant humans in this way? It is one of the world's great mysteries, a matter for considerable conjecture, but there is one generally accepted opinion – that the implants might act as transmitters or beacons so that when the aliens return they can trace their human subjects.

So far, though, hard evidence for implants is in short supply. Indeed, there is no conclusive proof that humans have ever been inside spaceships.

All the evidence is anecdotal, leading the sceptics to claim that the experiences reported by abductees are nothing more than lucid dreams. Yet how can we explain that the accounts of kidnappings by aliens number in their hundreds? Furthermore, the stories all bear a curious similarity.

Stories of abduction usually begin with the sighting of a UFO. The accounts that abductees give of dancing lights in the sky or cigar-shaped craft shooting overhead are sometimes verified by other people in the area.

BEAM OF LIGHT

Abductees then apparently walk, float or fly up into the spacecraft inside a beam of light. Inside, they find the craft brightly lit and clinically clean. They recount how the examination takes place in this surgical setting, with the human subject naked and quivering beneath the eyes of the aliens. It is presumably at this point that an implant is inserted. Afterwards, the human interlopers might be offered a tour of the craft. Attempts to remove a keepsake have always ended in failure, although the aliens are apparently friendly and keen to give advice that will benefit mankind.

A HAZY MEMORY

Returned to their homes or vehicles, the abductees typically discover they have been missing for hours or days, although it seems to them that only a few minutes have passed by. Immediately, the events inside the craft become a hazy memory, but then return in haunting and vivid dreams. After abduction experiences, people often sense that they are being observed, although they do not generally feel the surveillance has sinister motives.

Hypnosis is one of the methods used to understand what has happened to abductees – or experiencers as they are sometimes called – during the time lapse inside the spacecraft. In the absence of film footage or other incontrovertible evidence, this information would otherwise remain hidden in their subconscious. In the 1980s, 270 cases of claimed abduction were analyzed in detail using hypnosis. All accounts showed astonishingly close consistencies, especially given that those involved were from different backgrounds, professions and geographical locations. However, the accuracy of using hypnosis for the purposes of recall is not proven, and it is believed that interviewers' beliefs on the subject may influence the outcome. The results are open to debate.

MYSTERIOUS IMPLANTS

So what about the implants? Surely they must provide hard evidence of abductions. If experiencers submit to a second examination, the implanted particle or device can be analyzed. However, results have proved disappointing. One item believed to be an alien implant was sneezed out, and turned out to be a ball-bearing. Another was proved by chemical scrutiny to be a dental filling. There is no conclusive proof about the nature of implants, although recent accounts allude to small, tear-shaped rocks of an unknown substance.

Perhaps more worryingly, there is an oft-repeated allegation that women are implanted with sperm and become pregnant, only to be robbed of the foetus before giving birth. If the accounts of experiencers are to be believed, the aliens take a special interest in human reproductive organs.

THE ACCOUNTS OF EXPERIENCERS

In September 1961, Betty and Barney Hill were driving along the isolated Interstate Route 3 in New Hampshire when, as they relate, they encountered a

Betty and Barney Hill photographed at the time their abduction became known

spacecraft that looked like 'a big pancake'. Later, they were to reveal the details of their encounter while under hypnosis and their convincing stories became a kind of benchmark in terms of alien experience.

They recounted how they ended up aboard the craft, where there were uniformed men with large eyes, flat noses and lipless mouths. Betty, a social worker, was given 'a pregnancy test' by some futuristic machinery through the navel. Meanwhile, mail sorter Barney endured the extraction of his semen.

Although Barney died years later, Betty has always maintained that she was taken by aliens. Yet her approach remains underpinned by common sense. Her experience, she insists, does not reflect any extraordinary personal talents. 'I'm about as psychic as a dead fish,' she jokes.

Likewise Elaine Darlington, a former Royal Air Force servicewoman living in Newquay, Cornwall, enjoyed an ordinary life before her alleged contact with aliens. She recites four different encounters with aliens, and it was during the last of these that she said an 'operation' took place.

ALIEN OP

'They zapped me with a light on the centre of my forehead. They seemed to be able to manipulate matter or body energy,' she said, 'The operation began – I think it was on my stomach. There was no pain but they had some problem with my blood … I came round in my own bedroom with no side-effects, apart from one small blotch on my left rib cage. It vanished within 24 hours.'

Because the mark on her body disappeared so quickly, evidence was once again in short supply. However, Elaine's home was hit by power cuts around the time of the visits and she herself suffered electric shocks. Curiously, her local electricity board could find no problems with supply.

On a final alien encounter on Newlyn Downs, Cornwall, Elaine's husband Ian was there to share her experience. Elaine had woken in the early hours, convinced she was to make an excursion to the

The Hill abduction began as their car was followed along a remote country road by a UFO

Downs. On arrival, they recount how they both saw a bright light through the window of their vehicle and watched it shoot up at high speed into the sky.

The lack of hard evidence to prove alien abduction makes it all the harder for experiencers to convince sceptics, but they will not give up. 'My memories of being taken are real,' insists Elaine. 'It isn't like remembering dreams'.

Greys are described as having spindly bodies, with bulbous, bald heads and large, almond-shaped eyes

THE SINISTER GREYS

A spindly body with bulbous, hairless head and large, dark almond eyes. Sound familiar? Probably, since this is the uniform description given of alien life forms spotted here on earth. These beings are known as 'greys', after the colour of their smooth, rubbery skins. In recent years, reports of alien sightings have been relatively frequent, and it is striking how similar most descriptions are.

Typically, sceptics do not believe the image of the grey to be the real likeness of alien life-forms, but rather that which appeared in an ABC sci-fi show made in the early 1960s called *The Outer Limits*. They believe this image has somehow seeped into international consciousness as the definitive portrayal of extraterrestrial life, when previously the image was predominantly of 'little green men'. Yet surely this cannot explain that, even under hypnosis, literally scores of people have come up with the same descriptions?

The life forms they speak of communicate telepathically, have wasted muscles and closely resemble foetuses.

QUEST TO SAVE A DYING RACE?

There has been plenty of speculation about what part of space these extraterrestrials might come from. Among the most frequently cited places is Zeta Reticuli, a binary star, visible in the skies of the southern hemisphere, 39 light years away from earth.

Why would aliens want to visit earth? Perhaps they are on a quest to save their dying race, or maybe they want to clone human beings for an unknown purpose. It is doubtful that they would come here to wonder at our technology, since their own appears to be far superior. Nor does it seem to be their aim to share their knowledge with us, because the recall of abductees is often hazy.

Reports of UFOs began surfacing after the Second World War, when the world was gripped by the paranoia of the Cold War and fear of the atomic bomb. Rocket technology had advanced during the war years to a point where fast, long-distance flight appeared to be a distinct possibility for the first time. Americans were fearful of a communist invasion and they were sure that, in the event, both nuclear and psychological weapons would be dispatched by the USSR. It was in this climate of fear that pilot Kenneth Arnold saw what he described as 'flying saucers' soaring in formation above the Cascade Mountains in Washington State in June 1947. Arnold's testimony marked the beginning of a flood of UFO sightings in America and around the world.

ROSWELL

On 7 July 1947, these stories reached their climax, with the revelation of the now-notorious Roswell Incident. The wreckage of an odd-looking craft and its equally unusual humanoid crew was apparently discovered on the Foster ranch, near Corona, New

Rancher Mac Brazel inspects the wreckage; in real life the actual metal fragments carried symbols which no one could identify

Mexico. The following day a press officer for the nearby Roswell Army Air Fields announced that an alien vessel had crash-landed there. But a high-ranking military officer was swift to deny the claim, saying that an experimental balloon had gone down near Roswell. As he explained it, the bodies at the scene were in fact crash dummies. However, many people did not accept the official explanation, and they remained convinced that the US Government had evidence of aliens in its grasp.

The debate was fuelled in 1995 when a film allegedly showing an alien autopsy following the Roswell incident was unveiled. But there was

Government disinformation? Initial speculation about Roswell was quelled by this photo showing wreckage from a weather balloon.

immediate doubt about the film's authenticity, not least because the creatures which featured in it did not match descriptions given of them at the time.

Since then, theories about what really happened at Roswell have abounded, the latest being that emaciated Japanese prisoners of war were being used as test pilots on an experimental flight. This would certainly explain why the military were keen to have the whole incident hastily covered up.

The entire Roswell episode has been marked by

inconsistencies, controversy, claim and counter-claim. It is known that at least two crucial official documents from the era have gone missing. But if some of the original descriptions of the Roswell Army Air Fields crew are to be believed, then this was the first known human contact with greys.

SCINTILLATING FACT OR SCIENCE FICTION?

Since the Roswell incident, large numbers of stories involving contact with greys have circulated, some of which seem convincing, others less so.

In July 1952, Truman Bethurum was sleeping in his truck when he was woken by the voices of eight diminutive figures standing close by. Outside his cab, Truman was astonished to see a 90m-wide (300ft) spaceship, hovering soundlessly. The beings, he reported, had olive rather than grey skin. According to his account, they told him: 'Our homes are our castles in a faraway land'. Then they allegedly took him aboard the spaceship to meet its captain, Aura Rhanes, who told him they were from the planet Clarion, obscured from earth by the moon.

Ten years after this incident, a UFO that reportedly crashed south of Alamogordo, New Mexico, yielded the bodies of two greys. They have been described as being about 1m (3.3ft) tall with large heads, pink-grey skin, large eyes, small noses and mouths and holes for ears. It is said that the bodies were sent to a leading university hospital in America for analysis.

HUMANOID FIGURE

In 1973, student Masaaki Kudou was working as a security guard in a timber yard close to the sea on Hokkaido, Japan, when he apparently saw a space ship taking off from the water. He claims he saw one humanoid figure and another two that were smaller. Other spaceships joined the first before they sped off together, leaving Kudou astounded.

In 1989, mother Linda Cortile announced she was literally beamed up into a spaceship by aliens who were short and grey with round heads and apparently frail bodies. Curiously, the incident happened on Manhattan Island and reportedly had a host of witnesses. Alien appearances are more commonly associated with rural areas rather than metropolitan places like New York. Cortile recalled that during the abduction she was given a medical examination, before abruptly being returned to bed in her 12th-storey apartment. Scrutiny of Cortile's case continues even today.

ALIEN BLOGS

The internet has enabled the exchange of stories like these to proliferate. There are also many on-line tales from people who claim to have seen spaceships in US Air Force hangars and spoken to aliens captured from these craft. However, most of these are experiences related by a third person, rather than by first-hand witnesses, and are therefore less reliable.

Sceptics sneer at the stories of contact with aliens, sometimes known as 'close encounters of the third kind'. And some of the stories are so exaggerated that they are hard to believe.

Yet just as the cynics dismiss all claims of alien contact, so ufologists feel able to scoff at many of the earthly explanations given for episodes of this nature. When detailed descriptions of an alien encounter are given by several witnesses, the explanations that those involved mistook a fast-moving mystery disc for Venus in the night sky or for high-flying weather balloons do seem simplistic. To dismiss all reports of extraterrestrial contact is closed-minded, given the size of the universe and possibility of advanced life-forms existing far from earth. And the notion that alien sightings are the product of people's subconscious has yet to be proved to anyone's satisfaction.

INTO THE VOID

In 1927 the pioneer of genetics, J B S Haldane, famously observed that the universe is 'not only queerer than we suppose, it is queerer than we can suppose'. Today, eighty years on, there is little sign of science proving him wrong. Indeed, the more we probe the cosmos, the more baffling it seems.

At the heart of this great debate is the study of theoretical physics, where things happen for no reason and an event in one outpost of space can trigger an instant reaction light years away.

The Hubble telescope has transmitted pictures of the whirlpool galaxy M51. The dust nucleus is thought to hide a massive black hole

Traditionally, theoretical physics has been perceived as a dry and dusty subject, riddled with incomprehensible equations. Yet without it, we can never hope to tease out the secrets of the most mysterious phenomena in the known universe – black holes.

Current theories about what would happen to a manned spacecraft entering a black hole vary greatly. At one end of the argument is the view, held by most physicists, that it would be crushed to oblivion by immense gravitational forces. However, a respected minority believe that the craft could theoretically be spewed backwards or forwards in time, or even into a parallel universe, through distortions in the fabric of space caused by the black hole. These tunnels are known as 'wormholes'.

UNRAVELLING THE MYSTERY

To see what might happen to a spaceship in a black hole, it is important to take a look at our current understanding of how the universe works. Einstein produced huge advances in this area, although his Theory of Gravitation cannot explain the massive forces at work inside a black hole. The idea of black holes first emerged in 1916 when the German astronomer Karl Schwarzschild built on Einstein's work. Schwarzschild calculated the size of a star with a gravitational pull so strong that not even light, the fastest traveller of all, could escape from it. The speed needed to escape from this star, known as its 'escape velocity' was equal to the speed of light. According to Einstein's Theory of Relativity nothing travels faster than light, so such a star will be invisible. Moreover anyone, or anything, which becomes trapped in its gravitational field will be drawn

> **Schwarzschild calculated the size of a star with a gravitational pull so strong that not even light could escape from it**

inside and, according to most scientists, obliterated.

These 'stellar' black holes are essentially collapsed stars that have used up all their fuel. They have no material surface, because all their original matter has been shrunk to an infinitely dense point known as a 'singularity'.

Recent research led by Hubble space telescope astronomers suggests that there are millions of stellar black holes in our galaxy alone. It is also thought that every galaxy has a 'supermassive' black hole lurking at its centre, a monster whose mass was once millions of times larger than our sun. Supermassives are thought to play a pivotal role in the way a galaxy evolves.

STELLAR BLACK HOLE

However, Hollywood's portrayal of black holes as giant vacuum cleaners sucking up all matter (including planets) across many light years is a myth. If the sun were to become a stellar black hole tomorrow – and such an event is not due for several thousand billion years – the lack of light and heat would certainly destroy life on earth. However, the change in gravitational pull would be imperceptible. Unlikely as it sounds, you would have to get within a few kilometres of the sun to reach the point of no return.

Mainstream theories suggest that anything approaching a black hole is first torn apart by gravitational forces and then compressed into a flat rotational disc that spirals inside, a phenomenon known as a 'feeding' black hole. When this happens the material heats up (due to friction) and gives off X-rays detectable from earth. If the ring of material around a supermassive black hole contains lots of debris then it can produce an intense light source known as a quasar, one of the most distant objects ever observed. The nearest quasars are hundreds of billions of light years from earth, which gives some idea of the enormous energy they generate.

All this suggests the chances of a manned spacecraft surviving entry into a black hole are nil. Roughly the same odds, in fact, that a 19th-century aero-engineer had of landing a craft on the moon and bringing it home. The point is that no one can predict technological advances on the basis of current knowledge. What really matters here is the theory. So what if we assume a spacecraft could get through?

And this is where things get really tricky. Einstein's Theory of Relativity brought space and time together into a concept known, unsurprisingly, as 'spacetime'. This shows that we exist, in four dimensions – up, down, sideways and through the passing of time. If we can travel upwards, downwards and sideways in space, then why can we not do the same in time?

The best way to visualize spacetime is to imagine a rubber sheet stretched out with marbles rolling across it.

Imagine that the marbles are planets, or comets. They travel in straight lines except where they go near a heavy marble (a star) that causes the rubber to dip (a gravitational field). The marbles bend around that dip as they roll, illustrating that everything, including light, follows curved paths in spacetime.

Occasionally they come across a really heavy marble (a black hole). This does not just cause the rubber sheet to dip, it breaks right through it to the other side.

Similarly, the sheet itself may contain tiny holes, just as rubber does if viewed under a powerful microscope, allowing a passage through the barrier.

But what is on the other side of these wormholes? It could be the sheet folded back on itself, which would be a location back or forward in time. Or it might be a completely new universe.

The standard argument against time travel has always been the 'grandfather paradox', the idea that if you travelled back and somehow stopped your grandfather meeting your grandmother then your mother would never have been born… and neither

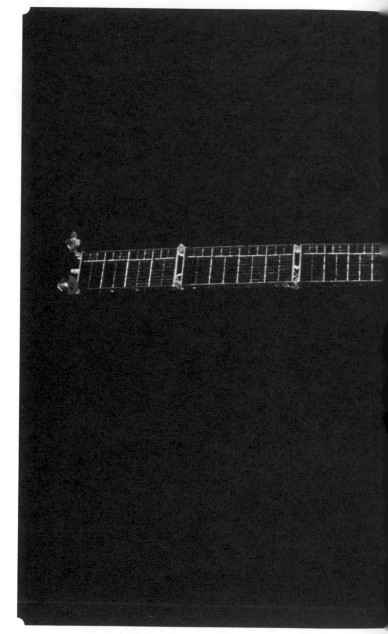

would you! If you never existed, then how come you are wandering around the past?

The notion of breaking into a separate universe altogether solves this conundrum. According to the theoretical model, anyone heading back in time through a wormhole arrives in a parallel universe with a completely new future.

The time traveller can now have no effect on the universe he left – he or she simply ceases to exist there – but can shape events in the new one. So

there could be an infinite number of universes accommodating an infinite number of time travellers...

To readers who have stuck with it this far – and nobody promised this section would be easy – the sad truth is that humankind has barely scratched the surface of cosmology and quantum physics. But scientists are already contemplating the possibility of teleportation, where particles move instantly from one point in space to another.

A spacecraft approaching a black hole would probably be destroyed, but not if the black hole were the portal to another universe...

They are also working on quantum computation, which will allow massively complex calculations to be performed in seconds rather than years. One day, they may answer the hardest question of all, namely what is time? It is possible that in the future, Haldane may be proved wrong.

SECTION 4

PARANORMAL PLACES

There are places on Earth that seem to attract the unnatural and paranormal. Some are ancient, mystic sites imbued with an aura of long-forgotten religion and ancient gods. Others hide very modern mysteries of vanishing ships and crashed aircraft where machines and crew simply vanish off the face of the Earth with no apparent explanation. Some are places that lure the visitor with promises of romance and magic, others are dangerous and best avoided, but they are all home to the unusual.

STONEHENGE

The towering, mysterious circle of rocks that rises out of Salisbury Plain has inspired awe in millions of people over the ages. But the reason for its existence baffles archaeologists to this day. Various theories suggest a ritual site, an astronomical observatory, or a focus for some mystical form of 'earth energy'.

ROCKY EVOLUTION

In piecing together the complex Stonehenge jigsaw, we can at least be confident of some basic facts. Using radiocarbon measurements, scientists have dated the earliest work on Salisbury Plain to around 3,100BC. At this time the site was far more primitive, comprising a circular 97.5m (320ft) diameter ditch, a single entrance and a central wooden 'temple' or sanctuary. Around the edge of the ditch were fifty-six holes, each containing cremated human remains. On the summer and winter solstices the whole structure aligned with rising and setting points of the sun.

By 2,500BC, the wooden sanctuary had been replaced with two circles of the famous bluestones that had been transported 390km (240 miles) from the Preseli mountains of south-west Wales. An entrance avenue of parallel ditches which aligned to the midsummer sunrise was added, together with outlying single megaliths such as the Heel Stone, Slaughter Stone and Station Stones. However, the

bluestones were pulled down within a century and recycled for a new design.

The new Stonehenge had a very different emphasis. At its centre was the Altar Stone (now fallen), a large sandstone shipped from the Cleddau Estuary in Pembrokeshire. Over the next 500 years, some of the re-used bluestones were raised around it in a horseshoe shape. Beyond these were placed five massive sarsen trilithons (two uprights bearing a horizontal), a ring of bluestone pillars and an outer ring of sarsen uprights linked by lintels. The bus-sized sarsen blocks are by far Stonehenge's largest, typically weighing 30 tons and at least one as much as 50 tons. Most are thought to have been transported from the chalklands of Marlborough Downs, some 32km (20 miles) west.

HEAVY WORK

According to some estimates these three building phases must together have required more than thirty million hours of labour. For Stone Age people to allocate this amount of time – even over two millenia – seems extraordinary. It suggests a level of co-operation far above what we might expect; a society in which Stonehenge labourers would have had to be fed, watered and sheltered in order to build a seemingly useless monument. How did they do it? More importantly, why did they do it?

The how is comparatively easy to fathom. Many of north-west Europe's neolithic monument builders used large quantities of stone transported from a great distance. The architects of Newgrange in the Irish Midlands, which pre-dates the Stonehenge megaliths by at least 500 years, brought quartz and granodiorite from sites 48km (30 miles) away. It seems likely that Stonehenge's bluestones were brought to Salisbury Plain by a combination of raft-borne river, sea and overland transport. Once the raw materials arrived, the construction of the circle itself would have required a phenomenal amount of manpower, relying on a levering system of wood and rope.

The huge bluestones for Stonehenge were dragged almost 400km

THE BUILDING OF STONEHENGE

The great block is being drawn on rollers by many labourers, who are cruelly whipped by the overseers. The architect standing on it is directing the teams of slaves and volunteers, so that the stone will turn over and fall into the big pit prepared for it.

It has been estimated that the three building phases of Stonehenge must have required more than thirty million man hours of labour

Manpower aside, the thorny question of quite why it was necessary to lug the bluestones 390km is far from clear. A study led by Geoff Wainwright and Timothy Darvill in 2004 suggests that the dolerite crags of the Preseli mountains would have held particular appeal. The stone is naturally fractured into 'ready-made' pillars, so they just needed to be levered off for removal. The stones themselves – strong, durable, and speckled with white feldspar – may have been invested with a symbolic, mythical power.

Which brings us back to the key question, what was Stonehenge for? It may well have had different functions at different times. But the prevailing archaeological view is that Stonehenge was a ritual and burial site, linked to astronomical observations. It was almost certainly not used to predict the agricultural crop cycle. In England the summer solstice occurs long after the start of the growing season and the winter solstice misses the harvest by a good three months.

PIGS AND DRUIDS

In 2005, tests on some neolithic pig bones showed that large numbers were slaughtered in the months of December or January. This lends weight to the idea that a winter solstice festival was held at Stonehenge. It also seems to have been an important burial site. Around the standing stones are a large number of burial mounds, and in 2002 an archer's grave was discovered that contained more than 100 precious items such as gold earrings, copper knives and pottery. Tests have shown that the deceased – dubbed the 'King of Stonehenge' – was born in the Alps around 2,300BC. This is the richest known burial of the age anywhere in Europe, and the implication is that the 'King' was a settler who played a key role in constructing the monument.

The link between Stonehenge and the ancient Druid religion has taken a battering in recent years. Experts believe this connection was always tenuous (based as it was on the observations of Julius Caesar) and it is now clear that the heyday of the Druids came a thousand years after work on Stonehenge ended. However, we cannot be certain how early the Druid traditions came into existence, so a link cannot be ruled out.

CELESTIAL CALENDAR

The idea that Stonehenge was used as a celestial calendar is simple to prove. If you stand in the centre of the circle at 5am on a clear Midsummer's Day you can see the sun rise precisely in line with the Heel Stone, 37m (121ft) beyond the ring. This is the most obvious and impressive of the circle's mysterious alignments.

During the 1950s and 1960s a further 23 alignments were recorded by Oxford University engineer Alexander Thom and the astronomer Gerald Hawkins. Hawkins speculated that Stonehenge was used to predict eclipses, although critics now say his methodology was flawed and that he overestimated the number of alignments.

ANCIENT KNOWLEDGE

What is clear is that the ancient architects of Stonehenge possessed a level of mathematical and engineering sophistication that defies explanation, knowledge that appears to have pre-dated both the Egyptian and Mesopotamian cultures.

How can we explain that 2,000 years before Euclid's Pythagorean 'breakthrough', and more than 3,000 years before Arya Bhata 'discovered' the value of Pi, neolithic Britons were using these concepts to construct Stonehenge?

MYSTERIOUS FORCES

Putting aside questions of science, another theory behind the existence of Stonehenge is that it focused some intangible 'earth energy', a natural force field that could be tapped by those in the know. Hard evidence for this theory is lacking, although footage of UFOs in the skies above the circle in October 1977 has never been properly explained. All we can say for certain is that Stonehenge seems to be in a significant place: it stands on a known 35km (22 mile) ley line, which also bisects three earthworks and three tumuli (burial grounds).

Maybe the greatest barrier to solving the mystery of Stonehenge lies in our own prejudices. Today we live a hectic urban lifestyle that isolates us from the subtle rhythms of nature observed by neolithic societies.

Perhaps we are concentrating too much on scientific knowledge, and our problem in unravelling the mystery of the mammoth stones is that we have started in the wrong place.

NEWGRANGE

The Megalithic tombs of Newgrange, in Ireland, are more than 5,000 years old, so they pre-date the pyramids of Egypt, and even the arrival of the Celts in Ireland. As is often the case with such ancient monuments, very little remains today to give a clue as to the greater purpose behind their construction and this fine Stone Age necropolis is a source of speculation and intrigue all over the world.

Located near the banks of the river Boyne, to the east of Slane, the Newgrange tombs are known in the native tongue as Bru Na Boinne. According to pagan lore, Newgrange was the dwelling of Aengus, the powerful god of love. The site is also associated with the mystical race of the goddess Danu, also known as the Tuatha De Dannan. According to local superstition, these nature-loving pagans have left something of their spirit in the landscape and it is thought that Cuchulain, the legendary hero of the Celtic warriors, was conceived at Newgrange.

The Newgrange tomb is said to be the burial place of the high kings of Tara. The ash remains of these rulers would have been contained in large bowls in each of the three recesses of the burial chamber.

The Newgrange tomb is said to be the burial place of the high kings of Tara. The ash remains of these rulers would have been contained in large bowls in each of the three recesses of the burial chamber

Although this chamber has been described as cruciform in shape, given the fact that the tomb pre-dates the birth of Christ by around 3,200 years, it is more likely that this layout reflects the clover form that is so prevalent in ancient Irish artworks.

The builders of these tombs demonstrated considerable devotion to their construction. First, they made use of materials that were not readily available – the quartz must have been quarried and transported from the Wicklow Mountains, a considerable distance from Newgrange. Second, the builders were involved in a huge project – it has been estimated that the construction of the monument would have taken a workforce of 300 men more than twenty years to complete.

In common with the people of other ancient cultures, the lives of the Newgrange community would have been closely regulated by the natural rhythms and cycles of the earth, with the summer and winter solstices assuming great importance. At Newgrange, during the winter solstice, the dawn sun shines through a 'roof-box', down a short, straight passage and into the heart of the burial chamber, illuminating intricate carvings that are believed to represent the sun and the moon.

Intriguingly, similar effects can be found at Stonehenge, in the pyramids of the Maya and Aztecs, and in King Khufu's pyramid in Egypt, where a curious shaft of light enters the tomb at the time of the solstice. It is unclear whether this shaft may have been intended to allow the king's soul to ascend to the heavens.

Did these cultures have a common spiritual identity, or is there simply something innate in human nature that discovered great profundity in the movement of the stars and the cycles of the planet? These ancient farming communities possessed a knowledge and understanding way ahead of their time. It is impossible not to marvel at the skill that enabled these people to make the precise calculations necessary in order to align the passages of the tombs with the light thrown out by the stars or the sun.

During the winter solstice, the dawn sun shines through a 'roof-box', down a short, straight passage into the heart of the burial chamber

It is hard not to marvel at the skills of those who built Newgrange

YONAGUNI

In 1985, a discovery was made in Japan that still baffles the scientific community today. A Japanese dive tour operator, Kihachiro Aratake, strayed from his regular area into the waters off Yonaguni Island, near Okinawa. About 30m (100ft) beneath the surface, he found a strange formation which, on further examination, appeared to be a man-made pyramid.

SOURCE OF CONTROVERSY

Ever since this date, the Yonaguni finding has been a source of immense controversy. Experts are unable to agree upon whether it is actually a man-made structure at all, or simply a remarkable natural formation.

If it can be confirmed to be man-made, it will undoubtedly revolutionize the way in which the history of our own species is viewed.

Scientists agree that this area of coastline became submerged by the rising oceans at least 10,000 years ago. Following the end of the last Ice Age, there was a huge global thaw that altered the world immeasurably and, over time, sea levels are believed to have risen by up to 30m (100ft).

This means that any civilization in place at that time would have been destroyed, engulfed by the rising waters, with all traces of it remaining hidden to this day.

Furthermore, it is known that human civilizations have thrived on coastlines for thousands of years, because the sea is not only an excellent source of food, but also facilitates important activities such as trading and transport.

Yonaguni would, therefore, have been a likely location for a settlement to arise. Such a civilization would, however, have pre-dated all known cultures by thousands of years, since the oldest known city is believed to be Sumeria in Mesopotamia, which dates back to around 5,000 years ago. To double the

A scuba diver embarking on exploration of the underwater world off Yonaguni Island

accepted timescale of human development is to take a drastic leap. This, however, is not impossible, especially if there is real evidence to support it, as Yonaguni might prove.

Perplexing scientists still further is the fact that similarities have been noted between the architecture that appears to exist at Yonaguni and that which can be found above the sea on the coast of Peru. Yet even the oldest of these Peruvian structures, built by the Moche people, are at the most 2,000 years old, leaving an inexplicable gap of many millennia.

Further controversy has arisen over the actual appearance of the Yonaguni structure. Underwater photographs of the site appear to show the presence of ramps, terraces and steps.

While American geologists argue that these are nothing more than natural formations, Japanese scientists have claimed that tool markings can be found along the structure, suggesting that it might have been tampered with.

BOTH SIDES OF THE ARGUMENT

One person, however, has seemingly taken both sides of the argument, asserting that the site is both natural and man-made. Dr Robert M Schoch, a geologist who made frequent dives to the site, actually suggested that the majority of the structure was indeed a natural formation, but one that had been chosen and modified by humans, in a process known as 'terra-forming'. The discovery of what appeared to be a small staircase on the site was prime evidence of such modification.

The discovery of structures beneath the sea always generates intrigue and excitement, with people proclaiming that the lost city of Atlantis has been uncovered. However, the location of Yonaguni means that it is unlikely to have been Atlantis. Rather, it would seem to have closer parallels to the lost continents of Mu or Lemuria, as both were said to exist in the region of Asia, spanning the Pacific and Indian oceans respectively.

Although the comparatively modern science of tectonics has largely discredited the notion that there were ever 'lost continents', many believe that they did, in fact, exist. Lemuria and Mu are supposed to have been destroyed by immense natural disasters that engulfed the continents.

It is not impossible that ancient myths telling of the demise of whole civilizations have become altered and enhanced over time to encompass the destruction of entire continents. In this respect it could actually be possible that the end of the Yonaguni culture could have been mythologized or exaggerated into a story such as that surrounding the island of Lemuria.

In drawing these parallels between Yonaguni and the mythical continents, the experts involved are hoping to advance the theory that there is a great lost culture of the Pacific. Tantalizing glimpses of such a culture are offered by the mysterious stone heads of Easter Island or the oral traditions of the Polynesian islands. Apparent similarities between Yonaguni and stone constructions on Hawaii and Tonga suggest a cultural bridge from pre-historic Japan to the coast of South America.

This theory also attempts to explain the similarities between many different cultures of the world, a large number of which shared a belief in astronomy and adopted the pyramid as a favoured type of construction. Some theorists, such as Graham Hancock, believe that this serves as evidence of an ancient seafaring culture that spread its wisdom around the globe. It is certain, however, that further proof will be required before the sceptical world of archaeology accepts such a drastic reinterpretation of man's early history.

Perhaps, if the site around the pyramid is explored further, this evidence might be found after all. Or, if not, it is possible that proof could be located at other formations that have been discovered on the sea-bed close to the Japanese islands of Kerama and Chatan, and in the Straits of Taiwan.

Now that technology is able to reveal more and more about global changes as a result of the Ice Age, it seems likely that further discoveries of this kind will be made in shallow coastal shelves around the world.

This offers us the exciting prospect of possible answers as to the nature of the origins of human civilization, but as always, each discovery is likely to raise further questions. Why, for example, has the pyramid been so evident in disparate cultures at different times of mankind's history? The answer to this question looks set to remain one of the greatest mysteries of the ancient world.

ATLANTIS

The most significant account of Atlantis is by the ancient philosopher Plato (427–347BC) in two stories called *Critias* and *Tinnaeus*.

The sceptics claim that the entire account is a metaphor, and that Plato is merely using the example of Atlantis to illustrate the disastrous fate of corrupt regimes. Yet significantly Plato says more than once that the stories he recites are true. Nowhere else in his work does he claim allegorical events to be real.

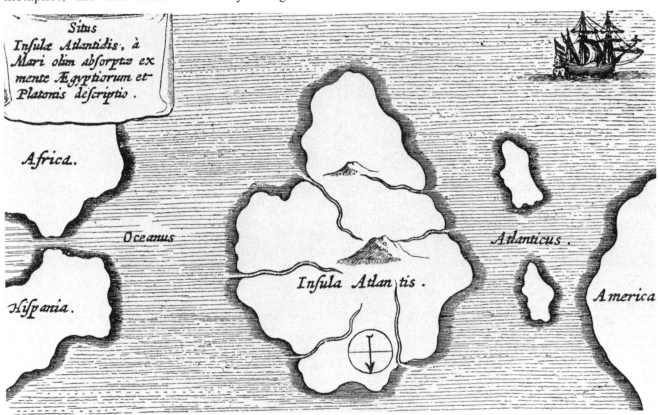

This seventeenth-century woodcut shows a supposed location of Atlantis. One more recent theory is that the civilization was in fact that of the Minoan people on Crete

ANCIENT UTOPIA

So just what does Plato say about this utopian Atlantis? Well, it was big – larger than Asia and Libya combined. Its people were virtuous, its soldiers skilful, its kings wise. There were fertile plains backed by picturesque mountains, hot and cold springs, horse racing and elephants. A central temple was adorned with golden statues. A system of deep-water canals enabled shipping to enter the city. Likewise, a man-made irrigation system kept crops green and abundant.

Curiously, Plato makes much of a precious metal called orichalcum that was mined in Atlantis and was a familiar decoration of the buildings there. It was, he says, second only to gold in value. But even by Plato's time, this prized commodity had vanished.

No one knows precisely what type of metal orichalcum is, although it is mentioned years later by the Roman commentator Josephus in relation to Solomon's Temple. But here too, evidence is scarce, and there is little archaeological data to confirm the materials used in that great temple. Whatever the physical properties of orichalcum, it seems certain that it was of great value to ancient cultures, and that Atlantis was rich in it.

According to Plato, Atlantis was an island once ruled by Poseidon, god of the sea. Poseidon fell in love with a native of Atlantis and she bore him five sets of twins. Admittedly, this part of his story does not seem to be anchored in reality, and the date is implausible. Plato dates the era of Atlantis to 9,000 years before his own day. Today, we have no knowledge of sophisticated civilizations existing so early in human history. It would have been a shining jewel in a Stone Age world.

A pair of monumental guard dogs flanks the entrance to the emperor's palace on the central island of Atlantis (artist's reconstruction)

DOOMED CIVILIZATION

But if Atlantis did exist, it was doomed to destruction. Plato's account tells how, within a single day and night, a natural disaster eradicated the entire civilization. This is entirely credible, since we know how powerful and ruthless nature can be. The island apparently disappeared into the depths of the sea, leaving only a shoal of mud that barred shipping from the area thereafter. Presumably an earthquake was to blame for the wholesale destruction, which would have extinguished the lives of countless thousands.

Initially it might sound like Plato was recycling some favourite myths that have cropped up down the ages. Atlantis bears some resemblance to a Garden of

The global cataclysm that abruptly ended the Bronze Age pushed human society everywhere to the edge of destruction. It may have accounted for the civilizations of Lemuria and Atlantis (above)

Eden, while its destruction might be likened to a great flood similar to the one in the Bible and in numerous other beliefs. But why then did Plato go into such historical detail about the civilization and the metal they mined? What if Atlantis was simply the ancient name for another culture that had been wiped out, one that we have evidence of today?

SO WHERE WAS IT?

For a long time it seemed as if Plato must have been referring to the Minoan civilization on Crete. This was named only relatively recently by an archaeologist, and no one knows what Plato's contemporaries would have called it. The Minoans had glorious palaces, paved roads and running water. A colossal volcanic eruption on the island of Thera 100km (60 miles) away from Crete caused wholesale destruction in the region, but it did not obliterate the Minoans immediately. Archaeological evidence

indicates they survived the tsunamis and the noxious sulphur clouds that must have followed the volcanic explosion, but fared poorly in the face of the ensuing climate change. By 1450BC the Minoan civilization had burnt out, succumbing either to starvation, insurrection or invaders.

Perhaps it was to the Minoans that Plato was referring? However, he confidently dates Atlantis to an era far earlier than that of the Minoan civilization on Crete. It leads one to speculate where the Minoans might have lived before migrating to the island.

Other sites for Atlantis have been put forward at various times throughout history, and these have been as farflung as Spain, South America, the Caribbean, Cyprus and the South China Seas. The evidence for Spain has been supported by satellite photographs, which appear to show concentric circles like those described by Plato. Although the size of the circles does not exactly match the philospher's description, this might be accounted for by a mistake in translating his unit of measurement, the stade, to present day measurements. The proposed site lies in salt marshes near Cadiz.

Ancient writings contain accounts of attacks on Egypt and the eastern Mediterranean by 'the Sea People'. One theory is that the Sea People, the Atlanteans and the Iron Age residents of southern Spain, known as the Tartessos, were one and the same people.

Tianhuanaco in the Bolivian Andes of South America has been earmarked as a possible Atlantis. Satellite photography has revealed it boasted hundreds of miles of inland canals. The residents are believed to have been of the Aymara tribe, a pre-Inca civilization. Such an investment in waterways implies they were a seafaring race who probably traded with Europeans and Africans. Generally, Tianhuanaco is thought to have dated from the middle of the first millennium (c. 500AD) but one researcher, Arthur Broznansky, was certain it was significantly older.

Elusive in place and time, it seems impossible, even using modern technology, to pin down Atlantis to one geographical location.

BELIEVERS

Nevertheless, many beliefs have sprung from the possible existence of Atlantis. Many people believed it to be the single root of all civilization. The odd coincidences of ancient history, like the way pyramids were built on both sides of the Atlantic and that various races chose to write in hieroglyphics, might have been explained by the existence of the great Atlantis. But there is no evidence of a linking civilization, and science has largely dismissed such claims.

This artist's impression of Atlantis from an aerial perspective shows a unique configuration of concentric rings of land and water

The Nazis believed the Atlanteans were a superior race and the ancestors of the Ayrans, those favoured by the unsavoury fanatics for peopling the earth. Hitler's henchman Heinrich Himmler was particularly taken with the theory and invested much in a fruitless search for antecedence.

There have even been claims that the Atlanteans were in fact highly advanced aliens. These assertions have proved popular, but evidence hard to come by. Edgar Cayce, the famous American psychic and healer, maintained that Atlantean existence focused on a giant crystal. This was used not only for healing but in a psychic sense for communication and teleportation. Disaster struck when the crystal exploded. Although they seem bizarre, Cayce's theories are backed by thousands of people today. He remains the inspiration behind the Association for Research and Enlightenment, based in America but present in sixty different countries.

If the mystery of Atlantis has retained its grip on human imagination for so long, it is because it remains a powerful symbol of the nature of human civilization, reminding us that, however wealthy and powerful nations become, the forces of time and nature will eventually overcome them.

NAZCA

Across a 434km² stretch of Peru's Nazca desert, archaeologists have identified 13,000 lines and pictures etched into the sun-baked surface. That these images were produced by an ancient civilization is beyond doubt. But their purpose is far harder to explain.

The designs were first noticed in the 1920s, as manned flights began to venture into South America. Pilots reported seeing straight lines which ran for miles, traversing mountains and occasionally ending on cliff edges.

Geometric shapes included triangles, rectangles, spirals, wavy lines and concentric circles. Animal geoglyphs included birds, whales, a dog and lizard. Some images were drawn on a truly vast scale: a 305m (1,000ft) pelican, a 285m (935ft) bird with a curiously zig-zag shaped neck and a monkey complete with 100m (328ft) spiral tail.

There were also more surreal pictures – specifically an 'astronaut' figure and a bizarre creature with two colossal hands, one of which had only four digits. Was this, as some have claimed, an attempt to record contact between prehistoric humans and alien beings?

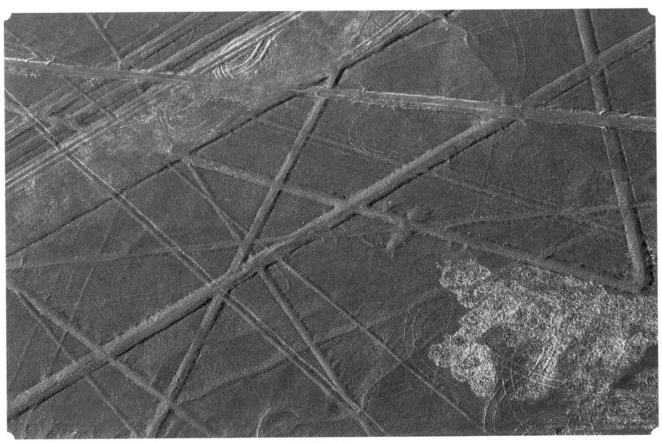

An aerial view of the Nazca lines criss-crossing the Peruvian desert. Could these really be some kind of communication for extraterrestrial visitors?

WHAT WE KNOW

Before considering this and other interpretations of Nazca, it is worth setting out areas of agreement among experts. Firstly, it is obvious that the lines were made by removing the desert's top layer of iron-oxide-coated stones to reveal lighter-coloured soil underneath.

Secondly, it is accepted that this must have been a colossal effort, perhaps lasting a thousand years, and that because of the scale of the work the artists could never have seen the full fruits of their labours from the ground. The lines are so unobtrusive that during the last century the pan-American highway was built straight through them without anyone noticing.

Although the back-breaking work of removing and rolling aside the rocks would have taken gangs of workmen much time and effort, the construction of the gigantic figures would not have required supernatural abilities. The majority of the figures are stylistically similar to drawings and paintings found on local pottery. To scale these pictures up from being a few inches across to being many hundreds of feet across is not as difficult as it may appear. What is needed is a basic knowledge of trigonometry, together with tools as simple as lengths of rope, wooden pegs and drawing boards. The mystery is not so much how the giant images were created, but why anybody should go to so much trouble.

Thirdly, it seems likely that the patterns were made by ancient Nazca Indians sometime between 400BC and AD600. This estimate is based on radiocarbon analysis of Nazca fire and ceramic debris, although it is not conclusive, since the lines themselves cannot be radiocarbon-dated.

GIANT GEOGLYPH

It is possible that an even older civilization did some of the hard work, perhaps evolving from the Paracas culture which blossomed in southern Peru between 1100–200BC.

The Paracas people are thought to have constructed the giant El Candelabro geoglyph. Also known as the Tres Cruces or the Trident, this form stretches to more than 120m (394ft) wide. It is situated on a slope overlooking the Bay of Paracas, together with some fifty figures – humans, birds, cats and monkeys – near the Peruvian city of Palpa.

SOUTH AMERICAN STONEHENGE?

The first academic to make a proper study of Nazca was Paul Kosok, an American who stumbled across the site in the late 1930s while researching prehistoric irrigation systems. He suspected that the lines were linked to astronomical alignments, a theory reinforced when in the late afternoon of the southern hemisphere's winter solstice (22 June) he and his wife witnessed the sun set precisely at the end of one line. Kosok enlisted the help of a German astronomer, Maria Reiche, and together they developed the idea that Nazca shapes were used as a calendar to help farmers calculate crop planting times.

SOLAR ALIGNMENTS

Another American scientist, Gerald Hawkins used a specialist computer program to calculate the number of significant solar alignments produced by the Nazca lines. He decided that alignments would have to point consistently to a specific celestial event, such as the rising or setting of stars, sun and moon. Neither was it enough merely for some lines to fulfil the criteria. If the astronomical link were to be proved, then it had to account for all the lines. Hawkins instructed his computer to show how many were aligned on extreme positions of the sun or moon. The answer was 39 out of 136, barely better than would be expected by chance.

Worse, only a few of these 39 alignments could be linked to significant solar or lunar positions. Hawkins tried a similar experiment with the stars, inputting a catalogue of their positions dating back to 10,001BC. Again, the alignments were statistically insignificant.

ALIEN SPACEPORT

In 1968, as Hawkins published his results, the Swiss writer Erich von Daniken inflamed the Nazca debate by claiming that the lines marked out a giant alien

One of the more bizarre geoglyphs has few recognizable features other than two huge hands, one of which has only four digits. Similar figures could be found on local pottery of the time

he constructed a 2,260m³ hot-air balloon, powered by heat from a bonfire on the ground. Together with the British balloonist Julian Nott, Woodman ascended to a height of 90m (295ft), neatly illustrating that Nazca designers could well have had the technology to fly and monitor progress of their work. This theory may sound far-fetched, but archaeologists have already shown that at least 500 years earlier, Paracas doctors were performing brain surgery through trephination – the removal of skull sections with a cylindrical saw.

WHY BOTHER?

Yet even if the ancient inhabitants of South America had the means to make the lines, this still does not explain what they were for. Few archaeological sites have spawned quite so many theories, and in recent years Nazca has been cast as a giant map of subterranean water sources, a focus for earth energies (rather like Stonehenge), a cathedral plan, an athletes' racetrack and even a giant loom on which vast teams of weavers produced cloths or nets. Even harder to grasp is the idea that the Nazca lines are located on a global 'Code Matrix' in which the world's significant ancient sites correlate precisely to the Great Pyramid at Giza. Evidence for this is reportedly found in the geometry of Nazca's layout.

spaceport. His book *Chariots of the Gods* essentially argued that it was impossible for ancient people, incapable of flight, to have produced the drawings themselves and that they must have been taught by visiting aliens.

Critics accused von Daniken of making the facts fit his theory. His cause was not helped by a television investigation into pottery fragments which, he claimed, dated from biblical times and depicted flying saucers. Unfortunately, von Daniken's fragments proved to be of more recent vintage, after television journalists found and interviewed the potter who made them.

SALT IN THE WOUND

As if to rub salt into his wounds, a flamboyant American publisher and adventurer called Jim Woodman set out to prove that Nazca people could, in any case, have known how to fly. Using cloth and rope based on samples found in Indian graves, and reeds cut from Lake Titicaca on the Bolivian border,

MAGICAL CEREMONIES

The most likely explanation is that the lines were linked to religious or magical ceremonies. Nazca was an agricultural society skilled in planting, irrigation, harvesting, storage and distribution, but it was also vulnerable to natural disasters and disease. Could the lines have been communal sites for appeasing or worshipping specific gods? Perhaps they served as a gentle reminder of the needs of the Nazca people, and a prompt for regular help from on high. The truth is that, even discounting the role of alien architects, the purpose of the lines remains frustratingly elusive.

BAALBECK

Temples have stood at Baalbeck, in Lebanon, for thousands of years, enduring the rule of numerous civilizations and the worship of many changing gods.

They have been altered, but never destroyed, because of their incredible beauty and grandeur. In fact, it is the sheer scale of the temples that has provoked such intrigue and wonder, with archaeologists the world over mystified as to how such impressive structures could have been built so long ago.

Baalbeck was originally a Phoenician settlement which became successively Greek, Roman, Byzantine and then Arab, through conquest. The Greeks occupied the town in 331BC, renaming it Heliopolis (city of the sun). Located on principal trading routes, the city flourished and became a large religious centre.

Wherever structures have survived this long, they have usually been built from stone with the express intention of permanence, and Baalbeck is no exception. In fact, this structure contains the largest cut blocks of stone in the world.

Some of these are so large, and quarried from so far away, that experts are mystified not only as to how they were transported to the site, but also how the temple was ever built.

The reason for the inconceivable vastness of the stones was Phoenician tradition, which dictated that the podium for the temple must consist of no more than three layers of stone.

When a large extension to the temple site was suggested, the ancient architects realized that they were going to have to work on a scale not previously imagined.

Undeterred by the daunting scale of their task, they commissioned the carving of what were in effect colossal building bricks, hewn from solid rock. Several of these are to be found on the western side of the podium, in the area named the 'Trilithon', after the three largest blocks. These stones are around 20m (65ft) long, 4.5m (15ft) high and 3.6m (12ft) deep, and each is estimated to weigh around 800 tonnes. By way of comparison, these stones are four or five times larger than those at Stonehenge, and approximately three hundred times heavier than those used to build the Egyptian pyramids.

1,000 TONNES

Amazingly, the largest of the stones was even heavier than this. At more than 1,000 tonnes, the size and weight of 'the stone of the pregnant woman' would test the greatest cranes in existence in the world today. However, this stone still remains in its quarry, as building work ceased before it ever came to be used.

Aside from the fact that the huge blocks of stone were transported more than a kilometre from their quarry and then raised more than 7m (23ft) into their final positions, there is yet another mystery attached to them. The craftsmanship shown in the construction is of such a high standard, with the stones arranged in such a precise fashion, without the use of mortar, that it is impossible to wedge even the slightest object between them.

The scale of Baalbeck has fired people's imaginations to such an extent that each successive culture to occupy the site has linked the Trilithon with some kind of popular myth, be it giants, biblical figures or even the intervention of extraterrestrials.

Whatever the explanation for the construction of this vast monument, it looks likely that Baalbeck will continue to draw countless visitors to the site in the future. No doubt these people, like thousands before them, will marvel at the beauty of this remarkable ancient monument, that suggests so much about the possibilities of human achievement.

*The remains of the Temple of Jupiter (foreground) and Bacchus (background) at Baalbeck; temples
have stood on this spot for thousands of years*

TINTAGEL

The legend of King Arthur is one we are all familiar with, but we are not so sure of the historical facts concerning his life. On 4 July 1998, an archaeologist working at Tintagel Castle in Cornwall unearthed an inscribed chunk of slate. It bore the name 'Arthnou' – an early version of Arthur – re-opening a furious academic controversy about where the 'Once and Future King' of the Britons resided.

TINTAGEL FINDS

The discovery of what became known as 'The Arthur Stone' caused a sensation in archaeological circles. The chief archaeologist of English Heritage, the government-backed body which manages the castle site in North Cornwall, declared it: 'the find of a lifetime'. Dr Geoffrey Wainwright added: 'It is remarkable that a stone has been discovered with the name "Arthnou" inscribed on it at Tintagel, a place with which the mythical King Arthur has long been associated.'

'SEALED CONTEXT'

What so excited Dark Age historians was that the stone emerged from a proven 'sealed context', meaning it had lain undisturbed since at least the seventh century AD. Measuring 20cm (8in) x 35cm (14in), and 1cm (0.4in) in depth, it was originally a plaque of some kind, and bore the Latin words: *Pater coli avi ficit artognov* – 'Arthnou, father of a

The ruins of Tintagel dominate the dramatic Cornish coastline… did King Arthur once live here?

descendant of Coll, has had (this) made/built/ constructed'.

Quite what he had constructed remains unclear, because the slate had been broken and re-cycled as a seventh-century drain cover. However 'Arthnou' was clearly once a leader of means and stature. In Britain of the Dark Ages, literacy was the preserve of monks and the educated nobility.

Previous excavations at Tintagel had produced fragments of wine and oil pots imported from the Mediterranean, suggesting that the castle was a high-status, secular site, possibly the royal court of a chieftain of Dumnonia (the ancient kingdom of southwest Britain). The slate's significance was that it proved people here were reading and writing Latin, and living a Romanized way of life, 200 years after the Romans left in AD410, which is exactly the period when King Arthur was supposed to have been in power.

THE LEGEND

In unravelling the mystery of the Arthur Stone, it is important to separate the legendary story of the King from the historical version (such as it is). Few other areas of ancient British history produce quite so much disagreement among scholars and given that there are at least nine competing claims for 'ownership' of Arthur – Brittany, Cornwall, Cumbria, Scotland, Somerset, three areas of Wales, Wiltshire, Warwickshire and Yorkshire – it is hard to see a consensus emerging.

What is clear is that Arthurian legend has been much reproduced and embellished over the years. Fantasies such as Malory's 15th-century tome

Le Morte D'Arthur, Tennyson's *Idylls of the King* and T H White's *The Once and Future King* have all contributed to Arthur's legendary status. In these books we learn how Arthur founds his court on the principle of 'might for right', valiantly defending his kingdom against the invading Saxons. He thrives under the counsel of the wizard Merlin, but is eventually betrayed by the adultery of his best friend, Sir Lancelot, with his Queen, Guinevere, and dies a hero's death in the 'last battle' against evil forces led

In unravelling the mystery of the Arthur Stone, it is important to separate the legendary story of the King from the historical version (such as it is)

by his nephew Mordred. Despite this, according to the old stories, he lies buried in a secret tomb and will return to aid his people in their hour of need.

The Arthur legend is loosely based on the writings of the 12th-century canon Geoffrey of Monmouth, whose *History of the Kings of Britain* was widely read in Europe. Geoffrey's declared aim was to promote patriotism by extolling the glories of the early Britons, but unfortunately the distinction between fact and myth is lost in his work. When Geoffrey wrote of Arthur's birthplace as Tintagel, he was mistranslating an earlier text which used the term 'din-dagol', an old Welsh word meaning 'double-banked hillfort'. He also wrongly believed the Cornovii tribe, supposed ancestors of the King, were based in Cornwall, although they actually controlled what is now the West Midlands. In fact some historians argue that Cornwall has the weakest claim of all to an Arthurian link.

WORD OF MOUTH

However, just because the written history of 6th- and 7th-century Britain is unreliable, this does not mean that traditional folk tales and oral records should be discounted. An oral system worked pretty well for the Vikings, who relied on it for centuries in matters of law and governance. In Iceland there was even an elected Lawspeaker whose job was to hold the law in his memory and recite a third of it each year, for three years, at the main annual assembly. The problem of course is that oral history is easier to manipulate.

HOLY GRAIL

The story of Arthur's quest for the Holy Grail is a case in point. Portraying the King as a defender of Christianity against pagan Britain was nothing more than skilful spin-doctoring by missionary monks keen to claim converts. Just as they built churches on sacred pagan sites, so they adapted traditional stories to suit their religious agenda. Arthur, if he ever existed, was almost certainly a pagan.

PLAGUE STALKS THE COUNTRYSIDE

And yet the legend of the Holy Grail may be an oral allegory for actual events. It draws heavily on the concept of a freezing wasteland where no crops grow, where famine is rife and plague stalks the countryside. Climatologists now believe that the Arthurian period may have seen just such a scenario, perhaps caused by a mass of debris from comets in the atmosphere which partially blocked light from the sun. Contemporary records from elsewhere in

Europe bear this out – the Mediterranean writer Zachariah for instance talks of 'fire from heaven' – and an analysis of oak tree rings suggests growth was severely curtailed between AD539 and 541.

SEARCHING FOR THE KING

So was there ever a 'real' Arthur figure? Many Dark Age historians now believe that a militarily successful and charismatic leader did emerge in Britain after the fall of the Roman Empire and that his name lived on in folk memory well before any meaningful written accounts. The 9th-century historian Nennius tells us that Arthur was a former Roman General, but offers little by way of explanation. To confuse matters further, it is likely that the name 'Arthnou' (which originally meant 'known as a bear, known to be a bear') was common among the ancient Britons.

MAGICAL SWORD

Could Arthur's court have been at Tintagel? There are certainly plenty of legends linking the King to Cornwall, among them a stone slab at Slaughterbridge, near Camelford, which is said to mark his grave.

Other stories claim his magical sword Excalibur lies at the bottom of either Dozmary Pool on Bodmin Moor, or Loe Pool near Helston, where it was thrown by St Bedivere as Arthur lay dying.

The waterfall at St Nectan's Kieve, near Tintagel, is supposedly the place where Arthur baptized his knights before they embarked on their search for the Grail.

English Heritage has been careful to play down any clear, evidential link between the Arthur Stone and either the historical or the legendary king. However as Dr Wainwright puts it: 'Tintagel has presented us with evidence of a court of the Arthurian period with buildings, high-status finds and the name of a person, Arthnou. Arthnou was here, that is his name on a piece of stone.'

Shrouded in mystery and yet somehow familiar, the Arthur stone is a unique archaeological find where, as Dr Wainwright put it, 'myth meets history'.

GREAT PYRAMID OF GIZA

The last surviving monument from the Seven Wonders of the Ancient World, the pyramid at Giza was built around 2560BC

There are perhaps no monuments more immediately associated with the concept of mystery than the great pyramids of Egypt. Although such structures are present all over the world, it is the Egyptian examples that are both the most ancient and spectacular and thus have the power to capture our imagination.

The most evocative pyramid of all is the largest, which marks the tomb of King Khufu at Giza in Egypt. King Khufu, the son of Sneferu and Queen Hetepheres I, was the second Pharaoh of the fourth Dynasty. Inheriting the throne while still in his twenties, he nevertheless immediately began the planning and construction of his tomb. He became the first Pharaoh to build a pyramid at Giza and in so doing began a period of monument building that was to span the ages. The clues offered by the great pyramid offer a tantalizing insight into the exact purpose of this kind of structure.

SHEER SIZE

The great pyramid took well over 20 years to complete, using around 2.3 million individual blocks of stone, weighing up to 2.5 tonnes each. The sheer size of the tomb may well have reflected the great power and respect enjoyed by this particular pharaoh. The entire process of mummification, monument building and ritual burial are aimed at the concept of granting the king a passport to the afterlife. In preparation for this, vast chambers were built within the tomb and filled with an immense variety of riches.

On further examining this pyramid, a number of factors have led many to suspect that there may be some hidden meaning contained within the structure. First, Khufu's personal burial chamber is larger than that of any other pyramid in the world and its construction is of the highest standard. In fact it is so intricate that it contains a small shaft, running all the way from the burial chamber up to the sky in a completely straight line.

The precision of the line is such that some Egyptologists believe it may have been intended as a conduit for the Ka, or spirit of the Pharaoh. It has also been suggested that the line of the shaft from the burial chamber would have aligned with the constellation of Orion at the time of the king's burial and, furthermore, that this pyramid and the two others built at Giza may actually form a representation on Earth of this particular constellation. Support for this theory is provided by the fact that Orion had particular importance for the Egyptians in terms of the afterlife.

There has also been much discussion about the supposed mathematical perfection of the pyramid's dimensions and position. Considering the religious importance of these factors to the Egyptians, these points may be worth considering. Each face of the pyramid is hyper-accurately oriented towards each of the cardinal compass points. The Egyptians used precise geographical North, which is aligned with the spin axis of Earth, rather than magnetic North. This fact demonstrates the Egyptians' advanced understanding of the world and suggests that they were aware that Earth was a sphere that rotated. The position of the great pyramid exactly straddles the 30th parallel latitude, setting it precisely one third of the way between the North Pole and the Equator.

Just as there seems to be a very precise positioning involved in the construction of the pyramid at Giza, so too can a curious alignment be seen in the temple of Amen-Ra at Karnak. Here, doorways to the monument have been built so that they line up exactly along the bearing 26° south of East, to 26° north of West, over the distance of almost one kilometre. This coincides exactly with the position of the rising and setting suns on the days of the spring and winter solstices.

MESSAGE

Such factors could be coincidental, but taken together they begin to suggest that perhaps the edifices of ancient Egypt contain some greater significance in their structure. The deliberately huge scale of the pyramids would moreover ensure that they defied the ravages of time and thus carry this message into subsequent millennia. Certainly, many Egyptian monuments would seem to demonstrate the importance to this ancient people of certain times of the year, such as the solstices. The Egyptian calendar also followed a kind of cyclical Zodiac that applied a particular cosmic importance to each particular day. This is in its essence very similar to the ideas expressed in astrology today in cultures all over the world.

The pyramids are a potent symbol of mysticism and inspire great curiosity all over the world. Their true meaning and purpose can only be guessed at, and we will probably never know the real answers. Perhaps what is most important, though, is that the pyramids prompt us to ask the right questions, questions about the power and wisdom of the ancients, the nature of civilization and the mysteries of the universe.

GREAT SERPENT MOUND

When European settlers began pushing into the Ohio Valley and adjacent areas of North America, they were surprised to come across vast man-made mounds and earthen platforms – signs that an advanced civilisation had once existed in the region. The local Native Americans were farmers living in a society based on clan or tribe society and showed no inclination to construct the massive structures found by the European settlers. The newcomers assumed that some previous race of civilized people had once lived in the area, only to abandon it centuries earlier. The truth turned out to be rather more complex.

The most famous remnant of this supposed

Located on a vast plateau in Ohio, the Serpent Mound is a huge earthwork effigy, but its exact function remains a mystery

vanished civilisation is the Great Serpent Mound, near Locust Grove, Ohio. This is a massive monument built out of earth and turf piled up to form an image of a snake that winds for 400m (1,300ft) while standing around one metre (3ft) tall. The head of the snake has an open mouth that encloses a large sunken oval around 40m (130ft) across. This has been identified as being an egg, a frog, the sun or a mere abstract shape.

SAVED

The Great Serpent Mound was discovered by two surveyors, Ephraim Squier and Edwin Davis when mapping potential farmland in the area in 1848. Unfortunately, the farmers who subsequently moved in did not value the many dozens of similar, but smaller mounds in the area and most of them were destroyed by ploughing. The Great Serpent Mound was saved when Frederic Putnam of Harvard University bought it in 1886.

Since Putnam's purchase, the mound has been subjected to several archaeological digs. The mound was built on top of a natural stone plateau that contains deeply folded and split bedrock unique in the area. Some think this may have had some significance to the mound builders. The excavations quickly established that the mound itself contained no burials, although several high-status burials were found close by. It was also found that the serpent's head pointed directly toward the spot on the horizon where the sun set on midsummer's day. Other alignments along the Great Serpent Mound's body point to various lunar alignments, though not all archaeologists accept these as being deliberate and suggest that they may be purely accidental.

Those who believe the Great Serpent Mound is primarily an astronomical structure suggest that it may represent a comet as it snakes its path across the sky. A radiocarbon date for burned wood found within the mound gave a date of AD1070, just four years after Halley's Comet was seen from Earth. Others suggest that the Great Serpent Mound represents the constellation known today as Draco –

which does have a serpentine shape with seven bends just like the mound.

Archaeologists now know that there were several native cultures in the Mississippi and Ohio valleys that centred on the construction of earthen mounds and platforms. Most of these mounds had a ritual use, with sacred enclosures being placed on top of them. The radiocarbon date for the Serpent Mound would place this within the culture known today as the Fort Ancient culture. This was based in the central Mississippi Valley, but outlying settlements were established on the Ohio. Despite the date, the Great Serpent Mound is untypical for the Fort Ancient structures. It contains neither burials nor votive offerings and it generally has a very low profile.

The other mound building culture to exist in this area was the Adena, which existed a thousand years earlier. The Adena were more prone to building mounds in the shape of animals, and moreover did not tend to bury their dead within the mound. However, nothing of Adena provenance has been found in the Great Serpent Mound.

SUPERNATURAL SERPENT

The local Native Americans had legends relating to the Great Serpent Mound and similar earthworks. They said that the works had been constructed by a tribe called the Allegheny who had inhabited the region in the remote past. These people were reported to have moved away many generations earlier. Anthropologists have taken these tales rather more seriously than have archaeologists. They have placed the migration of the Allegheny out of the area somewhere before 500BC. It is thought the Allegheny may be related to the Delaware tribe, known from historic times.

There is also a legend of a gigantic supernatural serpent named Uktena which once roamed the region dealing out death or favours to the local humans as it saw fit. Whether the Great Serpent Mound is a representation of Uktena is a matter of opinion.

Until or unless more evidence is found the origin, age and purpose of the Great Serpent Mound must remain a mystery.

EASTER ISLAND

On Easter Island links with history have disappeared and only the giant statues, the Moai, bear witness to the past

Located some 3,600km (2,237 miles) west of the coast of Chile, Easter Island is the most remote inhabited island in the world. The nearest island is Sala y Gomez which lies 415km (258 miles) east, but it is uninhabited. The island covers 163 square kilometres and although it has three lakes, there are no permanent streams or rivers. This would make Easter Island unusual enough, but it is the strange statues that make this place so special.

When the first European arrived here in 1722, the Dutch captain Jacob Roggeveen reported the island had 3,000 inhabitants and hundreds of standing statues. It was not until 1770 that a European ship called again, and reported that the statues seemed neglected. By 1825, when another ship called the statues had all been toppled. Disaster struck in 1862 when a fleet of Peruvian slave traders arrived and tried to enslave the entire population. The fighting and subsequent outbreak of smallpox reduced the island's population to around 800 and by 1890 there were only 111 left alive. The population has since recovered, but the chaos means that nobody can now read the writings left by the pre-1860 population and oral history of the time before the slave raid is confused.

Only the gaunt statues, the Moai, stare out to bear witness to the past.

STANDING TALL

There are a total of 887 statues on Easter Island, the tallest of which was 10 metres (33ft) tall and weighed 75 tonnes. Most were about half that size. Each statue was carved from a single block of stone and conformed to a set pattern. The statues all show a naked male from the waist up. The noses and lips protrude, while the ears are greatly elongated. The arms rest down the side of the body, with the hands resting on the stomach. Some show the traditional loincloth over the hips. The statues originally had eye sockets filled with coral and obsidian that produced staring eyes of startling power. Some statues show signs of having been painted.

The Moai were originally placed so that they stood on raised platforms of earth and stone called ahu. Most of the ahu were placed near the coast so that the statues gazed out to sea.

RULED BY THE GOD-KING

So far as can be gathered from the tales told to early European missionaries, the island was ruled until around 1780 by a god-king called the Ariki. This Ariki had absolute power over the islanders, enforced by his role in the cult dedicated to the god named Tangata Manu, which is usually translated as Birdman. It was the Ariki who ordered the construction of the Moai statues. They seem to have represented his divine ancestors and former rulers. The elongated ears were not an artistic abstraction, but an accurate representation of the ears of the Ariki and his family which were deliberately distorted by heavy weights in childhood.

FAILING HARVESTS

For reasons now unknown, but which were probably linked to a series of years when the harvests failed, the Ariki was overthrown by the leaders of his army. The army then began the Time of Statue Felling, or the Huri Moai. Not only were the statues tipped over to lie on their faces, but the various clans of the island began a series of vicious wars against each other. By 1850 all the statues had been toppled.

The key mystery about the statues was how they had been made and transported. There was no problem locating where they had come from for the quarry on the hill of Rano Raraku can still be seen. Dozens of half-completed statues are lying about in the quarry; a few completed statues stand outside the quarry as if awaiting transport. Work seems to have been abandoned when the Ariki was overthrown.

TUFF TREATEMENT

Most of the statues were carved from a volcanic rock called tuff. Given that the islanders had a Stone Age culture, the only way the stone could be worked was by pounding it with other stones. Tuff which has been exposed to rain and air for some time can be bashed away quite easily, but unexposed rock is very tough. To batter the statues out of the bedrock would have taken a vast amount of arm-aching work. Some have suggested that the islanders must have had some advanced technology, now lost, to enable them to make the statues.

LOST KNOWLEDGE

If the carving is a mystery, the transportation is even more so. By the time the statues were being produced and moved many kilometres across the island there were no trees left on Easter Island. The islanders have always maintained that the statues 'walked'. Leaving aside suggestions of magic or some unknown technology, this seems to mean that the statues were manoeuvred along while upright by swinging them from side to side with long ropes. An attempt to mimic this method in 1986 produced a daily 'walking' rate of around 90 metres (300ft), but inflicted some damage on the statue.

Perhaps the Ariki had some hidden knowledge long since lost.

BERMUDA TRIANGLE

The Bermuda Triangle is an infamous area of the western Atlantic that has its corners resting on Bermuda, Puerto Rico and Florida. To the oceanographer and cartographer there is nothing remarkable about the area. The Gulf Stream flows across it heading northeast and shipping lanes cross it to and from the ports of the Gulf of Mexico. To students of the paranormal, however, the area is one of the most mysterious and dangerous on Earth.

Over the years a large number of ships and aircraft have vanished without trace in the region. Although the shipping insurers Lloyd's of London does not charge extra premiums as overall loss rates for ships in the area are not unusually high, the number of craft that seem to vanish off the face of the Earth is abnormal.

SUDDEN STORMS AND POOR MAINTENANCE

Sceptics argue that there is nothing paranormal going on at all. They suggest that the various losses are nothing out of the ordinary and, although disturbing, are more to do with sudden storms and poorly maintained ships or aircraft than with any unusual or paranormal cause. Others are not so sure.

The earliest victim of the Bermuda Triangle of modern times seems to have been Joshua Slocum in his yacht *Spray*. Slocum was the first man to sail solo around the world, while his yacht had been recently overhauled and was in good repair. In 1909, Slocum set off in the *Spray* to cross the Triangle area heading south for Venezuela, but neither he nor his craft were ever seen again.

Nine years later the USS *Cyclops* set off from Barbados to sail north through the Triangle. Although it had the latest radio and safety equipment it was never seen again, nor were any of its 309 crew.

On 31 January 1921 two ships fell victim to the Triangle near Cape Hatteras. The weather was calm

and no high seas were running. The SS *Hewitt* vanished completely just hours after passing Cape

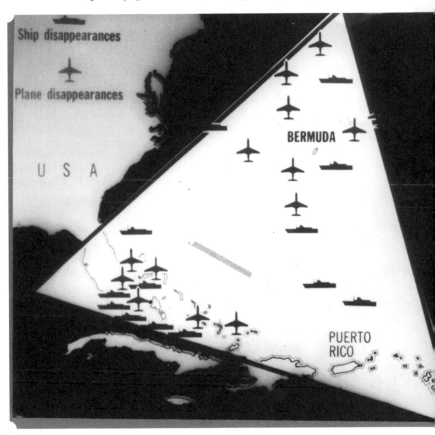

The disappearance of large numbers of ships and planes has led to speculation that paranormal events are taking place

Hatteras, while the schooner *Carroll Deering* was found hard aground on the Diamond Shoals. Her crew was missing and none have ever been found.

PERFECT CONDITIONS

A baffling disappearance occurred on 5 December 1945 when a training flight of Avenger bombers took off led by the highly experienced Lt Charles Taylor. This Flight 19 took off in perfect conditions of calm weather. The radio operators back at base listened to

Lost at sea: some people claim that giant whirlpools appear out of nowhere in the Bermuda Triangle to swallow up shipping vessels and drag them to the bottom of the ocean

it progressed on its way the pilot sent out the usual routine radio signals reporting his route and weather conditions. Nothing was wrong and the aircraft was tracked as far as the centre of the Triangle. Then radio signals ceased. No distress was sent out and no sign of the aircraft, crew or passengers was ever found.

On 28 December 1948 a DC3 passenger aircraft with 32 people on board took off from San Juan airport on Puerto Rico bound for Miami. It never arrived, no distress message was received and no trace of any wreckage was ever found.

Barely a month later a second Avro Tudor airliner, the *Star Ariel*, also went missing. Again no trace was ever found.

the messages coming back from Taylor as he led his men on a navigational exercise over the Atlantic. At first all seemed well, then something went wrong. The pilot's radio traffic began to report that there was something odd about the sea and the weather. Then land did not appear where it should have been. The base tried to raise Taylor by radio, but failed even though they continued to hear his voice. One of Taylor's final messages was baffling: 'We cannot be sure which way is west. Everything is wrong. Strange. We cannot be sure of direction. Even the ocean does not look as it should.' A few minutes later he called: 'It looks like we are entering white water.' After a while the radio traffic fell still and only an ominous silence prevailed.

VANISHED WITHOUT TRACE

On 30 January 1948 the Avro Tudor airliner, the *Star Tiger*, set out from the Azores to fly to Bermuda. As

'DANGER LIKE DAGGER NOW'

In 1955 the yacht *Connemara* was found drifting abandoned off Bermuda. No explanation was ever found as to what happened to it. On 4 February 1963 the large cargo ship, SS *Marine Sulfur Queen* set off from Florida to cross the Atlantic with a crew of 39. She was last reported passing the Keys, but thereafter vanished completely.

One hint of what might be going on in the Bermuda Triangle came in 1921 when the Japanese merchant ship *Raifuku Maru* was steaming through the Triangle area. The radio operator on another ship, the *Homeric*, picked up a distress call from the *Raifuku Maru*. After giving the recognized SOS signal and the ship's position, the Japanese operator sent the words 'Danger like dagger now. Come quick.' Then the radio fell silent.

What possible danger like a dagger lurks in the Bermuda Triangle?

INDEX

PICTURE CREDITS

Corbis: 10, 21, 22, 28, 29, 30, 31, 55, 60, 105, 107, 108, 118, 129, 148, 150, 154, 162, 177, 180, 181, 186, 187, 190, 192. 193, 194, 195, 197, 210, 211, 213, 214, 216, 232, 245, 270, 281, 285, 287, 290, 291
Getty: 13, 24, 25, 35, 36, 37, 38, 39, 40, 41, 43, 44, 45, 46, 48, 49, 50, 51, 53, 65, 73, 75, 84, 110, 131, 134, 137, 142, 146, 156, 184, 200, 201, 217, 218, 219, 220, 222, 224, 226, 261, 279, 289, 295
Mary Evans: 33, 52, 57, 81, 85, 92, 99, 120, 128, 144, 152, 183, 188, 189, 198, 203, 206, 208, 227, 231, 234, 237, 242, 244, 246, 255, 256, 257, 258, 262, 263, 265, 266, 275
Bill Stoneham: 124, 125, 127, 260, 282, 283, 284
Rex Features: 58, 67, 68, 71, 72, 268
Science Photo Library: 172
Photos.com: 159
Shutterstock: 9, 26, 274, 277, 278, 293, 297
Tamasin Reno: 253, 264
Topfoto: 66, 78, 87, 88, 94, 96, 97, 101, 103, 113, 122, 139, 140, 168, 204, 236, 299, 300